M000107533

Les formes géométriques dans le graphisme

Las formas geométricas en diseño gráfico

GRAPHIC DESIGN ELEMENTS

WANG SHAOQIANG ED.

Shapes

Geometric Forms in Graphic Design

promopress

Shapes

Geometric Forms in Graphic Design
Les formes géométriques dans le graphisme
Las formas geométricas en diseño gráfico

Editor: Wang Shaoqiang
English preface revised by: Tom Corkett
Translators of the preface:
Leïla Bendifallah, French translation
Jesús de Cos Pinto, Spanish translation

Promopress is a brand of:
Promotora de Prensa Internacional S.A.
C/ Ausiàs March, 124
08013 Barcelona, Spain
Phone: 0034 93 245 14 64
Fax: 0034 93 265 48 83
info@promopress.es
www.promopresseditions.com
Facebook: Promopress Editions
Twitter: Promopress Editions @PromopressEd
Sponsored by Design 360°
– Concept and Design Magazine
Edited and produced by
Sandu Publishing Co., Ltd.
Book design, concepts & art direction by
Sandu Publishing Co., Ltd.
info@sandupublishing.com

Cover design:
spread: David Lorente

ISBN 978-84-16504-54-1

Printed in China

Contents

Big Ideas in Simple Shapes

By Genis Carreras
Founder of Studio Carreras

When I design, I always use the same approach, whether what I am working on is a personal project or a commission, whether it is for a big client or a small one, or whether it involves creating a single poster or a whole visual identity. I design by instinct and rationality, and I use a minimal amount of visual elements – color, shapes, and type – and give meaning to each of them. In a world that is so visually saturated, a whisper can stand out more than a scream.

Geometry just comes naturally to my working approach. For me, geometric shapes are the building blocks that I use to visualize my thoughts. I usually start a project from scratch and use the simplest shapes: circles, squares, and triangles. I spend a lot of time playing with the same simple elements and changing their size and composition until I achieve something visually interesting. Sometimes these shapes will turn into something more complex, while at other times they will stay the way they are: pure, unaltered, and rational.

We are all attracted to geometric shapes. The order and harmony of these shapes are pleasing to the eye in a world of imperfection and chaos. They show us something direct, clear, and true. Designers know this and have been using these shapes since the very beginning of our profession as a tool for communication and visual impact. In this book, you will find many examples of why geometry is still very much relevant in today's graphic design industry and of how it is a crucial part of our visual language.

De grandes idées dans des formes simples

Par Genis Carreras
Fondateur de Studio Carreras

Quand je crée, j'utilise toujours la même approche, que je travaille sur un projet personnel ou une commande, qu'il s'agisse d'un gros ou d'un petit client, ou que je doive créer une seule affiche ou une identité visuelle entière. Je crée avec instinct et rationalité, j'utilise une quantité minime d'éléments visuels (couleurs, formes et polices) et je donne un sens à chacun d'entre eux. Dans un monde saturé visuellement, un murmure peut se démarquer davantage qu'un cri.

La géométrie accompagne naturellement mon approche de travail. Les formes géométriques sont les piliers que j'utilise pour visualiser mes pensées. Je commence généralement un projet en partant de rien et j'utilise les formes les plus simples: des cercles, des carrés et des triangles. Je passe beaucoup de temps à jouer avec les mêmes éléments simples et à changer leur taille et leur composition jusqu'à obtenir un résultat visuellement intéressant. Parfois, ces formes se complexifient alors que d'autres fois, elles restent telles quelles: pures, intactes et rationnelles.

Nous sommes tous attirés par les formes géométriques. L'ordre et l'harmonie de ces formes apaisent l'œil dans un monde d'imperfection et de chaos. Elles nous montrent quelque chose de direct, de clair et de vrai. Les designers le savent et utilisent ces forment depuis les débuts de notre profession comme un outil de communication et d'impact visuel. Dans cet ouvrage, vous découvrirez de nombreux exemples démontrant que la géométrie est toujours très importante dans l'industrie graphique actuelle et qu'elle représente une partie essentielle de notre langage visuel.

Prefacio

Grandes ideas, formas simples

De Genis Carreras
Fundador de Studio Carreras

Ya se trate de un proyecto personal o de un encargo, de un trabajo para un cliente importante o para uno modesto, de la creación de un solo póster o de toda una identidad visual, mi enfoque del diseño siempre es el mismo. Diseño por instinto y con racionalidad, y utilizo una cantidad mínima de elementos visuales –color, forma y tipografía– a los que doy significado. En un mundo tan saturado de imágenes, un suspiro puede decir más que un grito.

La geometría es un elemento natural de mi trabajo, las formas geométricas son los bloques de construcción que utilizo para visualizar mis pensamientos. Suelo empezar los proyectos desde cero y uso las formas más sencillas: círculos, cuadrados y triángulos. Paso mucho tiempo jugando con los mismos elementos simples y cambiando su tamaño y su composición hasta que consigo algo visualmente interesante. En ocasiones, esas formas se convierten en algo más complejo, mientras que otras veces se quedan tal como son: puras, inalteradas y racionales.

Las formas geométricas nos atraen a todos. En un mundo de imperfección y de caos, el orden y la armonía de esas formas resultan placenteros a la vista. Nos muestran algo directo, claro y auténtico. Los diseñadores lo saben y han venido usando esas formas desde los orígenes de la profesión como herramientas de comunicación y de impacto visual. En este libro el lector encontrará muchos ejemplos que muestran por qué la geometría sigue siendo hoy muy importante en la industria del diseño gráfico y es una parte esencial del lenguaje visual.

Shapes as Transformational Elements

By Korbinian Lenzer
Cofounder of Moby Digg

Shapes enjoy huge popularity in graphic design. Their multidimensional nature and simplicity have been fascinating creators since design's earliest days, and they have left their mark on historical visual works and zeitgeisty creations alike. Beyond its color and size, the form of a shape transmits subconscious messages, determining the character and the mood of a layout. The creative possibilities that shapes offer are limitless, and viewers are continuously interpreting them consciously and unconsciously. To give just a few examples, rectangles may stand for symmetry and order. Squares, with four equal sides and angles, could represent calmness and neutrality. And circles might reflect perfection and infinity.

When we at Moby Digg start working on a new project, shapes present a fundamental step in finding the initial design language. And so we often start with collecting, presenting, and discussing moods from different fields in which the construction and design methods are frequently based on shapes – for example, architecture or product design. This first step generates initial insights into the project's intended perception, and it helps us to evaluate the visual direction in an "abstract" way. Naturally, it is not possible to transfer the concepts from architecture and product design to the world of graphic design with one-to-one equivalence, but the process offers an idea of the design impact.

Interestingly enough, these initial shapes from the early stages of projects are often included in the final presentation of our design works and guide our process of creation throughout the project. Shapes not only give us visual direction but work as a guideline from the beginning of a design project until its final realization.

Moby Digg has its origins in digital design. In our digital projects, we add another dimension to our design work: interaction and motion. Animations can change the appearance of shapes drastically, affecting their symbolic language and meaning. The added motion guides the viewer's focus and influences the hierarchical and spatial relationship between different shapes. Animation in design can express dynamics and transformation. Additionally, motions connected to users' input, such as gestures on mobile applications or hover states and clicks on websites, enhance these effects. The result is a greatly enriched user experience. These principles are now extensively used and have become a popular design trend.

I warmly recommend to designers that they start experimenting with shapes and use them as a starting point for a different kind of design process. Many different design areas have at some point applied this creation method. The ubiquity of shapes, which are not just one of the first design elements taught in design schools but also the starting point even in experienced designers' creation processes, tells us much about their salience in the world of design.

Les formes : des éléments de transformation

Par Korbinian Lenzer
Cofondateur de Moby Digg

Les formes sont très populaires dans le graphisme. Leur nature multidimensionnelle et leur simplicité fascinent les créateurs depuis les débuts du graphisme et elles ont laissé leur marque dans des œuvres visuelles historiques tout comme dans des créations contemporaines. Au-delà de sa couleur et de sa taille, la structure d'une forme transmet des messages subconscients, déterminant le caractère et le ton d'un dessin. Les possibilités créatives qu'offrent les formes sont illimitées, et le public les interprète constamment de manière consciente et inconsciente. Par exemple, les rectangles peuvent signifier la symétrie et l'ordre ; les carrés, avec leurs quatre côtés et angles égaux, pourraient représenter la sérénité et la neutralité ; les cercles, eux, peuvent refléter la perfection et l'infini.

Chez Moby Digg, lorsque nous entamons un nouveau projet, les formes constituent une étape fondamentale pour trouver le langage graphique initial. Nous commençons donc souvent par recueillir, présenter et discuter d'ambiances provenant de différents domaines dans lesquels les méthodes de construction et de conception sont fréquemment fondées sur les formes, comme dans l'architecture et la conception de produit, par exemple. La première étape donne une vision initiale de la perception voulue du projet et nous aide à évaluer la direction visuelle de manière « abstraite ». Il est naturellement impossible de transférer directement des concepts de l'architecture ou de la conception de produit au monde du graphisme, mais ce processus nous permet d'avoir une idée de l'impact de la création.

Il est intéressant de constater que ces formes initiales émergeant dans les premières phases du projet sont souvent incluses dans la présentation finale de nos travaux de conception graphique et guident notre processus de création tout au long du projet. Les formes ne nous donnent pas seulement une direction visuelle mais servent également de fil rouge du début d'un projet de conception graphique jusqu'à sa réalisation finale.

Moby Digg trouve son origine dans la conception numérique. Dans nos projets numériques, nous ajoutons une autre dimension à notre travail de conception : l'interaction et le mouvement. Les animations peuvent radicalement modifier l'apparence des formes en changeant leur sens et leur langage symboliques. Le mouvement ajouté guide l'attention du public et influence la relation spatiale et hiérarchique entre différentes formes. L'animation dans la conception peut exprimer la dynamique et la transformation. De plus, les mouvements connectés aux données introduites par l'utilisateur, comme les gestes sur les applications mobiles ou les *hover states* et les clics sur les sites internet, augmentent cet effet. Le résultat en est une expérience beaucoup plus riche pour l'utilisateur. Ces principes sont maintenant largement utilisés et sont devenus une tendance de conception populaire.

Je conseille vivement aux designers de continuer d'expérimenter avec des formes et de les utiliser comme point de départ pour un processus de création différent. De nombreux domaines de création ont appliqué cette méthode à un moment ou à un autre. L'omniprésence des formes, qui ne sont pas seulement les premiers éléments de conception enseignés en école de design, mais également le point de départ des processus de création même pour les designers expérimentés, en dit long sur leur influence dans le monde du design.

Las formas como elementos transformacionales

De Korbinian Lenzer
Cofundador de Moby Digg

Las formas gozan de gran popularidad en diseño gráfico. Su naturaleza multidimensional y su simplicidad han fascinado a los creadores desde los primeros tiempos del diseño y han dejado su huella tanto en obras visuales intemporales como en creaciones fruto de una época determinada. Más allá de su color y su tamaño, la forma de un objeto transmite mensajes al subconsciente y determina la atmósfera y el mensaje de un diseño. Las posibilidades creativas que ofrecen las formas son ilimitadas y los espectadores las interpretan sin cesar, de manera consciente e inconsciente. Por citar algún ejemplo, los rectángulos representan simetría y orden; los cuadrados, con sus cuatro caras y ángulos iguales, denotan calma y neutralidad, y los círculos reflejan perfección e infinitud.

Cuando mis compañeros de Moby Digg y yo empezamos un proyecto nuevo, las formas son un factor fundamental en la búsqueda del lenguaje de diseño inicial y a menudo empezamos por reunir, examinar y discutir muestras procedentes de distintos campos –por ejemplo, arquitectura o diseño de producto– en los que los métodos de construcción y diseño suelen basarse en las formas. Esta primera fase genera ideas sobre el aspecto que queremos darle al proyecto, lo cual nos ayuda a evaluar la dirección visual de una manera *abstracta*. Naturalmente, no es posible trasladar los conceptos de la arquitectura o del diseño de producto al mundo del diseño gráfico de un modo equivalente, pero el proceso nos proporciona una idea del impacto que aspiramos a crear con el diseño. Es interesante notar que estas formas surgidas en las primeras etapas de los proyectos terminan con frecuencia figurando en la presentación final de nuestros trabajos de diseño y guían el proceso de creación a lo largo del camino. Las formas no sólo nos marcan una dirección visual sino que actúan como líneas maestras desde el principio del proyecto de diseño hasta su realización final.

El diseño digital está en los orígenes de Moby Digg. En nuestros proyectos digitales añadimos otra dimensión a nuestro trabajo de diseño: interacción y movimiento. Las animaciones pueden cambiar drásticamente la apariencia de las formas y afectar a su lenguaje simbólico y a su significado. El movimiento de la animación dirige la atención del espectador e influye en las relaciones jerárquicas y espaciales entre las distintas formas. En diseño, la animación expresa dinámicas y transformación. Además, los movimientos debidos a la interacción con el usuario, por ejemplo, las acciones con los dedos en los móviles o los cambios al pasar el ratón y los clics en los sitios web, refuerzan estos efectos y se traducen en una experiencia del usuario más rica. Estos principios se usan ya ampliamente y se han convertido en una tendencia popular en diseño.

Recomiendo encarecidamente a los diseñadores que experimenten con las formas sin cesar y que las usen como punto de partida para desarrollar procesos de diseño diferentes. Muchas áreas del diseño han aplicado en algún momento este método de creación. La ubicuidad de las formas –que son no sólo uno de los primeros elementos de diseño que se enseñan en las escuelas sino también el punto de partida en el proceso de creación incluso de los diseñadores más experimentados– nos dice mucho de su importancia en el mundo del diseño.

Points & Roundness

Studio Niccolai

Design: *Studio AH—HA*
Photography: *Diogo Alves / Studio AH—HA*

Communication project and website for Studio Niccolai, an Italian consultancy firm operating in the field of fashion, luxury goods and design.

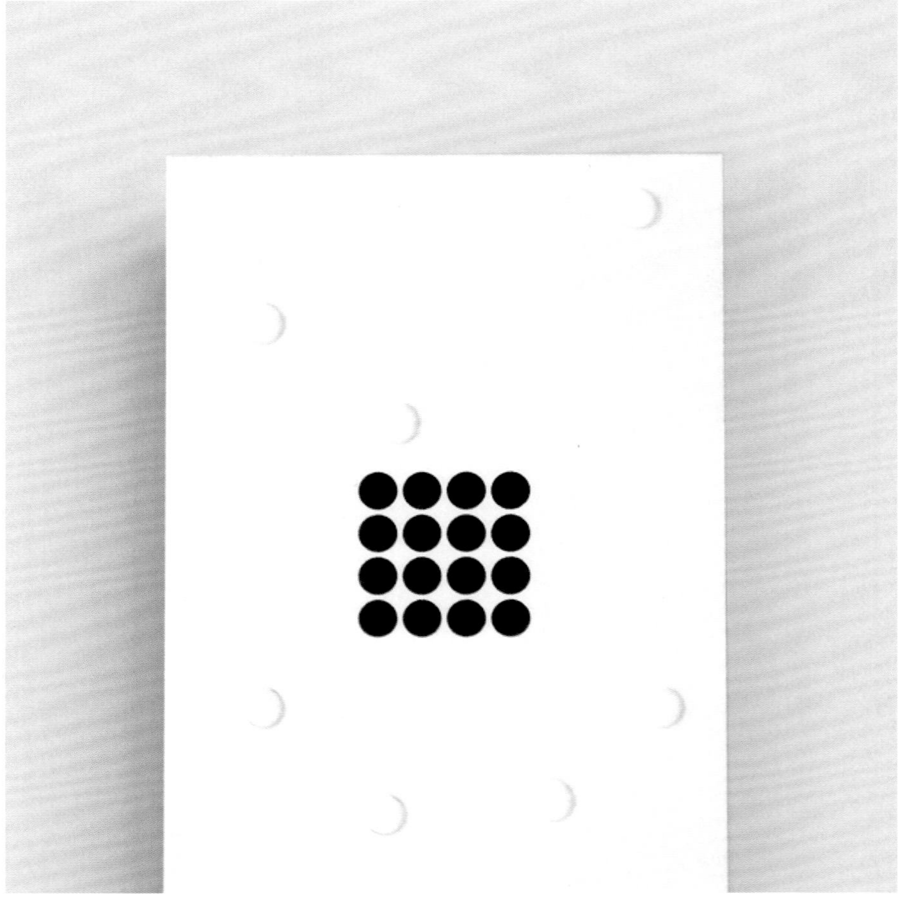

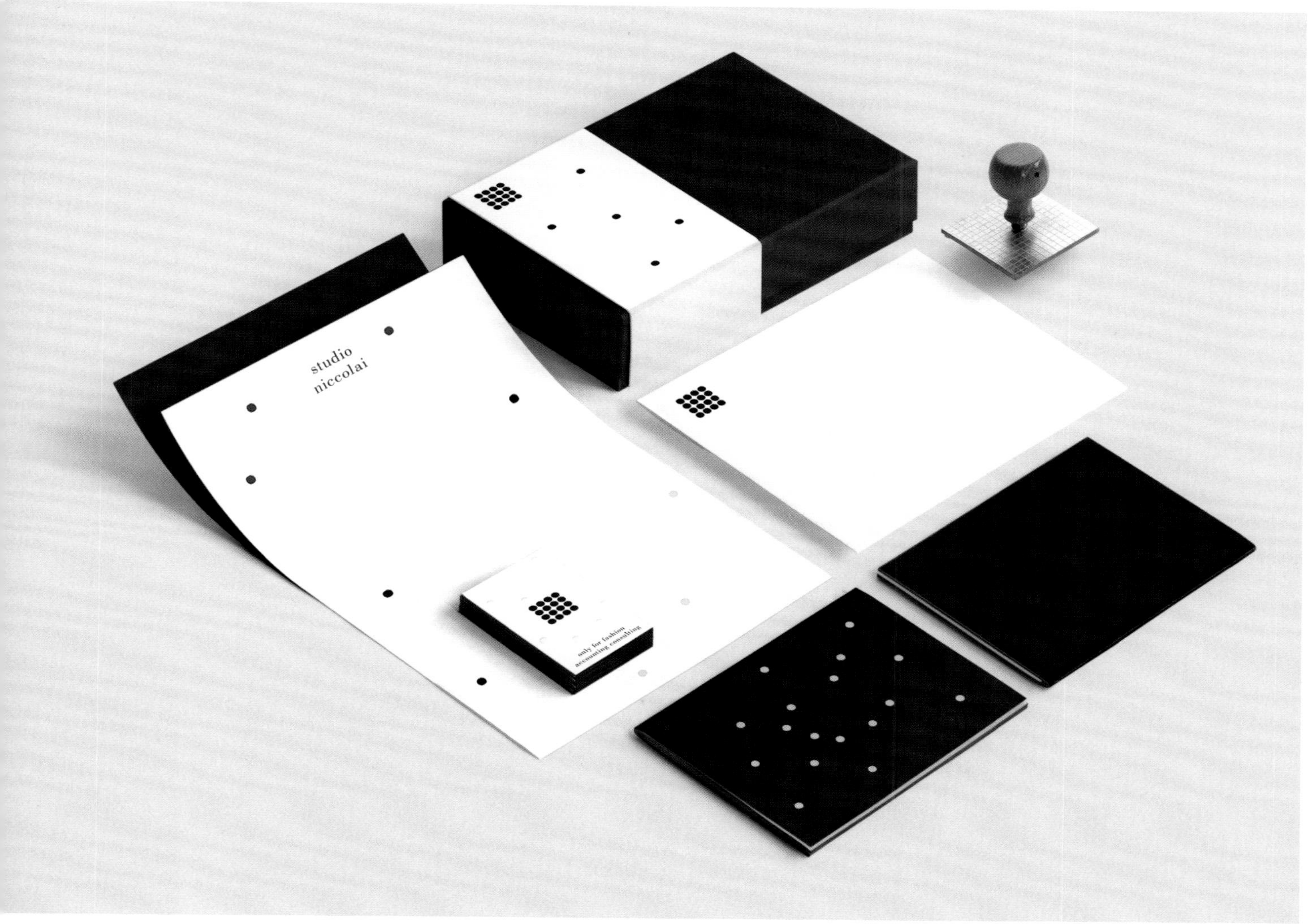

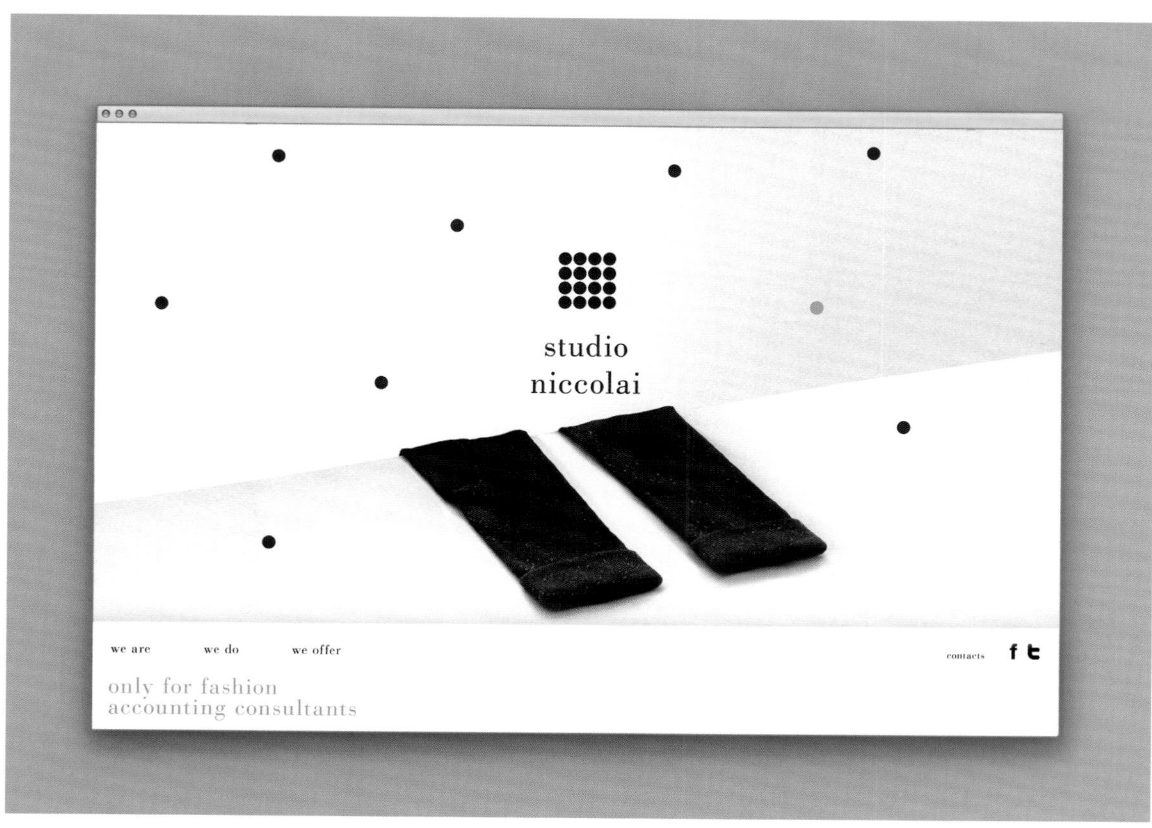
studio
niccolai
we are
we do
we offer
contacts
only for fashion
accounting consultants

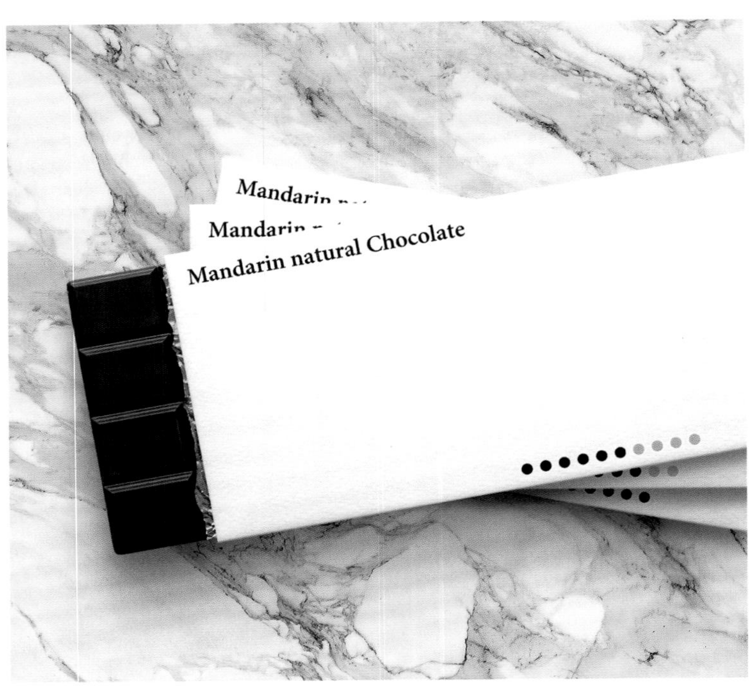

Mandarin Natural Chocolate

Design: *Yuta Takahashi*
Photography: *Yuta Takahashi*

Mandarin natural chocolate makes "bean to bar" chocolates, employing chocolate consistently working on the entire manufacturing process from the roasting of cacao beans to the finished chocolate bar.

This modernistic brand expresses itself through stunning white, an understated elegance and modernistic graphic design. The distinct identity, borne of an obsessive refusal to compromise, integrates a minimalistic elegance with a contemporary impression thus bringing the experience of a lovely, new brand to you.

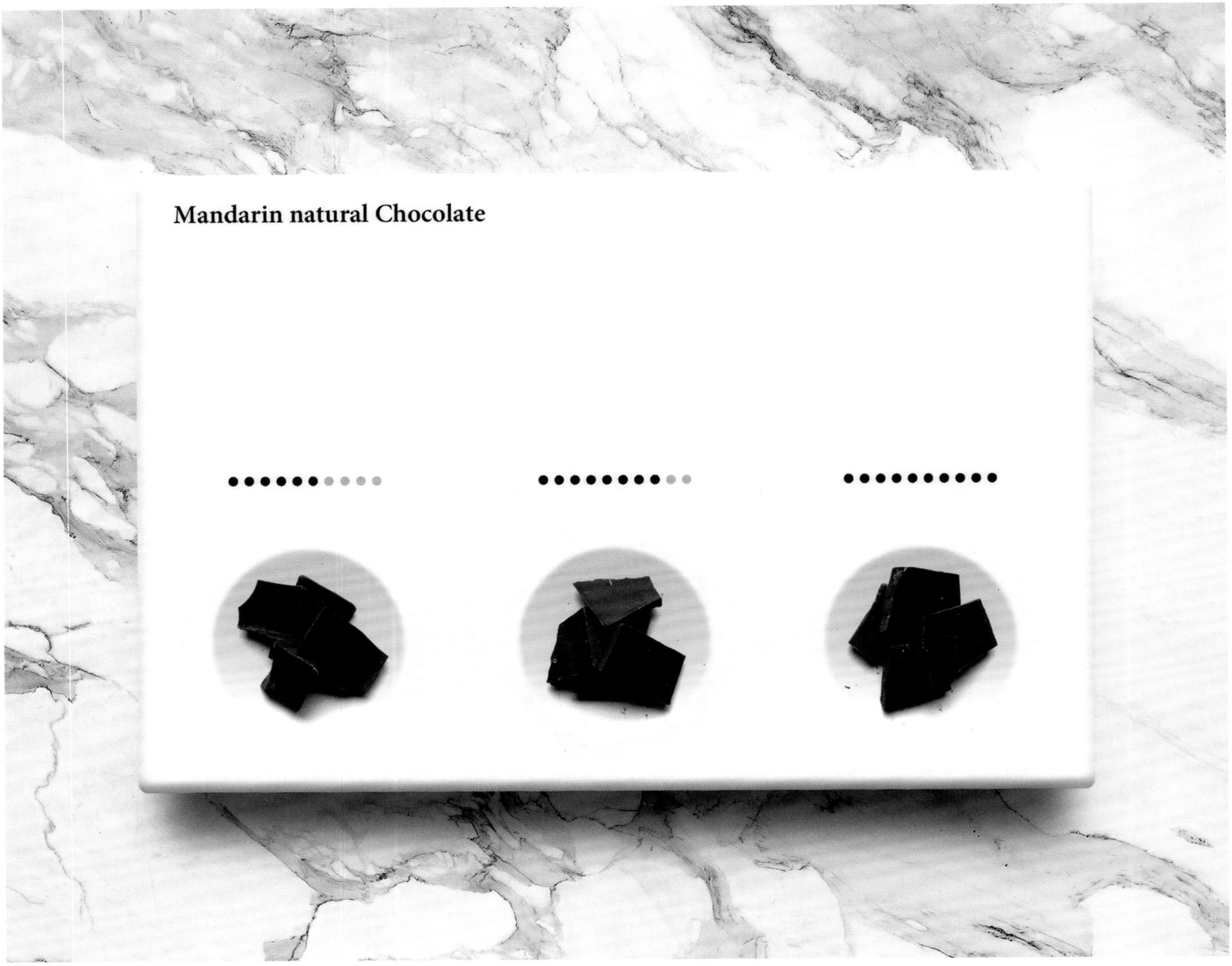

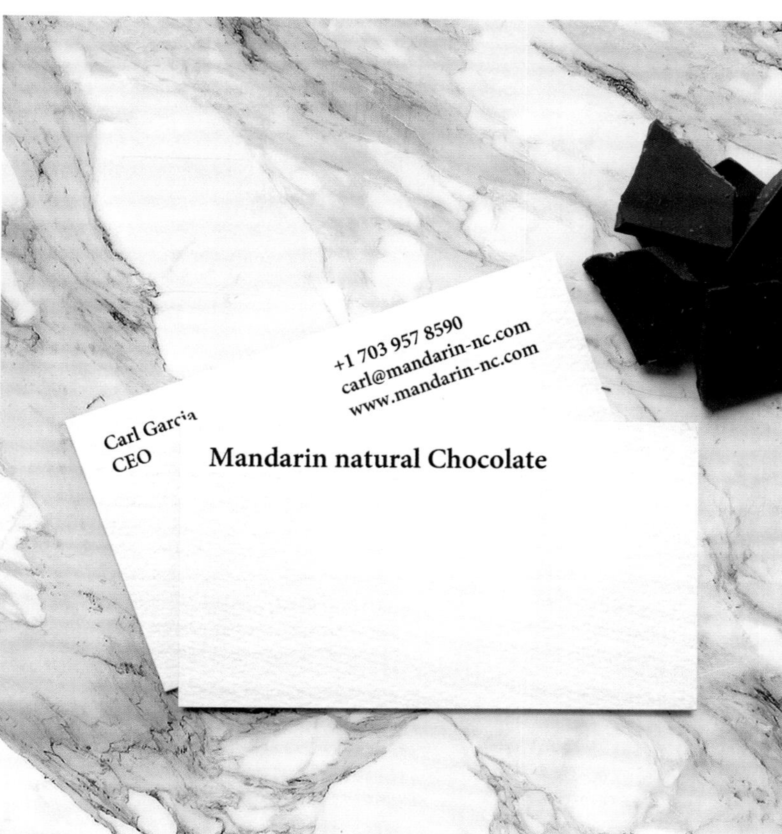
+1 703 957 8590
carl@mandarin-nc.com
www.mandarin-nc.com
Carl Garcia
CEO
Mandarin natural Chocolate

Mandarin natural Chocolate

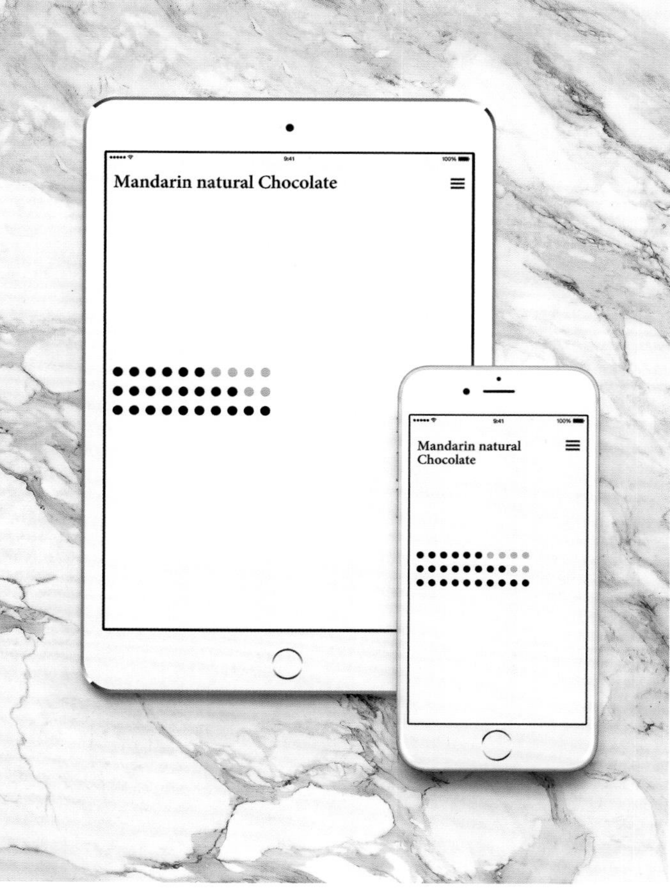
Mandarin natural Chocolate
Mandarin natural
Chocolate

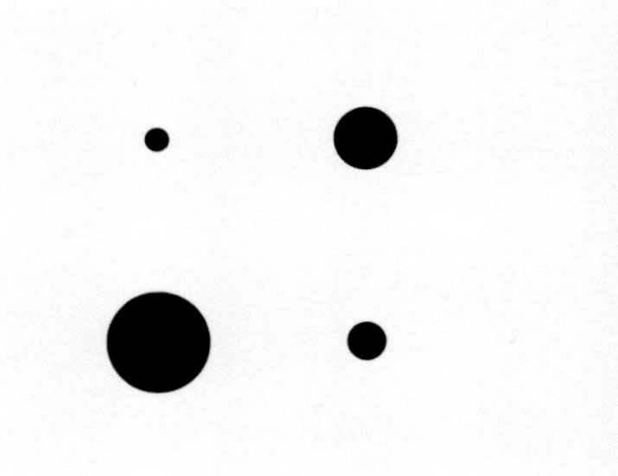

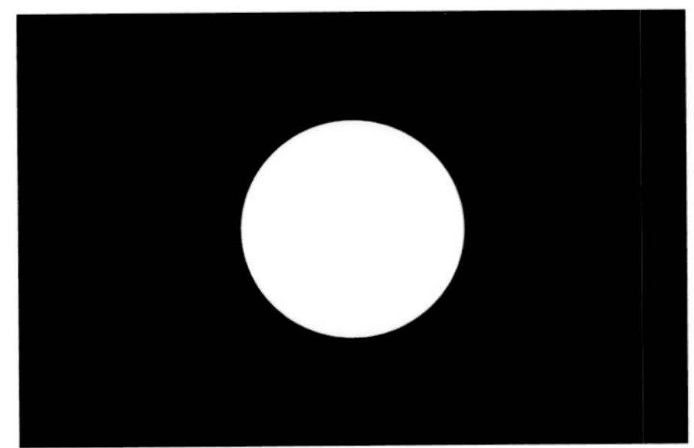

Polka

Design: *Yuta Takahashi*
Photography: *Yuta Takahashi*

Polka brings a global product selection that is carefully curated to Japan. When creating the identity of Polka, the usage of dots for the identity was utilized in a modern and joyful way which can be seen with each piece of the identity from the business cards and stationary. By used of polka dot that is the origin of the name of Polka, the designer produced the logotype that is full of modernity and joy. Then, by extracting the dots, the designer created the original pattern of random arrangement of large and small four dots. It expresses the interests, pioneering spirit, passions, funs, the claims of individuality of Polka.

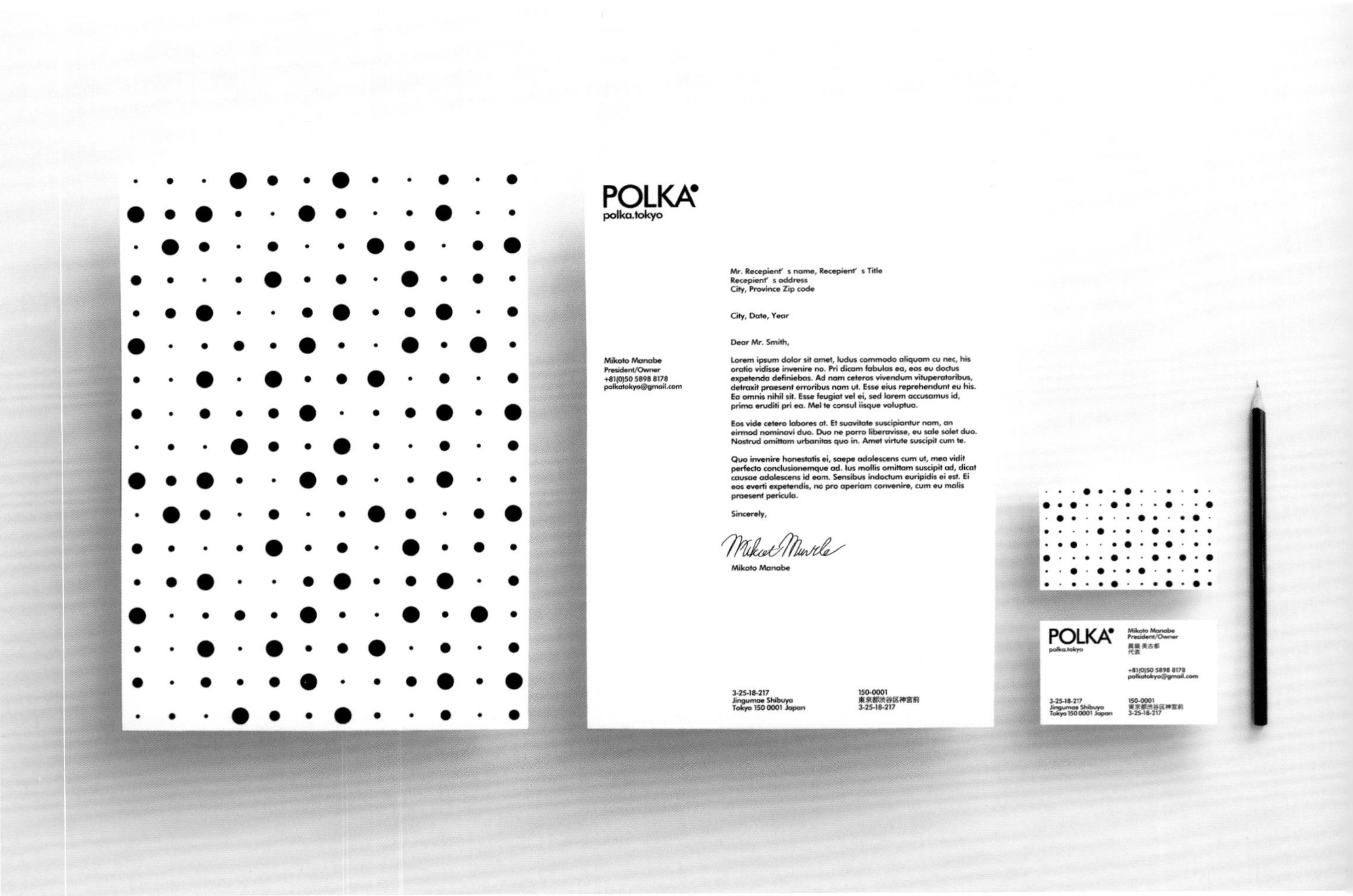

POLKA

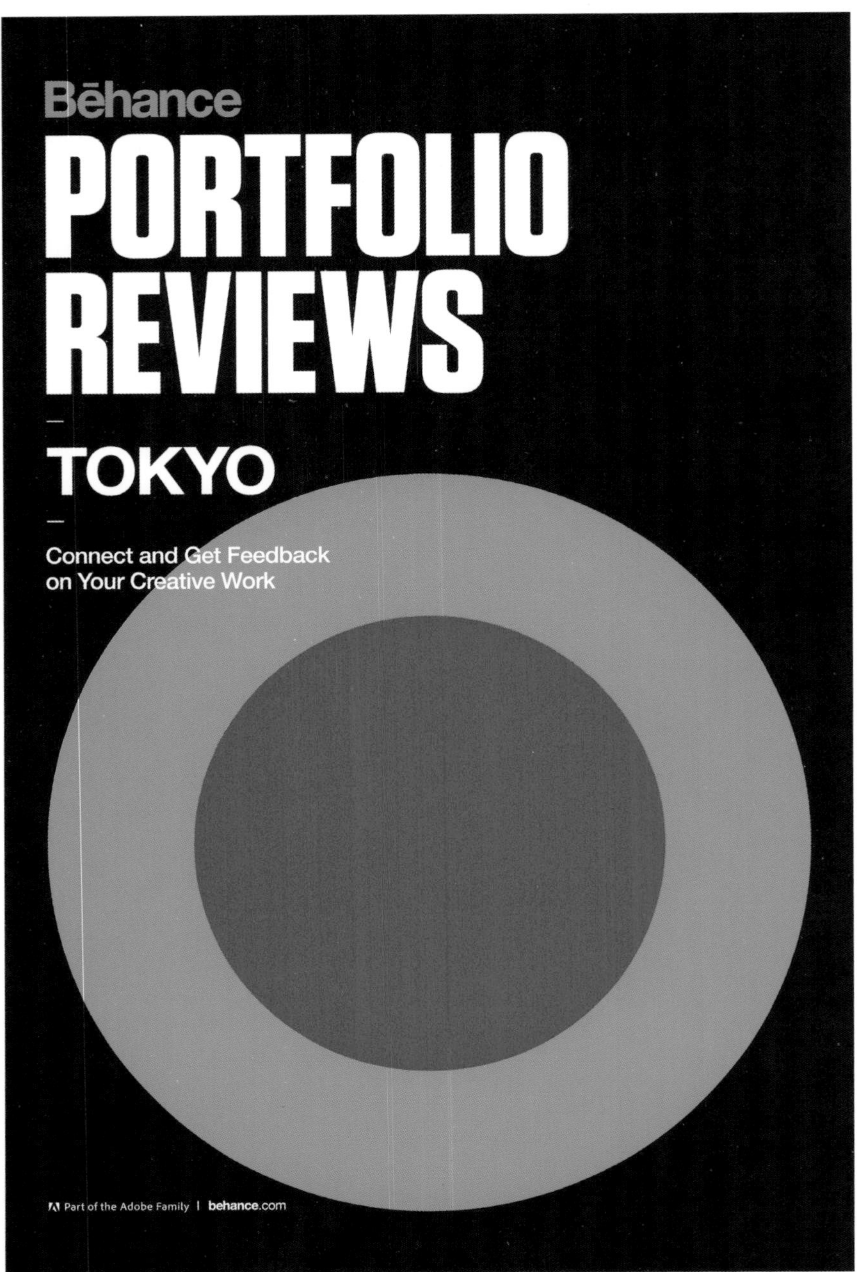

Behance Japan Community Portfolio Reviews #5

Agency: *Enhanced Inc.*
Art Direction: *Hiromi Maeo*

These artworks were created for the "Behance Japan Community Portfolio Reviews # 5". The mission of the Behance Japan Community is to create events and stimulate creators to share and connect leading to various opportunities, to encourage creators to take advantage of the Behance platform and to promote the creators overseas outside of Japan.

In order to obtain a strong visual effects, the designer tried a simple design structure as much as possible. The red circle in this visual symbolizes the Japanese identity. The overlap and spread of the circle represent the spread of ideas through dialogue and exchanges.

Symbol os Japanese flag = Blood
(Source of Japanese identity)

Spread of Japanese identity
to overseas

Conversation of a creators and reviewers
(World creators and Japanese creators)

Bēhance
PORTFOLIO
REVIEWS
TOKYO
Connect and Get Feedback
on Your Creative Work
May 10, 2014
5:00PM - 9:00PM
T-SITE GARDEN Gallery, Daikanyama
Tokyo, Shibuya-ku, Sarugakucho 16-15
Part of the Adobe Family
behance.com

Bēhance
PORTFOLIO
REVIEWS
TOKYO
Connect and Get Feedback
on Your Creative Work
May 10, 2014
5:00PM - 9:00PM
T-SITE GARDEN Gallery, Daikanyama
Tokyo, Shibuya-ku, Sarugakucho 16-15
Part of the Adobe Family
behance.com

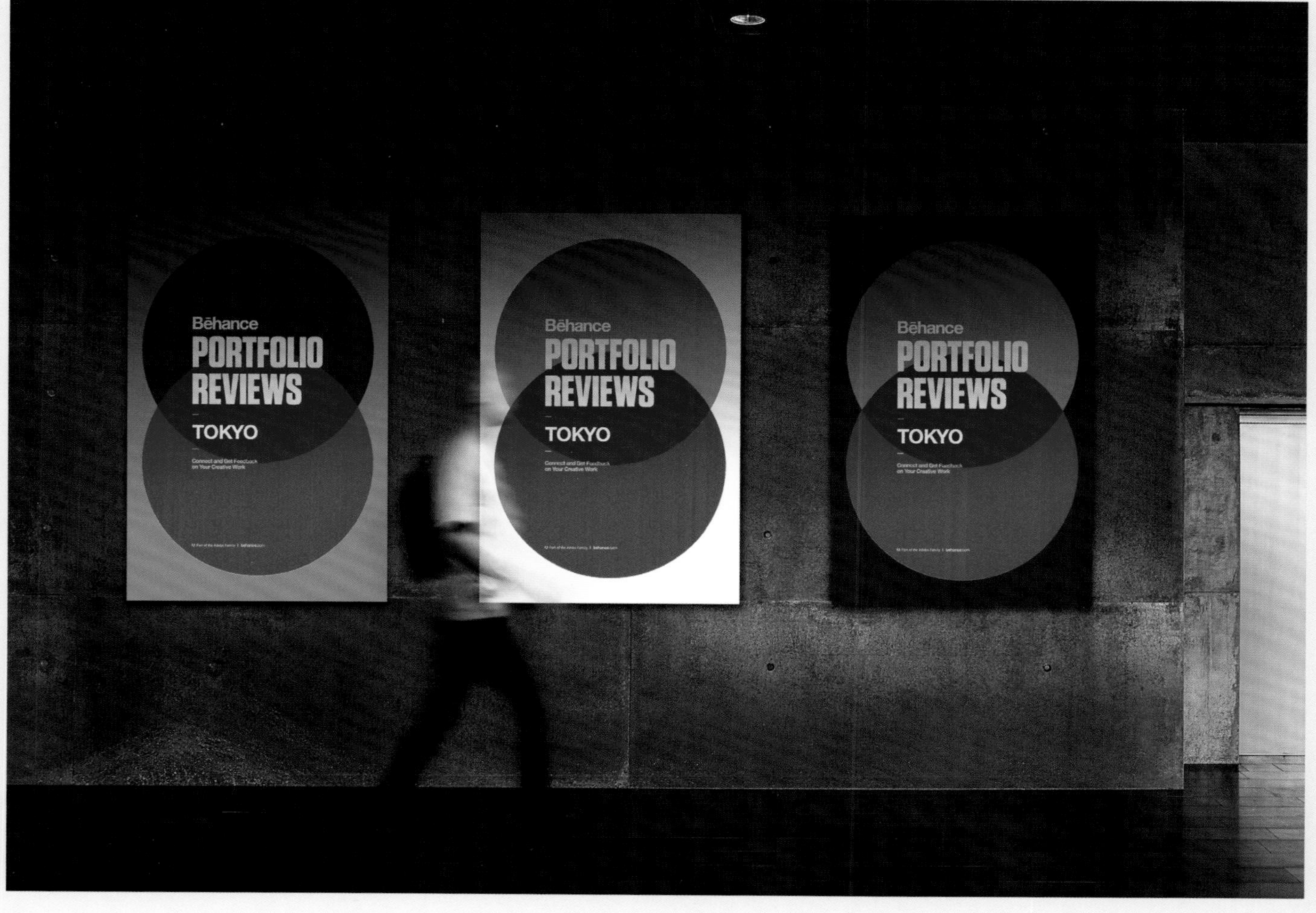

STREIB

Agency: *ADDA Studio*
Creative Direction: *Christian Vögtlin*
Photography: *Stephanie Trenz, LSDK*

Refreshing the corporate design, the designers had to expand the visual range due to the extended treatments and additional dentists. Each dentist and treatment keeps his friendly signal color on business cards and appointment cards which the designers also keep in the established quadratic dimensions. The corporate color system is being used as a menu. Optimized for tablet and smart phone the one-pager makes every message easily accessible.

STREIB & KOLLEGEN
T 07130 . 45 30 13
M info@praxis-streib.de

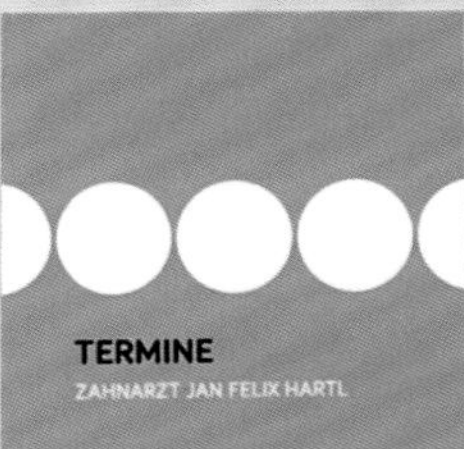

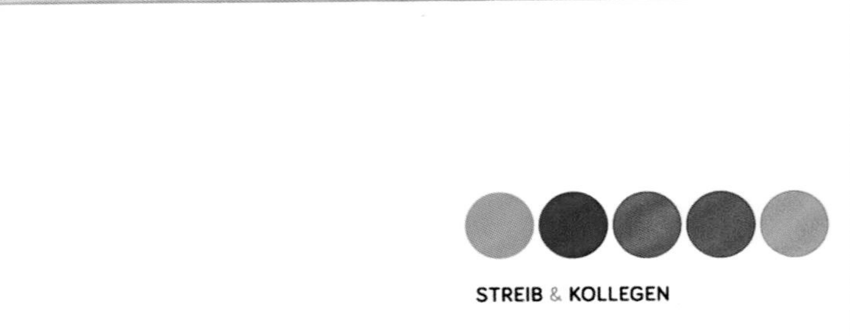

STREIB & KOLLEGEN
Hangstraße 2 · 74182 Obersulm-Affaltrach
T 07130 . 45 30 13 · F 07130 . 45 30 23
M info@praxis-streib.de · I praxis-streib.de

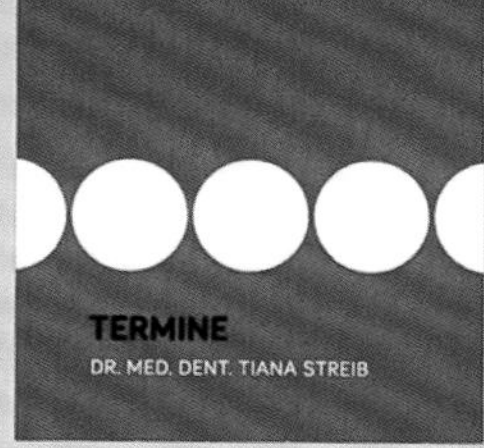

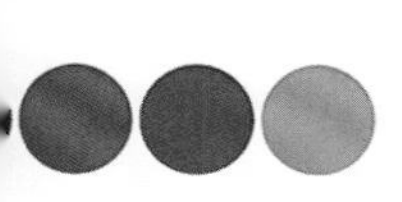

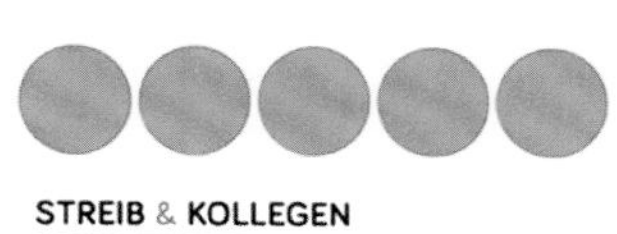

STREIB & KOLLEGEN
SPEICHELTEST

STREIB & KOLLEGEN
PROPHYLAXE
Für junge Erwachsene zwischen 18 und 35 Jahren.

WIE OFT SOLLTE EINE PROFESSIONELLE ZAHNREINIGUNG DURCHGEFÜHRT WERDEN?

Eine PZR dauert ungefähr 45-60 Minuten. Bei gesundem Zahnfleisch ist die PZR im Abstand von 6 Monaten eine ideale Ergänzung zur häuslichen Zahnpflege. Je nach individuellem Erkrankungsrisiko erstellen wir aber auch alternative Zeitintervalle.

WARUM PROFESSIONELLE ZAHNREINIGUNG?

Karies und Zahnfleischentzündung, die Hauptursachen für einen Zahnverlust, sind vermeidbar. Die PZR unterstützt Sie dabei und zusammen sorgen wir dafür, dass Eingriffe erst gar nicht nötig werden. Die vollständige Entfernung des Zahnbelags und die regelmäßige Pflege der Zähne sind die wichtigsten Eckpfeiler für gesunde Zähne und Zahnfleisch.

WAS WIRD GEMACHT?

Nach dem sichtbar machen der Zahnbeläge mit einem Farbstoff werden alle Zähne schonend gereinigt. Mit Handinstrumenten, Ultraschall- oder Pulverstrahlgeräten entfernen wir Zahnstein, Plaque und Ablagerungen. Wir polieren alle Oberflächen mit einem weichen Polierer und Polierpaste. Dadurch erhalten die Zähne nicht nur einen schönen Glanz, sondern die Anhaftung von Belag wird damit stark verringert. Fluorid-Gel härtet die Zähne und Chlorhexidin-Gel schützt die Zahnzwischenräume wirksam vor schädlichen Bakterien. Im Anschluss beraten wir Sie ausführlich, worauf Sie bei Ihren Zähnen zu achten haben und wie Sie diese zu Hause optimal pflegen können.

KOSTEN GESETZLICH VERSICHERTE

Je nach Zeitaufwand kostet die professionelle Zahnreinigung zwischen 50.00 und 80.00 €.

KOSTEN PRIVATVERSICHERTE

Sie erhalten eine Rechnung nach der Gebührenordnung, die in der Regel von den Versicherungen übernommen wird.

STREIB & KOLLEGEN
PROPHYLAXE

Für Kinder unter 6 Jahren oder Kinder mit hohem Kariesrisiko.

STREIB & KOLLEGEN

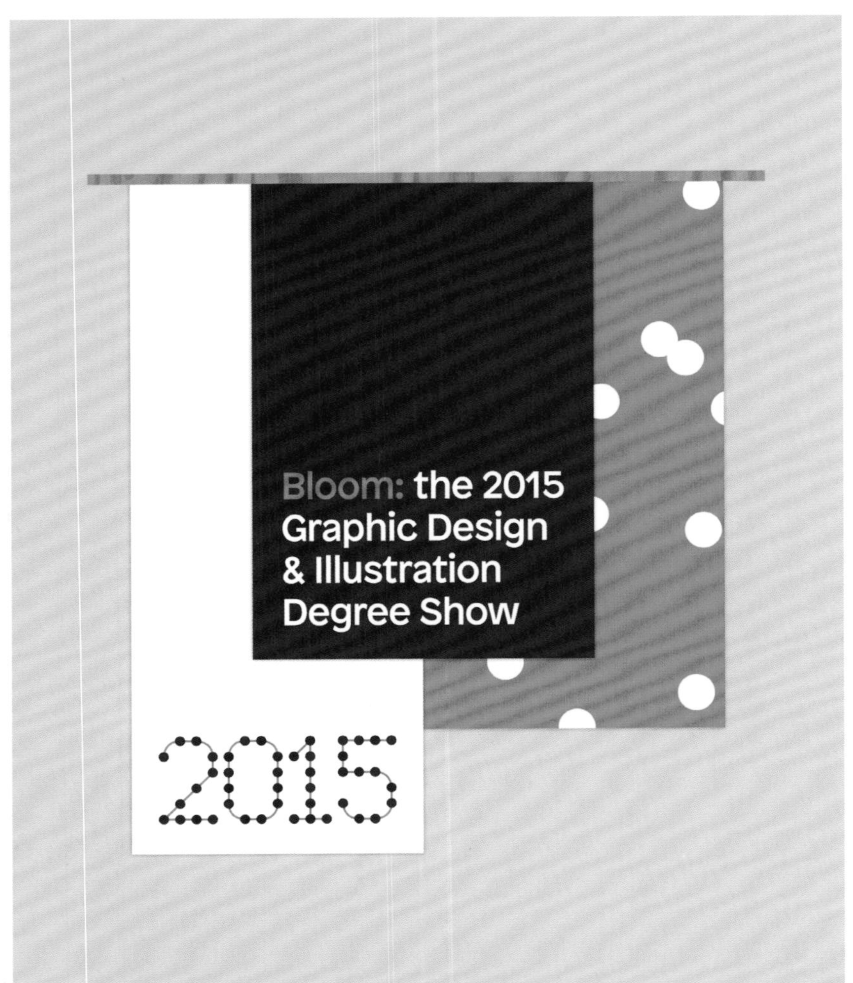

Bloom

Design: *Moving Studio*
Photography: *Moving Studio*

De Montfort University commissioned Moving Studio to create a Degree Show Identity for their 2015 Graduates. The students worked with Moving Studio to create concepts that were strengthened and refined through group meetings to produce a cohesive identity. The show, entitled Bloom, used promotional materials featuring a 132 pages brochure with die-cut cover, neon posters using reverse printing to highlight each area of the course (design and illustration), A5 flyers, and hand crafted way-finding boards.

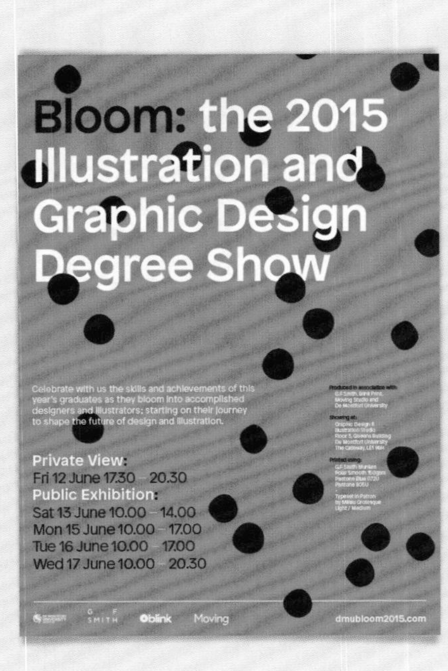

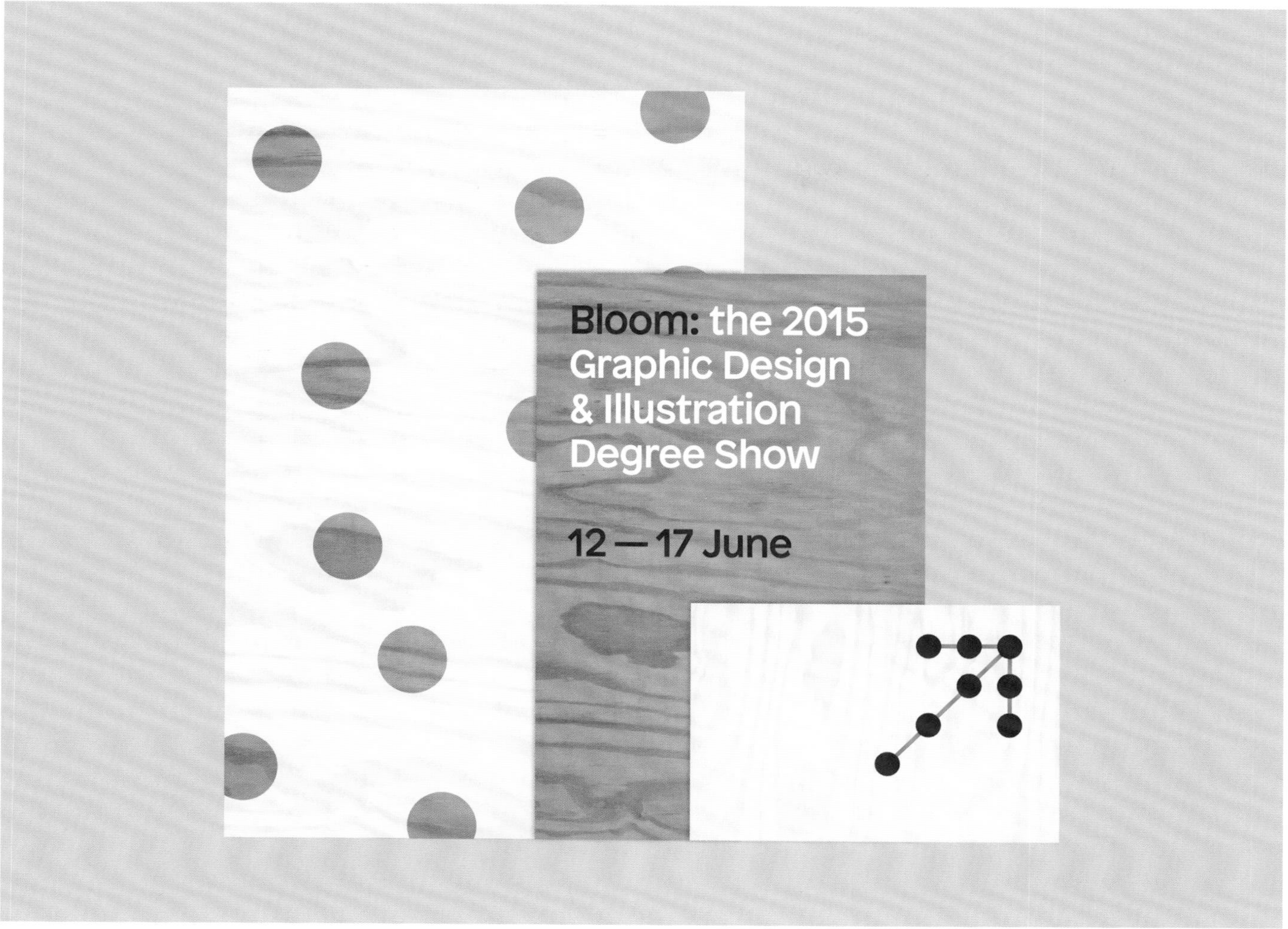

Bloom: the 2015
Graphic Design
& Illustration
Degree Show

12 — 17 June

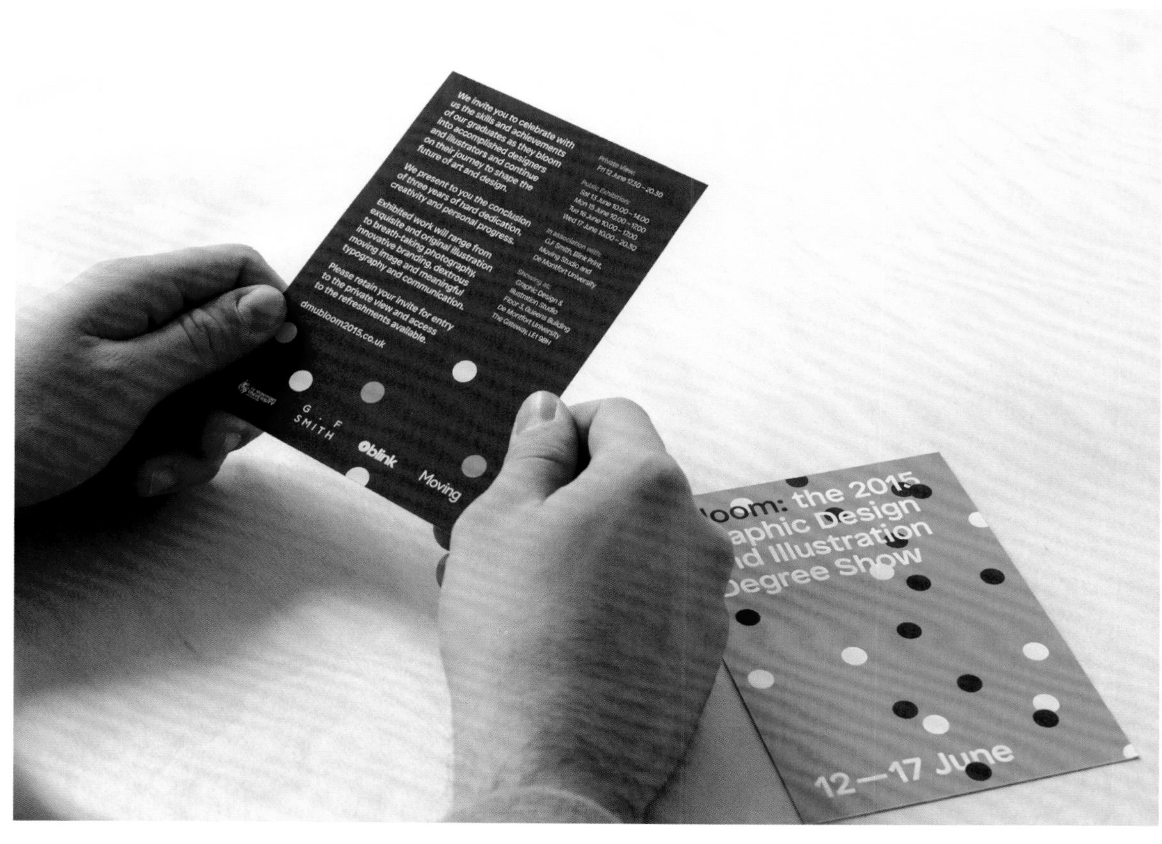

United Nations Climate Change Conference – COP20

Agency: *Brandlab*
Art Direction: *Andres Nakamatsu*
Design: *Jhesse Franco*

The Ministry of the Environment commissioned Brandlab the development of the identity for The XX International Conference on Climate Change Event that was held in Lima, Peru. Conceptually, the designers decided to put the problem and the solution in the brand, a wakeup call for all the leaders attending the event; Graphically, the designers developed an identity based on 20 rings representing the different temperatures currently on Earth. The inner rings represent the current temperatures and external represent the goal of reversing the current trend.

LIMA COP20 CMP10
UN CLIMATE CHANGE CONFERENCE 2014

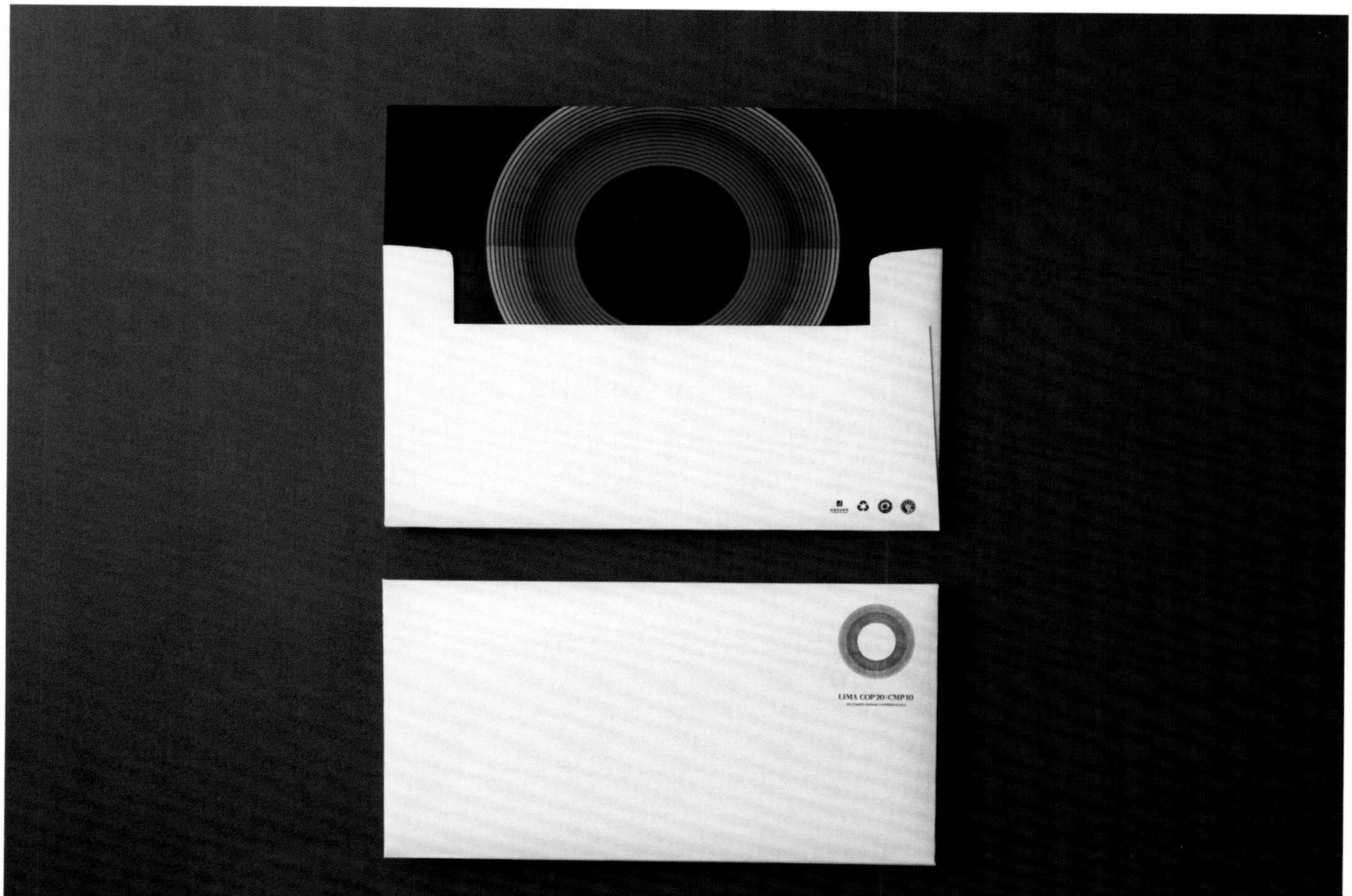
LIMA COP20 CMP10

Panama Plus

Design: *Moby Digg*

The Panama Plus Festival is an annual subculture festival, featuring the creative work of various artists, musicians, performers, writers, and cinematographers. Moby Digg mainly were responsible for the branding of the festival, which included the production of the poster artwork, the corporate identity, a redesign of the logo, ticket design, and banner design and so on. Key indicators for the visual identity were the vivid and colorful character of the culture festival. Therefore, the designers created a playful typography and a simple but strong color theme. The typography can be used as a single item for branding or in combination with the colorful key visuals. The key visuals were constructed out of circles filled with gradients and then randomly transformed through a coded glitch generator.

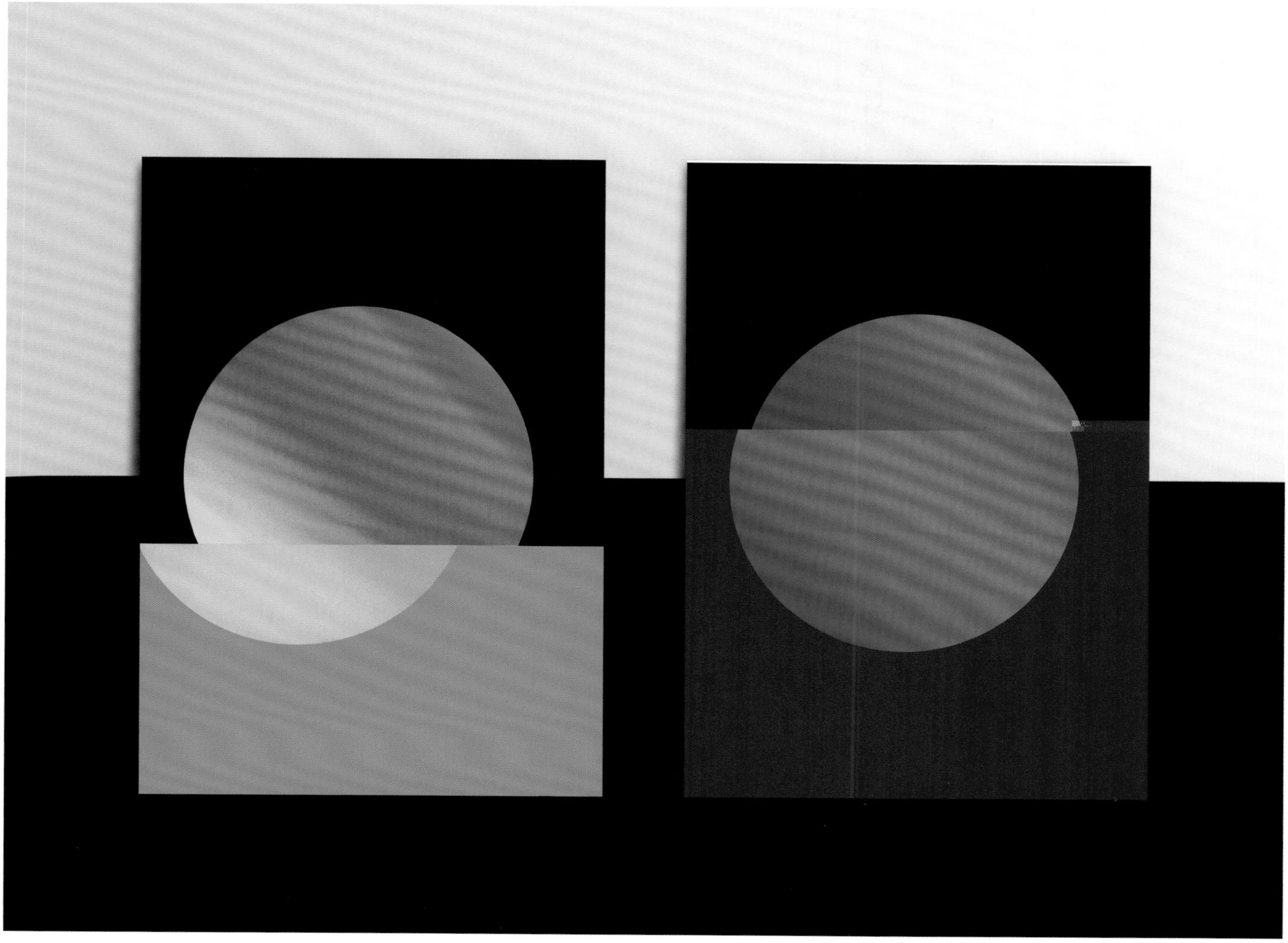

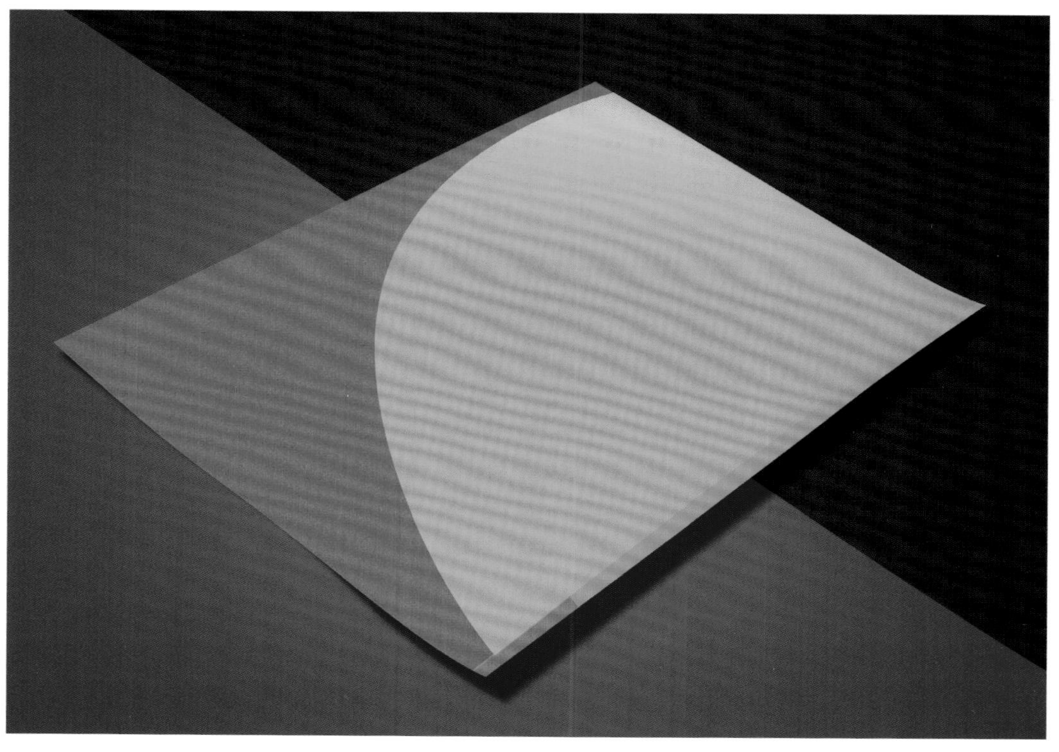

IIT Architecture Chicago

Design: *Mainstudio*

Since the appointment of Dutch architect Wiel Arets to its helm, the Illinois Institute of Technology's College of architect has introduced a new graphic design identity. It emanated from Nowness, which was translated into the design of the school's communication tools, as its lecture posters and event invitations.

Four varying – "information zones" – alongside contrasting colors and dots of many sizes, are basic components of its organizational system. Dots are often patterned to create form, by placing them in each zone, in varying sizes and colors. The identity makes use of the typeface Theinhardt, a Grotesque typeface designed by François Rappo, which reflects the rigid system of grids favored by the school's founder, Mies van der Rohe. Lectures posters are deconstructed into smaller posters, and the school's digital communications, such as the design of its website. Select posters within the series are designed with two colors to denote special events, some with a white background.

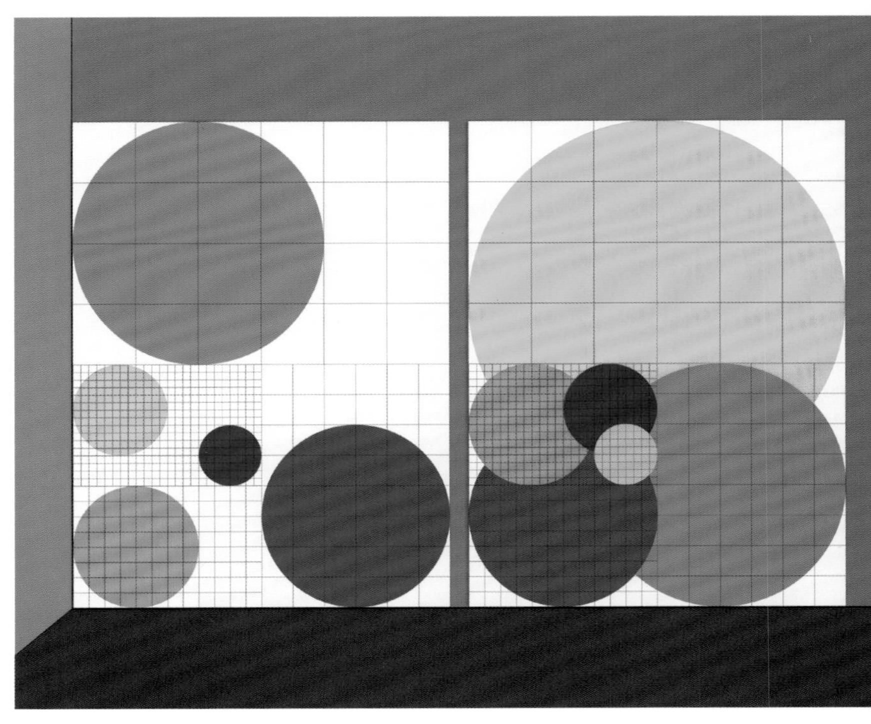

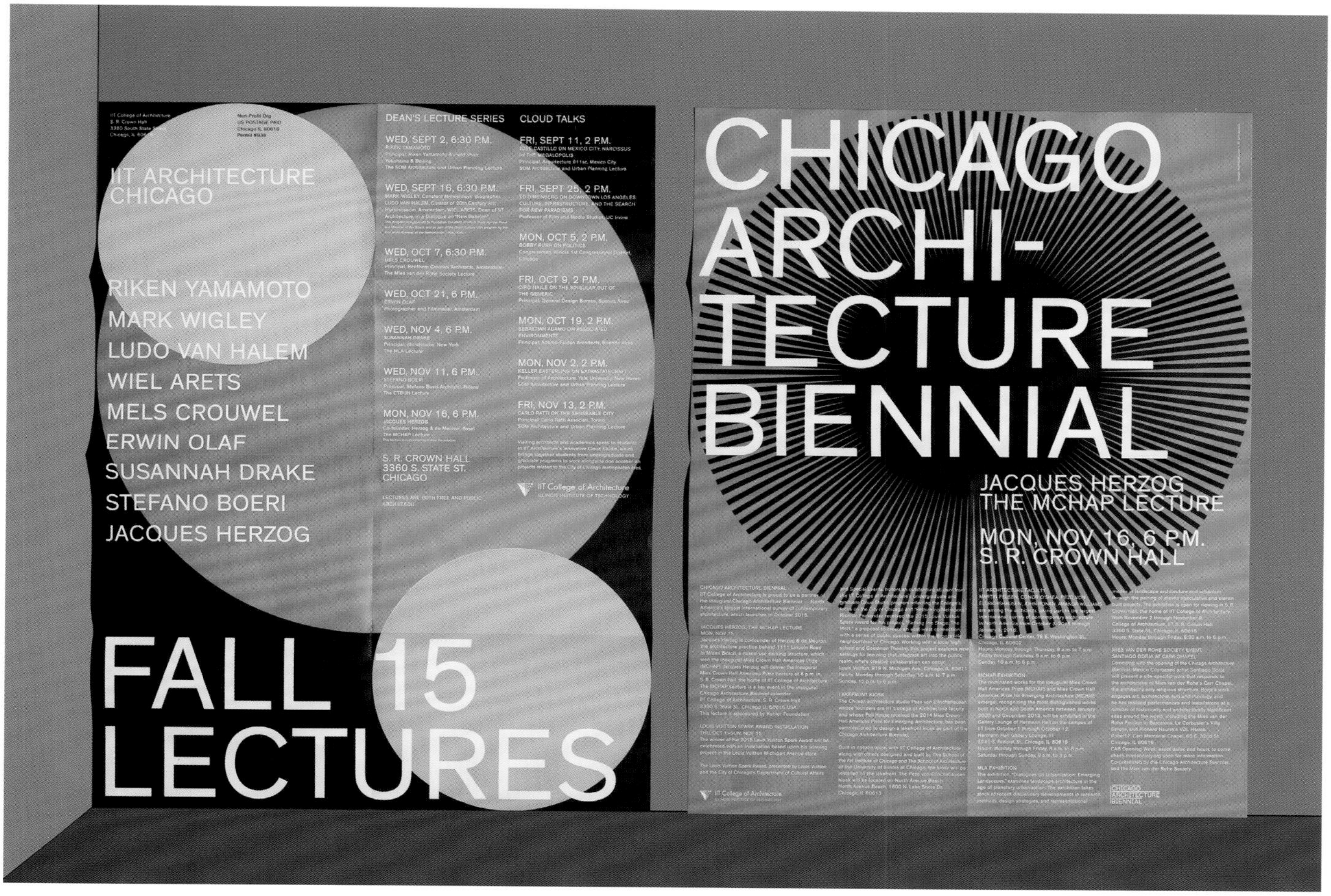

IIT ARCHITECTURE
CHICAGO

RIKEN YAMAMOTO
MARK WIGLEY
LUDO VAN HALEM
WIEL ARETS
MELS CROUWEL
ERWIN OLAF
SUSANNAH DRAKE
STEFANO BOERI
JACQUES HERZOG

DEAN'S LECTURE SERIES

WED, SEPT 2, 6:30 P.M.

WED, SEPT 16, 6:30 P.M.

WED, OCT 7, 6:30 P.M.

WED, OCT 21, 6 P.M.

WED, NOV 4, 6 P.M.

WED, NOV 11, 6 P.M.

MON, NOV 16, 6 P.M.

S. R. CROWN HALL
3360 S. STATE ST.
CHICAGO

CLOUD TALKS

FRI, SEPT 11, 2 P.M.

FRI, SEPT 25, 2 P.M.

MON, OCT 5, 2 P.M.

FRI, OCT 9, 2 P.M.

MON, OCT 19, 2 P.M.

MON, NOV 2, 2 P.M.

FRI, NOV 13, 2 P.M.

IIT College of Architecture

FALL 15
LECTURES

CHICAGO
ARCHI-
TECTURE
BIENNIAL

JACQUES HERZOG
THE MCHAP LECTURE

MON, NOV 16, 6 P.M.
S. R. CROWN HALL

OPEN
HOUSE
ANNUAL
STUDENT
EXHIBIT
FRI, MAY 8, 2015
5 P.M.
AWARD PRESENTATION
5:30–8 P.M.
OPEN HOUSE

IIT ARCHITECTURE
CHICAGO
WINY MAAS
JORGE FRANCISCO
LIERNUR
ADRIAAN GEUZE
MARCELO FERRAZ
WIEL ARETS

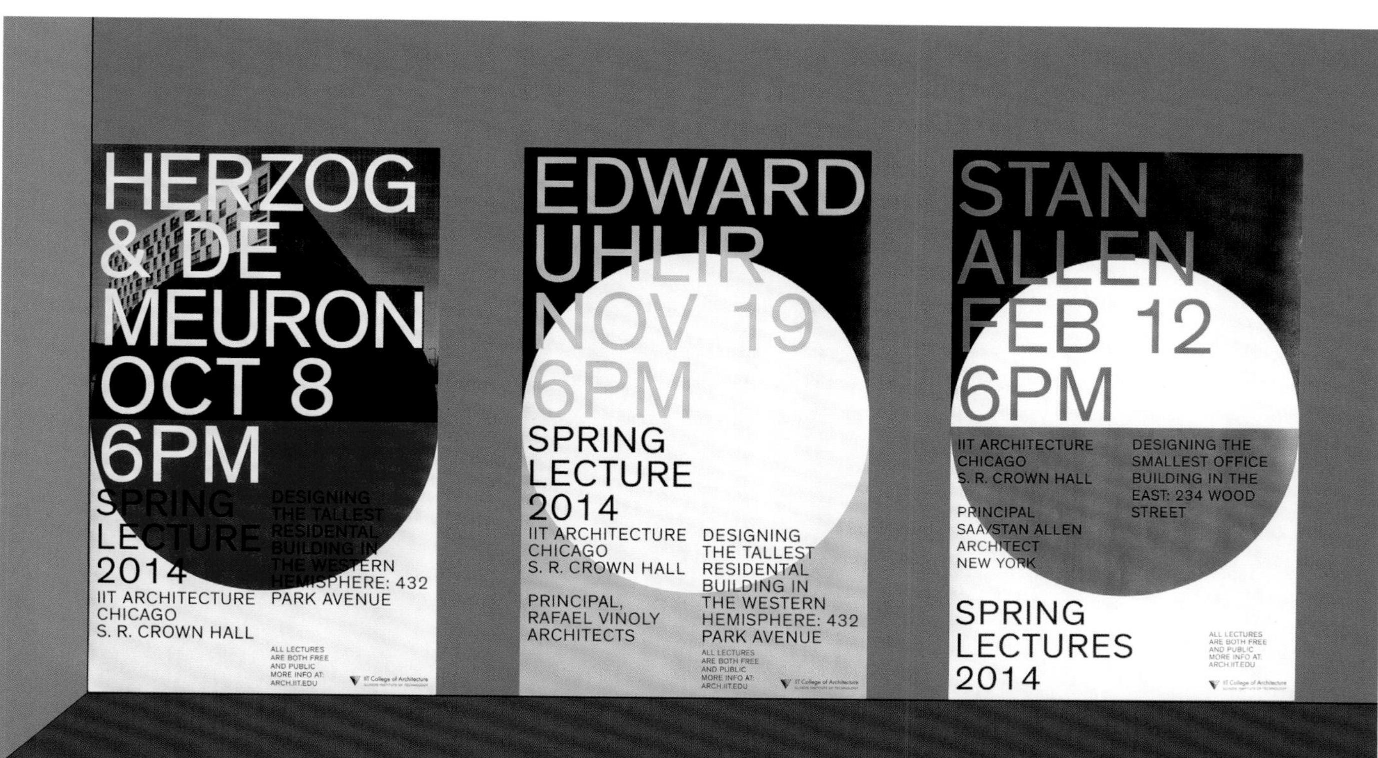

IIT
ARCHITECTURE
CHICAGO
BIENNIAL
PROGRAMS

CHICAGO

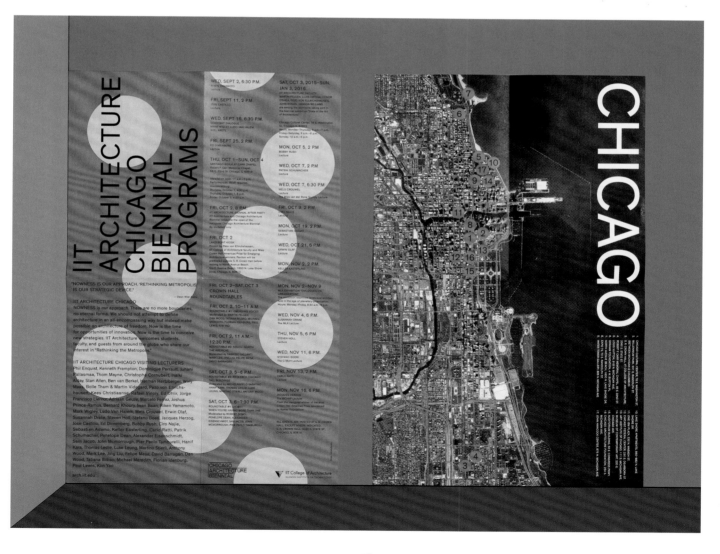

Ted × Poznan

Design: *Natalia Zerko*

The main concept for the logo and the overall identity is a graphic illustration of the theme – Reborn. The designer took one of the first associations which came to mind – the concept of reincarnation and played with it a bit, using simple geometric shapes. The circle, as the perfect shape, was selected as the main element.

TEDx Poznań
Reborn.
You have to die
a human being,
to be Reborn
an individual.

Each night,
when I got to sleep,
I die.
And the next morning,
when I wake up,
I am Reborn.
TEDx Poznań
Reborn.

TEDx Poznań
Reborn.
You have to die
a human being,
to be Reborn
an individual.
Each night,
when I got to sleep,
I die.
And the next morning,
when I wake up,
I am Reborn.

Rewire Festival

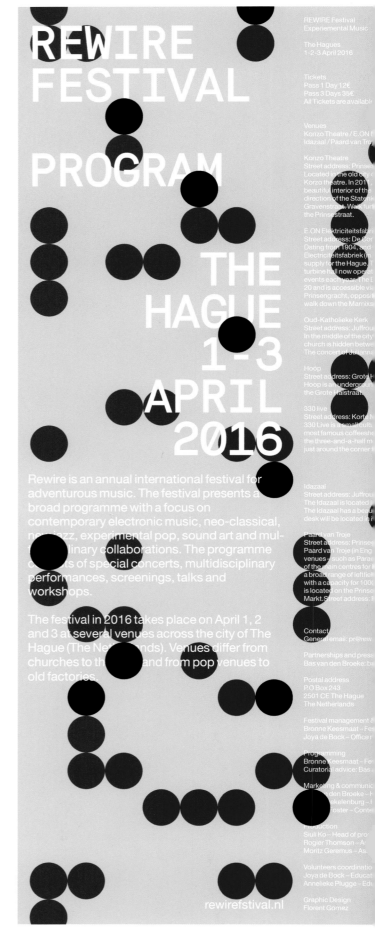

***Design:** Florent Gomez*

Rewire is an annual international festival for adventurous music. The festival presents a broad programme with a focus on contemporary electronic music, neo-classical, new jazz, experimental pop, sound art, and multidisciplinary collaborations. The programme consists of special concerts, multidisciplinary performances, screenings, talks, and workshops.

REWIRE FESTIVAL

PROGRAM

THE HAGUE 1-3 APRIL 2016

rewirefestival.nl

ebsite www.rewirefestival.nl

itsfabriek / Oud-Katholieke Kerk / Hoorp / 330 live /

he Hague, on the Prinsestraat, lies the alluring
ovation of the theatre was finished, in which the
as created. Korzo is accessible with tram in the
ram 17 stops in front of the station. Get out at stop
there, the street to your right before the post office is

becqueplein 20
ally altered over the following century, the
electricity factory") was built to regulate the electricity
ng has been owned by E-On since the millenium. The
onumental arts venue, hosting a select number of
itsfabriek is situated at De Constant Rebecqueplein
You can catch the Grote Markt stop on the
rd van Troje. dstraat West, and then
Joseph Ledel

at 7
The Hague lies this old Catholic parish church. The
uses of the Moelnstraat and the Juffrouw Idastraat.
will take place in this beautiful old church.

ated in the city-basement under the old city-hall at

at 2
m and -stage situated in the former basement the
Hague: Café Crémers. The 330 in it's name refers to
basement lies below the surface. 330 Live is located
o Theatre.

at 2
courtyard accross the street from Korzo theater.
ic hall for performances, and the tickets and info
ard.

rojan Horse) was founded gside other
weg, 013 and Vera – the P ed as one
usic in the Netherlands; and s for booking
lerground music. The Paard has two stages, one
the other holding 300. The venue also has a café and
The Hague, diagonally opposite the lively Grote
cht 12.

.nl

efestival.nl

ment
ctor

ator
n, Martijn Buser, Rogier Thomson

arketing & communications
keting & communications

ction manager

tion
inator
ordinator

MON, 1 APRL
–

96wrld (LIT)
10:00 am – hall 1
Konzo Theatre

Addison Groove (UK)
11:30 am – hall 3
E.ON

Akka (NL)
1:00 pm – hall 2
Konzo Theatre

Alessandro Cortini (IT)
2:00 pm – hall 3
E.ON

Antenna (NL)
4:00 pm – hall 1
Konzo Theatre

Aisha Devi (CH)
5:30 pm – hall 2
E

Blue Daisy (UK)
7:00 pm – hall 2
Konzo Theatre

Bronze Teeth (UK)
10:00 am – hall 2
Oud-Katholieke Kerk

Casperelectronics (US)
10:00 am – hall 6
Oud-Katholieke Kerk

FilosofischeIStilte (NL)
10:00 am – hall 1
330 live

Garoeda (NL)
10:00 am – hall 1
I

G Louw (NL)
10:00 am – hall 1
Oud-Katholieke Kerk

Gnod (UK)
10:00 am
Konzo Th

Godspeed You!
Black Emperor (CA)
10:00 am – hall 1
Oud-Katholieke Kerk

Grouper (US)
10:00 am – hall 1
E.ON

Gut & Irmler (DE)
10:00 am – hall 1
Oud-Katholieke K

HOEK (NL)
10:00 am – hall 1
Idazaal

Holly Herndon (US)
10:00 am – hall 1
Oud-Katholieke Kerk

Chris Corsano (U
Mette Rasmussen (DK)
10:00 am – hall 1
Hoop

Cliff Lothar (SE)
10:00 am – hall 1
Hoop

Cloudface (CA)
10:00 am – hall 1
Oud-Katholieke Kerk

Dandana (NL)
10:00 am – hall 1
Hoop

De Tuinen (NL)
10:00 am – hall 1
Oud-Katholieke Kerk

DJ Sniff (JP)
10:00 am – hall 1
Hoop

DJ Stingray (US)
10:00 am – hall 1
Oud-Katholieke Kerk

Evian Chris (UK)
10:00 am – hall 1
Hoop

FETTER (US/NL)
10:00 am – hall 1
Oud-Katholi

IVVVO (PT)
10:00 am – hall 1
Oud-Katholieke Kerk

Jac Berrocal +
David Fenech +
Vincent Epplay (FR)
10:00 am – hall 1
Hoop

Jenny Hval & Susanna (NO)
11:30 am – hall 3
Oud-Katholieke Kerk

Julianna Barwick
Expanded (US)
1:00 pm – hall 2
E.ON

Klankman (NL)
2:00 pm – ha
Konzo Theat

Lorn (US)
4:00 pm – hall 1
Konzo Theatre

Marsman (NL)
5:30 pm – hall 2
E.ON

Blue Daisy (L
7:00 pm – hall 2
Konzo Theatre

TUE, 2 APRL
–

Mbongwana Star (CD
10:00 am – hall 2
Oud-Katholieke Kerk

MGBG (FR/IS)
10:00 am – hall
Oud-Katholiek

Neneh Cherry &
Rocketnumberine (SE/UK)
10:00 am – hall 1
Hoop

Omer Eilam (ISR)
10:00 am – hall 1
E.ON

Oren Ambarchi (AU)
10:00 a 1
Oud-K Kerk

Organisms (NL)
10:00 am – hall 1
330 live

Paul Panhuysen (NL)
10:00 am – hall 1
Hoop

DJ Sn
10:00 1
Hoop

DJ Stingray (US)
10:00 am – hall 1
Oud-Katholieke Kerk

Pearson Sound (UK)
10:00 am – hall 1
Konzo Theatre

Powell (UK)
10:00 am – hall 1
Konzo Theatre

Ron Morelli (US)
10:00 am – hall 1
330 live

RP Boo (US)
10:00 am – hall 1
Idazaal

RSS BO
10:00 am
Oud-Katholieke Kerk

Saskia Lankhoorn /
Kate Moore (NL/AU)
10:00 am – hall 1
Hoop

Shabazz Palaces (US)
10:00 am – hall 1
E.ON

Shit and Shine (US/UK)
10:00 am – hall 1
330 live

Siinai (FI)
10:00 am – hall 1
Idazaal

WED, 3 APRL
–

Sima Kim (KR)
10:00 am – hall 1
Konzo Theatre

Stoka Ensemble (NL)
10:00 am – hall 1
Oud-Katholieke Kerk

Svengalisghost (US)
10:00 am – hall 1
Hoop

TCF (NO)
10:00 am – hall 1
Konzo Theatre

The Bug (UK)
10:00 am – hall 1
Idazaal

The Cult of Dom Keller (UK)
10:00 am – hall 1
Konzo Theatre

The Void Pointers (NL)
10:00 am – hall 1
Idazaal

Thomas Ankersmit (NL)
10:00 am – hall 1
E.ON

Tomaga (UK)
10:00 am – hall 1
Hoop

Thomas Jarmyr (SE)
10:00 am – hall 1
330 live

Total Life
10:00 am
Oud-Katholieke Kerk

Unit Moebius
Anonymous (NL)
10:00 am – hall 1
E.ON

Yes... PinkPink (NL)
10:00 am – hall 1
330 live

Yodok III (NO/SE/BE)
10:00 am – hall 1
Konzo Theatre

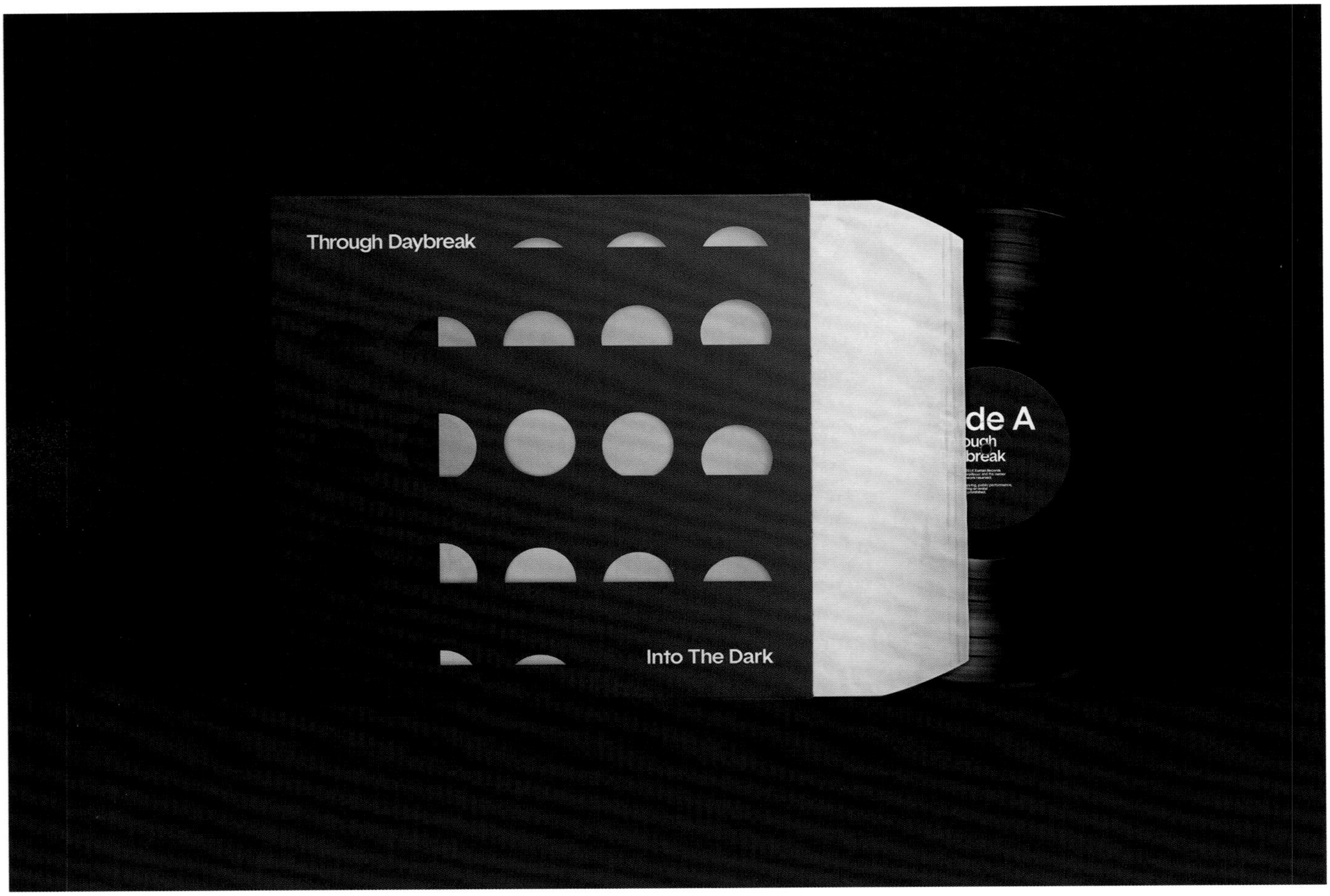

Everything is Made in China Singles

Design: *The Bakery Design Studio*

The Bakery Design Studio was approached by Eimic – one of the biggest indie bands in Russia – to design a cover for their new single. The designers' idea was inspired by the titles of the tracks. One is named Through the Daybreak, the other Into the Dark. The designers created a bold visual interpretation of a sun's day cycle. The following Remixes EP utilizes the same artwork, but in a reworked/rearranged visual form.

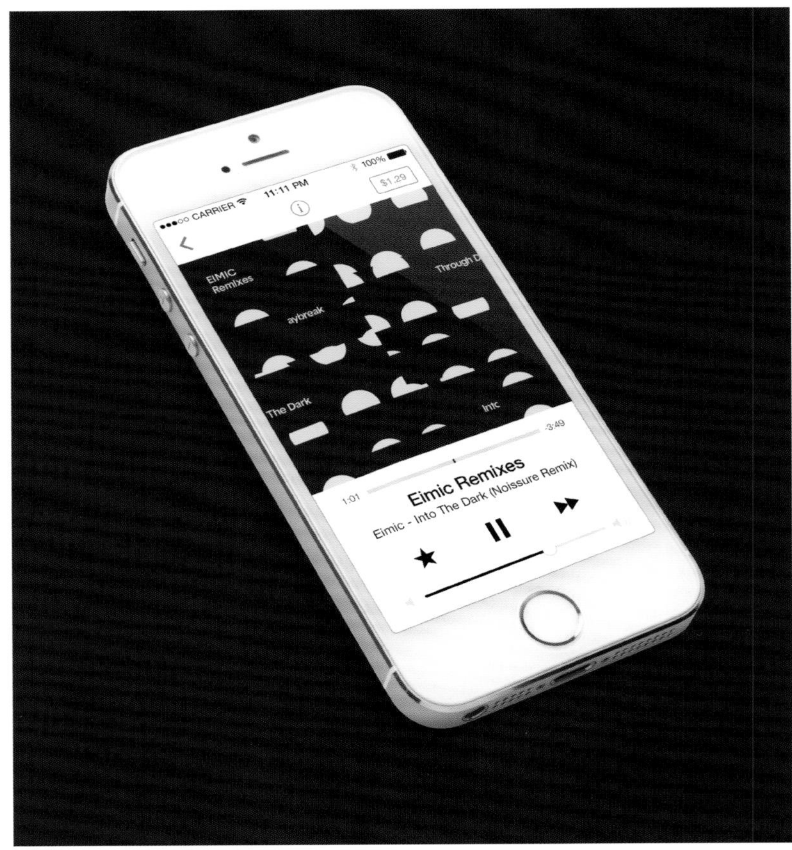

Sidra Variety

Design: *Typical Organization*

Packaging and poster design for a new crossed variety Sidra – a unique, small lot, rare coffee of superior quality edited by Taf Roastery. The design direction could be compressed in one quote: "The beauty of the universe consists not only of unity in variety, but also of variety in unity." — Umberto Eco, *The Name of the Rose*.

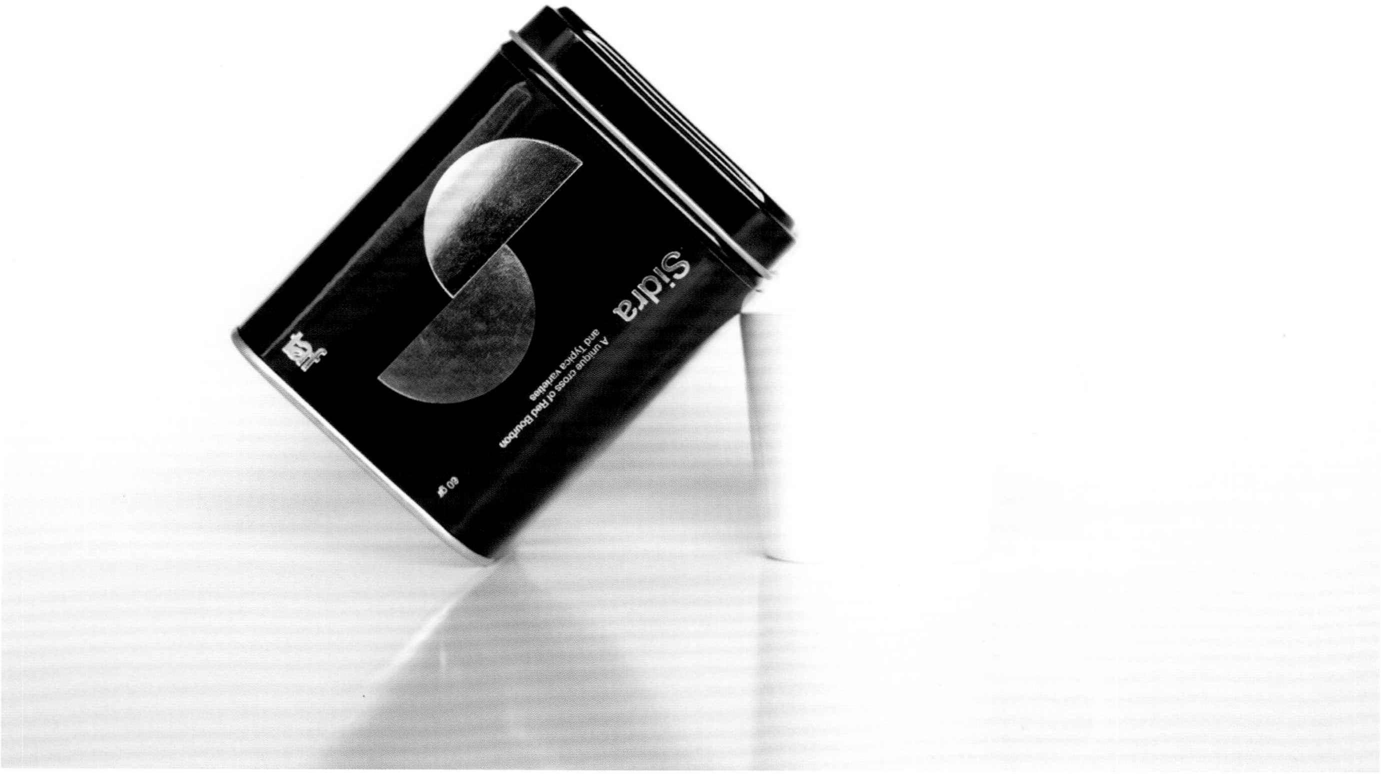

Erica Marley Lamps

Design: *Lid&Wiken*

Erica Marley makes lamps from natural, high quality material she finds at flea markets and second hand stores. She uses material such as marble, metal, leather, and wood that tends to get prettier as the time goes by. The lamps are handmade by Erica herself. The designers have made a visual identity and website for Erica Marley. The logo is minimalistic with the small dot as a finish touch. The dot is a part of the "I" that becomes a detail and symbolizes the shape of Erica Marley's lamps.

ERICAMARLEY
HANDMADE

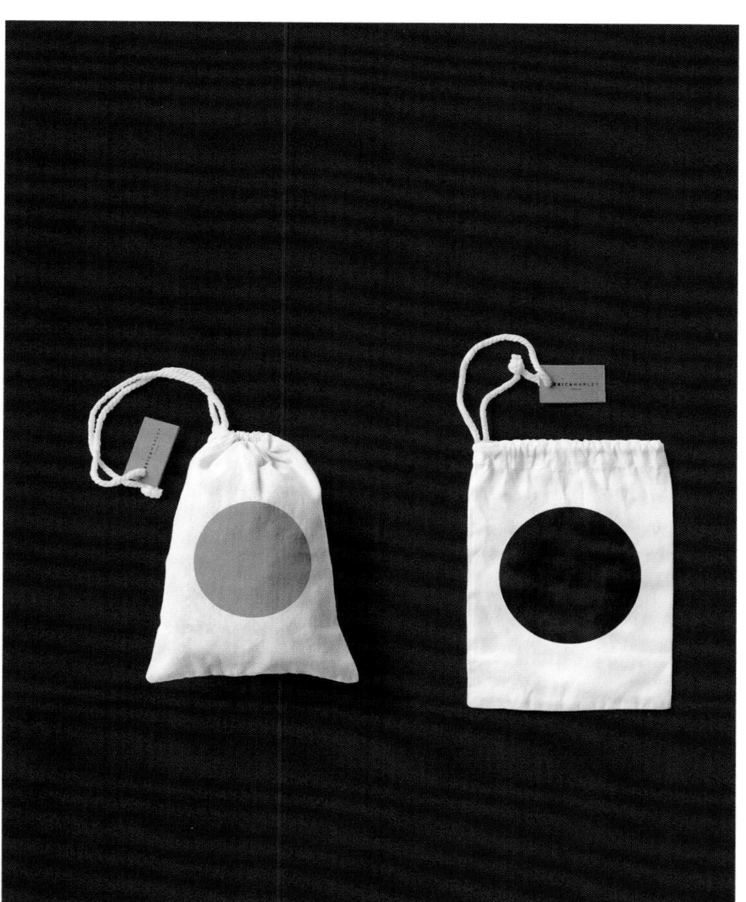

ERICAMARLEY
HANDMADE
ERICAMARLEY
HANDMADE

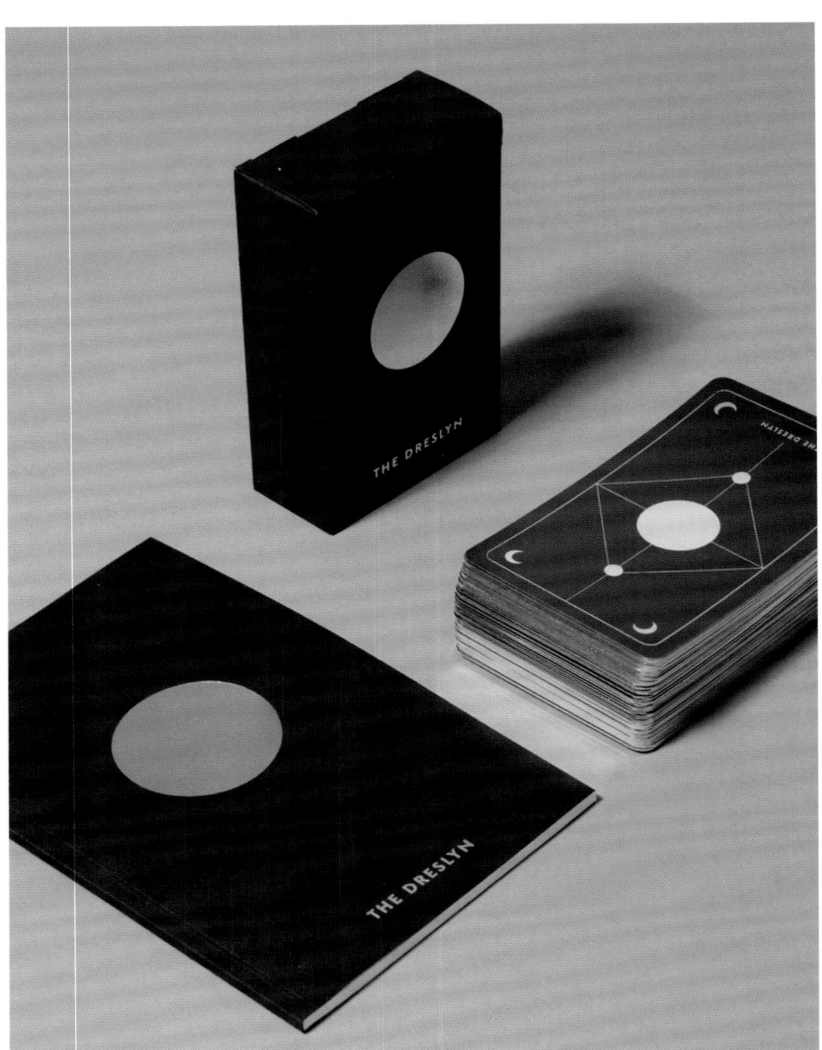

The Dreslyn Tarot

Design: *Kati Forner, The Dreslyn*

In an area that is saturated with ornate and complex illustration, the designer and The Dreslyn wanted to create something that was minimal and unique to The Dreslyn. They have joined their minimalist aesthetic with the intuitive art of Tarot.

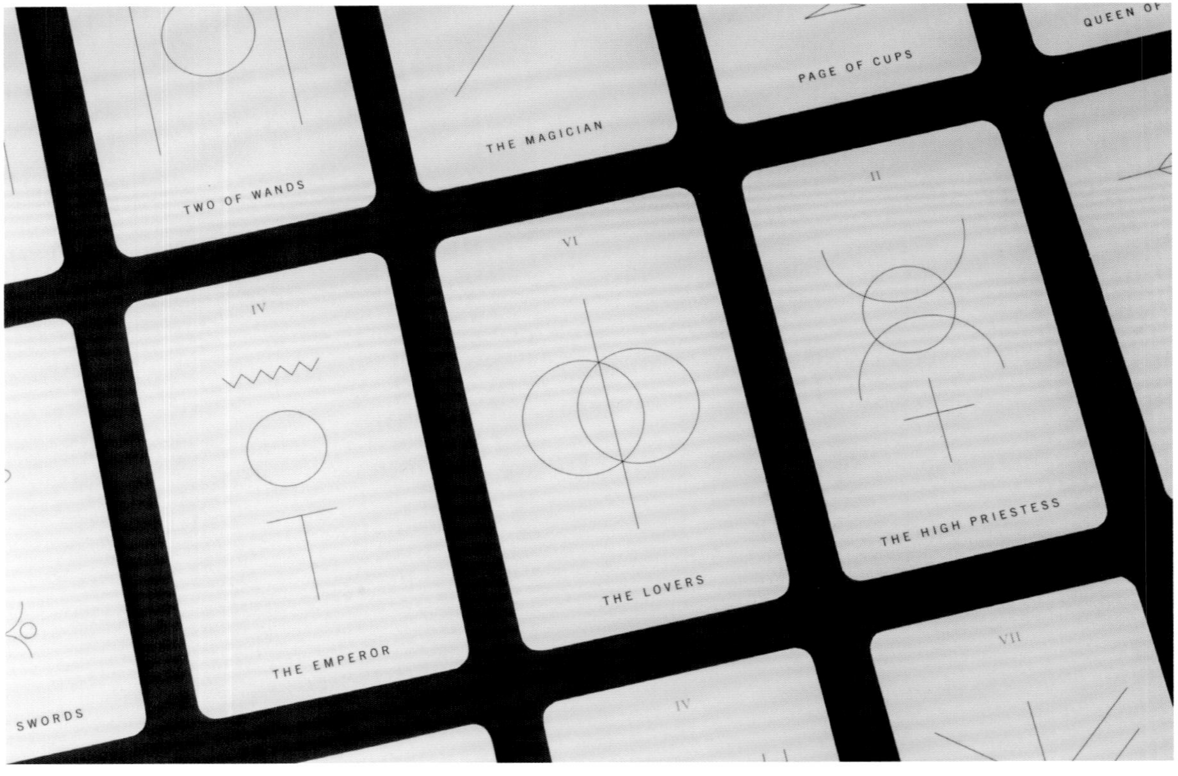

THE DRESLYN

Spectaculoos Speculoos
MAISON
DANDOY
Depuis 1829
Rue au Beurre
Bruxelles
Speculoos Spectaculoos

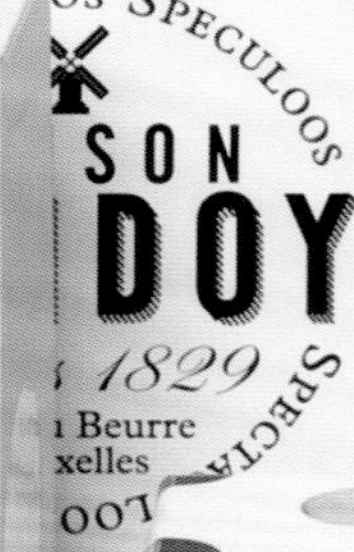

Spectaculoos Speculoos
MAISON
DANDOY
Depuis 1829
Rue au Beurre
Bruxelles
Speculoos Spectaculoos

Maison Dandoy

Agency: *Base Design*
Design: *Slow Food Editore, Giunti Editore*
Photography: *Atelier KZG*

Founded in 1829, Maison Dandoy is a family-owned artisanal bakery based in Brussels. They asked Base Design for a modest redesign, but after a series of strategic discussions, the designers decided to pursue a total makeover instead. The designers built a generous brand universe together, ranging from the brand identity, tone of voice and website to campaign videos, co-branding strategies and the new boutique design.

Fursetgruppen Catering

Agency: *Pocket Oslo*
Design: *Nicklas Haslestad*

Fursetgruppen Catering is a full-service caterer delivering restaurant-quality food to a wide range of events and happenings. After the client's desire to become Norway's leading caterer, the designers felt an urge to challenge the visual language in the catering industry. The concept of the identity is carved down to the bone, with the single keyword "plate" – from which food is eaten or served – in mind. A plate of food is the connection between the entire restaurant industries. This geometric form gave the designers an idea to create a universe of abstract circles to emphasize the different characteristics of FG Catering, including full-service: from A to Z catering, overall quality, sustainability, agricultural economics, humility and positivity. The circular shapes act differently based on the environment they appear in.

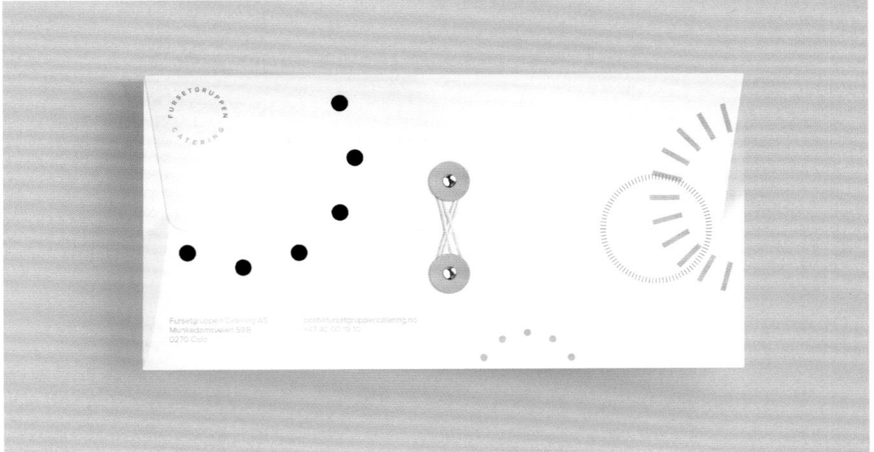

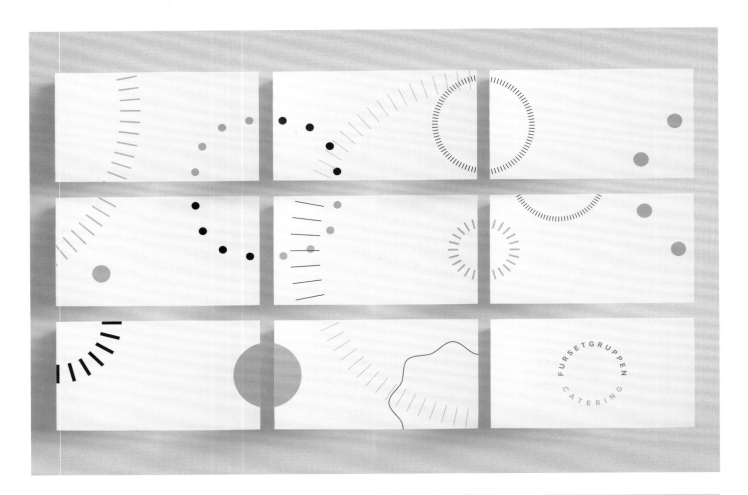

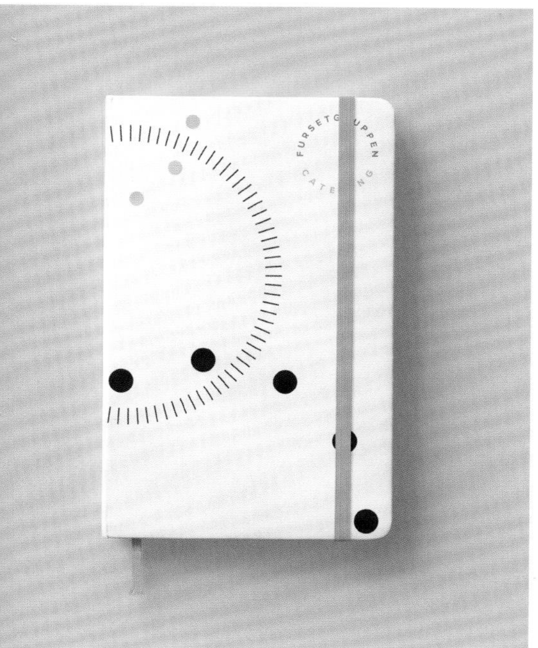

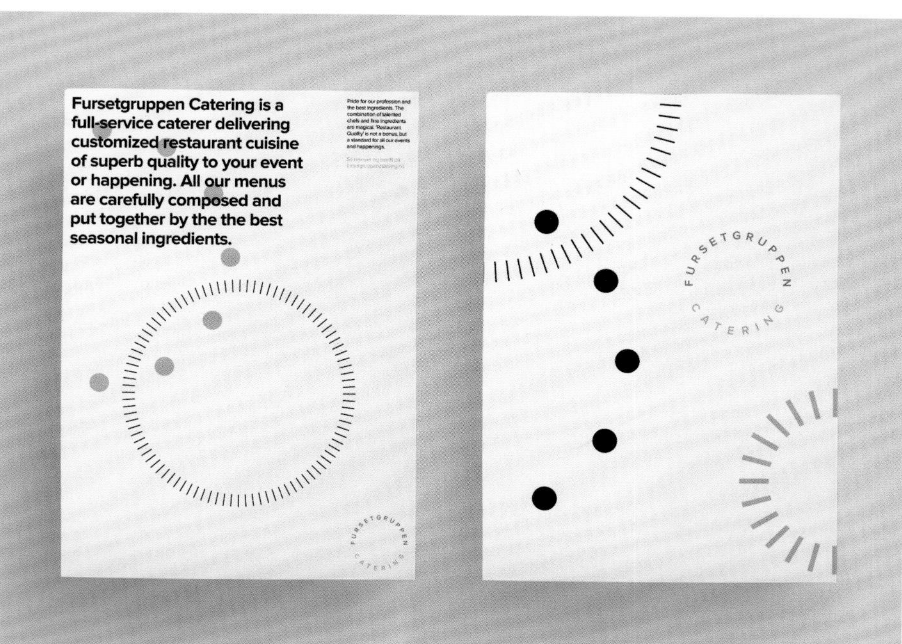
Fursetgruppen Catering is a full-service caterer delivering customized restaurant cuisine of superb quality to your event or happening. All our menus are carefully composed and put together by the the best seasonal ingredients.
FURSETGRUPPEN
CATERING

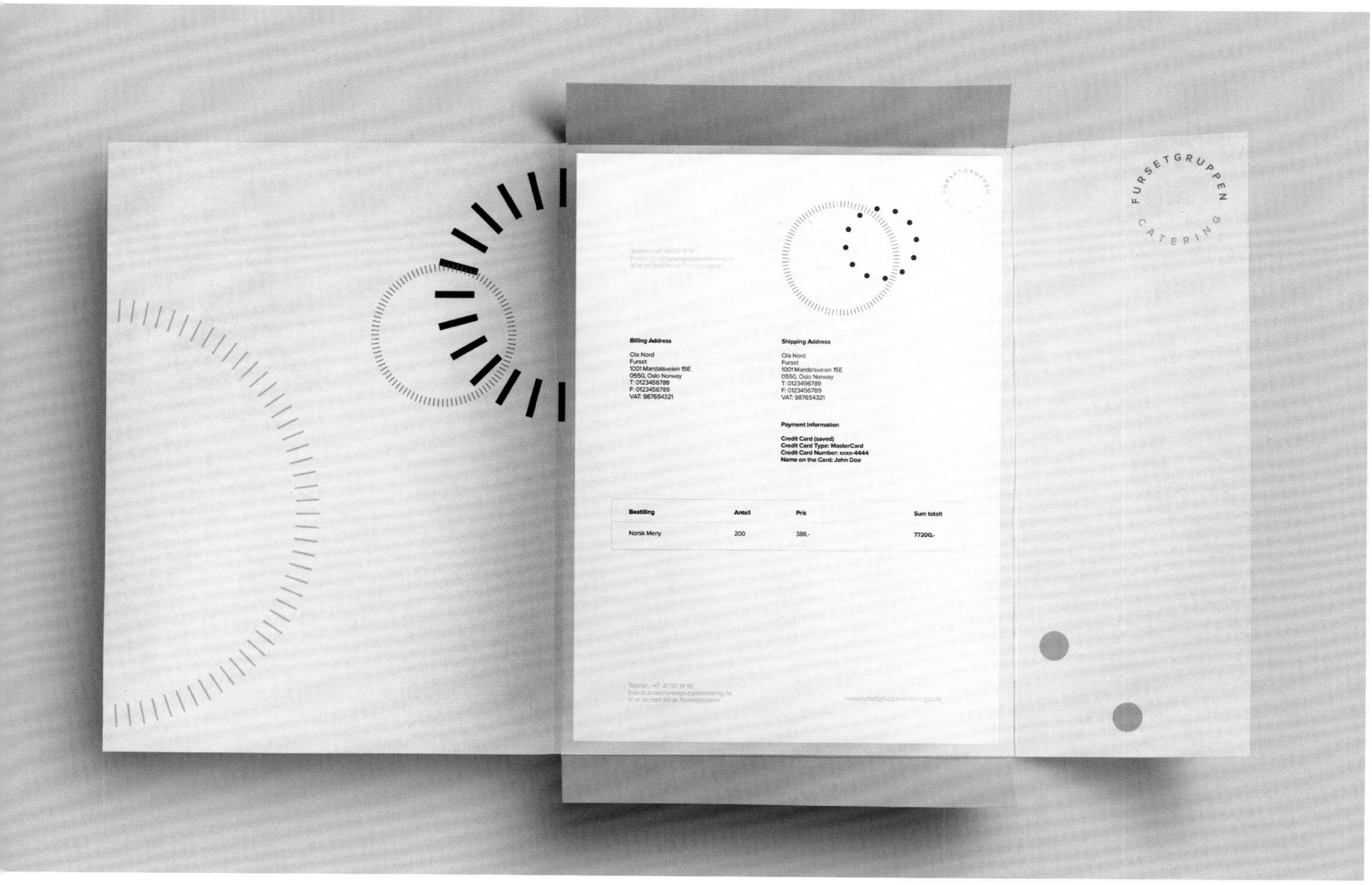

Brandon Pictures Corporate Identity

Agency: *Studio Flag*
Art Direction: *Cheolhee Hwang*

Corporate Identity designed for Brandon Pictures. The "B" and "O" were expressed in the basic shape of a circle to emphasize the meaning of "Brand + On" consisting of a compound word of "Brand" and "On". The combination of the semicircle, circle graphic and the neat yellow color shows the image of a young company.

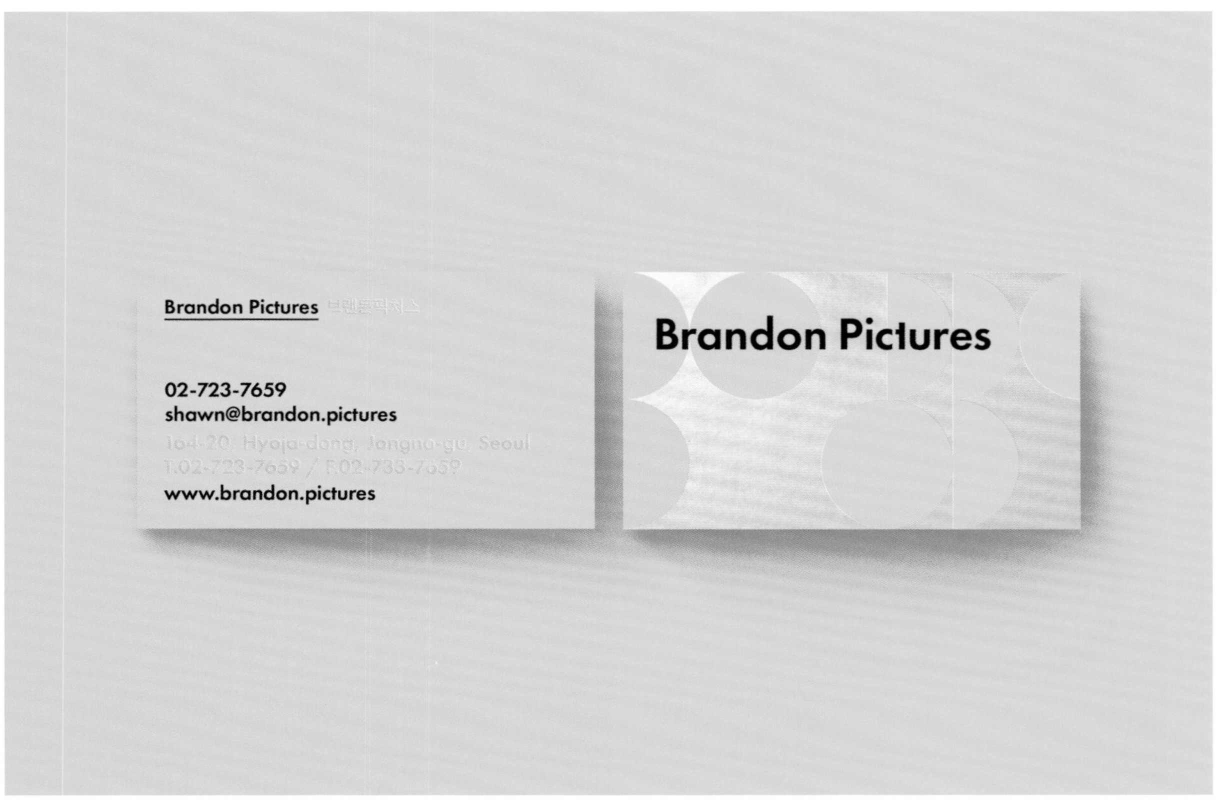

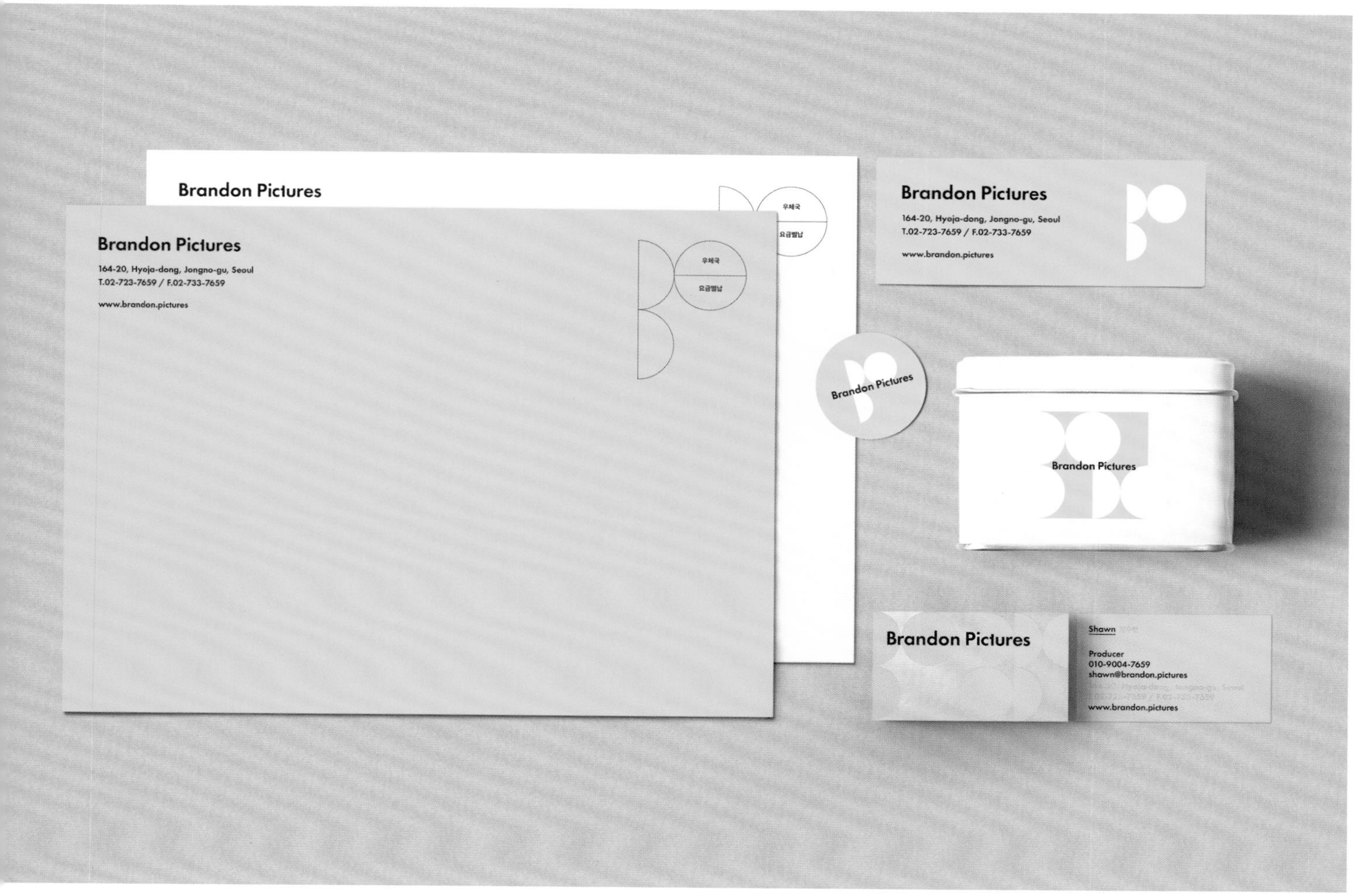

Brandon Pictures

Brandon Pictures discovers the unique personality of brands and creates astonishingly attractive brand images.

Vincit Beer – Special Limited Edition

Design: *Marco Vincit*
Copywriter/Concept: *Marcos Oliveira*
Photography: *Lara Dias*

Vincit Beer is a gift for the designer's customers, partners, and friends. It was conceived to celebrate all 2015's victories and to celebrate the arrival of 2016. It is also a tribute to the poet Publius Virgilius Maro, whose quotes served as inspiration to the designer's last name. The designer's best wishes to everyone who's by his side, every day, learning, and achieving amazing things together.

Global Diplomacy Lab

Agency: *mischen*
Design: *Harri Kuhn*

The Global Diplomacy Lab was initiated by the Foreign Office, the BMW Stiftung Herbert Quandt, the Robert Bosch Stiftung, and the Stiftung Mercator with the goal of finding out what diplomacy could look like in the future. Labs are regularly held where members from around the world gather to intensively discuss questions about sensitive political and social issues.

The corporate design is flexible and playful in order to loosen the solid structures that are characteristic of politics. The five circles are permanently in movement and can be seen as the continents, as minds or as ideas. Fresh green symbolizes the process of growth and avoids any connotation of flags or nationalities.

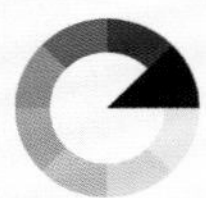

Proper Produksjoner

Design: *Lid&Wiken*

Proper Produksjoner is a production company based in Nordmore, Norway. It delivers artistic and technical solutions within the cultural field. The designers have made a visual identity and website for Proper. The values of Proper Produksjoner are dynamic, playful and colorful. Sound is the main element of this identity, and the concept is based on the ripple effect where the production is the core.

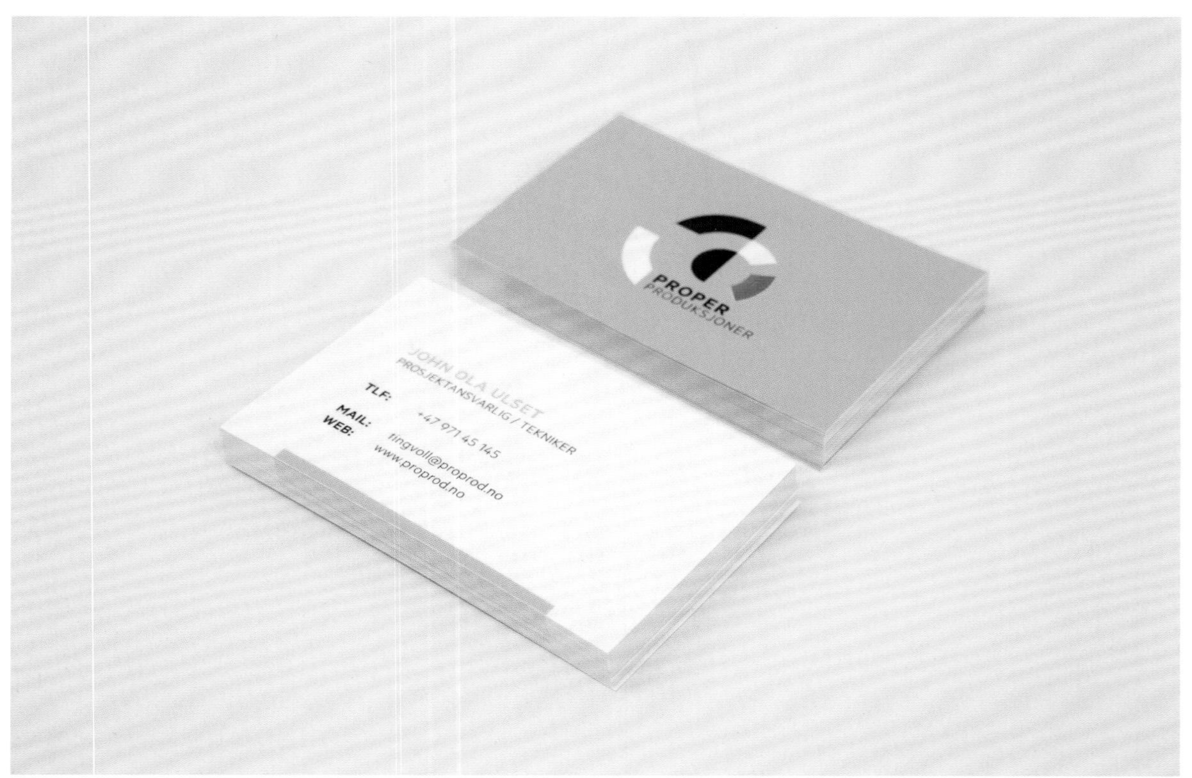

PROPER
PRODUKSJONER

PROPER
PRODUKSJONER

Museum of Broken Relationships

Design: *Savvy Studio*

Savvy Studio was chosen to rebrand the Museum of Broken Relationships with the mission of tropicalizing its identity to fit the lifestyle and culture of a North American audience without sacrificing the raw emotional essence of the original identity.

The branding's structure is based on three brand values: familiarity, basic emotions, and high aesthetic value. These values were defined based on the universality of the subject, the museum's location and cultural context, as well as our own philosophy as a design studio.

The logotype expresses simply and abstractly the feeling of being broken and out of place. It's the break of a cycle, of continuity and harmony. The printed material, together with its desaturated colored paper, photographs and typographic selection conveys a sense of nostalgia and intimacy that roils the viewer, making them feel intrusive by delving into other's personal lives.

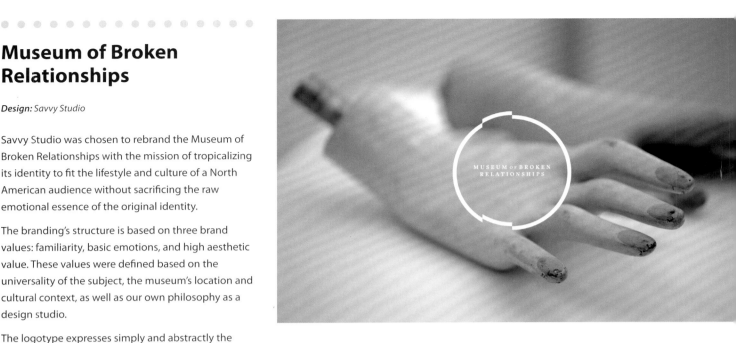

MUSEUM OF BROKEN
RELATIONSHIPS

MUSEUM OF BROKEN
RELATIONSHIPS
6751 Hollywood Boulevard Los Angeles, CA 90028 USA
www.brokenships.la

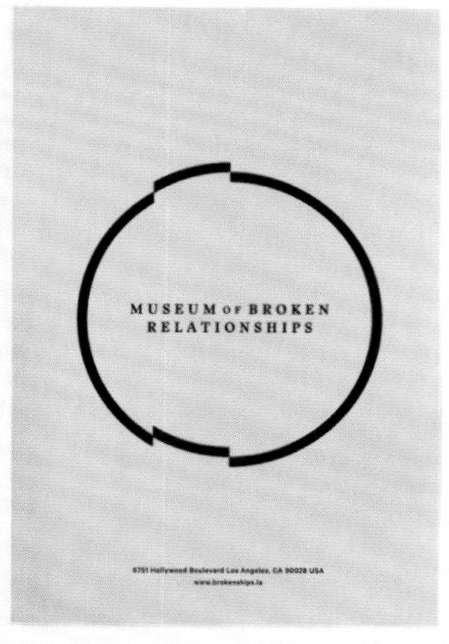
MUSEUM OF BROKEN
RELATIONSHIPS

Beton Foundation

***Agency:** UVMW*
***Creative Direction:** Robert Mendel, Jacek Walesiak*
***Design:** Robert Mendel, Jacek Walesiak, Michal Malolepszy, Marta Czuban*

The designers looked for forms, which could be easily associated with the activities of Beton Foundation and that wouldn't limit them to the raw material of "beton" (Polish for concrete). The foundation envelops a wide variety of interests starting with the beginning in the 20th century and the modernist legacy as well as different ways of depicting architecture in film, computer games, unfinished projects projects, and futuristic utopias.

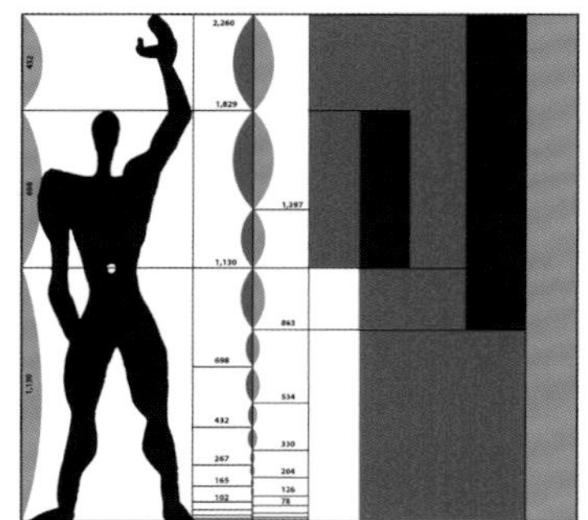

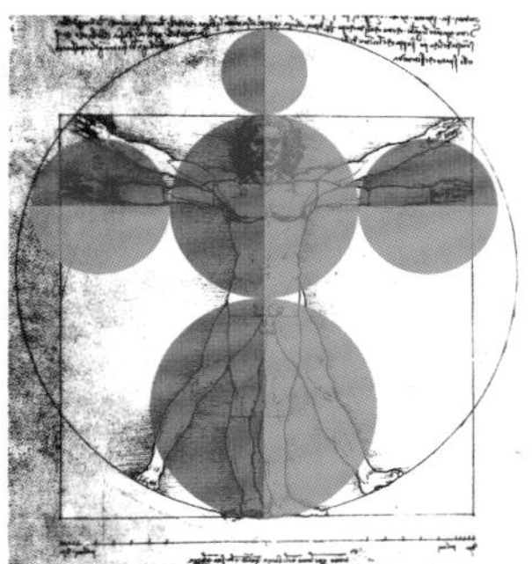

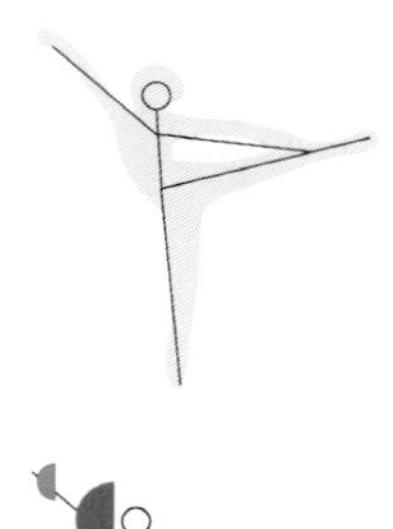

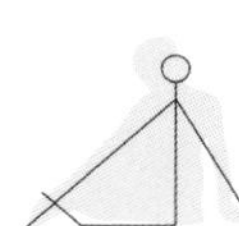

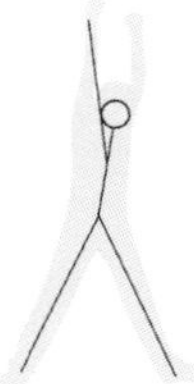

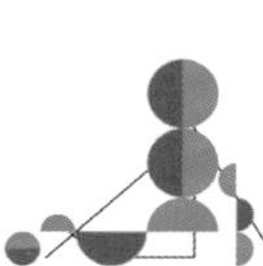

betonik
Architecture workshops for kids
Warsztaty architektoniczne dla dzieci
betonff.pl
Karnety Gość
już dostępne na
kinoluna.pl!
betonik
Beton Film Festival 2015
Niemożliwe konstrukcje
10.04
Kino Luna
Warszawa
betonff.pl
Beton Film Festival 2015
betonff.pl
Architektura radykalna
09.04
Kino Luna
Warszawa

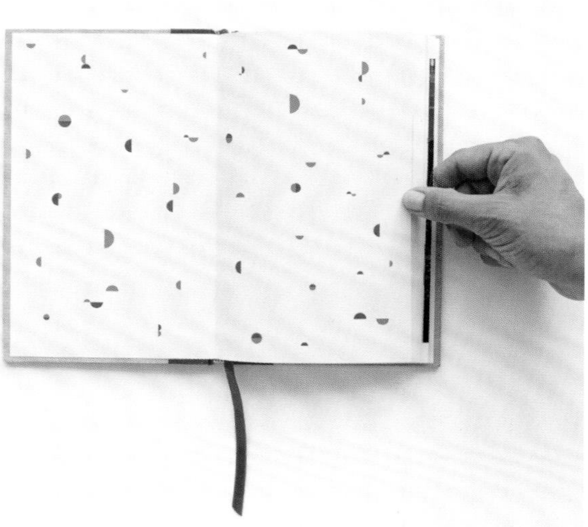

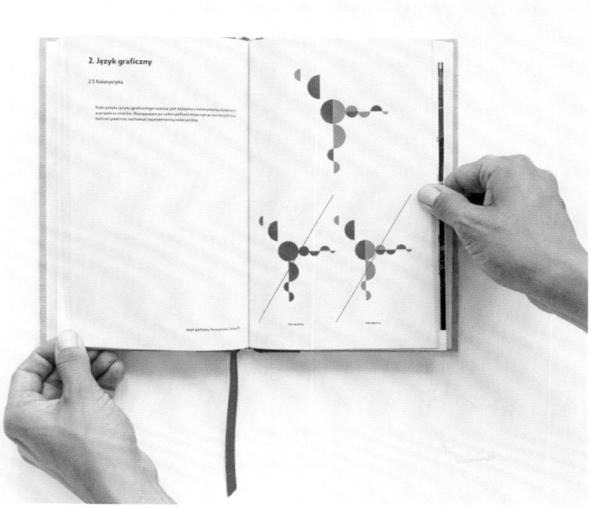

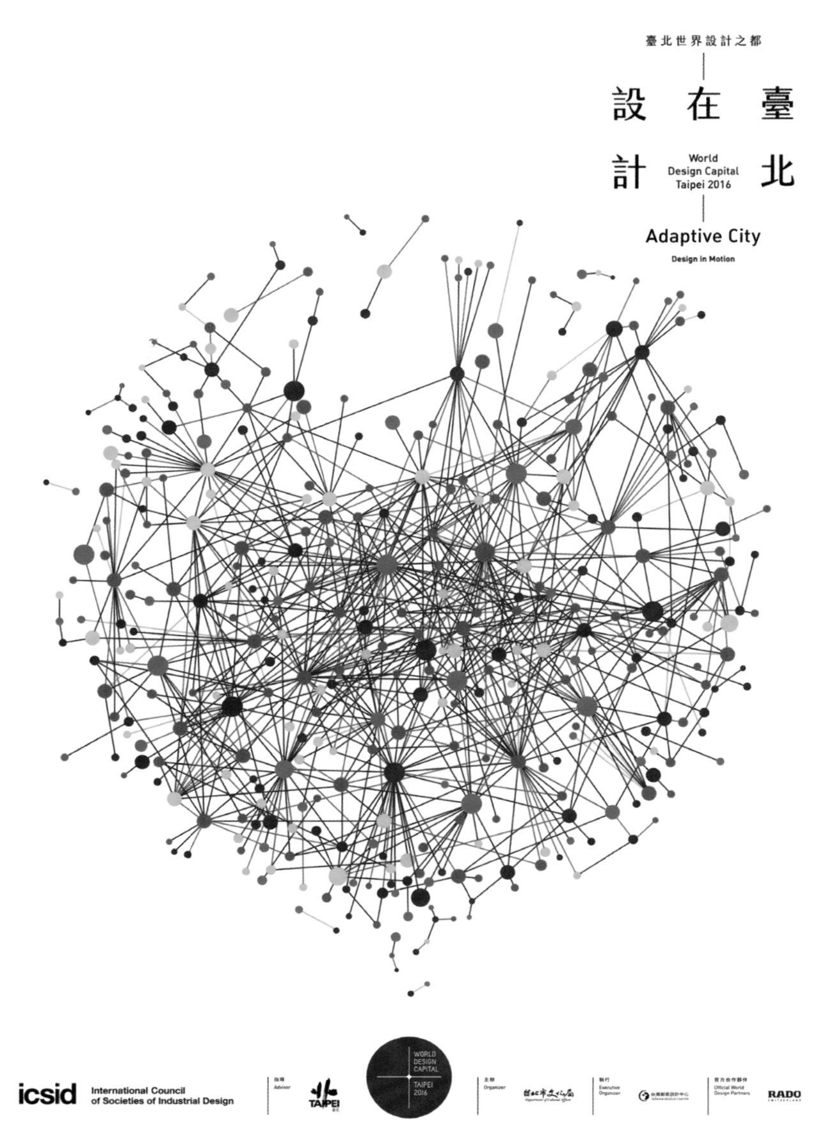

World Design Capital Taipei 2016

Creative Direction: *JL DESIGN*
Art Direction: *Lance Wei*
Lead Design: *Hsiang Ju Hung*
Graphic Design: *Jarvis Lim, Ivan Fang*

One of the plans going forward is to engage its residents in discussion on the betterment of the city. The future of the capital lies in its ability to evolve, to adapt, and to set the wheels in motion. Hence the design for the Taipei City logo is a reflection on a capital whose vision of its future is still taking shape. The logo takes the form of an imperfect circle, a derivative of the WDC logo, with design elements in the state of reaching the final form. Three themed logos addressing on the ways the city can go forward are titled "Engaging the Community", "Connecting Information", and "A City Reborn". An adaptive city, sets its designs in motion.

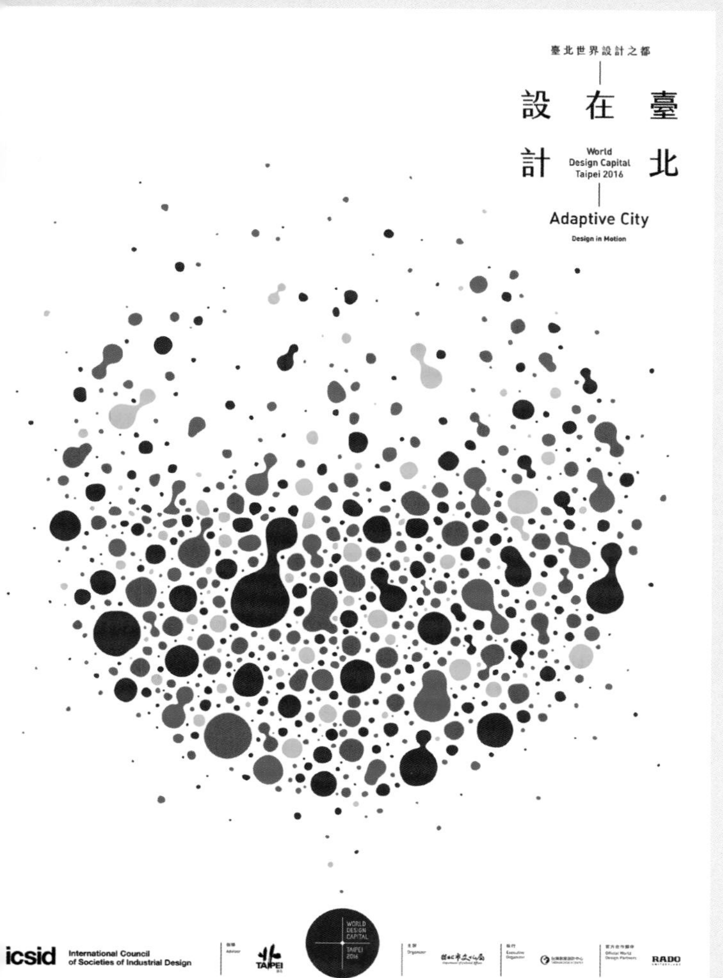
臺北世界設計之都
設 在 臺
計 北
World
Design Capital
Taipei 2016
Adaptive City
Design in Motion
icsid International Council of Societies of Industrial Design
RADO

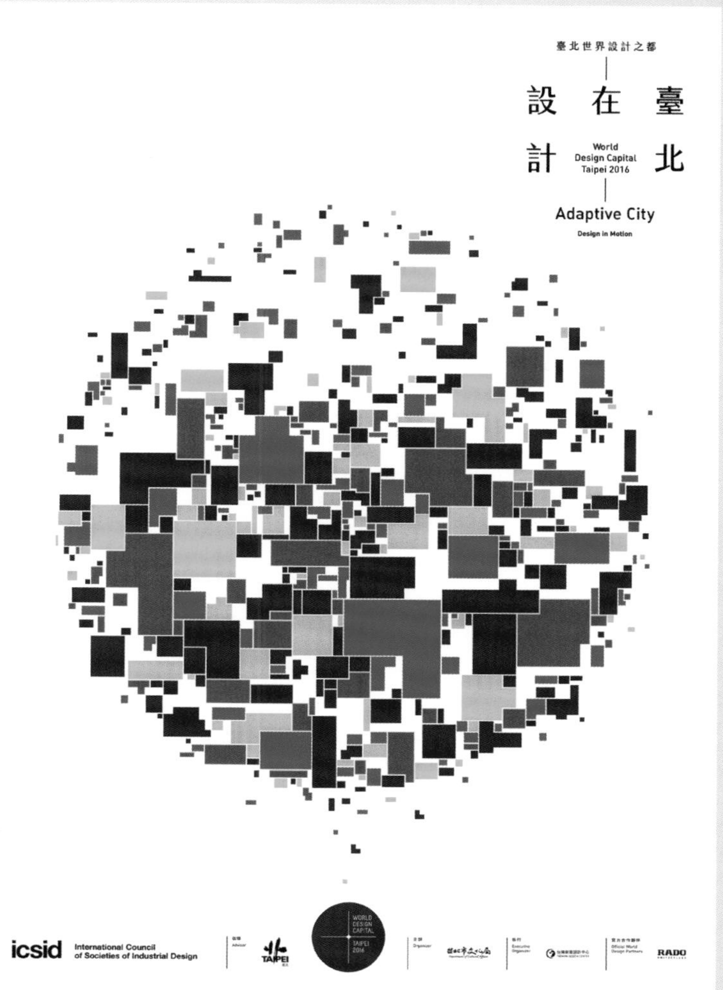
臺北世界設計之都
設 在 臺
計 北
World
Design Capital
Taipei 2016
Adaptive City
Design in Motion
icsid International Council of Societies of Industrial Design
RADO

WORLD
DESIGN
CAPITAL
TAIPEI
2016
臺北世界設計之都
設 在 臺
計 北
World
Design Capital
Taipei 2016
Adaptive City
Design in Motion

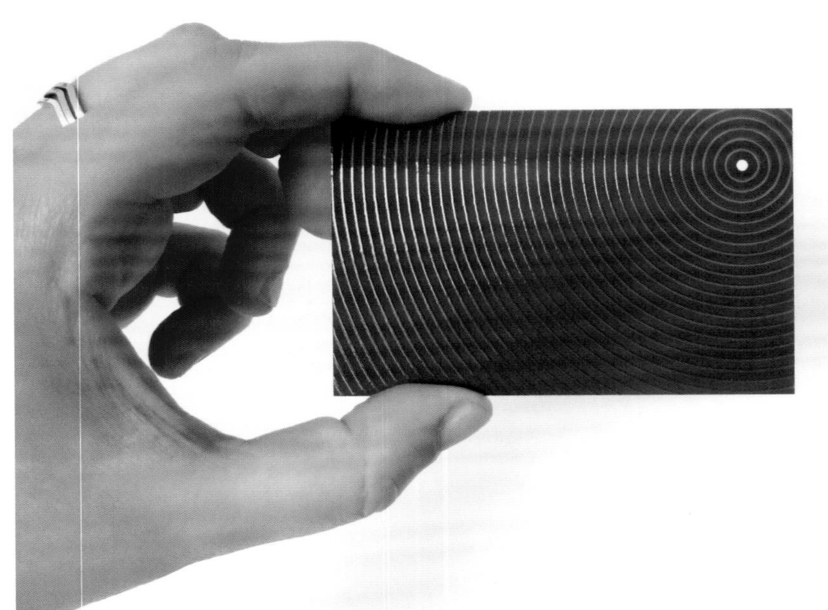

Shine Bright!

Agency: *Puntuale*
Design: *Silvia Virgillo*

Shine bright little business cards!

Business cards for personal promotion, with shiny details in raised spot gloss.

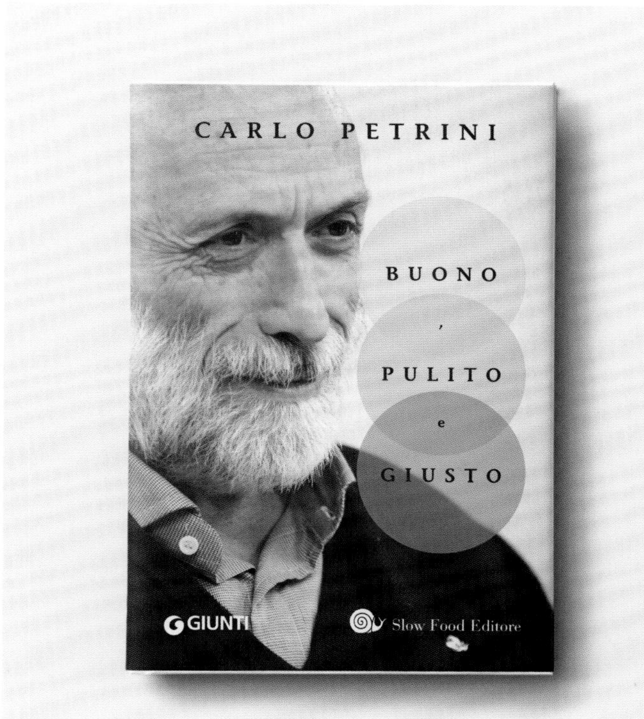

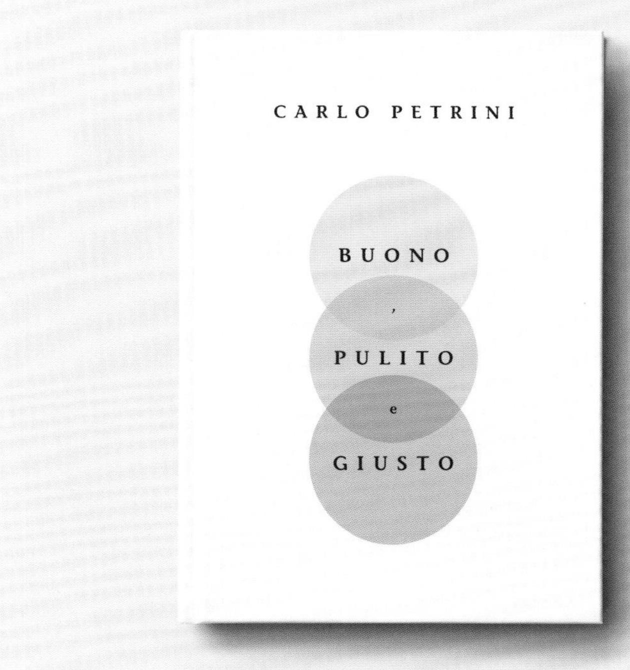

Buono, Pulito e Giusto

Agency: *Puntuale*
Design: *Silvia Virgillo*

After 10 years since the first release, Buono, Pulito e Giusto, a book that has deeply marked Slow Food history and reinvented the contemporary gastronomy, has been updated and published with a new cover and layout. Three adjectives, three circles, three colors.

OCG

Design: *Tadas Bujanauskas*

OCG stands for Owen Cheese Guild, a cheese company located in USA. It's a rebranding of company's identity. The project involved simplification and lots of attention to minimalism. So naturally the concept came using the fundamental shapes of geometry.

OWEN
CHEESE GUILD
KENNETH OWEN
504 Park Ave
Ridgely, MD 21660
p. 202-575-0159
f. 202-575-2358
owencheese.com
Bleu

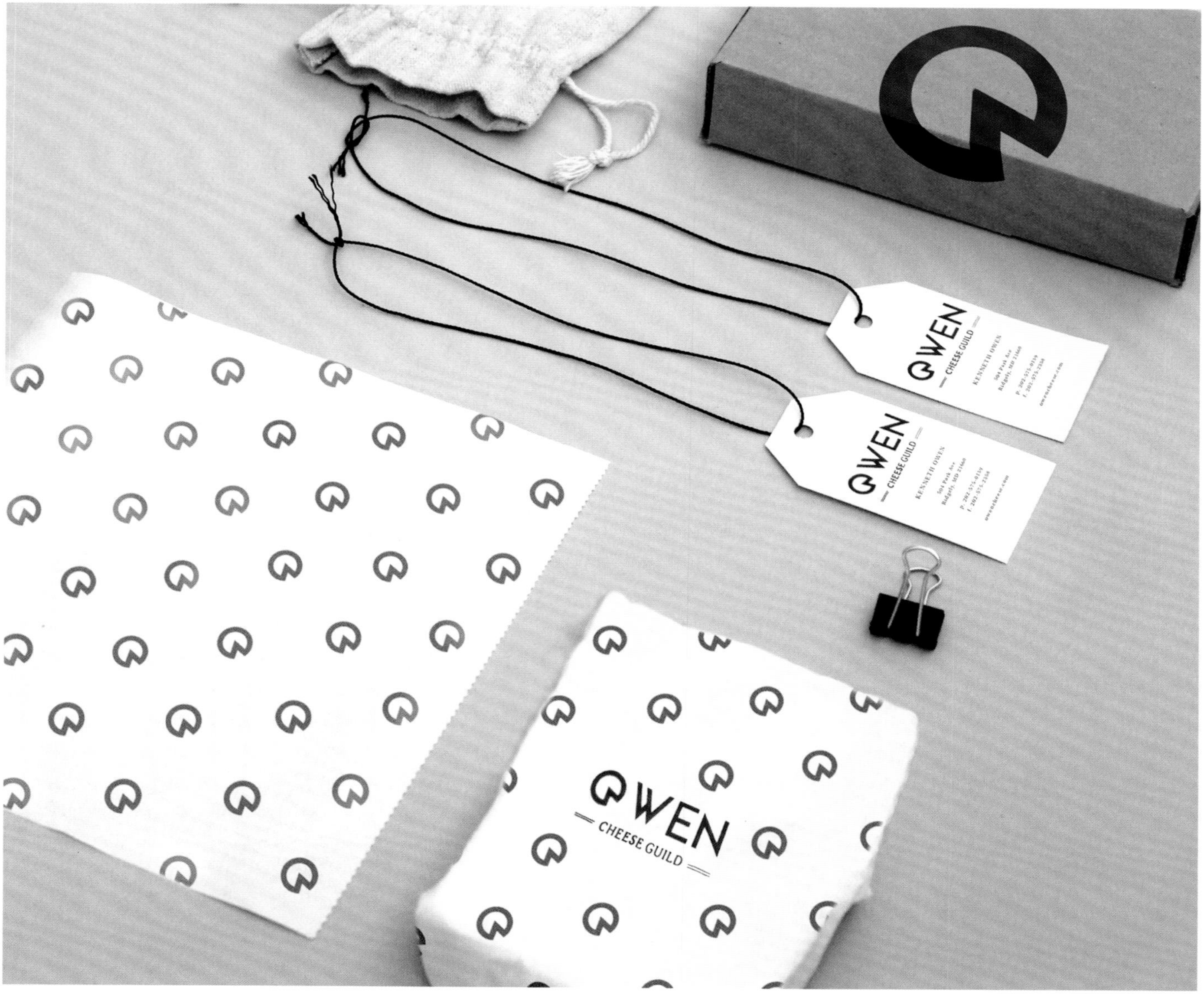

Wonder.full

Design: *Studio AH—HA*
Photography: *Diogo Alves / Studio AH—HA*

Identity and website design for Wonder.full, a Lebanese brand that offers its customers several different experiences. Each box serves as a theme, a color, an image, and a library of shapes. The idea is to take the client to another world, with surrealist images and different layers of information.

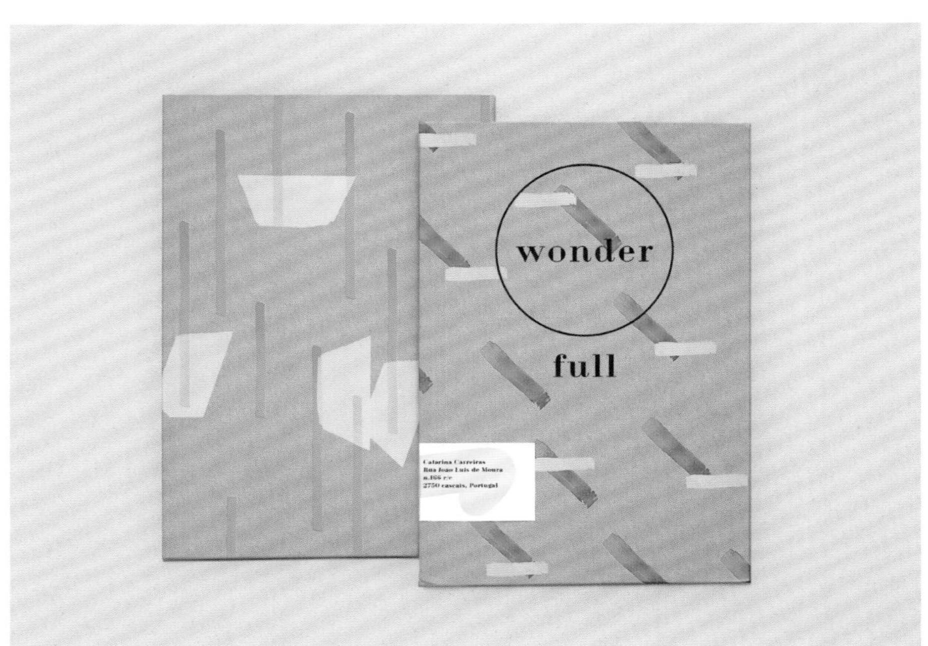

wonder
full
awesome
adventure
wonder
full
beyond
harmony
wonder
full
glitter
glamour
wonder
full
FINE
GOURMET

wonder

Landestheater Niederösterreich

Agency: *13&5*
Creative Direction: *Melanie Kraxner, Simon Lemmerer, Markus Jausovec*
Art Direction: *Melanie Kraxner, Simon Lemmerer*
Photography: *Marion Luttenberger, Lupi Spuma*

The design concept is eye-catching, adaptable as well as playful and mirrors the variety of the theatre plays. The designers shortened the long name of the theatre for conceptual and design reasons and created an acronym. It is very well integrated into the entire concept and the diacritics also provide the key visual. Lively, variable, contemporary – those are some of the concepts guiding the redesign of the brand image.

As an additional visual element, the designers added a cone of light, as light is not only the base of visual images, but also an important component of a theatre play. The cone, in combination with the logo, is used as key visual and together with the illustrations for the plays it forms the basic compositional element of the design. The combination of the different elements, the matching typography and the reduced colors create a unique image for the theatre – modern and diverse, just as the plays are.

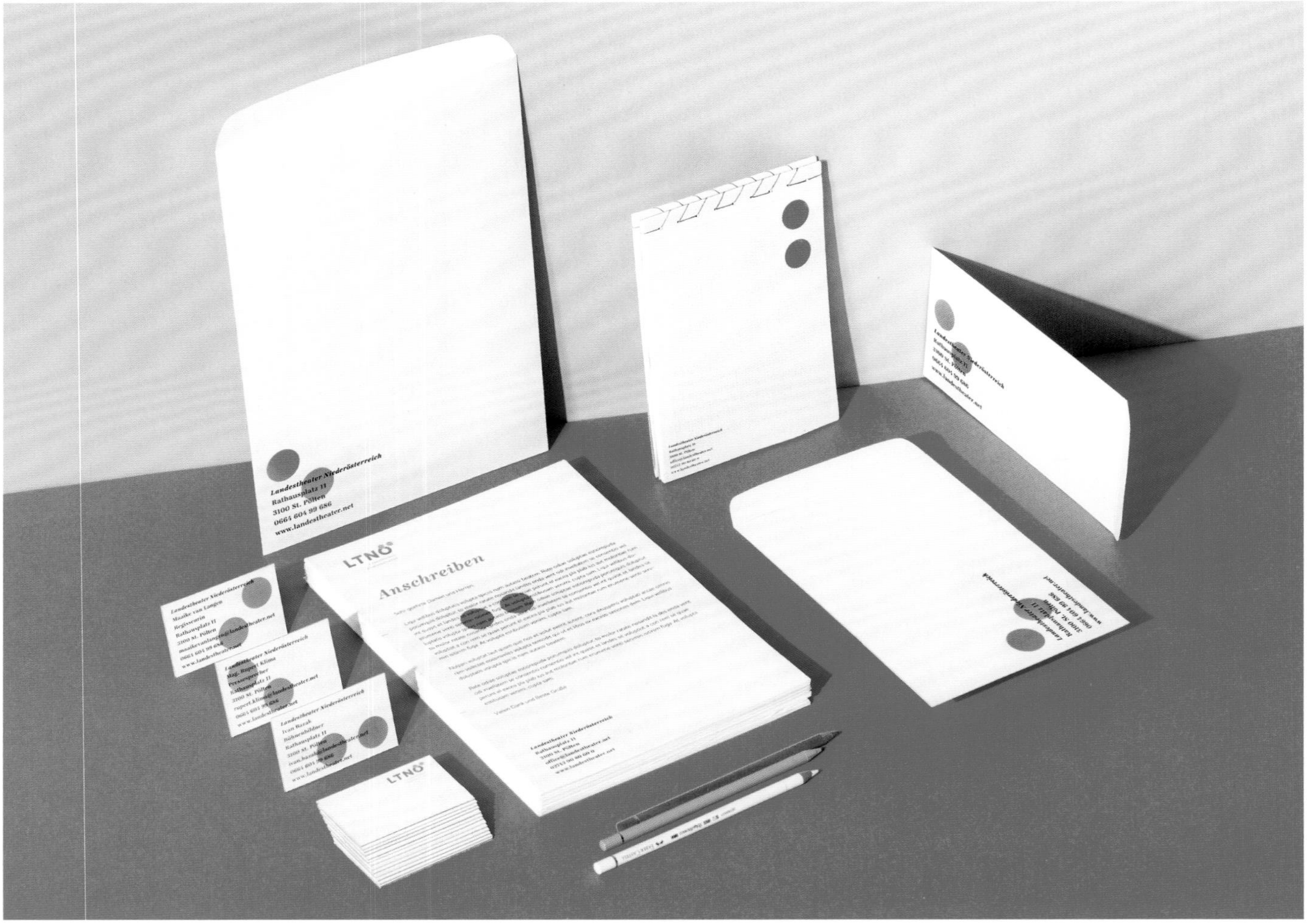

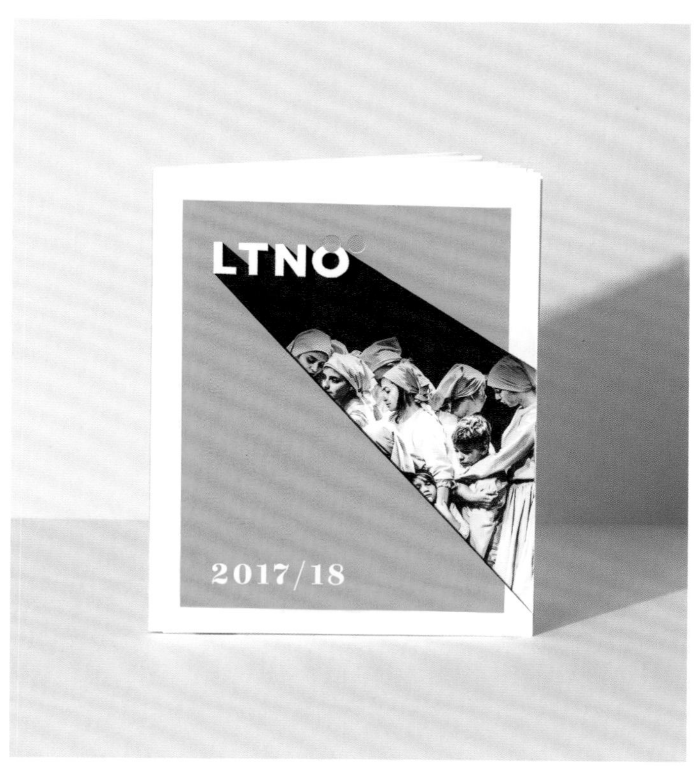
LTNO
2017/18

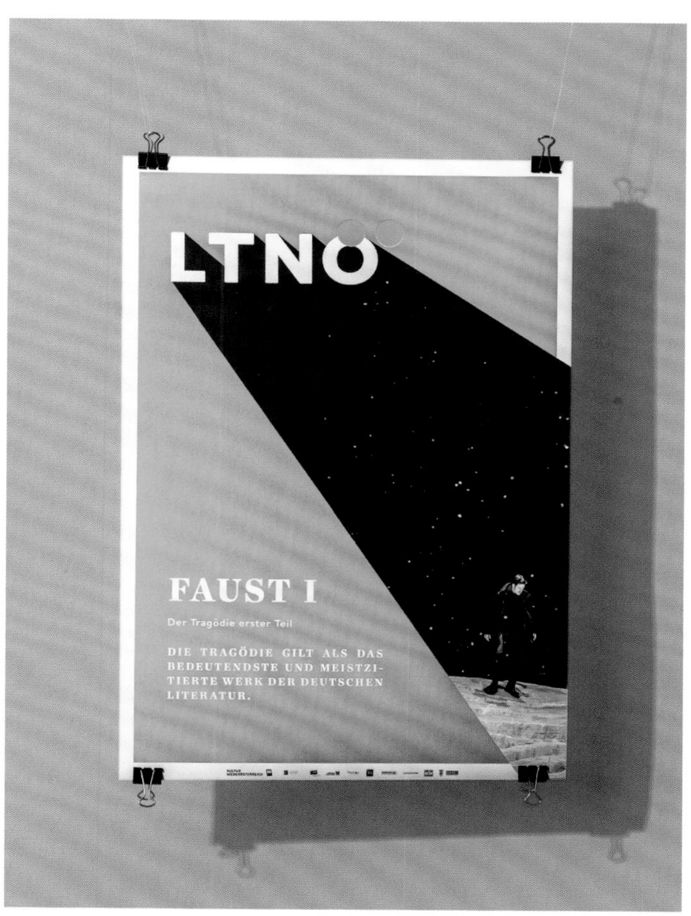
LTNO
FAUST I
Der Tragödie erster Teil
DIE TRAGÖDIE GILT ALS DAS BEDEUTENDSTE UND MEISTZITIERTE WERK DER DEUTSCHEN LITERATUR.

OKTOBER 20 17 OKTOBER

Wedding Solution

Agency: *MTN Company*
Design: *Max Lippolis*

Wedding Solution is a company specialized in the production and rental of equipment and sets for events. A precious partner for anyone who wants to create a detailed customized event, giving shape to their creativity, thanks also to the valuable work of craftsmen carpenters and experienced tailors in the creative showroom. It's from simple and infinite shapes, like a circle, which came to life the new brand and the new image. A combination of basic elements and different shades of colors that can support the perpetual search for new directions and a new world to create with imagination.

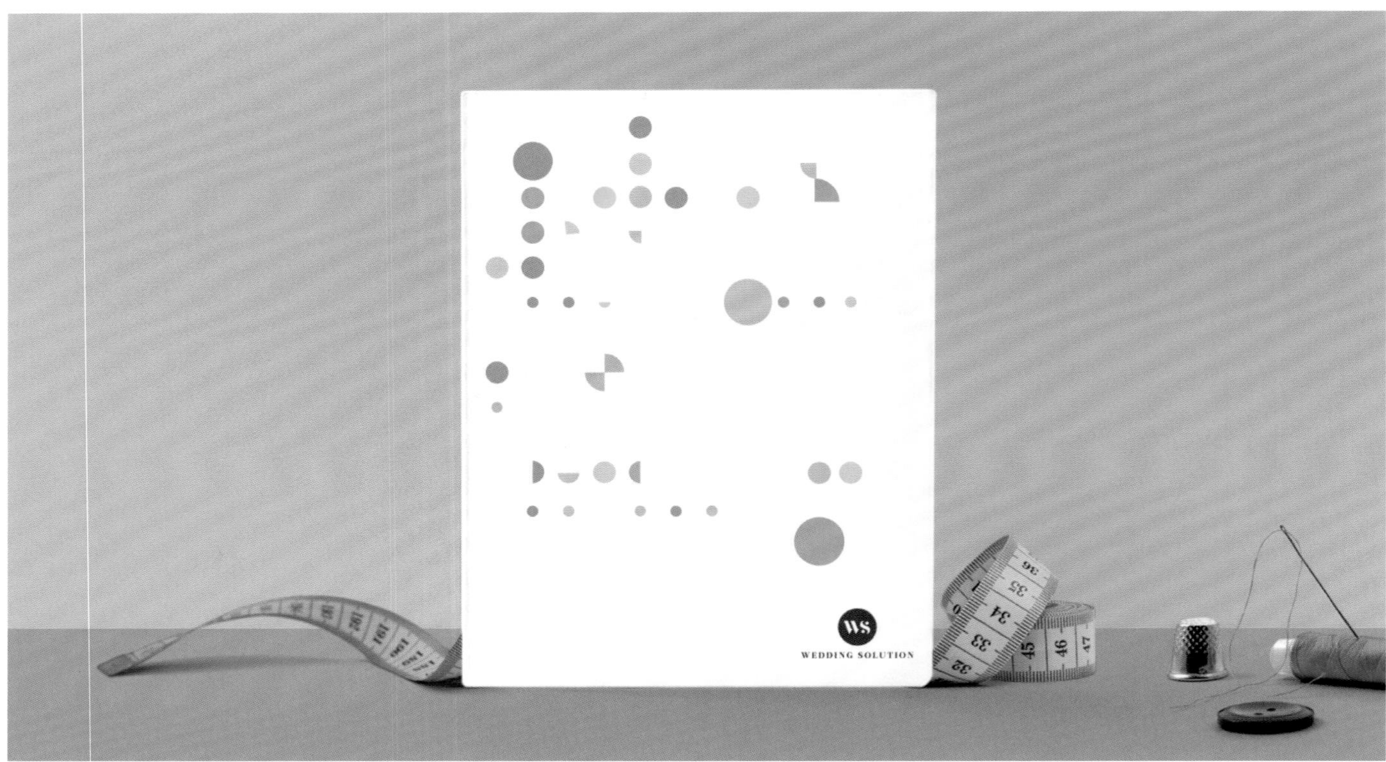

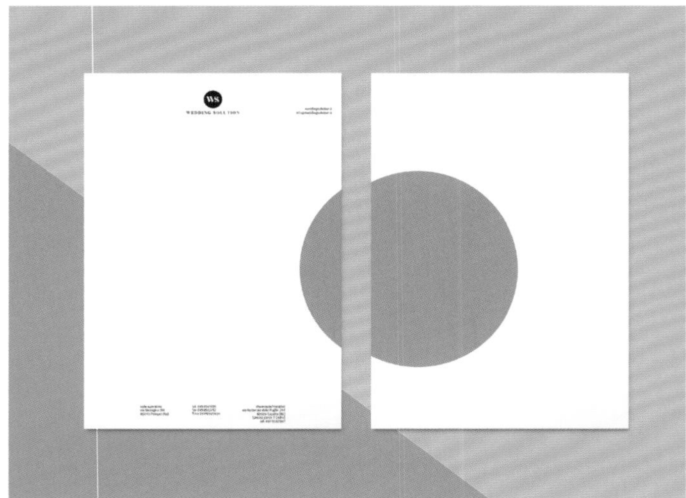

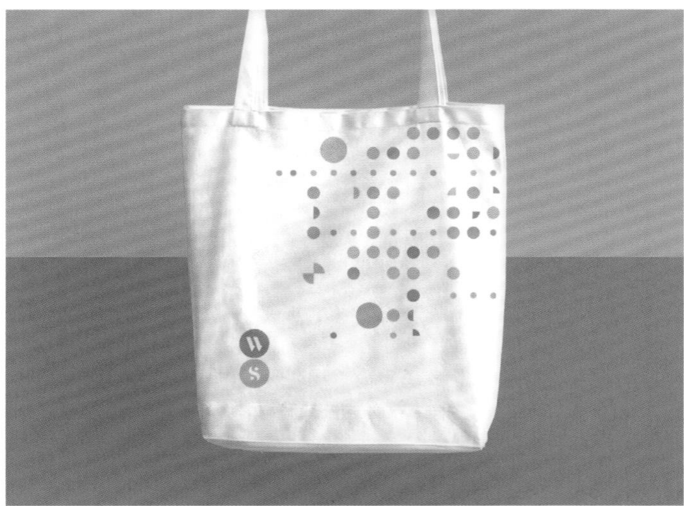

ANDREA RICCIO
MISTER SOLUTION

Digi.logue

Agency: *Fol Studio*
Design: *Volkan Olmez*
Motion Graphic: *Mustafa Gundem*
Photography & Video: *Neslihan Gunaydin*

Digi.logue – discovery and innovation in new media and art. The design project includes visual identity, posters and motion graphic design for Zorlu Holding.

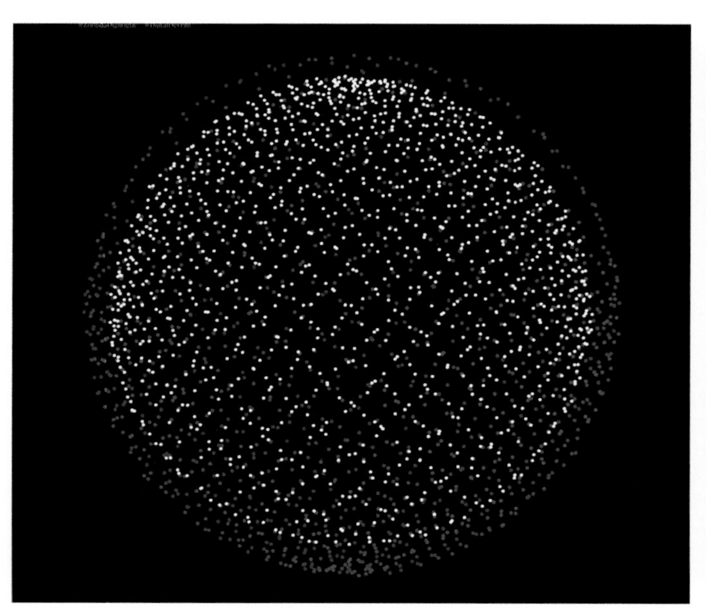

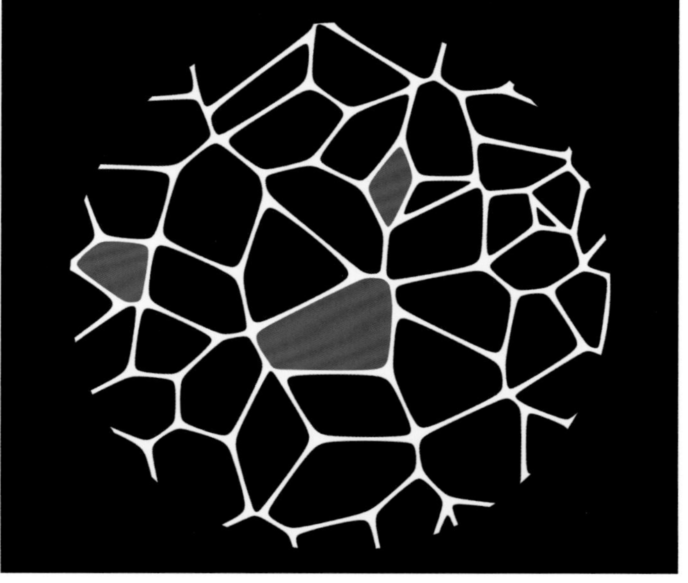

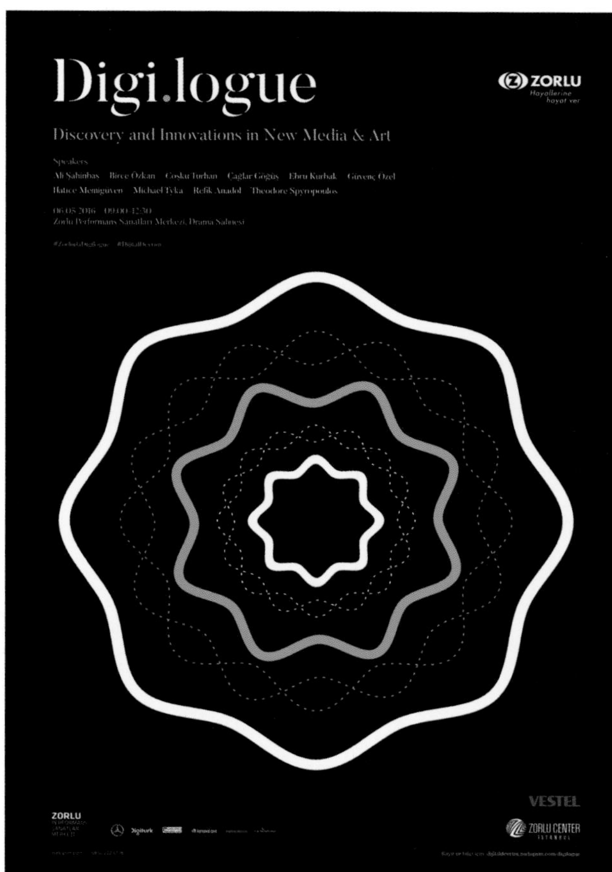
Digi.logue
ZORLU
Hayallerine hayat ver
Discovery and Innovations in New Media & Art
Speakers
Ali Şahinbaş Birce Özkan Coşku Turhan Çağlar Göğüş Ebru Kurbak Güvenç Özel
Hatice Memigüven Michael Tyka Refik Anadol Theodore Spyropoulos
06.05.2016 09:00-12:30
Zorlu Performans Sanatları Merkezi, Drama Sahnesi
VESTEL
ZORLU CENTER
ZORLU

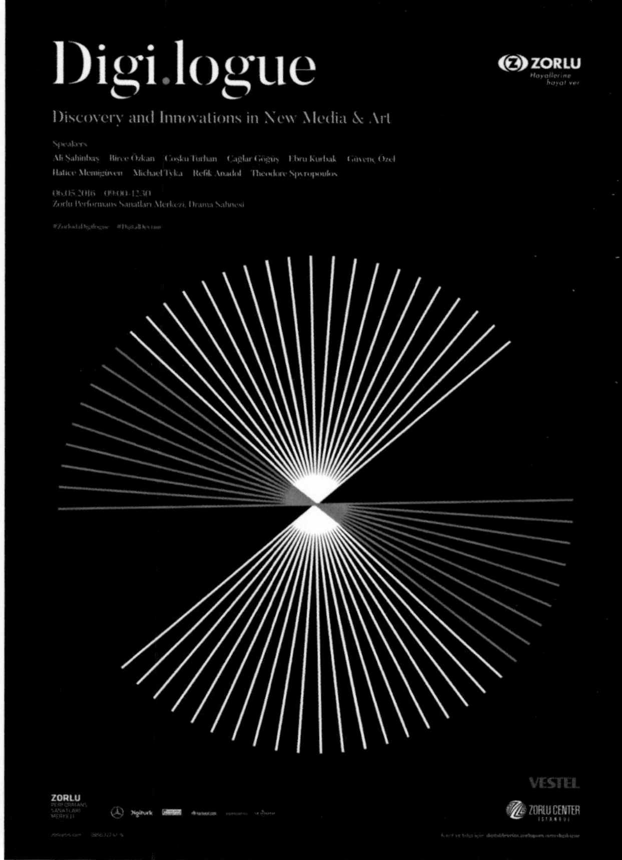
Digi.logue
ZORLU
Hayallerine hayat ver
Discovery and Innovations in New Media & Art
Speakers
Ali Şahinbaş Birce Özkan Coşku Turhan Çağlar Göğüş Ebru Kurbak Güvenç Özel
Hatice Memigüven Michael Tyka Refik Anadol Theodore Spyropoulos
06.05.2016 09:00-12:30
Zorlu Performans Sanatları Merkezi, Drama Sahnesi
VESTEL
ZORLU CENTER
ZORLU

Digi.logue
ZORLU
Hayallerine hayat ver
Discovery and Innovations in New Media & Art
Speakers
Ali Şahinbaş Birce Özkan Coşku Turhan Çağlar Göğüş Ebru Kurbak Güvenç Özel
Hatice Memigüven Michael Tyka Refik Anadol Theodore Spyropoulos
06.05.2016 09:00-12:30
Zorlu Performans Sanatları Merkezi, Drama Sahnesi
VESTEL
ZORLU CENTER
ZORLU

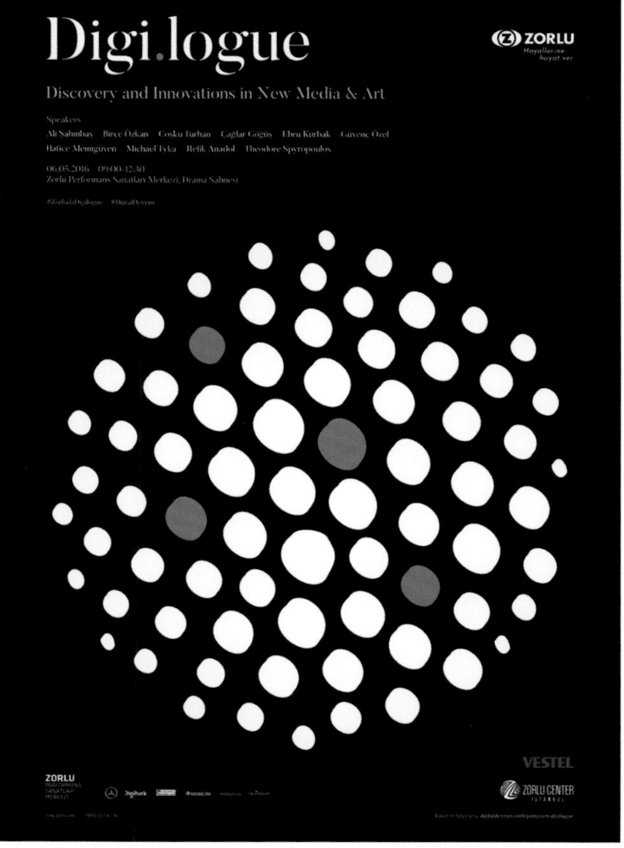
Digi.logue
ZORLU
Hayallerine hayat ver
Discovery and Innovations in New Media & Art
Speakers
Ali Şahinbaş Birce Özkan Coşku Turhan Çağlar Göğüş Ebru Kurbak Güvenç Özel
Hatice Memigüven Michael Tyka Refik Anadol Theodore Spyropoulos
06.05.2016 09:00-12:30
Zorlu Performans Sanatları Merkezi, Drama Sahnesi
VESTEL
ZORLU CENTER
ZORLU

CASAHANA

Agency: *1983ASIA*
Design: *SUSU & YAO*

CASAHANA is a food manufacturer of Malaysia specializing in pastries for "festivals and ceremonies". Now it faces the challenge of international brand positioning and younger customer base, and hopes to improve its brand image by branding. Therefore, it needs a "universal" story.

From its history, the designers have extracted the concept of "delight & moon". Twelve full moon days not only deliver the brand's original intention of "one ceremony one month" but also serve as the carrier of the brand's diverse development and highlight its unique presence in the marketplace.

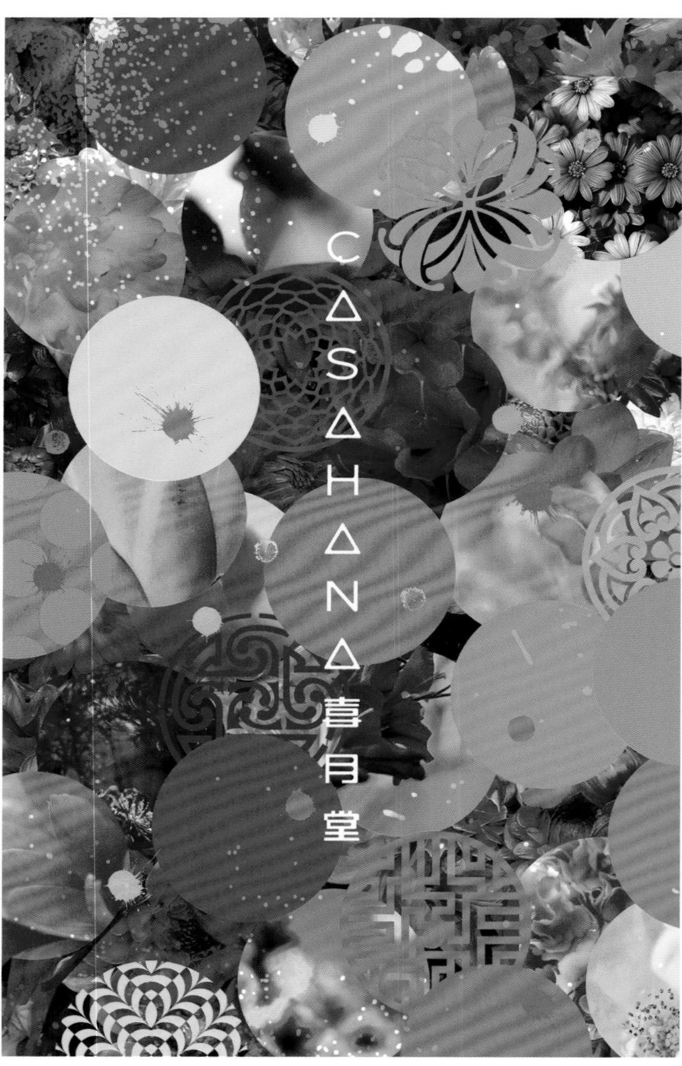

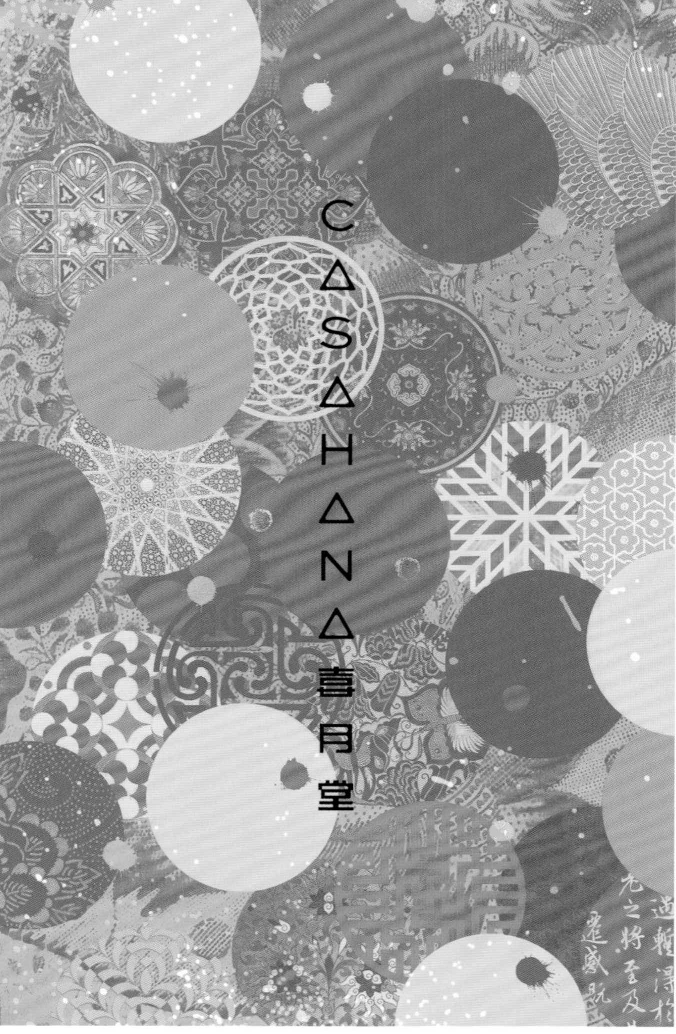

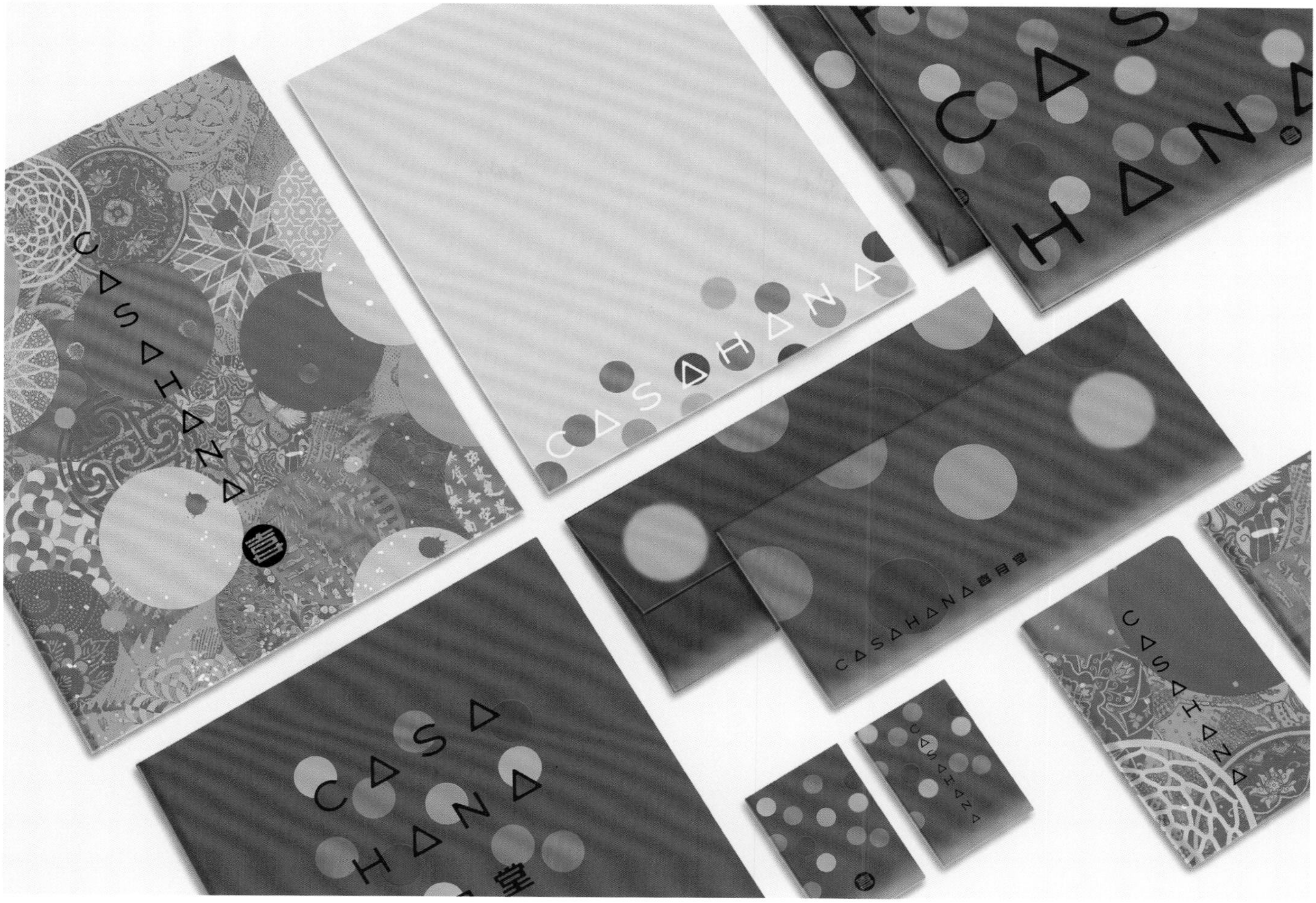

Dunkin Donuts

Designer: *Sara Knipström, Hanna Sköld*

The designers have updated Dunkin Donuts visual identity and packaging and turned it into a modern cafe. The new design goes back to the basics and fits the Scandinavian market as well as the global. With a simplified logo, geometric shapes and bright colors the design communicates fun, simple and playful.

DUNKIN
DONUTS

DUNKIN

DUNKIN
DONUTS
DUNKIN
DONUTS

Troom

***Design:** Andrii Kurylo*

In the logo, the designer focuses on the double "O". For this, the designer placed it one on one and chose the simplest form. After that, the other letters were made using the grid and the same simple forms. The emphasis in the logo was chosen as the identifier. A simple form makes it easy to interact with it and repeat it outlines. Positive youth mood of identity is achieved by means of color and emotional photos.

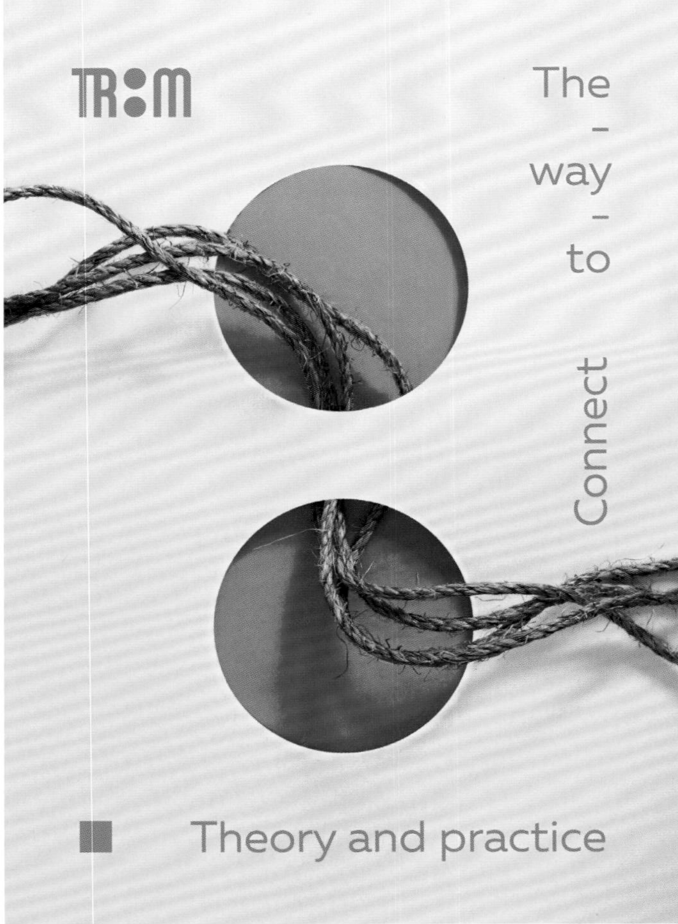

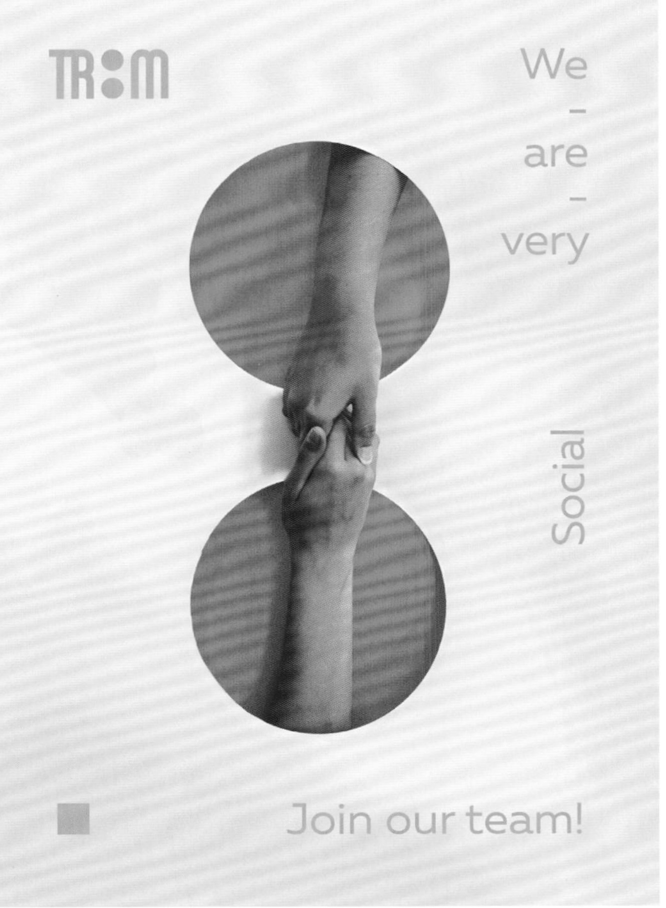

TR:M
If
–
you
–
are
Emotional
Come here!
TR:M
If
–
you
–
are
Confused
Come here!
TR:M
If
–
you
–
are
Little crazy
Come here!

TR:M
13
–
06
–
16
Old books sale
18.30

Francesco Mircoli. Psicofarmaci

Design: *Davide Parere*

Francesco Mircoli is an Italian emerging songwriter. In order to promote his first debut album "Psicofarmaci"(Italian word for psychotropic drugs), the designer created a clean and modern monogram in addition to the visual identity of the album, including some merchandising stuff.

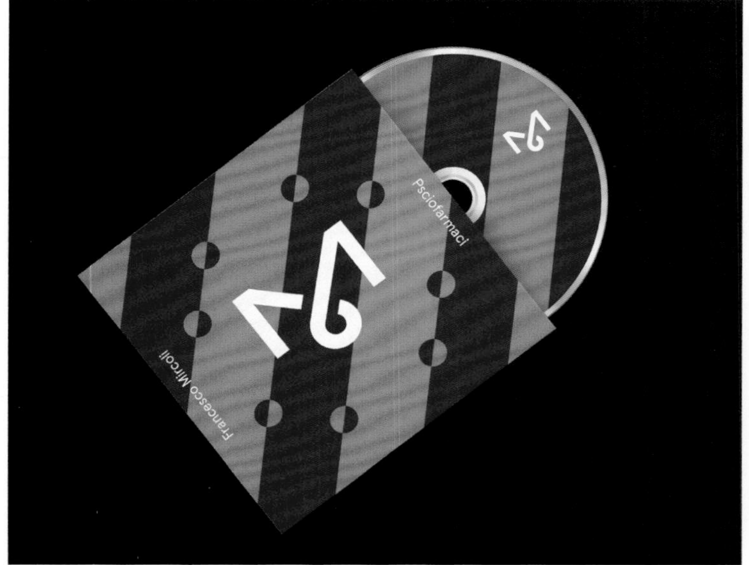

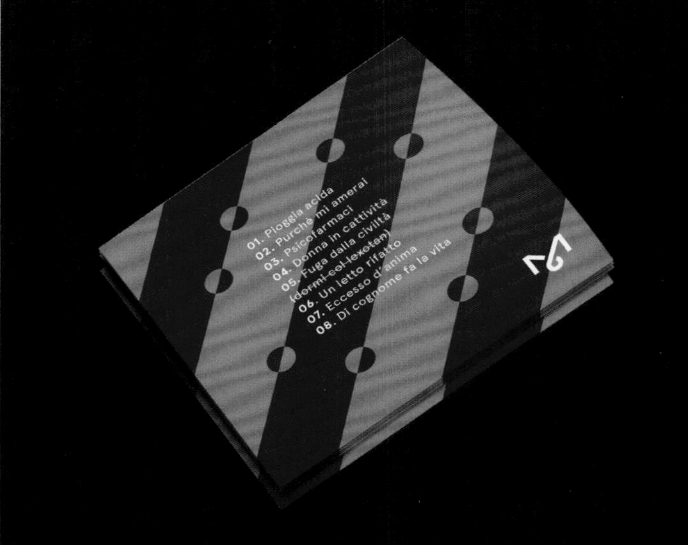

PSICOFARMACI
200 mg

Francesco Mircoli

PSICOFARMACI
200 mg

Francesco Mircoli

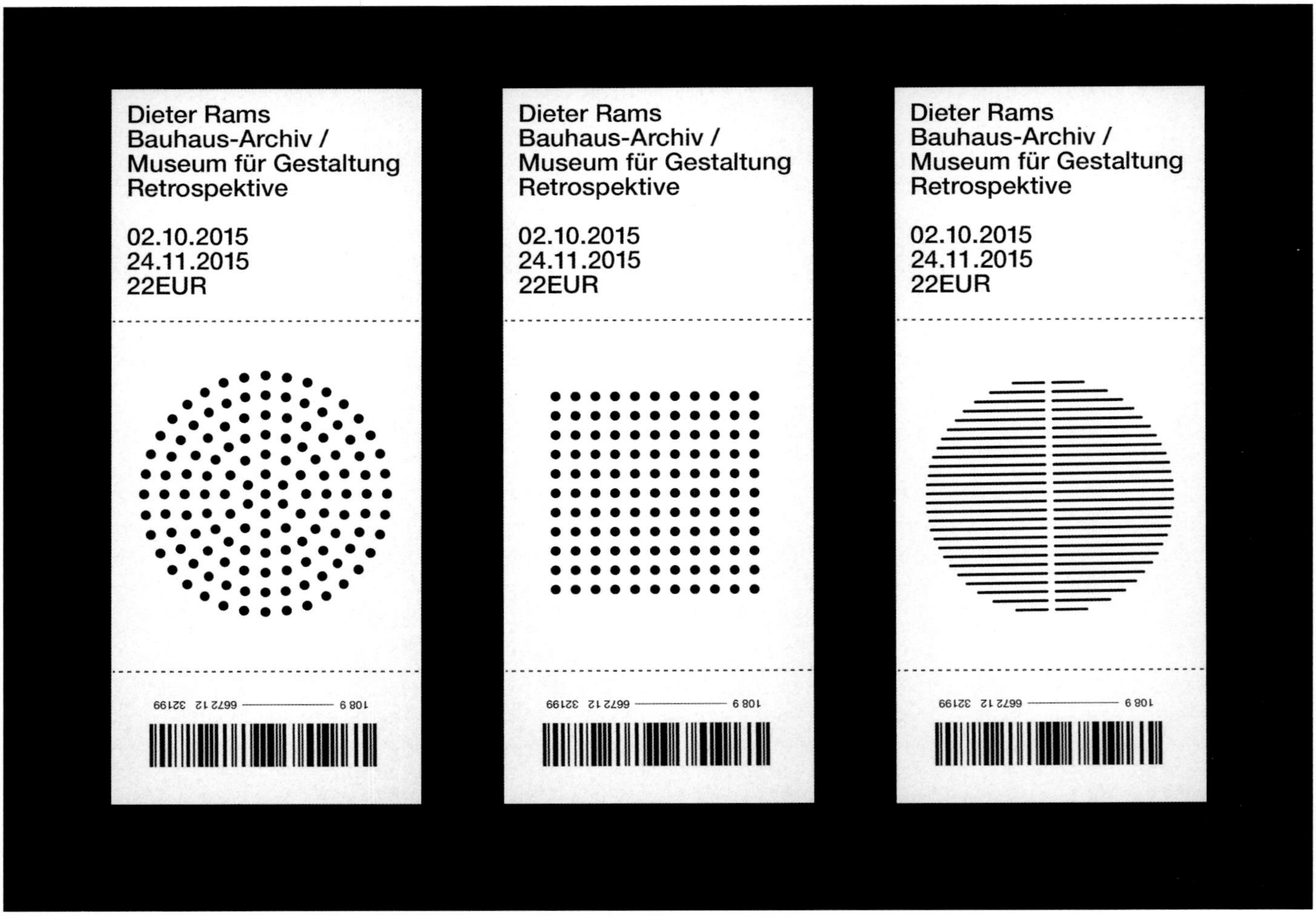

Dieter Rams
Bauhaus-Archiv /
Museum für Gestaltung
Retrospektive

02.10.2015
24.11.2015
22EUR

Dieter Rams

Design: *Florent Gomez*

The idea was to design a branding that responds to the ten principles to good design by Dieter Rams. Design is not a finite way, measuring it strove to express the ten fundamental principles of what he considered be good design. Here they are: good design is innovative. Good design makes a product useful. Good design is aesthetic. Good design makes a product understandable. Good design is unobtrusive. Good design is honest. Good design is durable. Good design is accurate down to the smallest detail. Good design is respectful of the environment. The good design is as little design as possible.

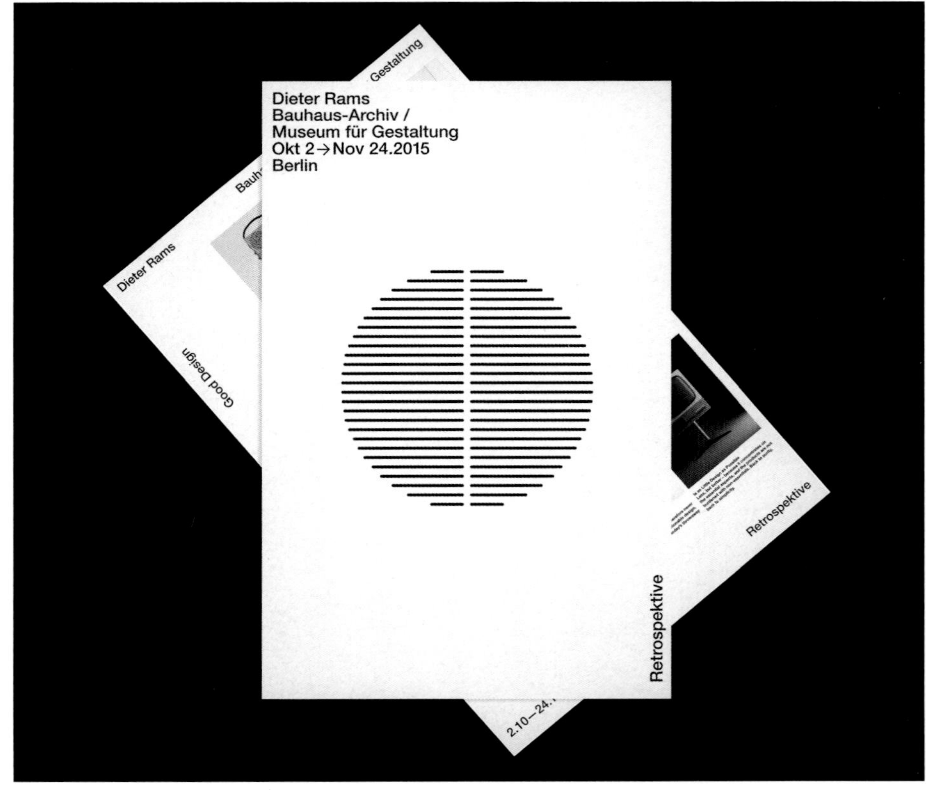

Triangles, Rectangles & Polygons

Self Rebranding

Design: *Riccardo Vicentelli*

Personal branding design. The logo is not a simple triangle. It is the letter V (initial of the designer's last name) vertically reflected, because it recalls the shape of a mountain. The mountain has several meanings for the designer. In addition to being a great lover of snow and cold, the mountain means: the summit, the uniqueness, the peak, the roof of the world.

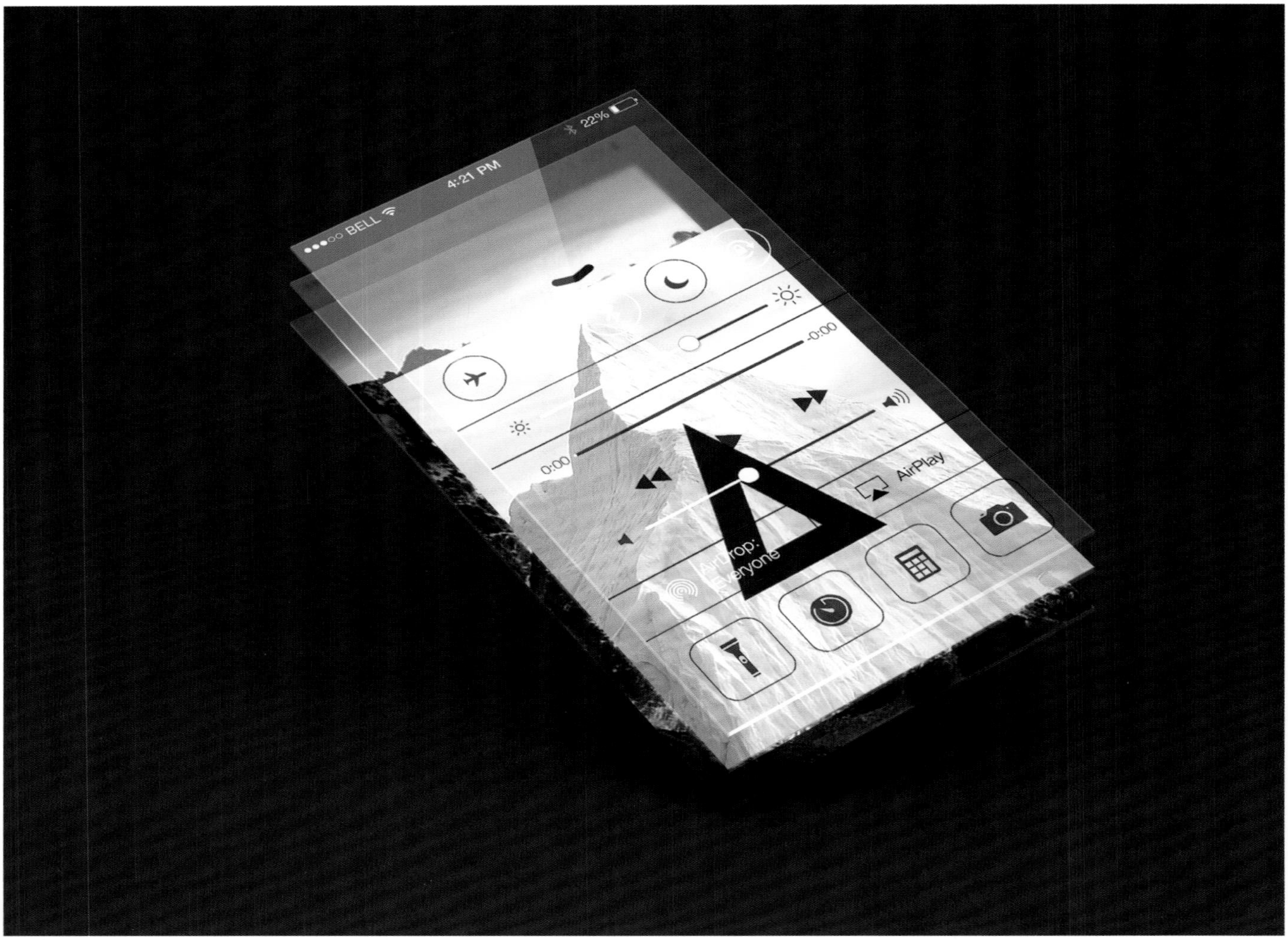

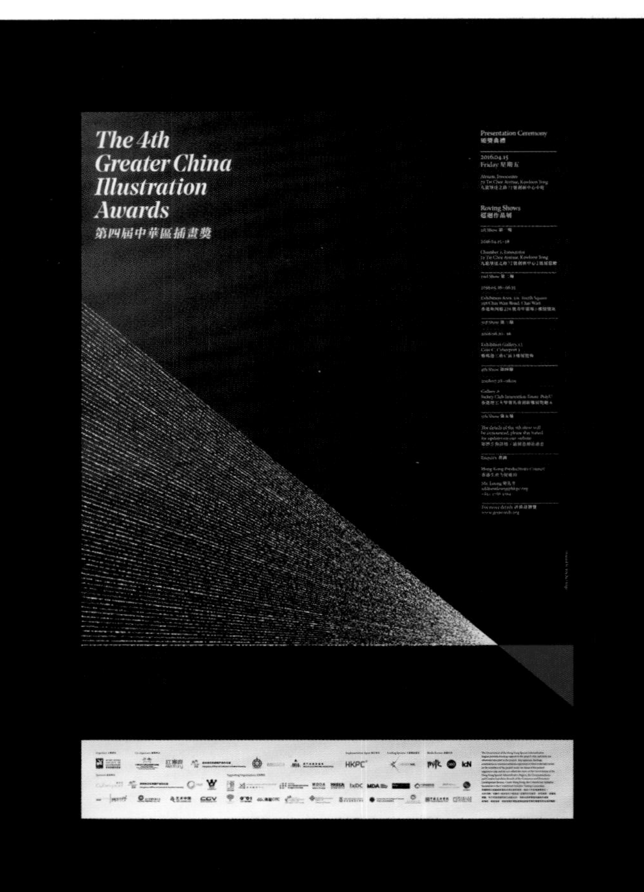

The 4th Greater China Illustration Awards

Design: *Toby Ng Design*

Based on the theme "A Vibrant Transformation A Meticulous Masterpiece", the designers created the identity and all the printed matter related to the Awards. The design, comprised of a set of 4 graphics, depicts a small color – coded triangle that radiates into a big triangle through a variety of patterned organic lines. The small triangle represent the illustrator's hand / pen / brush and the big triangle, with its various organic, hand crafted line patterns symbolizes creativity and possibilities.

Four colors and four patterns created a color code to distinguish the different award categories and sections; these were used in the small triangles to reinforce the competition's award identity.

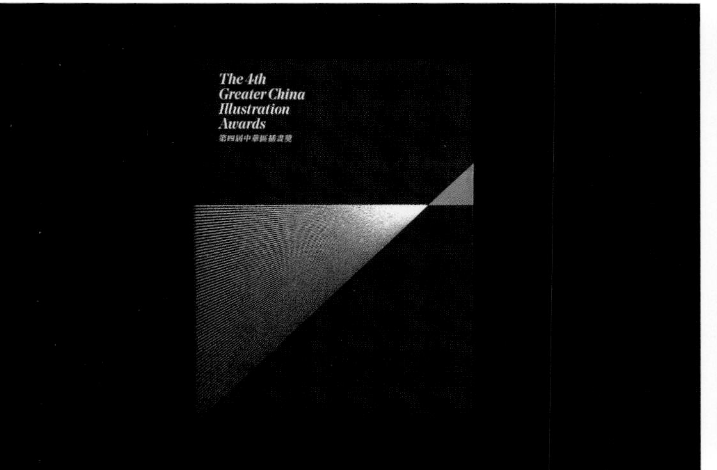
The 4th
Greater China
Illustration
Awards

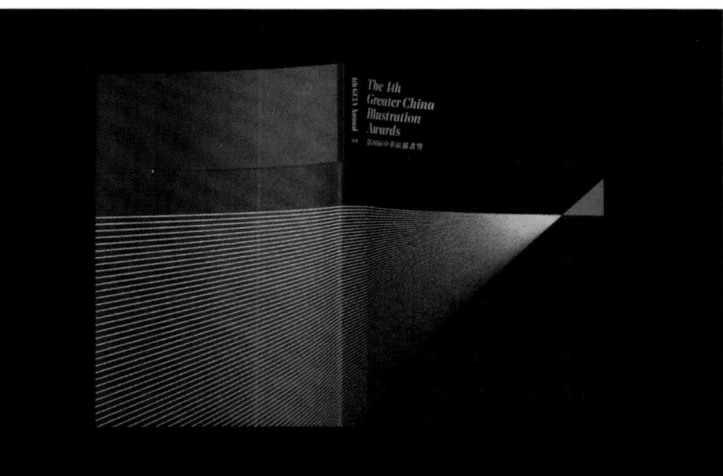
The 4th
Greater China
Illustration
Awards

The Best
Illustration
(Judges' Choice)
Award
WEN Peng

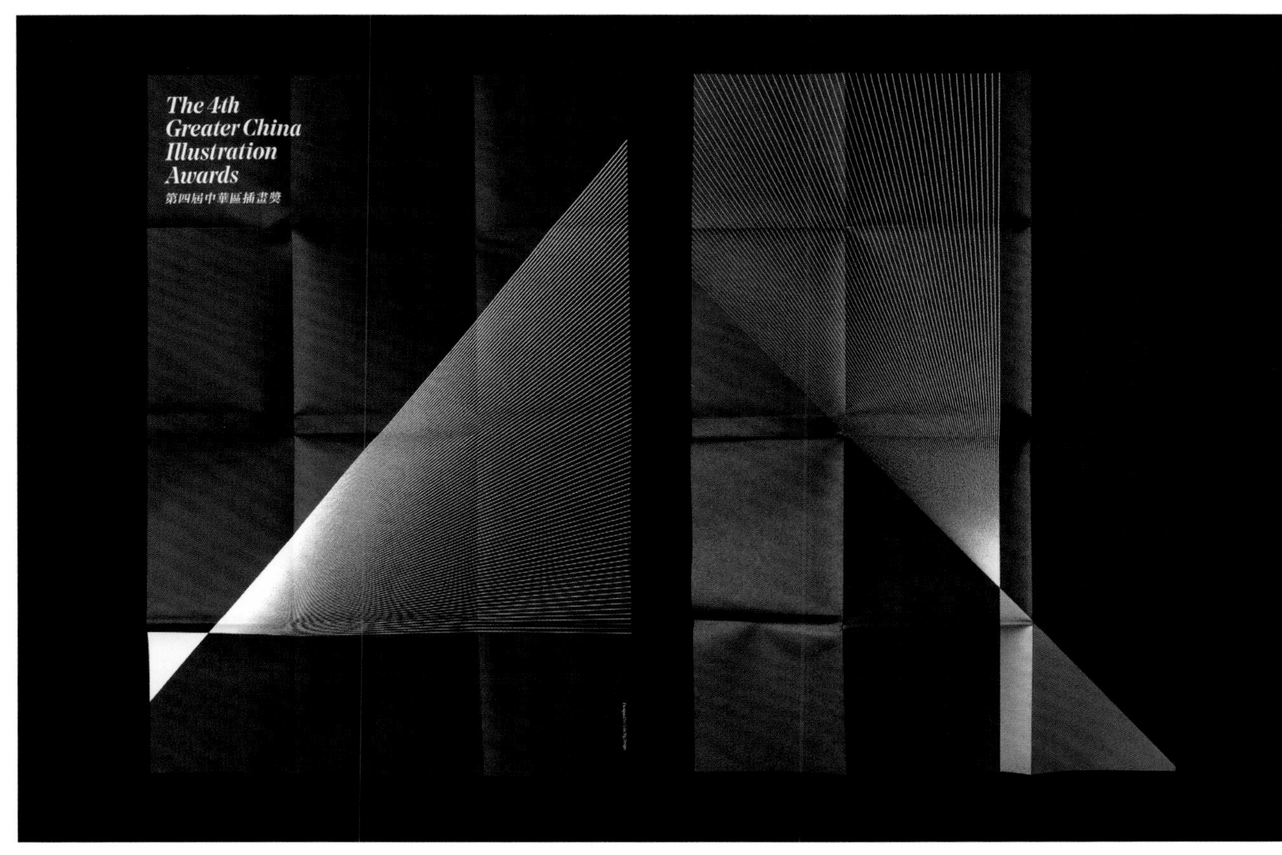
The 4th
Greater China
Illustration
Awards
第四屆中華區插畫獎

Flow

Design: *Studio Hands*
Photography: *Johnny van Bergen, Sabine Metz*

The logo represents the musical areas of house music Flow represents: Deephouse, Tech House, and House in general. For the typography, the designers used a font that matches the triangular shape – Cassanet. This font is now the main font of Flow. Flow organizes stages at festivals, but also club nights. Therefore, the designers have divided it in color. For festivals, the designers use a colored background and the club nights a black one.

FLOW
TIVOLI D8
DUBLIN
WWW.LISTENTOFLOW.COM
FLOW
05.02.2016
THE EGG
LONDON
WWW.LISTENTOFLOW.COM
FLOW
11.07.2015
A DAY
AT THE PARK
WWW.LISTENTOFLOW.COM

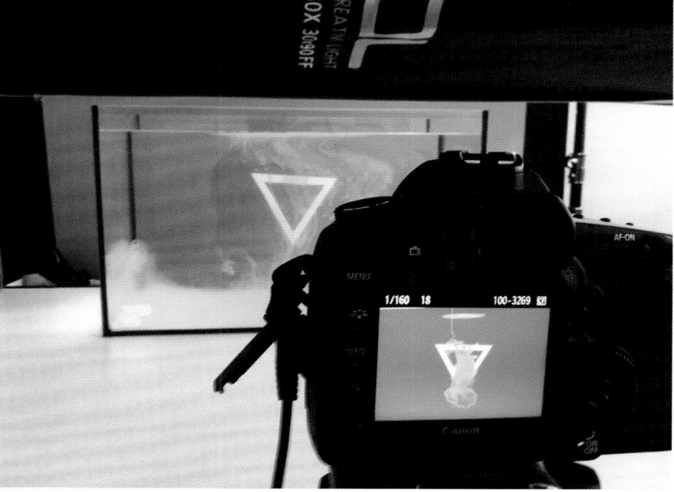
MENU
AF-ON
1/160 18
100-3269

Boticário – Play It

Agency: *Taste.ag*
Design: *Pedro Gonzalez*

Boticário, the world's largest cosmetic franchise, hired Taste.ag to create an innovative brand experience for its communication partners. The goal was to obtain a moment of break and discussion regarding the new direction of their brand communication. The most challenging part, however, was to provoke a complete disruption in the visual identity, and this was achieved by completely ignoring Boticário's visual guidelines, as requested by the client himself.

play it
ONE WAY

play it

Donots – Karacho. LP Artwork.

Design: *Rocket & Wink*

Here is the new artwork for the new donots album: Karacho.

DAS NEUE ALBUM
DONOTS
KARACHO
20.02.2015
DAS NEUE ALBUM
DONOTS
KARACHO
20.02.2015
OLDSC
DAS NEUE ALBUM

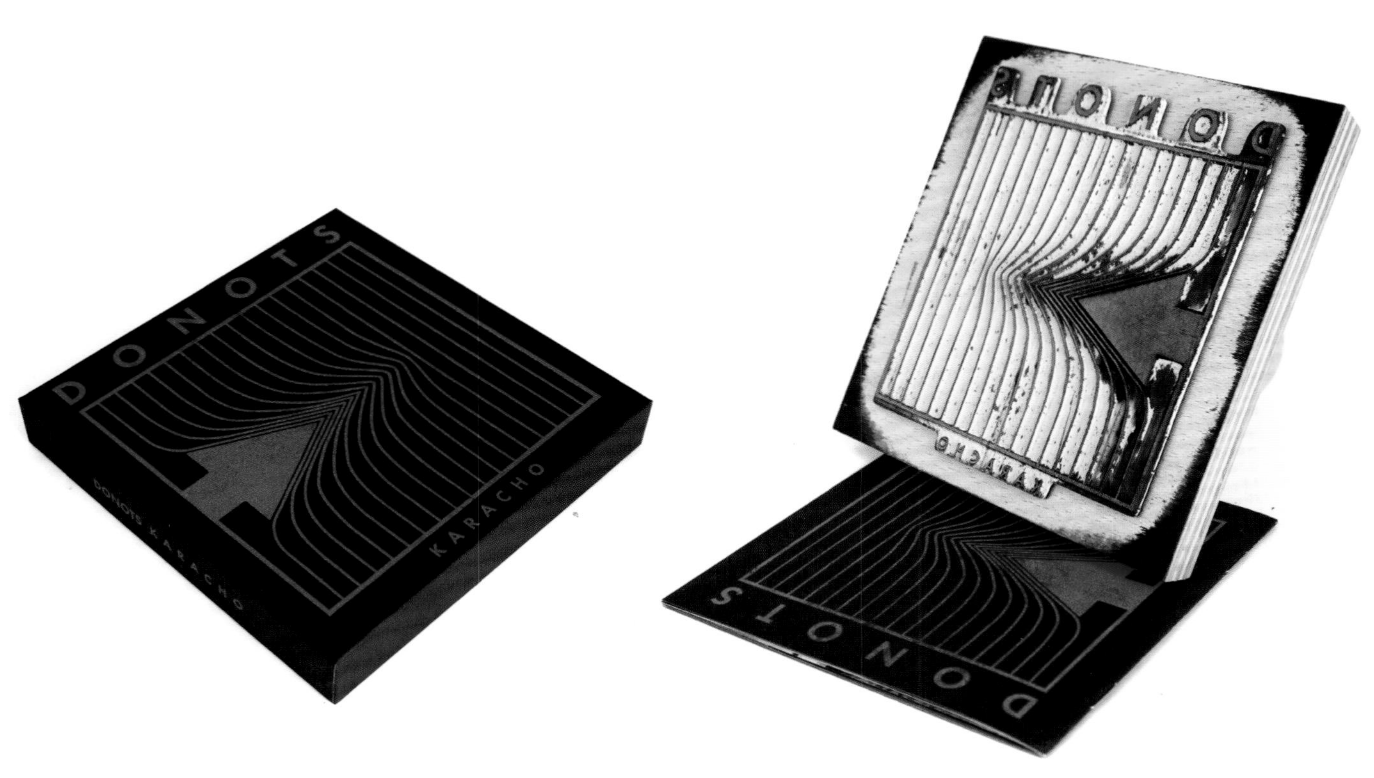
DONOTS
KARACHO
DONOTS KARACHO
DONOTS

Kubique

Design: *Vasilis Pallas*

The name Kubique is a combination of Marina's (the designer of the bags) love to geometry and cubism, the director Stanley Kubrick and the French ending "ique". The logo is inspired by the characteristic pattern which is used in every Kubique bag, tribute to simplicity and geometry and the initial letter K. The symbol is accomplished with a light monospace typography, which reflects the elegant aesthetic of the brand. The identity follows the same values.

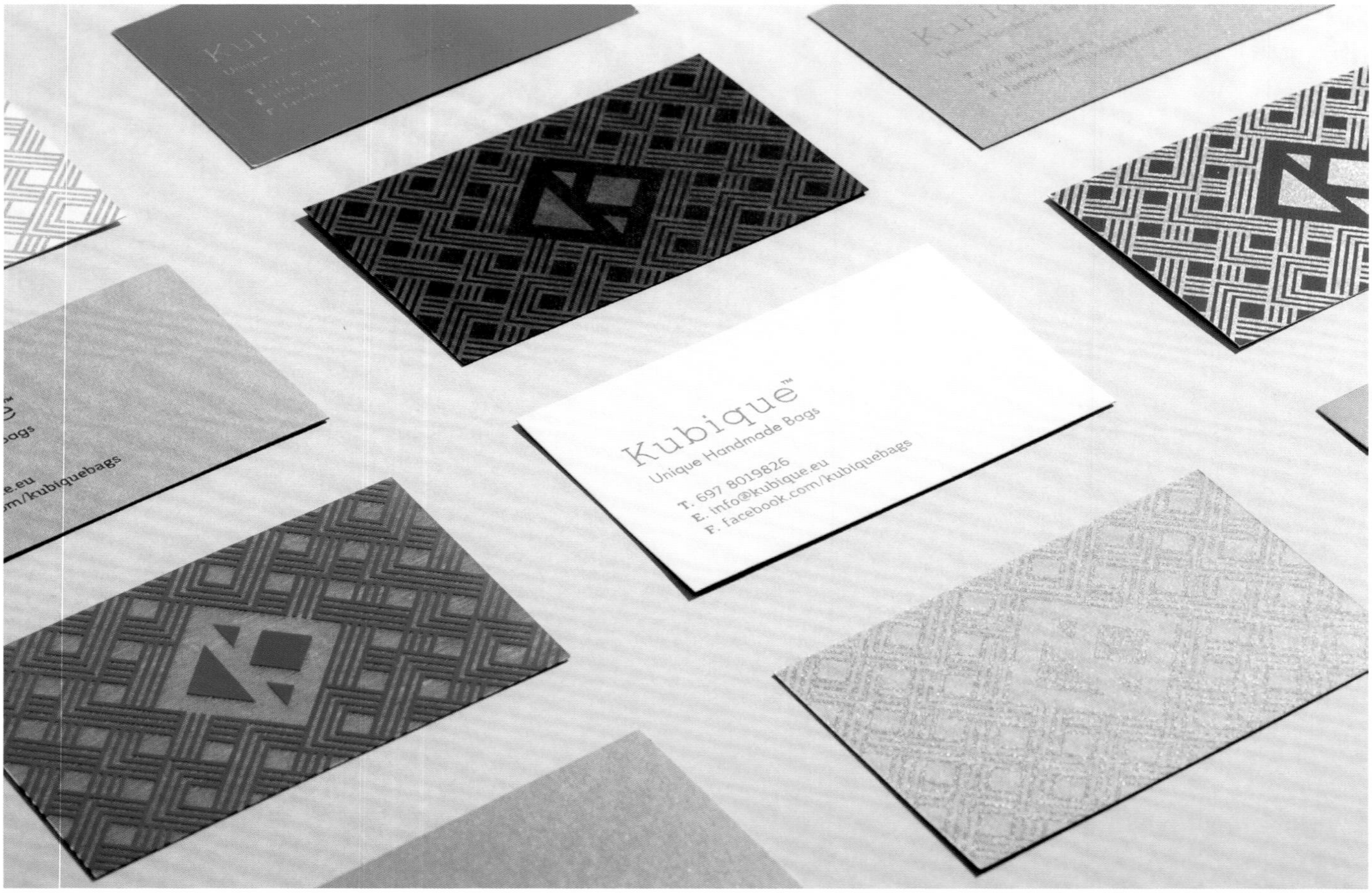

Έναρξη έκθεσης
Σάββατο 04 Απριλίου
ώρα 20:00
Kubique™
H I B 1st T I O N
04 - 19 Απριλίου
ANANTI CITY RESORT
Λογγάκι, Τρίκαλα 42100
Bags

Kubique™
Unique Handmade Bags

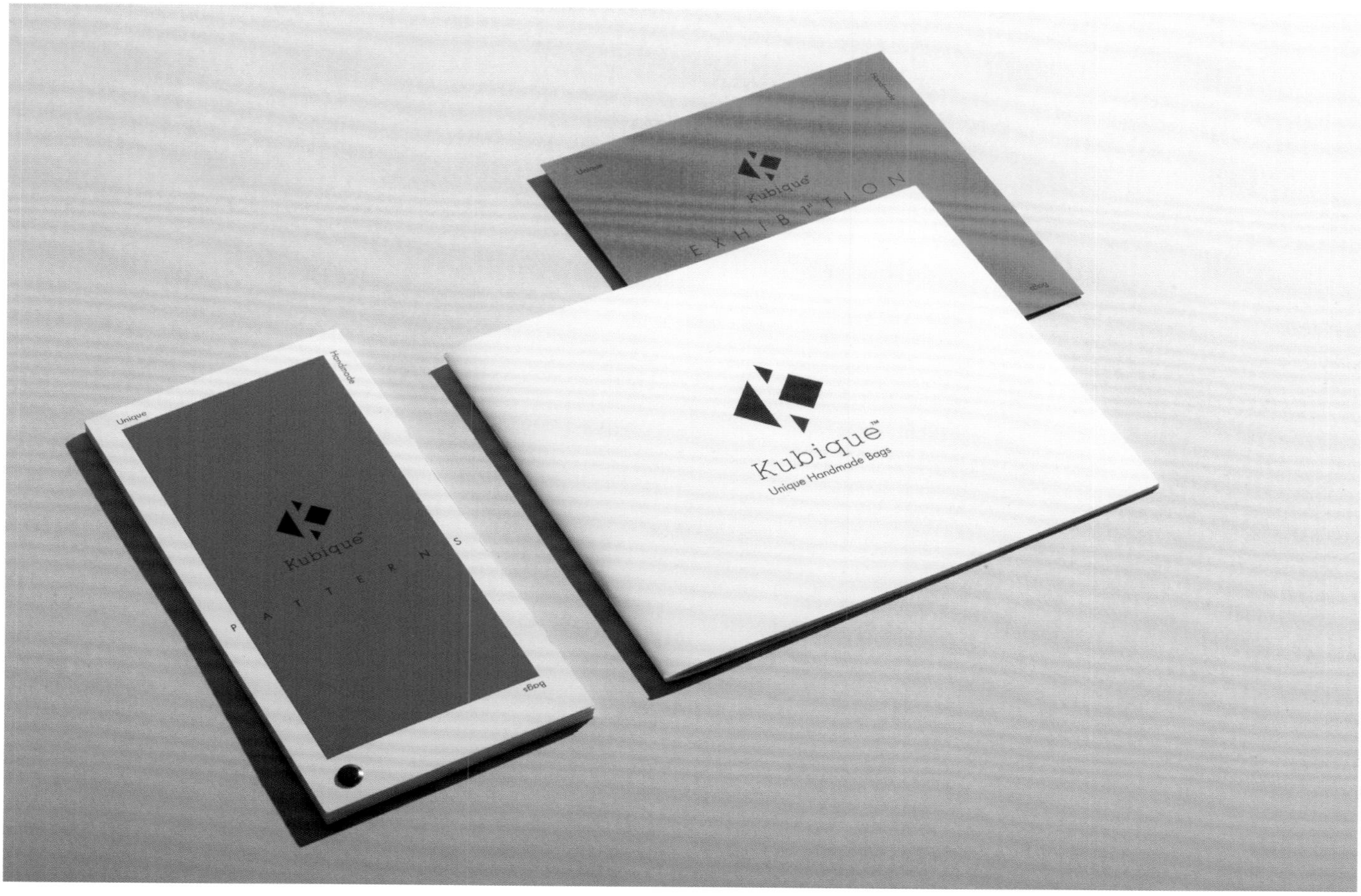

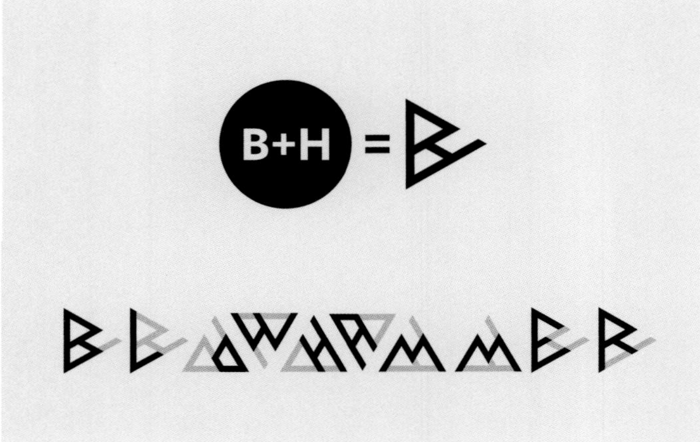

Blowhammer

Design: *Maurizio Pagnozzi*

The ultimate goal of the rebranding of Blowhammer was the creation of a mark that could be iconic and memorable, wearable and suitable for possible future expansion of the brand, such as accessories, brooches and more. Always paying attention to the spirit of the brand "Choose a style which can scream who you are to the world. Change your rules. Live Blowhammer."

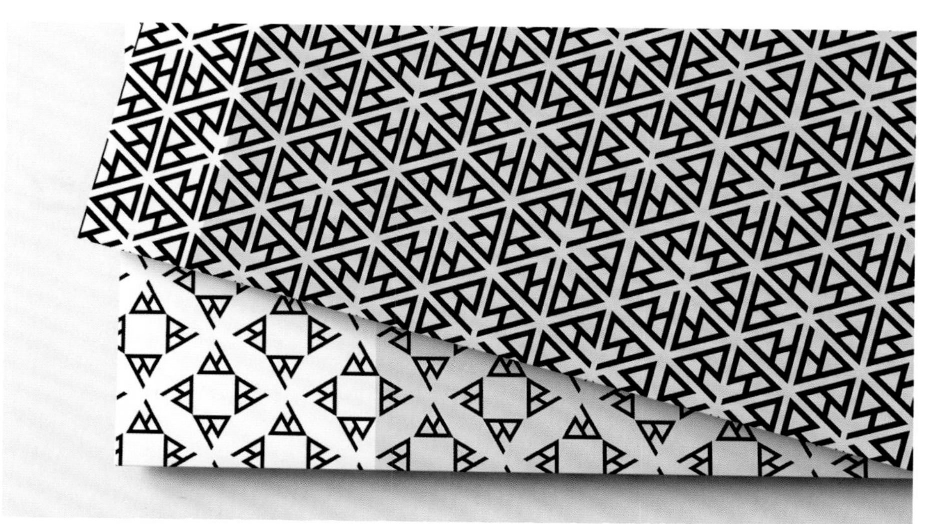

BLOWHAMMER
BLOWHAMMER

BLOWHAMM
MAN/WOMAN
2015
THSIRT // TANK TOP // SWEATSHIRT

BLOWHAMMER

Knights Paving & Landscaping

Design: *JB Studio*

Identity created for Knights Paving & Landscaping, inspired by a simple paving pattern, which is used to create a unique (letter K) logo mark, whilst also referencing the nature of the company's business. The identity was applied to various media including stationery, website, site boards, staff uniforms, and vehicle livery.

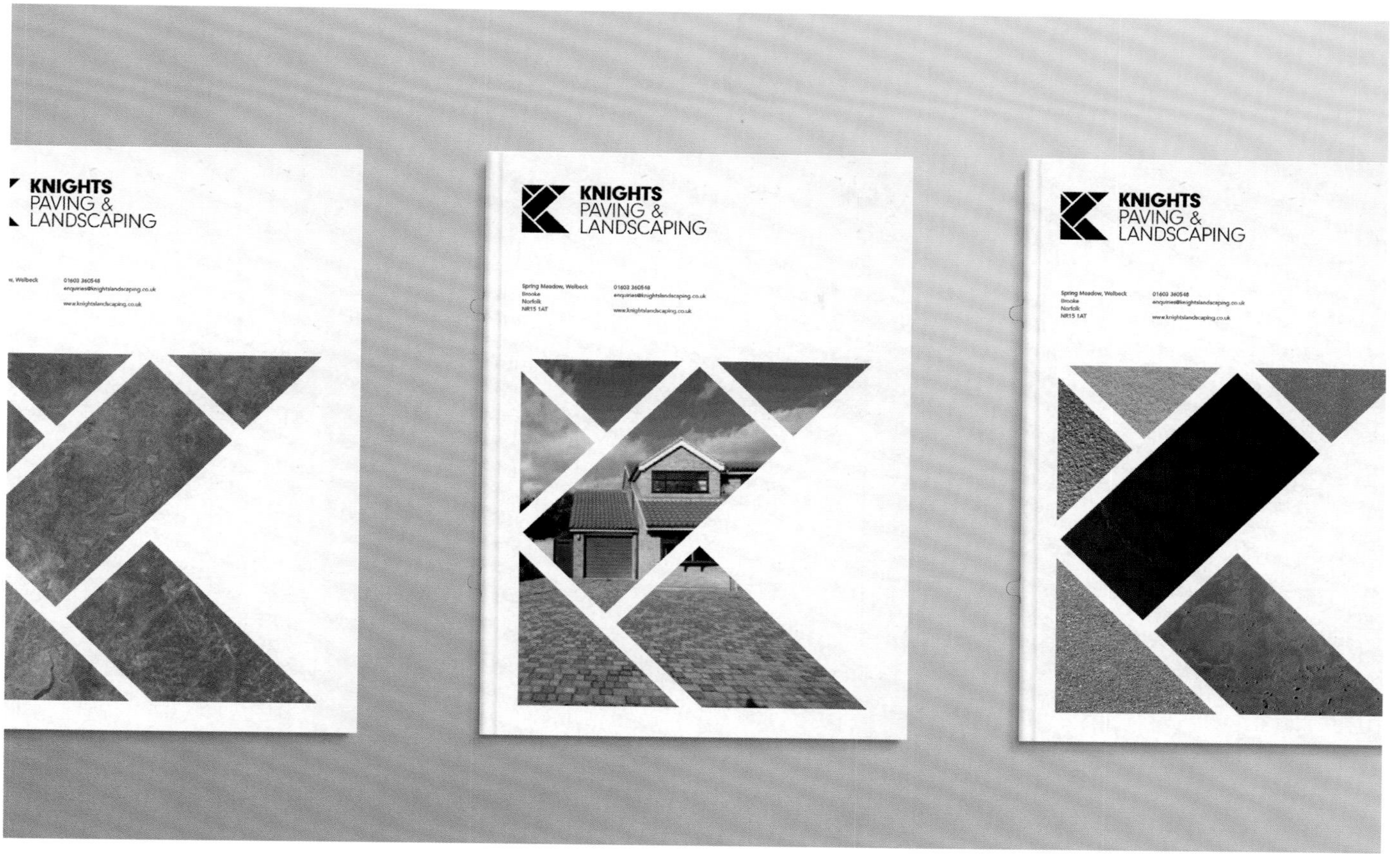
KNIGHTS
PAVING &
LANDSCAPING

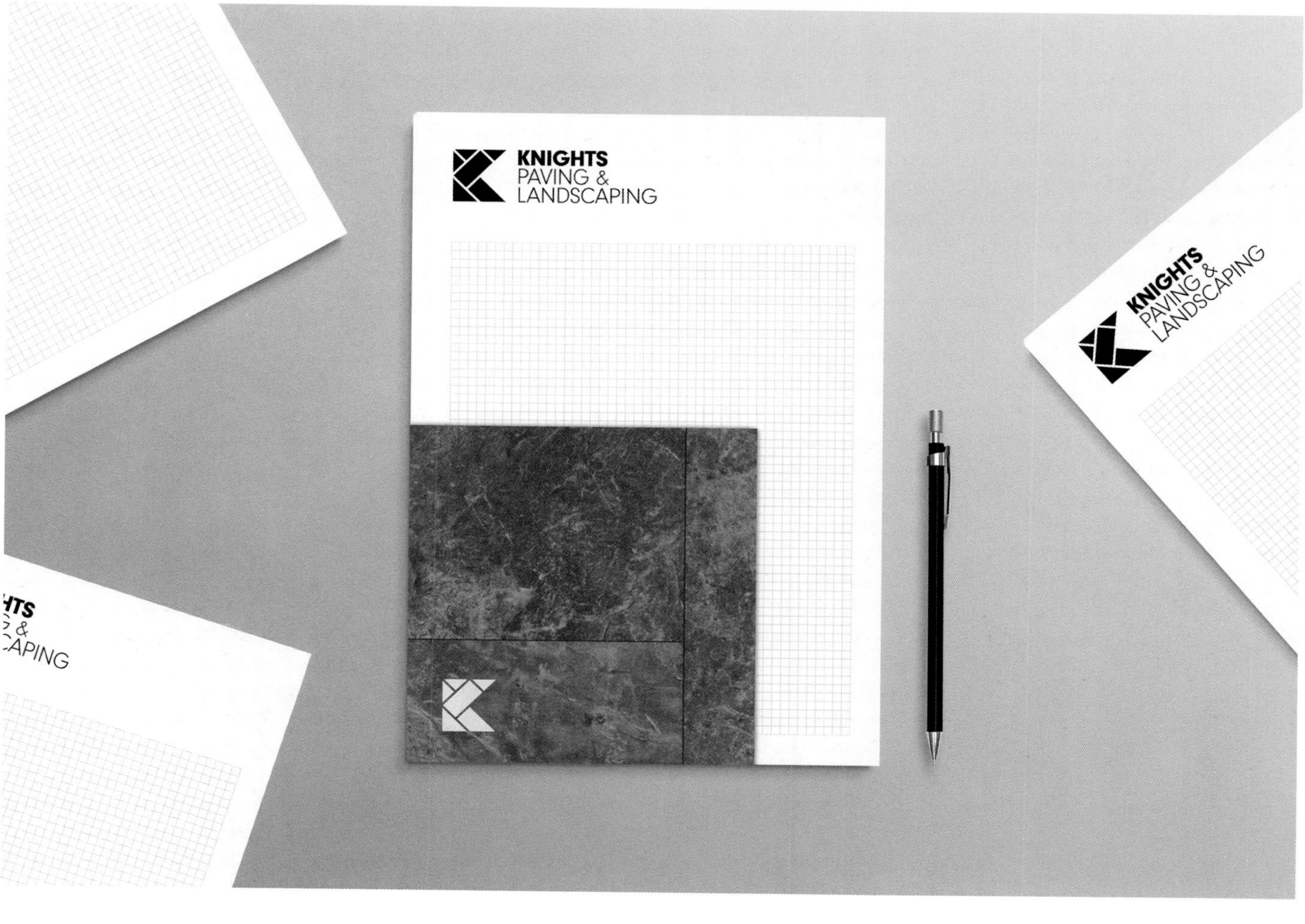
KNIGHTS
PAVING &
LANDSCAPING

THINK
OUTSIDE
THE

Google Squared

Design: *Jack Morgan*

Google Squared is a disruptive new digital education initiative developed by Google in London and piloted. It encourages learning by doing and action over theory; training participants to affect change by understanding how technology impacts society.

The conceptual brand identity for Google Squared was unveiled by independent designer Jack Morgan. These concepts later led to a multi-year partnership between Jack Morgan and Google, including the full rebrand of Google Squared and the launch of new global innovations in education such as the Google Digital Academy.

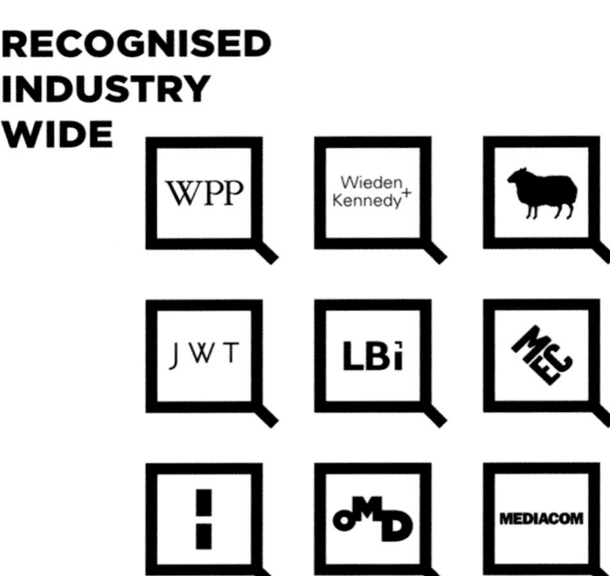

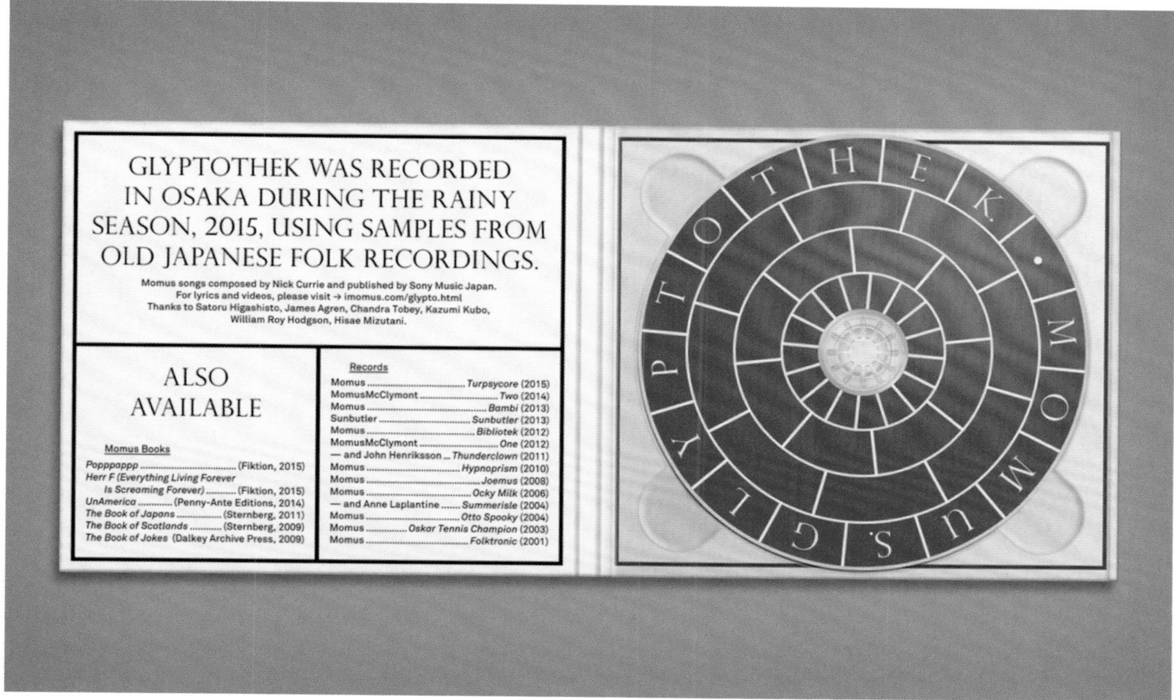

Momus: "Glyptothek"

Design: *Hagen Verleger*

On "Glyptothek," recorded in Osaka during the rainy season, Momus has ransacked his colorful pile of Japanese folk 45s for samples and wrapped a series of cautionary tales for the internet age around the thunder of Shinto festival drums, the keening wail of rural flutes, the tinny riffing of massed shamisen, the clacking of summery claves, and the wild backing vocals of kimono-clad village maidens. The results sound like a UNESCO World Heritage site incongruously taken over by the ghosts of Hilaire Belloc, Cocteau, Kafka, Jarry, Kantor, Petronius, DH Lawrence, Bolan and Bowie.

Poly-Copies

***Design:** Dimitris Kostinis*

Poly-Copies is a small printing center which offers an extensive range of copying and digital services: Photocopying black/white and color, Printing on different sizes (A8 to A0), digitization, printing plans and many more.

With a young and dynamic team this small family business offers a large range of quick and qualitative printing to students and individuals.

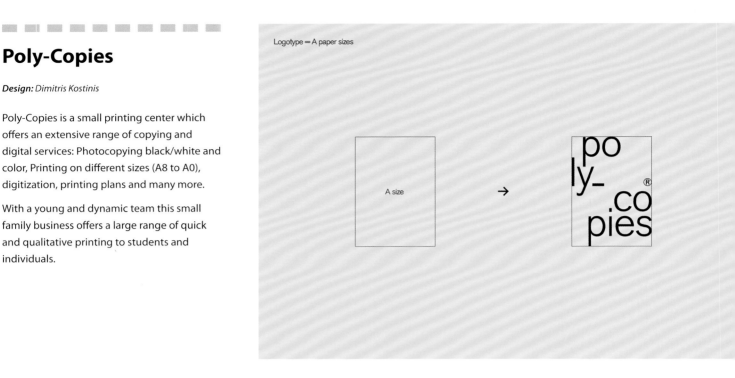

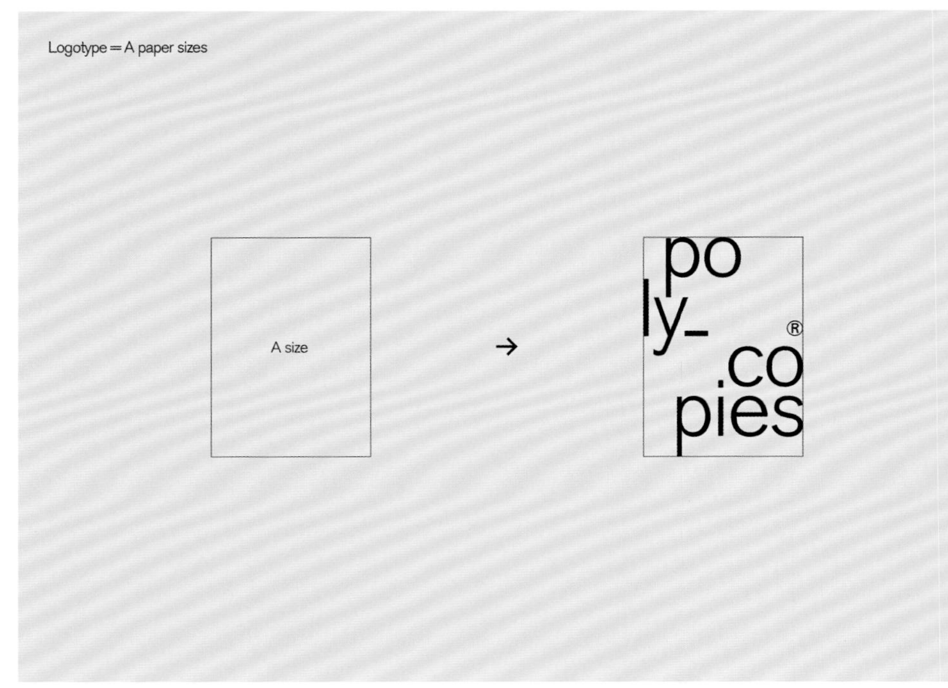

Impression
Numérique
De qualité
Couleur
& N/B
Photocopies N /B
Couleurs
Tirages A4, A3, .. A0;
Reliures
Plastification A4, A3;
Papeterie
Lundi au vendredi de 7h30
à 18h. Samedi de 10h00 à
14h00.
po
ly-
.co
pies

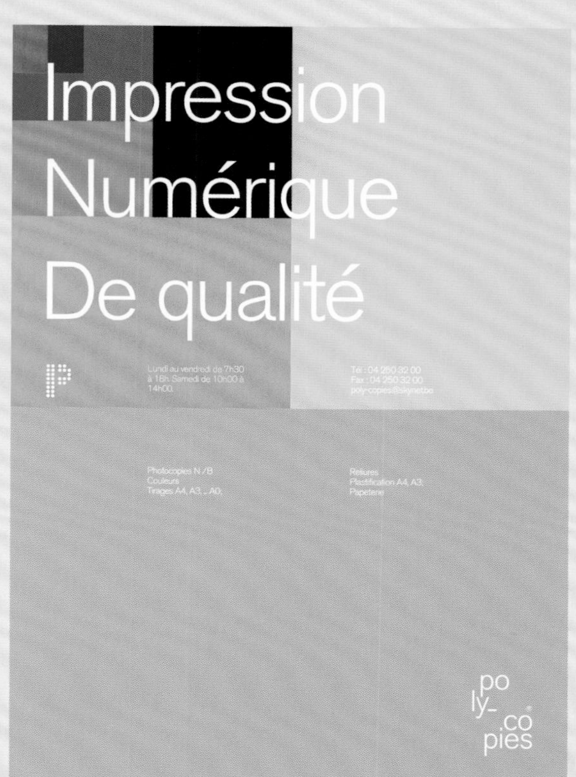

Idea : To use the size chart illustrating the ISO A series

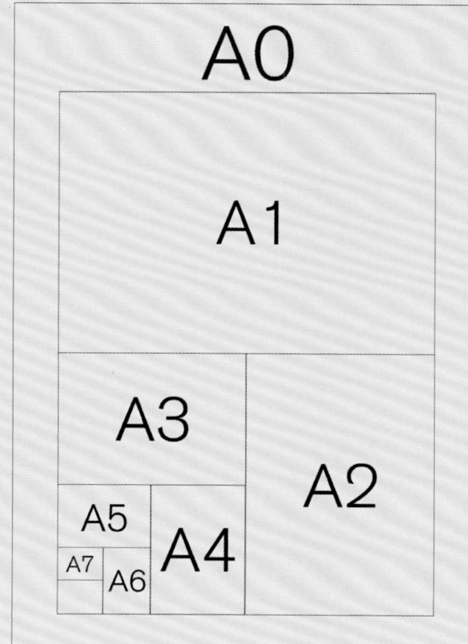

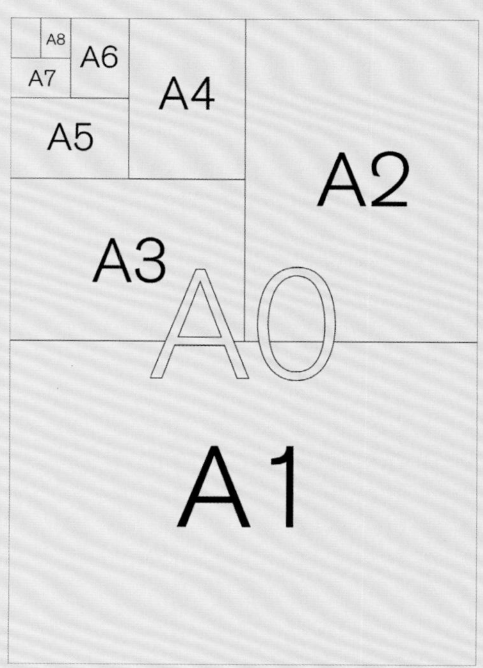

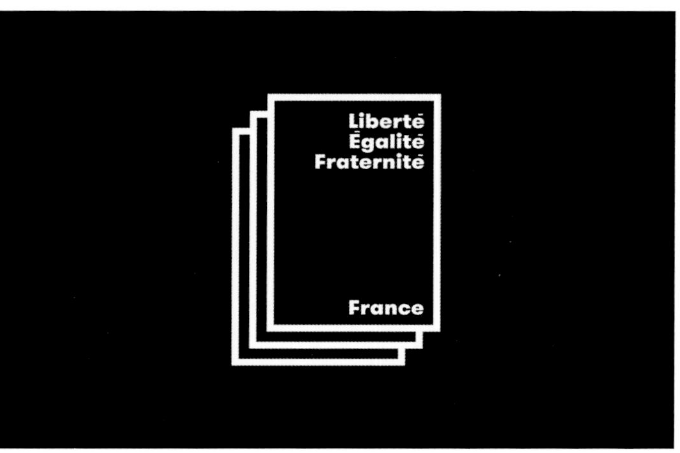

Francia País Invitado de Honor

Agency: *Brandlab*
Art Direction: *Andres Nakamatsu*
Design: *Jhesse Franco*

The twentieth edition Lima Book Fair took place and the French Embassy in Peru assigned Brandlab their Identity design to be presented as a guest of honor. The concept takes as its pillar the official motto of the French Republic Liberty, equality, fraternity, and being a cyclical order, the designers represented with three stacked books.

The designers applied the identity in all parts they designed, from bags to architectural space. The designers also produced a series of posters representing graphically the work of each author who assisted the fair.

Liberté
Egalité
Fraternité
France
Francia
país
invitado
de honor
FIL
2015

Liberté
Egalité
Fraternité
France
Deville

Liberté
Egalité
Fraternité
France
Ledu

Liberté
Egalité
Fraternité
France
Cailleaux

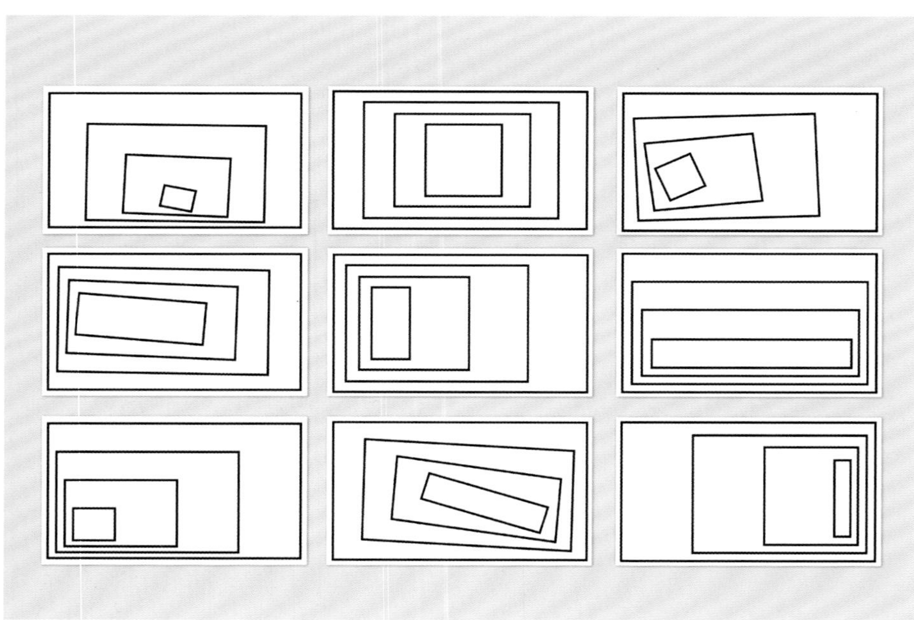

Little Prince Museum of Surrealism

Design: *Leo Porto*

The Little Prince Museum is a fictional museum of art and design that showcases Surrealist works from all over the world. The museum is named after The Little Prince book, by Antoine De Saint-Exupery.

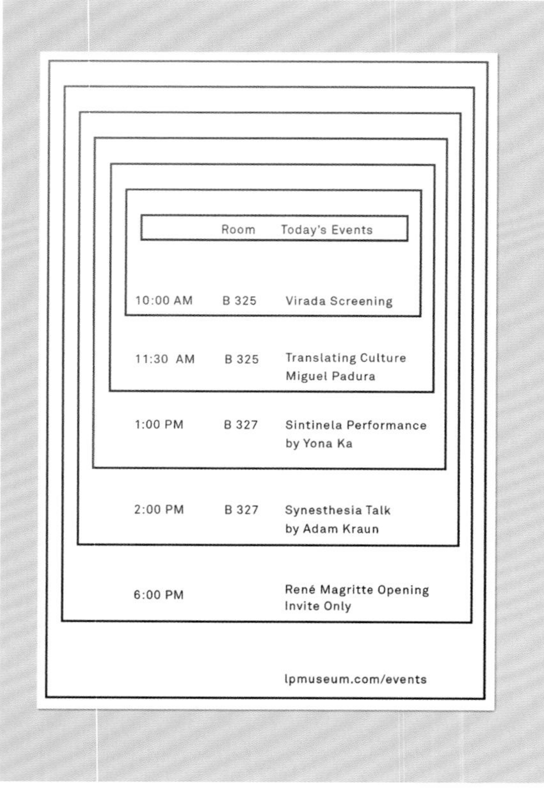

Room Today's Events
10:00 AM B 325 Virada Screening
11:30 AM B 325 Translating Culture
Miguel Padura
1:00 PM B 327 Sintinela Performance
by Yona Ka
2:00 PM B 327 Synesthesia Talk
by Adam Kraun
6:00 PM René Magritte Opening
Invite Only
lpmuseum.com/events

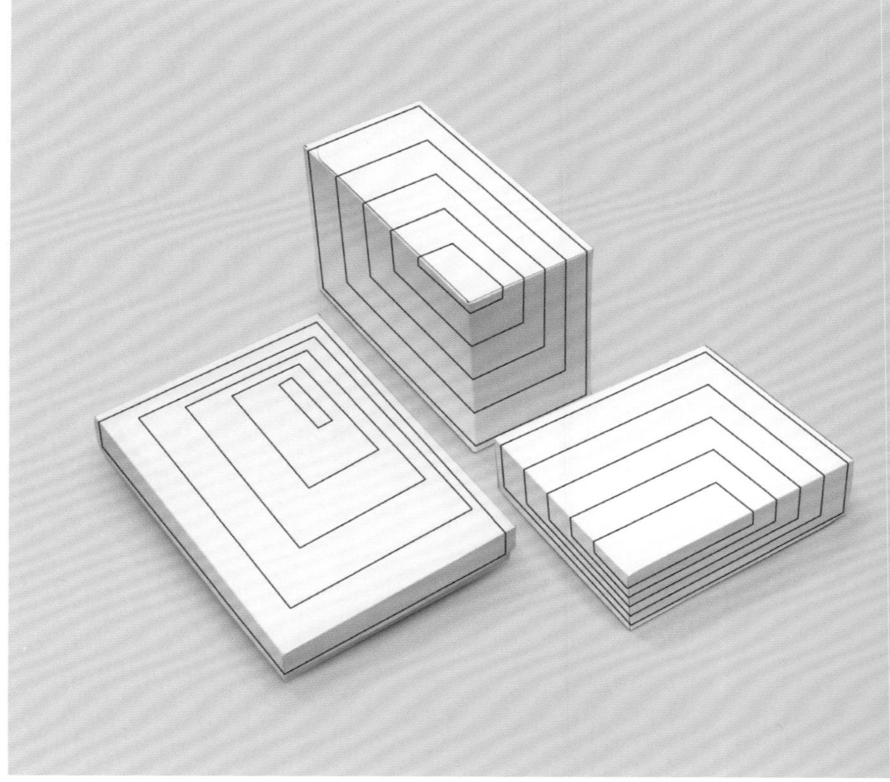

B.Visible – Okulus Drift

***Design:** Daniel Triendl*

Okulus Drift was a visual identity project, including album artworks for Vienna based music artist B.Visible. The goal was to build a strong identity influenced by his personal character and his album tracks. To keep the identity together, all visual key elements for example the typography and illustration style is based on the lines of the logo. To boost a visual similarity, the designer also used a bold color palette for B.Visible's identity system.

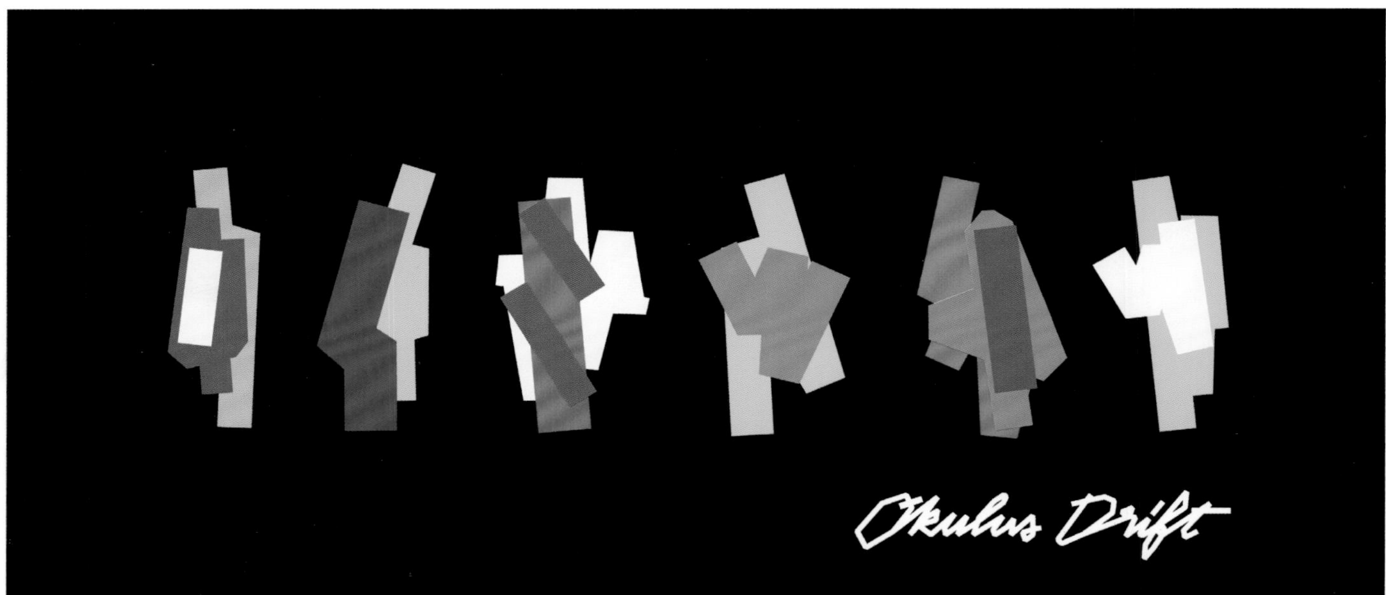

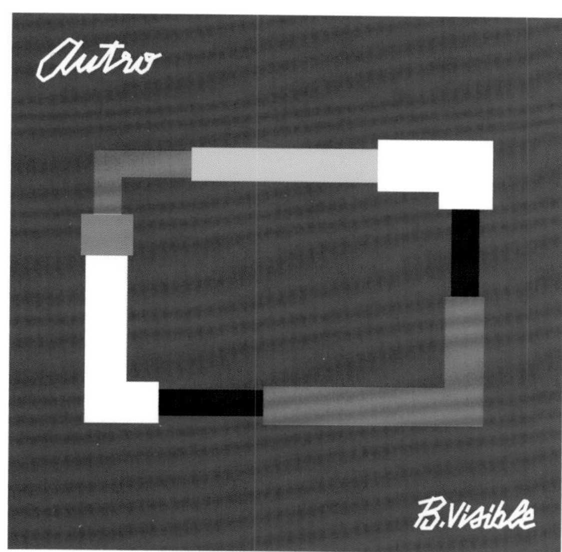
Autro
B.Visible

Hott
B.Visible

Nashi
B.Visible

Concrete Proof
B.Visible

Bcn
B.Visible

Mayr

Design: *Moby Digg*

For Mayr Investment Managers, the designers developed a full branding set, including logo design, key visual, branding guidelines a corporate website based on a one-pager system, corporate letter, v-cards, signage, and so on. The minimalistic corporate identity was based on simple line-graphics and a decisive color combination. The clean approach represents the clients' vision of his finance services and brand core. The animated website stands out in comparison with competitors and helps Mayr Investment Managers to differentiate its brand and position itself as a thought leader.

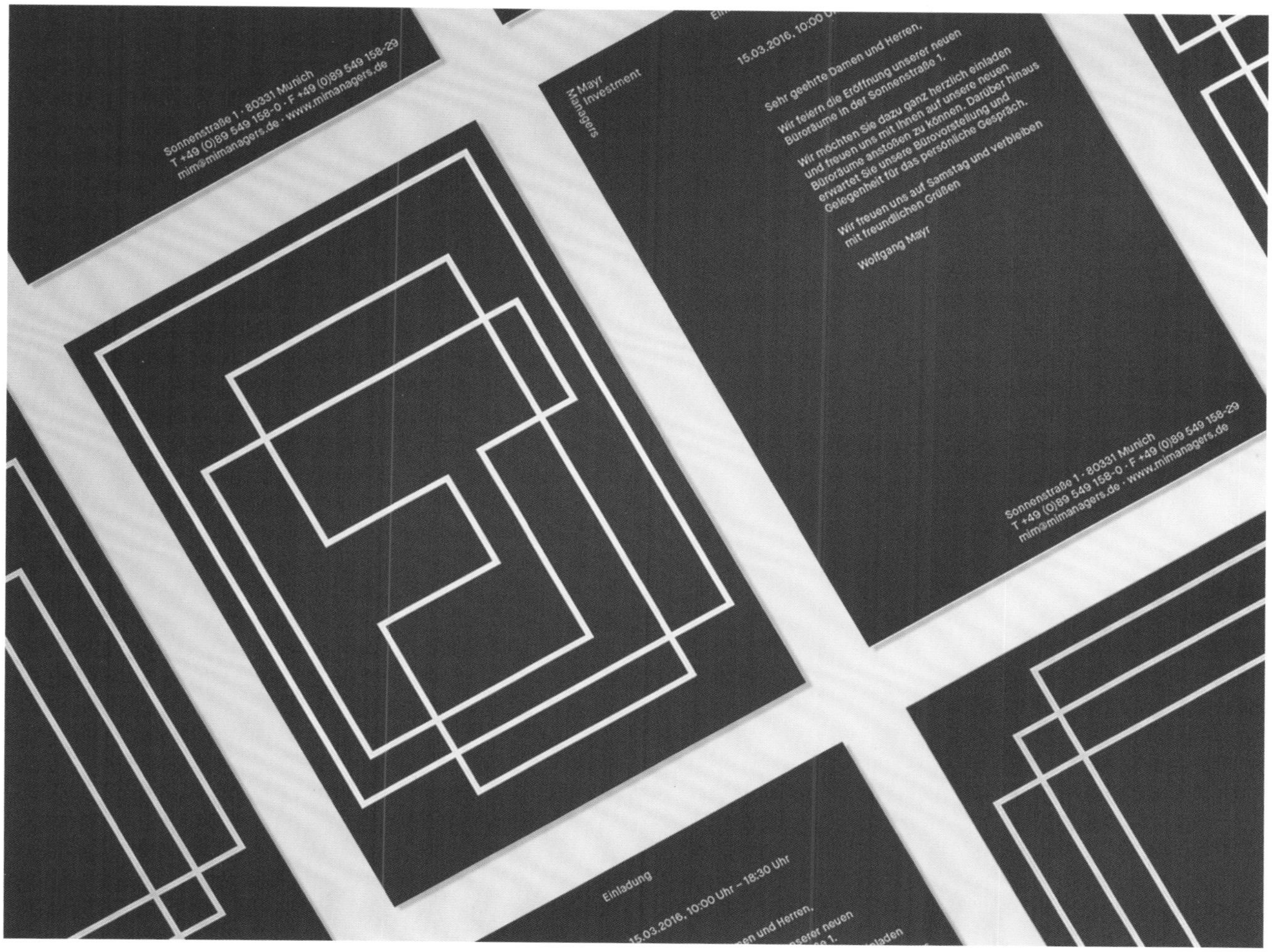

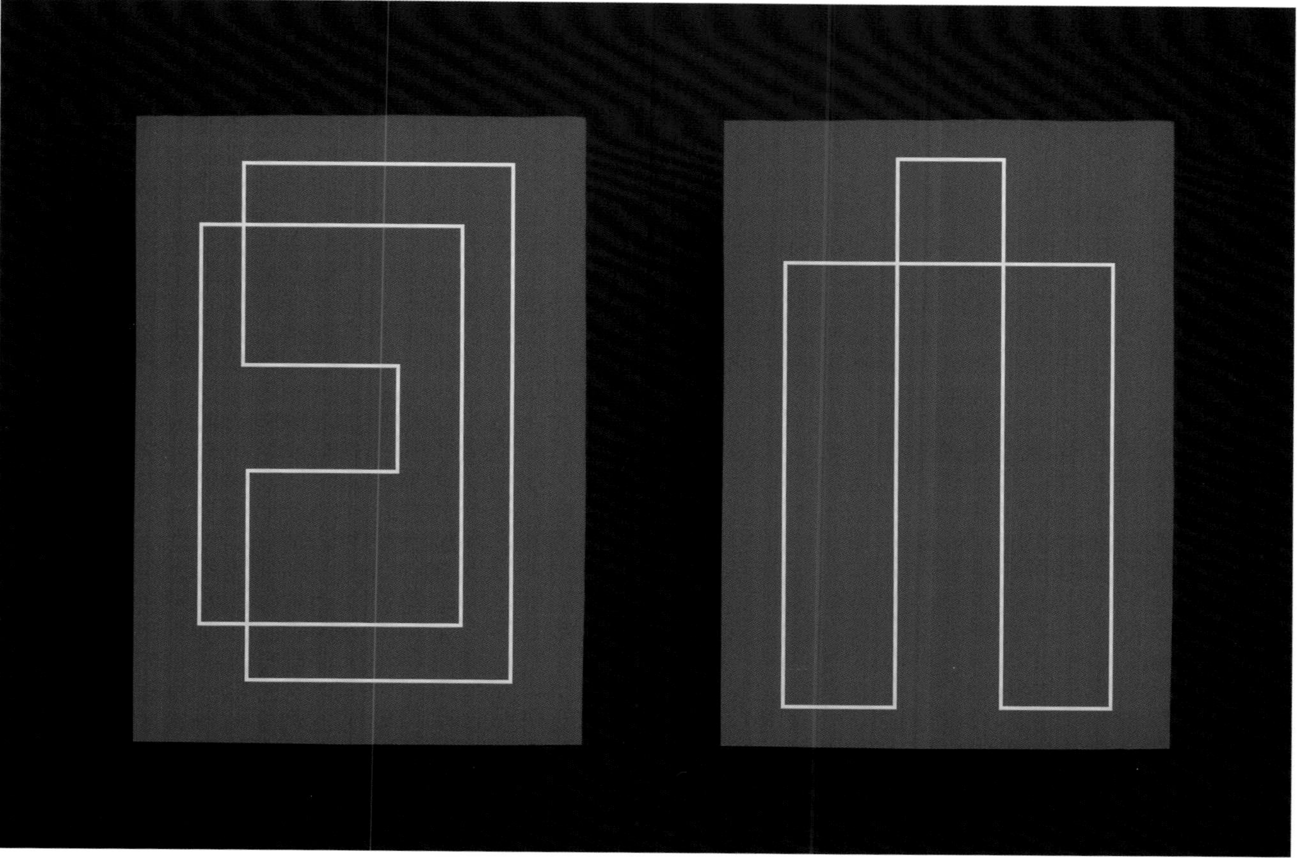

Acqua e Territorio

Design: *Studio Iknoki*

Studio Iknoki designed all the communication materials for the exhibition and the conference "Acqua e Territorio" curated by Latitude Platform, a non-profit organization that focuses on urban and territorial research and design. The exhibition wanted to inquire the relationship between rivers in Veneto region in Italy and their surrounding areas from an environmental, social, cultural and economic point of view.

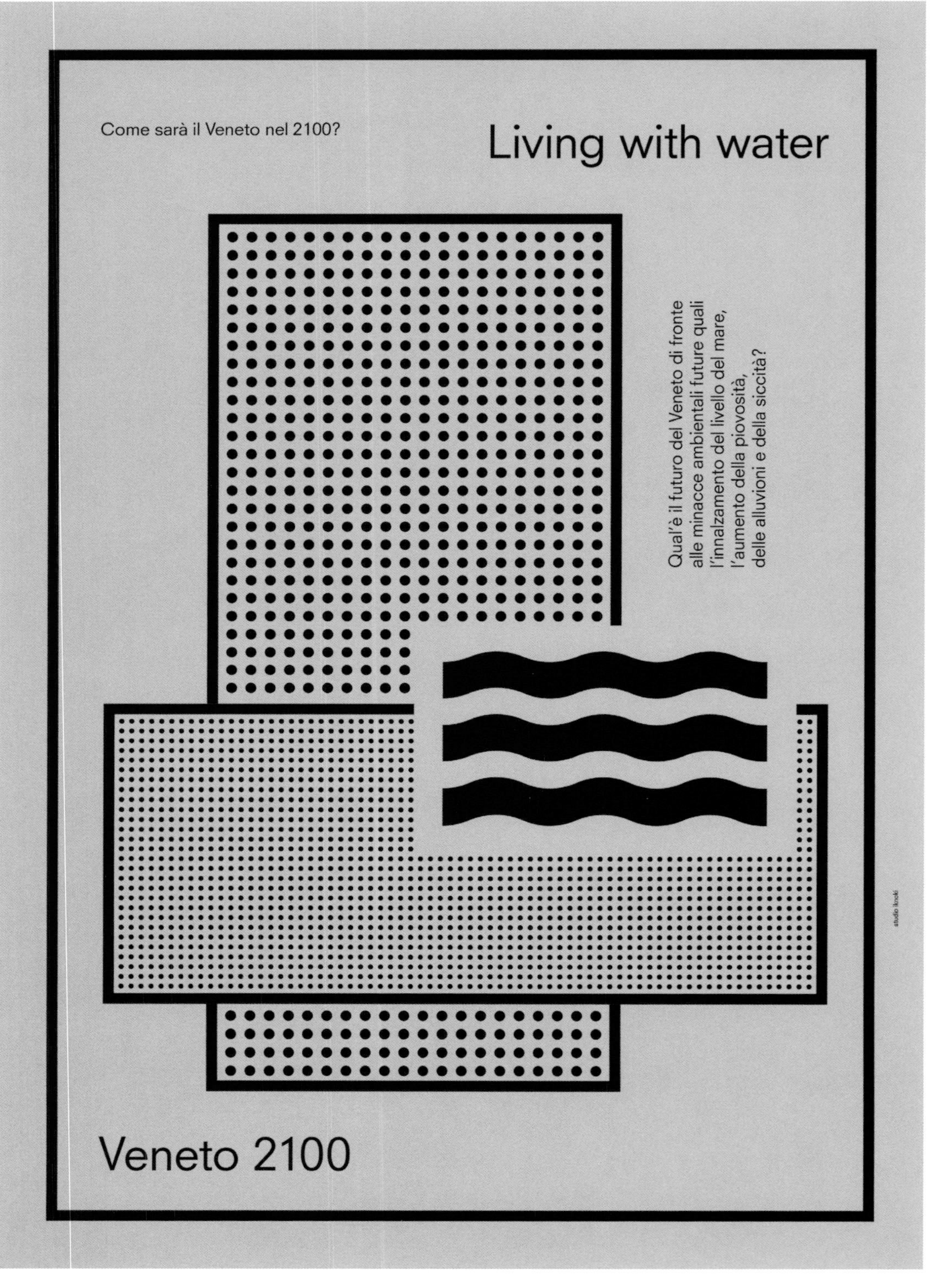

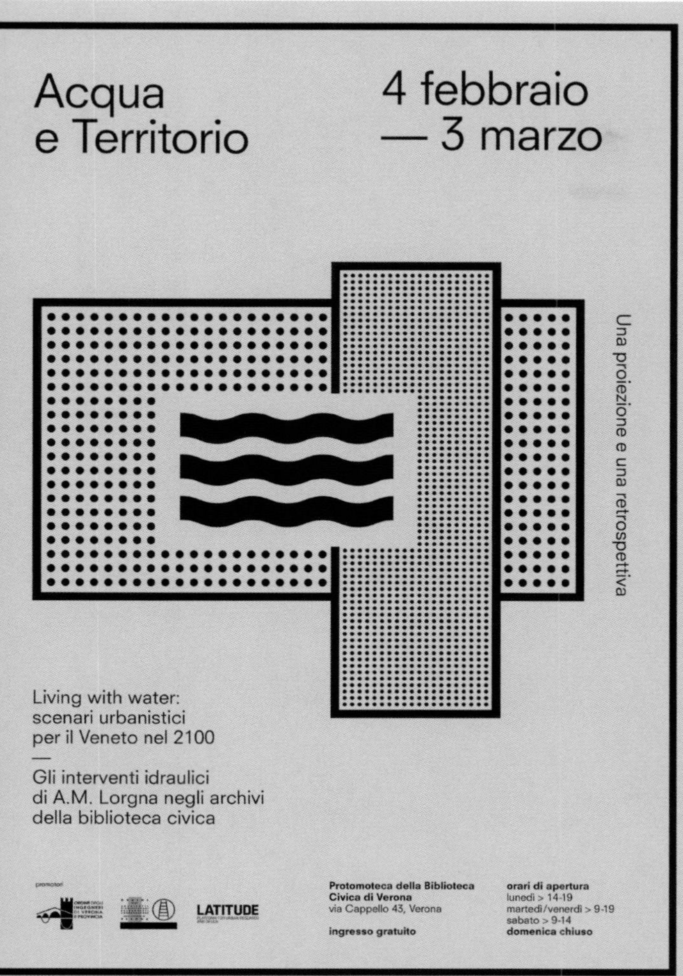
Acqua
e Territorio
4 febbraio
— 3 marzo
Una proiezione e una retrospettiva
Living with water:
scenari urbanistici
per il Veneto nel 2100
—
Gli interventi idraulici
di A.M. Lorgna negli archivi
della biblioteca civica
promotori
LATITUDE
Protomoteca della Biblioteca
Civica di Verona
via Cappello 43, Verona
ingresso gratuito
orari di apertura
lunedì > 14-19
martedì/venerdì > 9-19
sabato > 9-14
domenica chiuso

Acqua
e Territorio
15 febbraio
— convegno
Living with water
introducono
Dott. Agostino Contò
Biblioteca Civica di Verona
Arch. Arnaldo Toffali
Presidente Ordine Arch. PPC Verona
Ing. Ilaria Segala
Presidente Ordine Ingegneri Verona
intervengono
Arch. Pietro Laureano
Presidente ITKI (International Traditional
Knowledge Institute) dell'UNESCO
Ing. Luca Guarino
Autorità di Bacino dell'Adige -
settore Assetto Idrogeologico
Prof. Alessandro Paoletti
Politecnico di Milano –
Centro Studi Idraulica Urbana
Ing. Roberto Bertoldi
Dirigente Generale Dipartimento
Protezione Civile Provincia Autonoma
di Trento
Arch. Fabio Vanin, Arch. Marco
Ranzato
Latitude, platform for urban research
and design
modera
Ing. Filippo Toso
Ordine Ingegneri Verona -
commissione rischi del territorio
Acqua come risorsa e come
bene prezioso per l'ecosistema;
acqua come forza impetuosa
e fonte di catastrofi.
Il convegno è a margine della mostra
"Living with water: scenari urbanistici
per il Veneto nel 2100 - Gli interventi
idraulici di A.M. Lorgna negli archivi
della biblioteca civica" allestita presso
la Protomoteca della Biblioteca Civica
sino al 03.03.13
15 febbraio > ore 14.30
Sala Farinati della Biblioteca
Civica di Verona
via Cappello 43 Verona
ingresso libero
promotori
LATITUDE

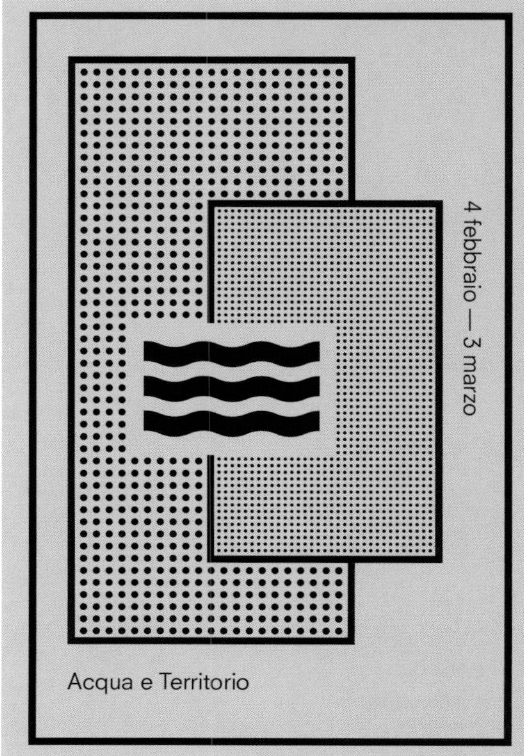
4 febbraio — 3 marzo
Acqua e Territorio

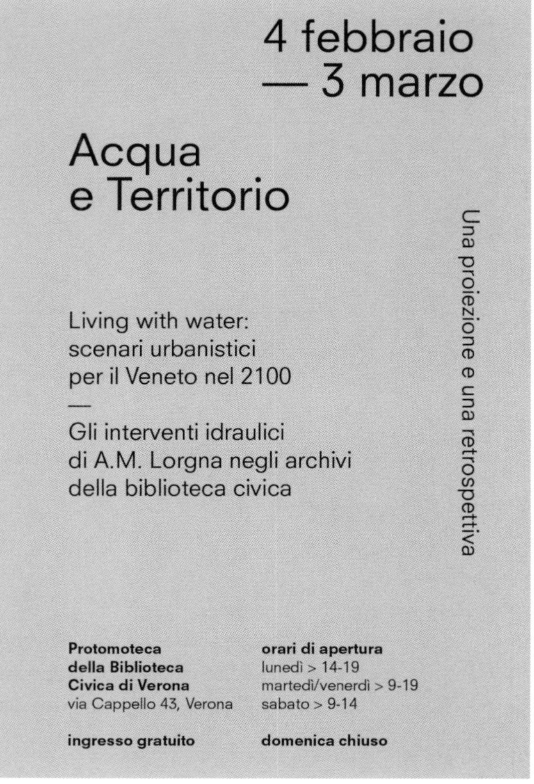
4 febbraio
— 3 marzo
Acqua
e Territorio
Una proiezione e una retrospettiva
Living with water:
scenari urbanistici
per il Veneto nel 2100
—
Gli interventi idraulici
di A.M. Lorgna negli archivi
della biblioteca civica
Protomoteca
della Biblioteca
Civica di Verona
via Cappello 43, Verona
ingresso gratuito
orari di apertura
lunedì > 14-19
martedì/venerdì > 9-19
sabato > 9-14
domenica chiuso

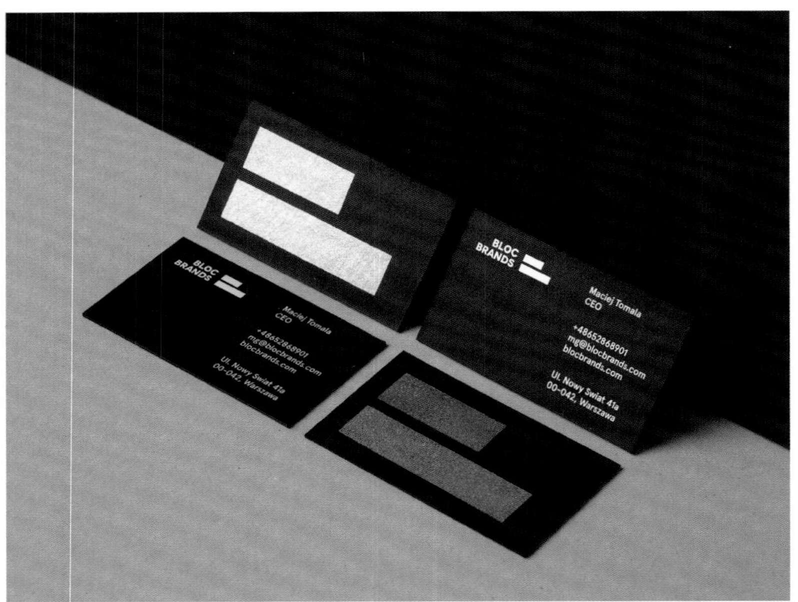

Bloc Brands

Design: *Noeeko*

Bloc Brands is a publisher focused on design activity from communist era, covering all countries which were under Soviet Union jurisdiction. Noeeko created a comprehensive brand identity system, responsive website and direct-to-consumer packaging.

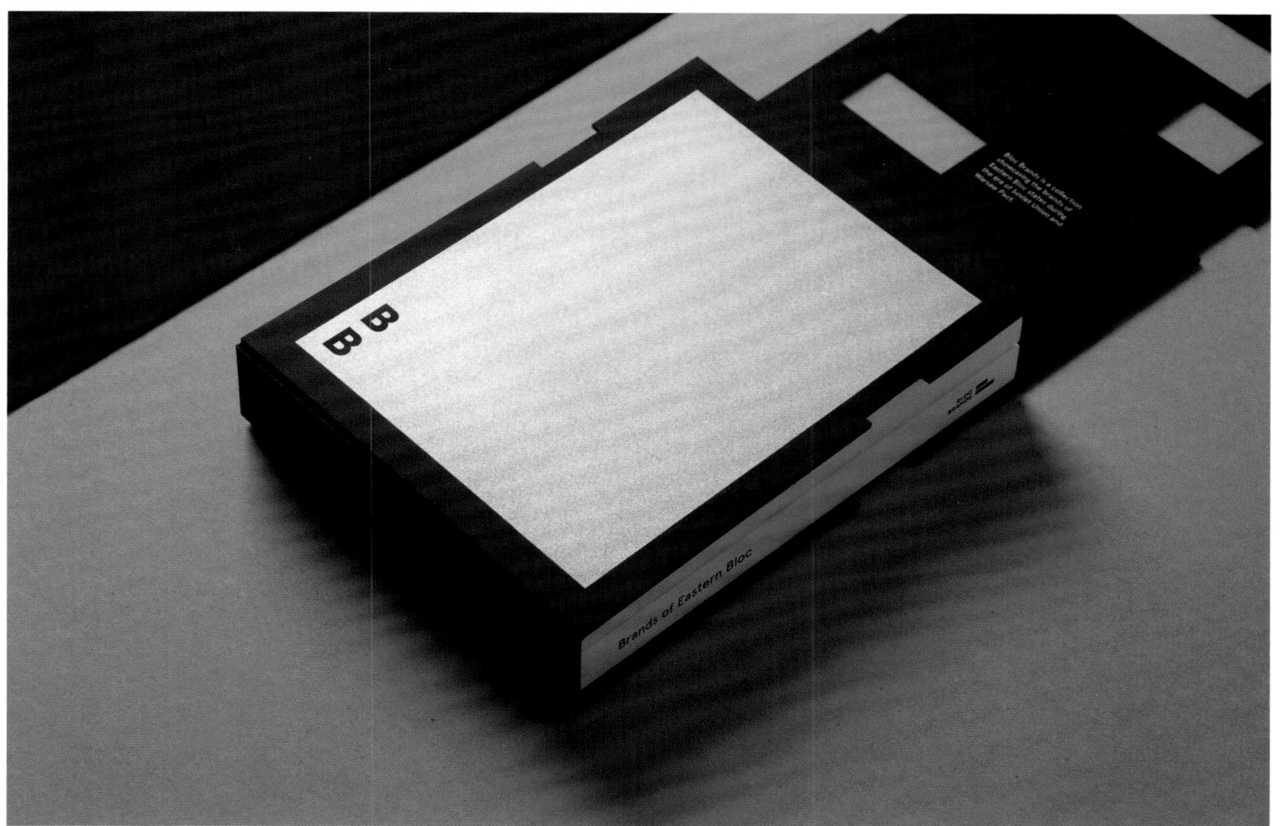
B
B
Brands of Eastern Bloc

Brands of Eastern Bloc

info@blocbrands.com
blocbrands.com
Bloc Brands is a collection showcasing the brands of Eastern Bloc states during the era of Soviet Union and Warsaw Pact.

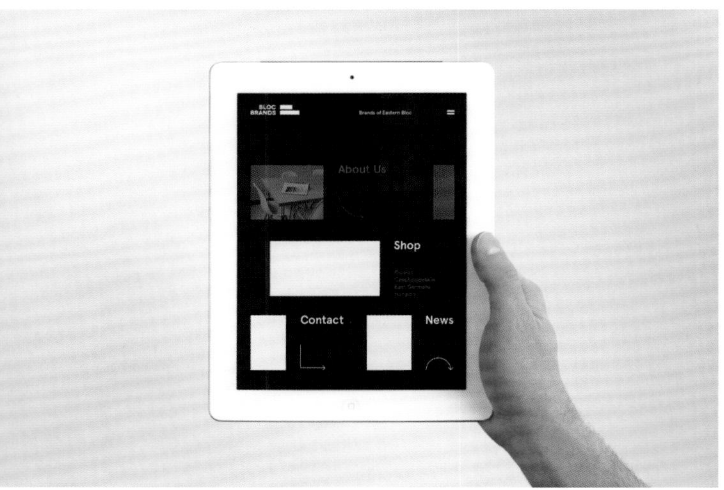
BLOC
BRANDS
Brands of Eastern Bloc
About Us
Shop
Contact
News

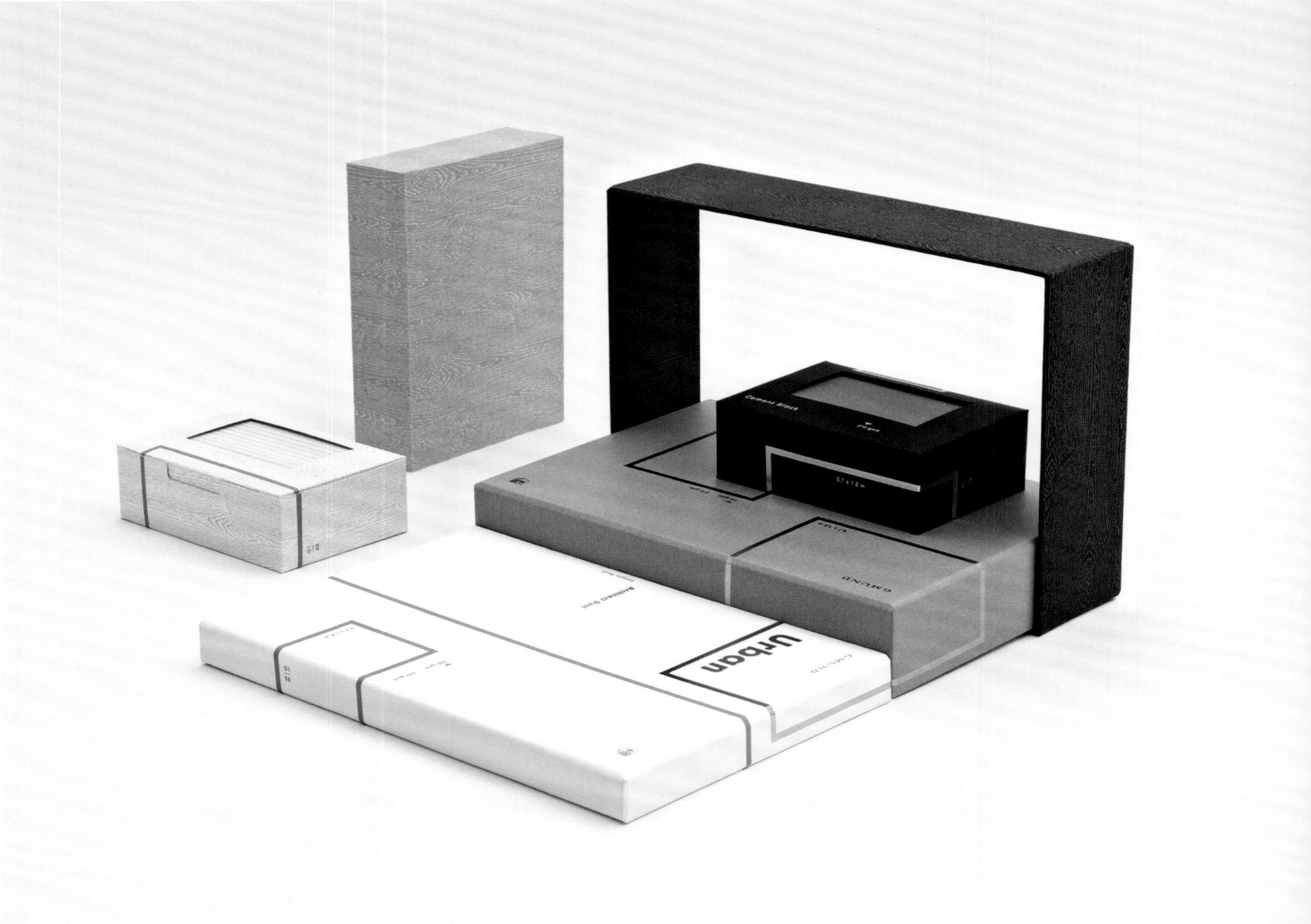

Gmund Urban

Agency: *Paperlux*
Art Direction: *Daniela Gilsdorf*
Creative Direction: *Max Kuehne*
Photography: *Michael Pfeiffer*

The basic concept of the design is the element of the line, which links all design disciplines in the modern living space – regardless of whether it speaks of architecture, interior design, or product design. The line connects things or excludes them, the spaces in between are filled with building materials.

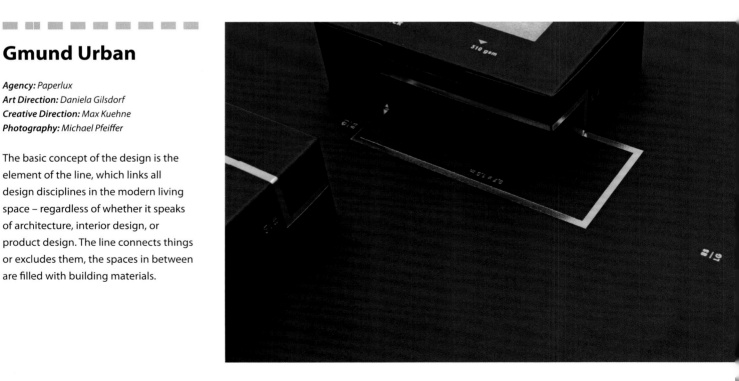

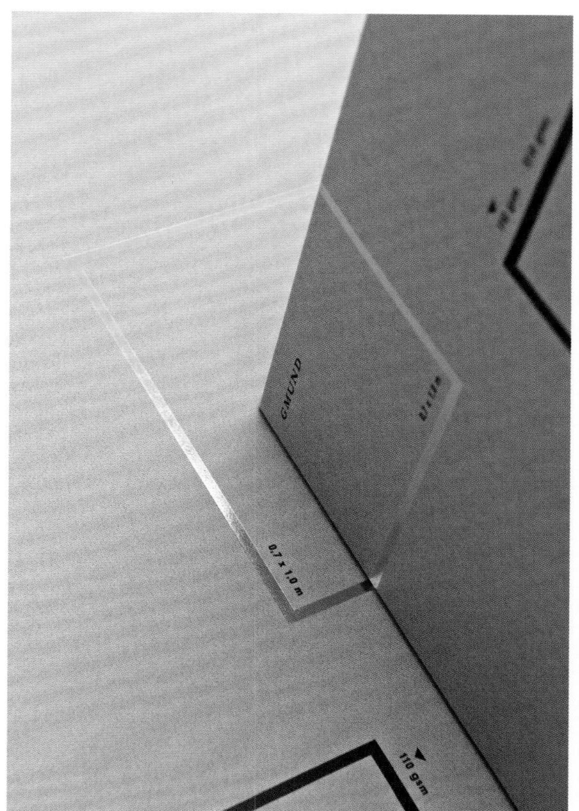
GMUND
0,7 x 1,0 m
110 gsm

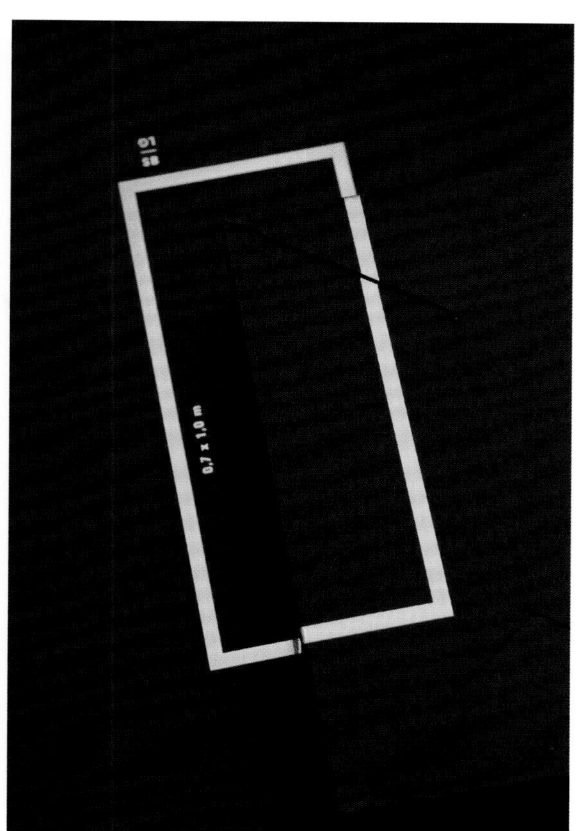
0,7 x 1,0 m

Broou

Creative Direction: *Caio Mattoso, Rodrigo Mendes, Leonardo Balbi*
Design: *Luiz Henrique Galbiatti, Rômulo Caballero*

Broou cast is the most accurate surf forecast in Brazil. It's also the first one developed with a mobile first mindset. And the only one to acknowledge that surfing is a social experience, considering the surfer friends to indicate the surfing conditions of a particular spot.

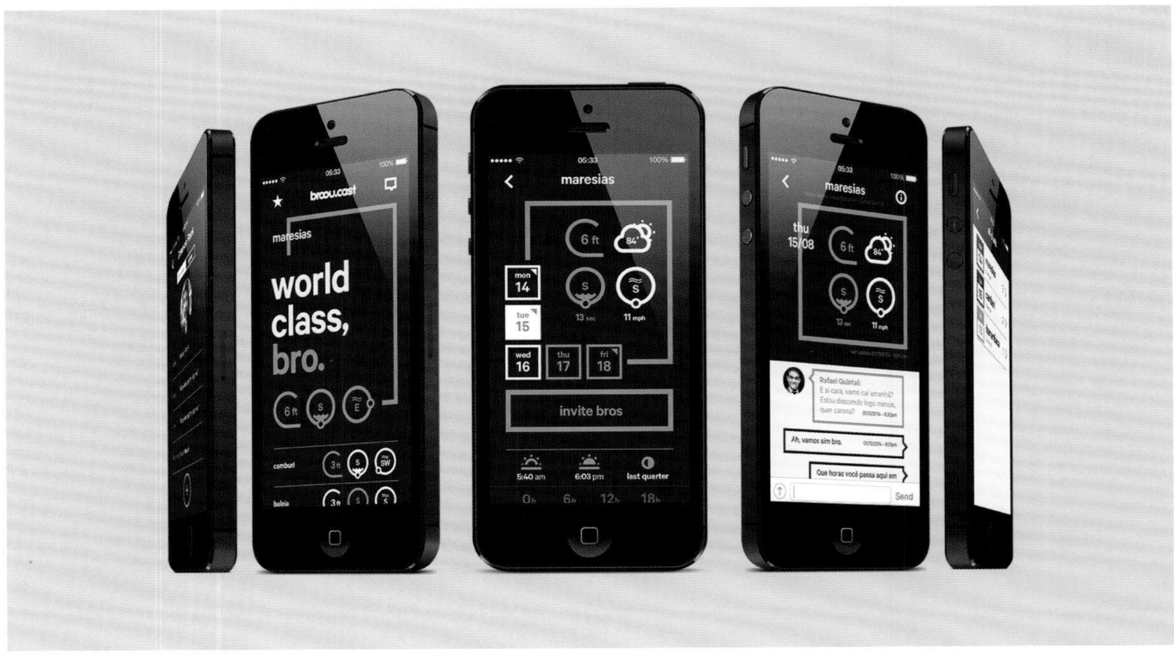

broou.tour
Donavon
Frankenreiter
17.01 belo horizonte
18.01 vitória
22.01 são paulo
24.01 xangri-la
25.01 rio de janeiro
de 15 a 25
de janeiro
ingressos em:
broou.com/tour
broou

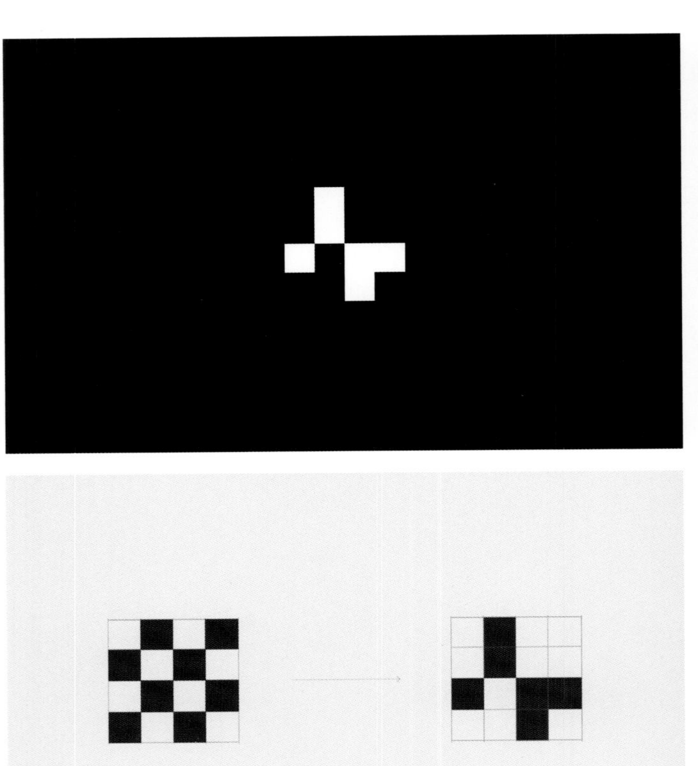

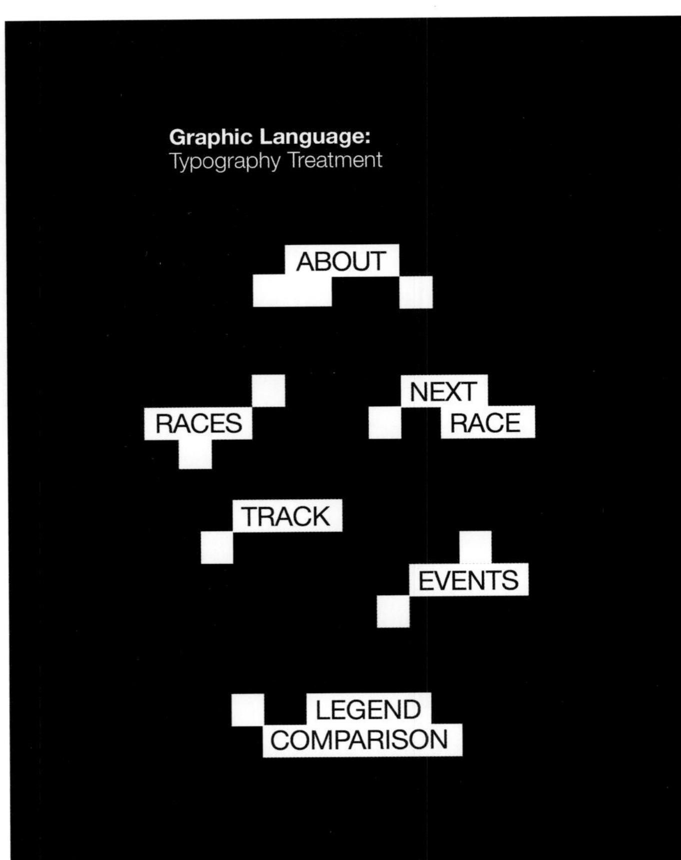

Racing Driver Branding: Jordan Cane

Agency: *Twelfthman London*
Design: *Thomas Wightman*

Jordan Cane is a 14 year old race car driver who has been competing in F1600 series. As he is young and still growing into his profession, it was important to create a timeless brand identity that will grow with him. Jordan's progress is determined by success on the track. The chequered flag is one constant symbol of achievement throughout this journey. The key words are: preparation, training, effort, dedication, progress. The chequered flag defines Jordan's racing spirit in his quest to be number one. An iconic and minimal application allows the identity to grow as Jordan's career progresses, whilst avoiding trends to remain timeless. The logo also remains abstract enough to not be exclusively "motor racing".

JordanCane.

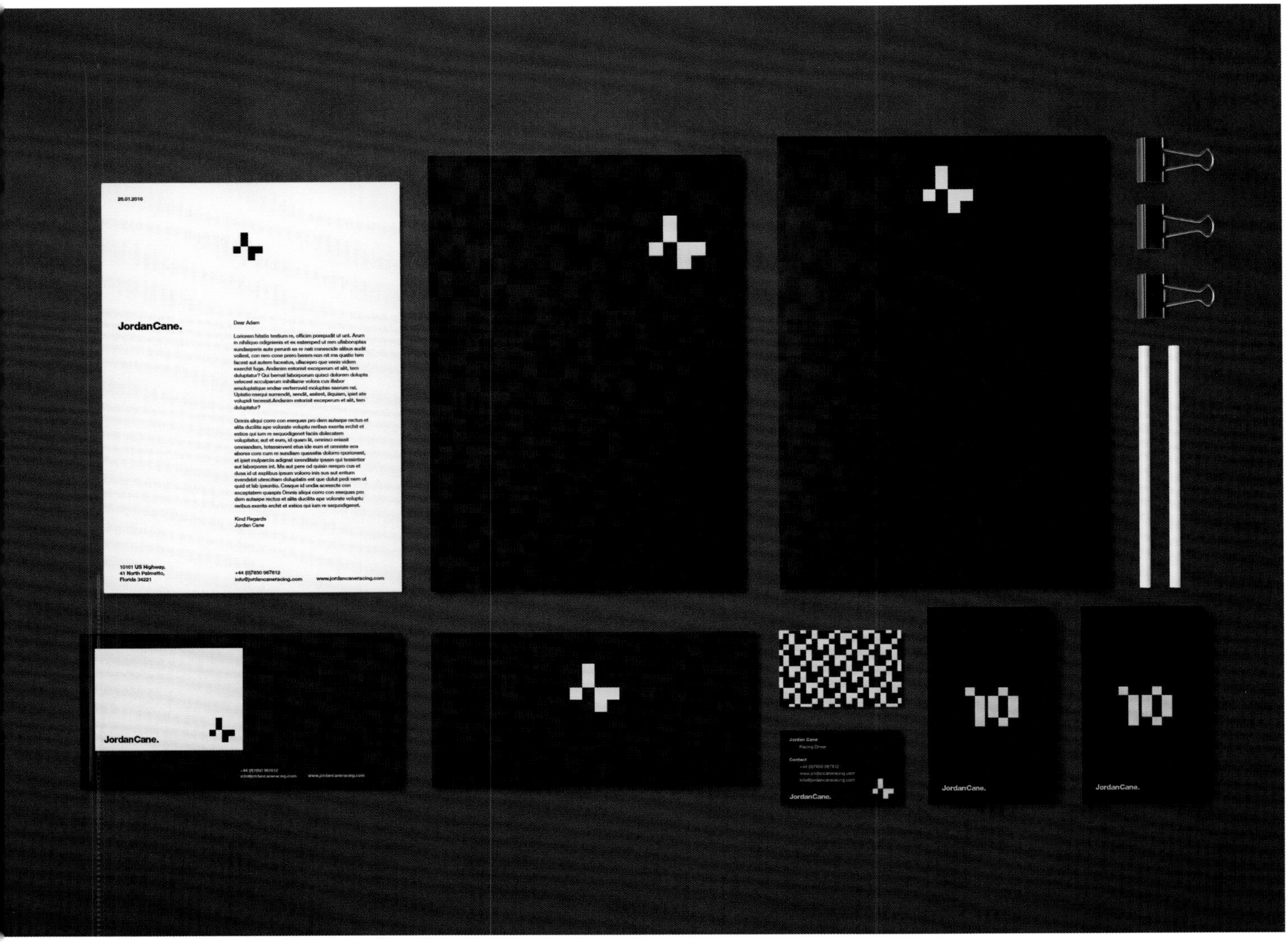

Arcadia Data

Design: *Casey Martin*
Animation: *Brent Clouse, Jonathan Corriveau*
Photography: *Jonathan Corriveau, Eric Louis Haines*

Big data is not static – it's exciting, dynamic, and even beautiful. That became the goal: to show that Arcadia Data translates raw information into something meaningful, compelling, and personal. It's clean, modern, smart, and compelling. The fonts, color choices, and design had to align with their product goal: to take a subject that very quickly tends to turn off many people and make it simple and clear.

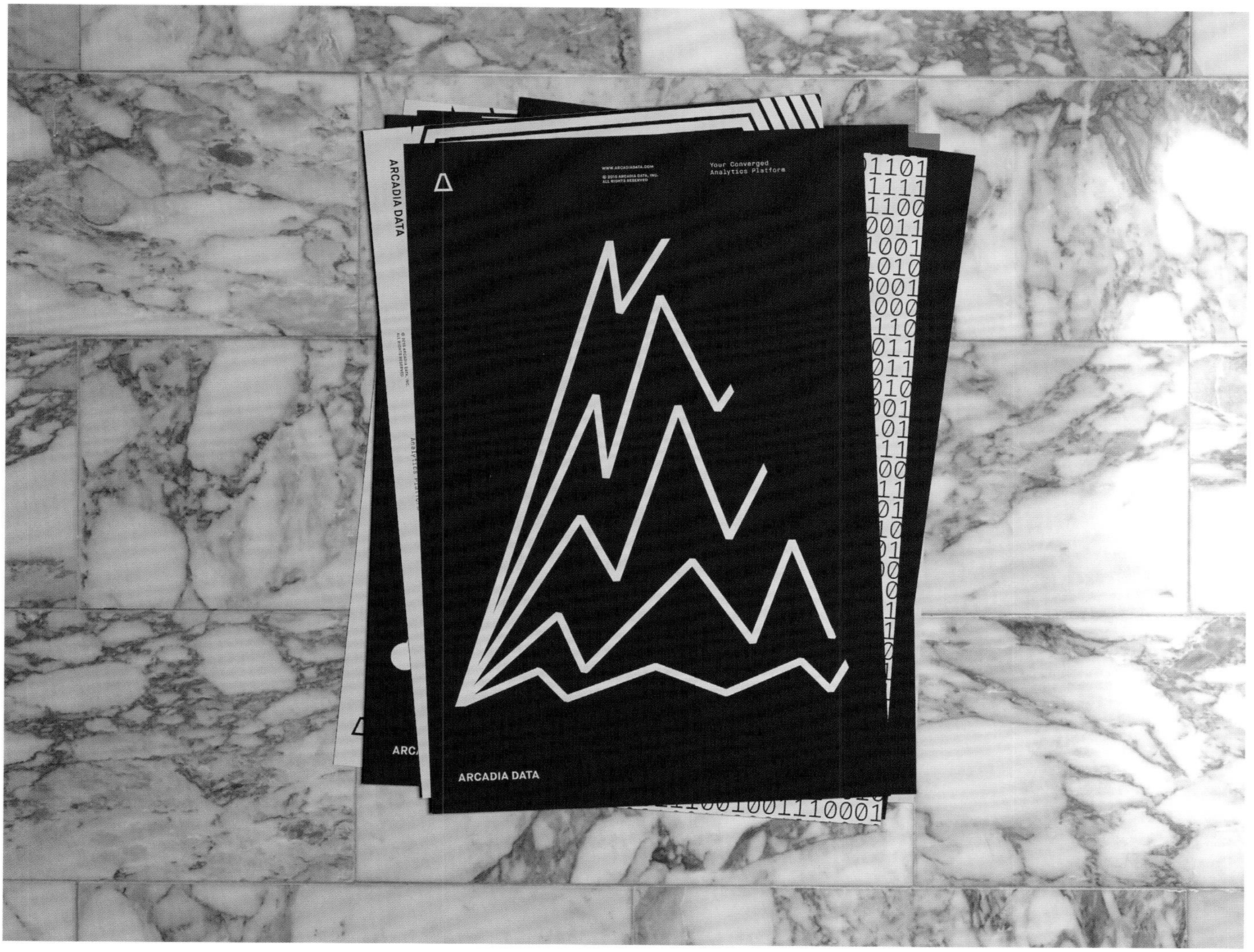
Your Converged
Analytics Platform
ARCADIA DATA
ARCADIA DATA

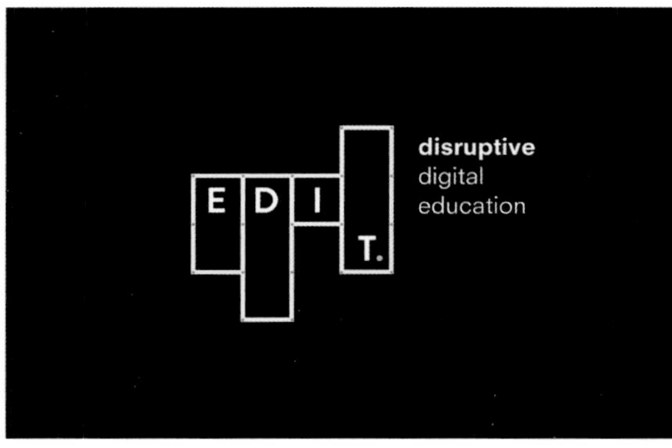

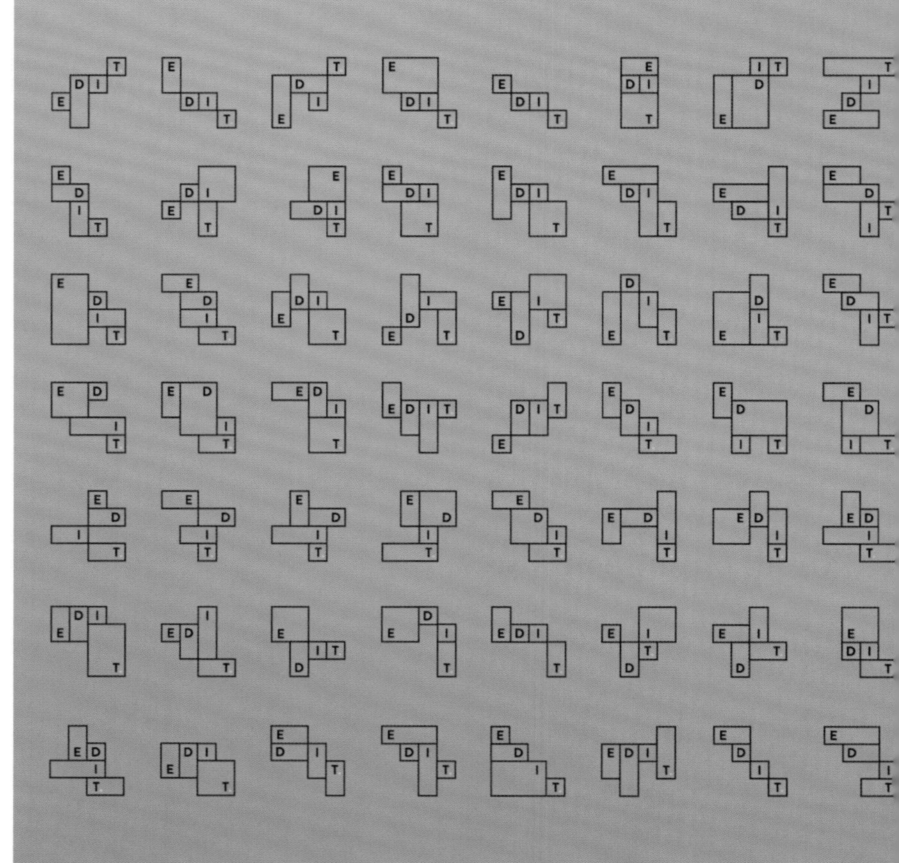

EDIT Disruptive Digital Education

Design: *VOLTA Brand Shaping Studio*

EDIT is a school dedicated to the areas of digital design, marketing and creativity. They asked VOLTA to create a new (responsive) identity for the school, using their very recognizable color scheme (yellow and black), the yellow dot, and a new signature: Disruptive Digital Education.

The designers based their work in a 4×4 grid, with each square working as a metaphor for the most basic digital element, the pixel. Each EDIT letter has its own frame: it expands and contracts, interacting with the other frames. The combinations between the frames sizes and positions (always within the 4×4 grid) are endless and truly respond to EDIT's request of having a "responsive" identity that portrays their 100% digital attitude.

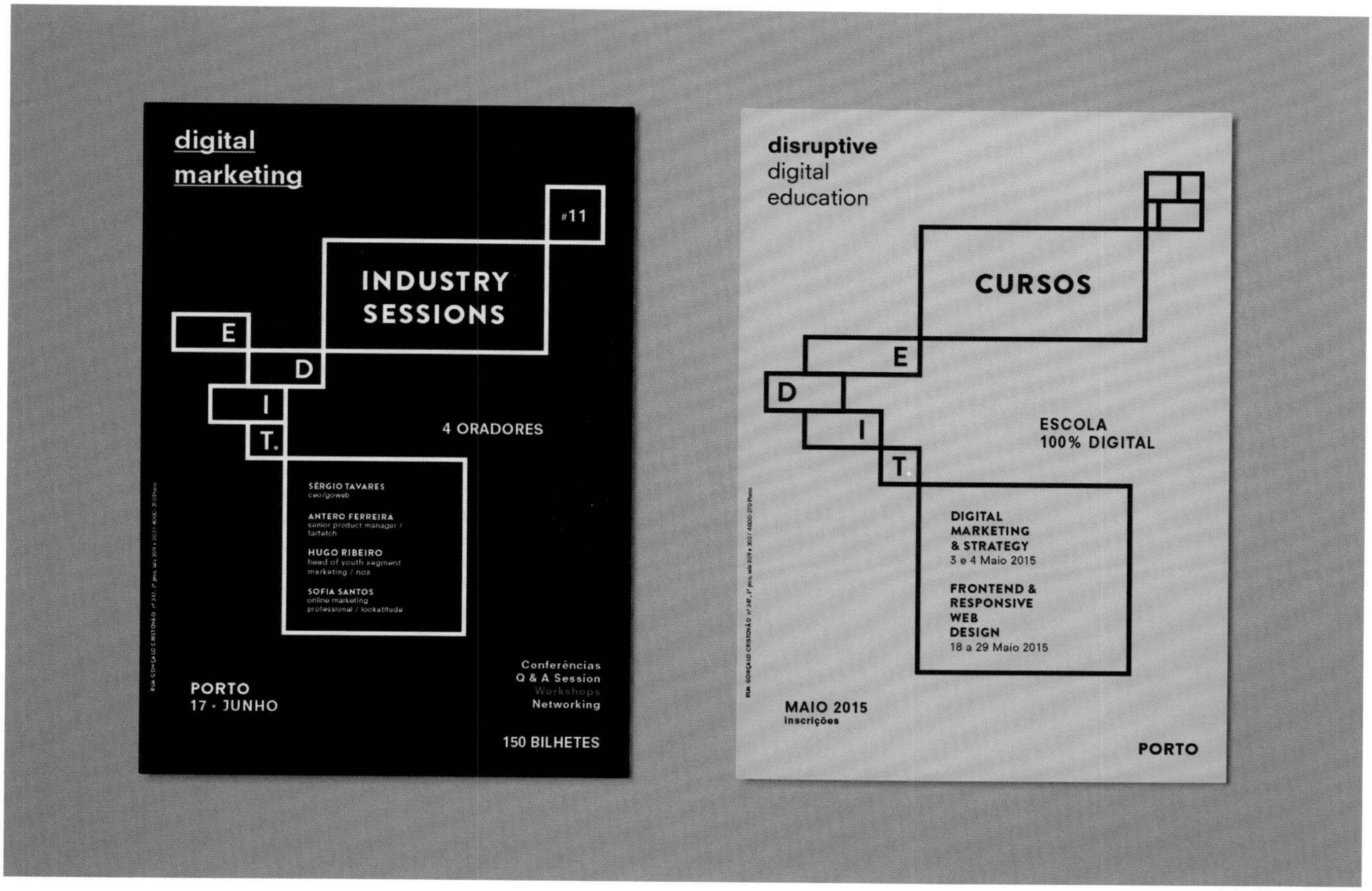

digital
marketing

#11

INDUSTRY
SESSIONS

E
D
I
T.

4 ORADORES

SÉRGIO TAVARES
ceo/goweb

ANTERO FERREIRA
senior product manager / farfetch

HUGO RIBEIRO
head of youth segment marketing / nos

SOFIA SANTOS
online marketing professional / lookatitude

PORTO
17 · JUNHO

Conferências
Q & A Session
Workshops
Networking

150 BILHETES

disruptive
digital
education

CURSOS

E
D
I
T.

ESCOLA
100% DIGITAL

DIGITAL
MARKETING
& STRATEGY
3 e 4 Maio 2015

FRONTEND &
RESPONSIVE
WEB
DESIGN
18 a 29 Maio 2015

MAIO 2015
inscrições

PORTO

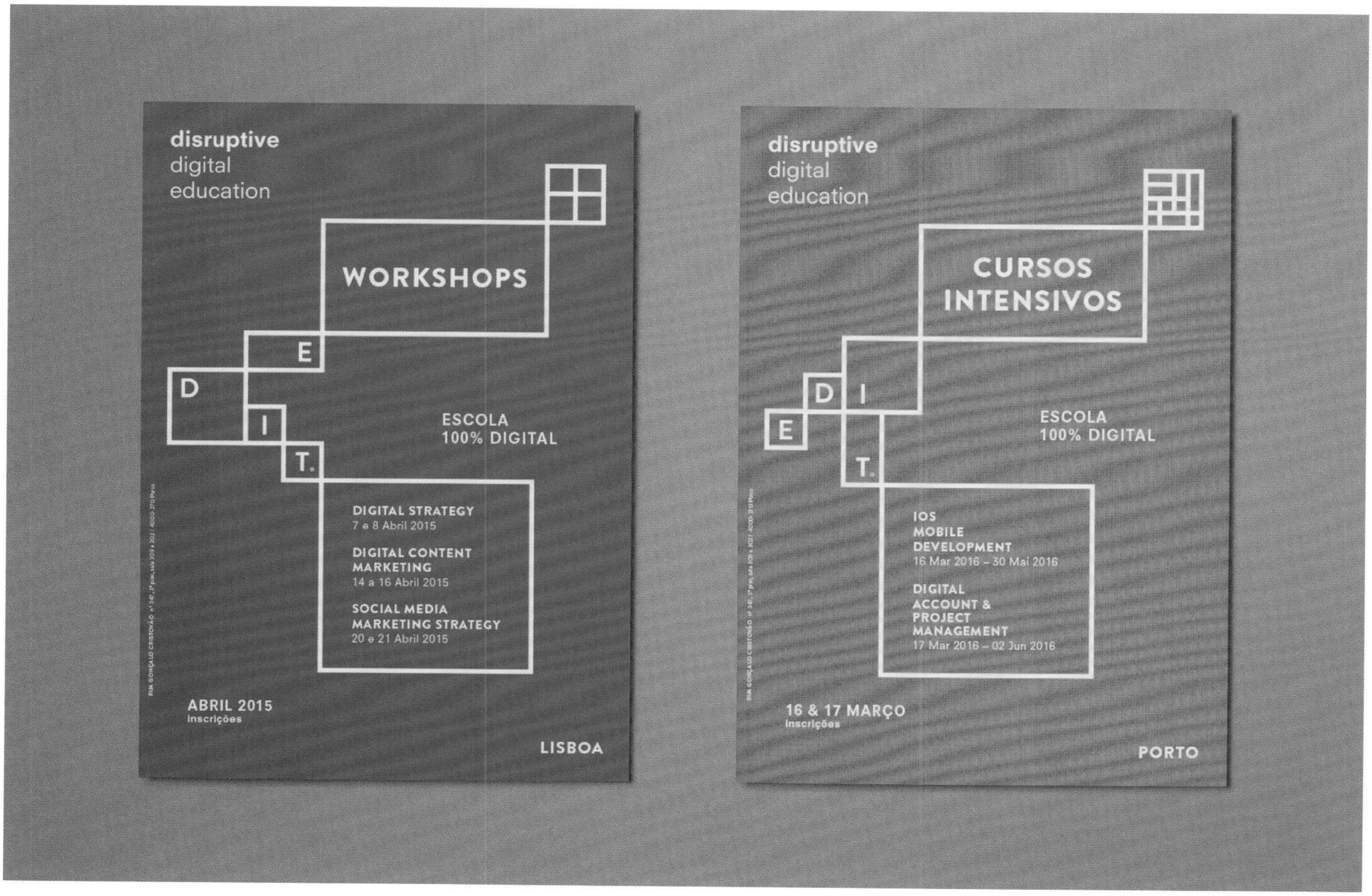

disruptive
digital
education

WORKSHOPS

E
D
I
T.

ESCOLA
100% DIGITAL

DIGITAL STRATEGY
7 e 8 Abril 2015

DIGITAL CONTENT
MARKETING
14 a 16 Abril 2015

SOCIAL MEDIA
MARKETING STRATEGY
20 e 21 Abril 2015

ABRIL 2015
inscrições

LISBOA

disruptive
digital
education

CURSOS
INTENSIVOS

D
I
E
T.

ESCOLA
100% DIGITAL

IOS
MOBILE
DEVELOPMENT
16 Mar 2016 – 30 Mai 2016

DIGITAL
ACCOUNT &
PROJECT
MANAGEMENT
17 Mar 2016 – 02 Jun 2016

16 & 17 MARÇO
inscrições

PORTO

Festival of New Spanish Cinema Posters

Design: *Toormix*

Poster design and communication of the Festival of New Spanish Cinema 2015 and 2016, the most important festival regarding to the Spanish independent cinema in USA. It is an itinerant festival which has been present in five cities around the USA during the 2015 and 2016 editions, including Chicago, Portland, Houston, Puerto Rico, and Washington. For the communication, the designers have built a modular graphic code characterized by the typography, identifying and customizing each poster with each city initials. Between both editions, the designers have opted for upgrade the chromatic gamma at all communication, appropriating in this way of the graphic code.

FESTIVAL
OF NEW
SPANISH
CINEMA
The official traveling
festival about the new trends
in Spanish Cinema
MARCH 4–31 / 2016
AS PART OF THE CHICAGO EUROPEAN UNION FILM
FESTIVAL AT GENE SISKEL FILM CENTER
BUY TICKETS AT
INFO & PROGRAM
PRAG
DA
FESTIVAL
OF NEW
SPANISH
CINEMA
The official traveling
festival about the new trends
in Spanish Cinema
MARCH 10–13 / 2016
RICE CINEMA
6100 MAIN STREET, HOUSTON
FREE ADMISSION
INFO & PROGRAM
PRAG
DA
FESTIVAL
OF NEW
SPANISH
CINEMA
The official traveling
festival about the new trends
in Spanish Cinema
FEBRUARY 11–27 / 2016
AS PART OF PORTLAND INT'L FILM FESTIVAL
AT NORTHWEST FILM CENTER
934 SW Salmon St, Portland
BUY TICKETS AT
INFO & PROGRAM
PRAG
DA
FESTIVAL
OF NEW
SPANISH
CINEMA
El festival itinerante oficial
de las nuevas tendencias
del cine español.
6 – 13 DE ABRIL / 2016
DENTRO DEL FESTIVAL DE CINE EUROPEO DE PUERTO RICO
DE LA ALIANZA FRANCESA / FINE ARTS MIRAMAR
COMPRA DE BOLETOS
INFO & PROGRAMA
PRAG
DA

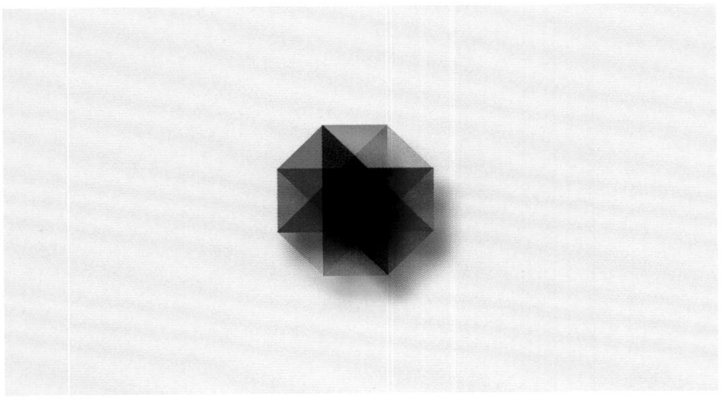

TDS. Braille Board

***Design:** H3L Studio*

Braille board branding project for INNOVAR – National Competition of Innovation. The main goal was to develop TDS system identity. The new image design and the elaboration of a new isotype was included as part of the corporate stationary and complementary pieces. The environment textures create an imaginary world. The color is an attribute perceived by the rest of the senses.

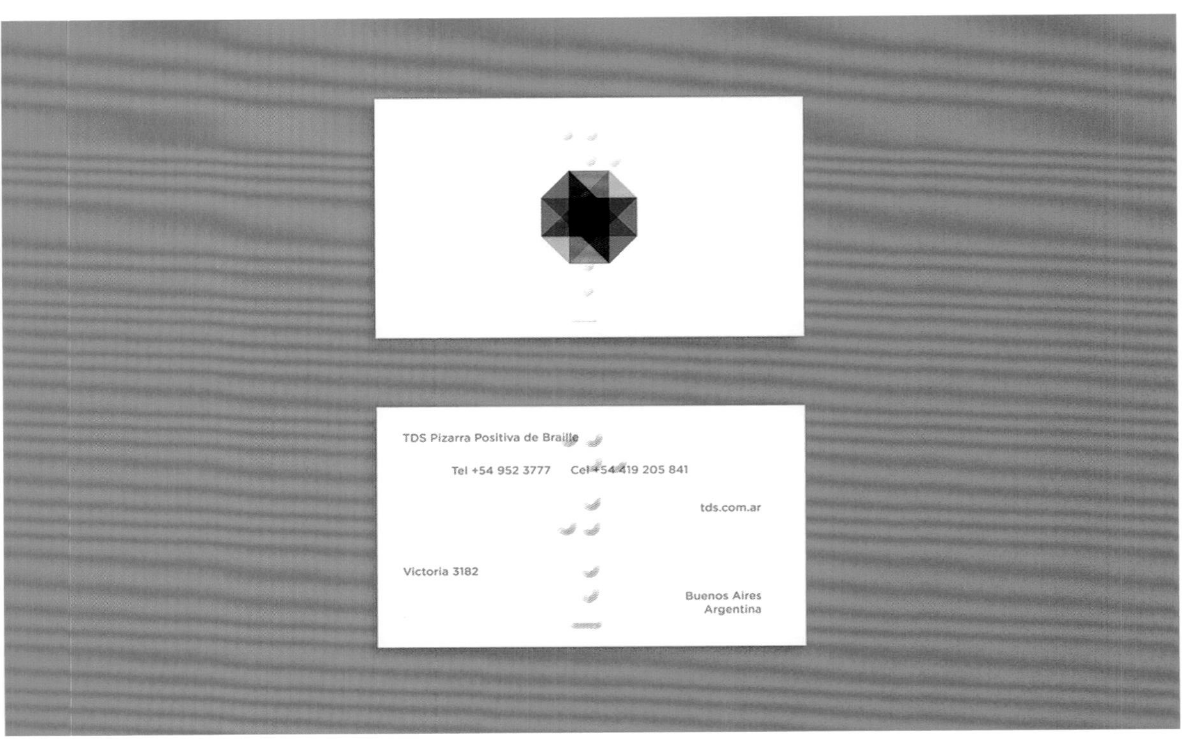

TDS Pizarra Positiva de Braille
Tel +54 952 3777 Cel +54 419 205 841
tds.com.ar
Victoria 3182
Buenos Aires
Argentina

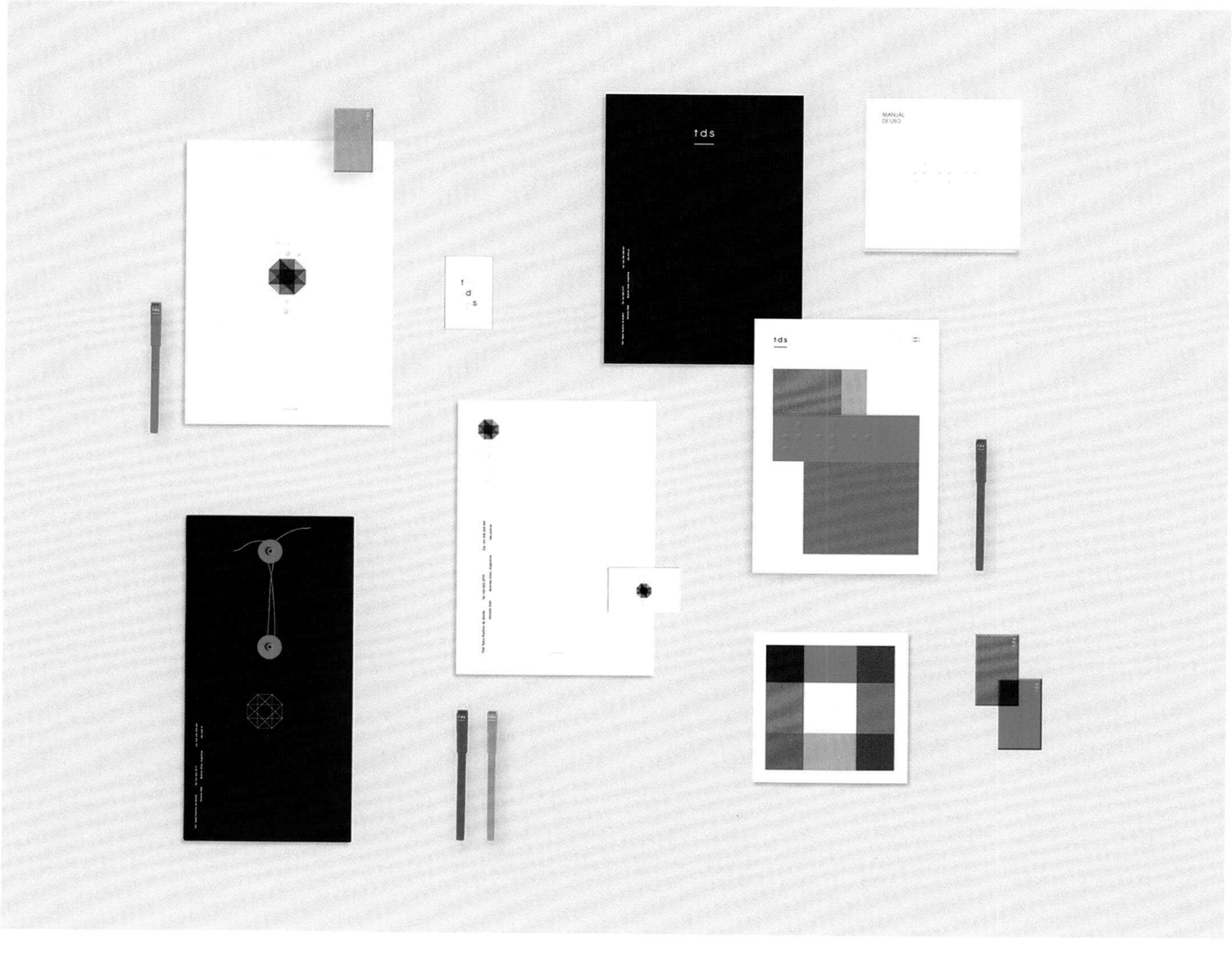

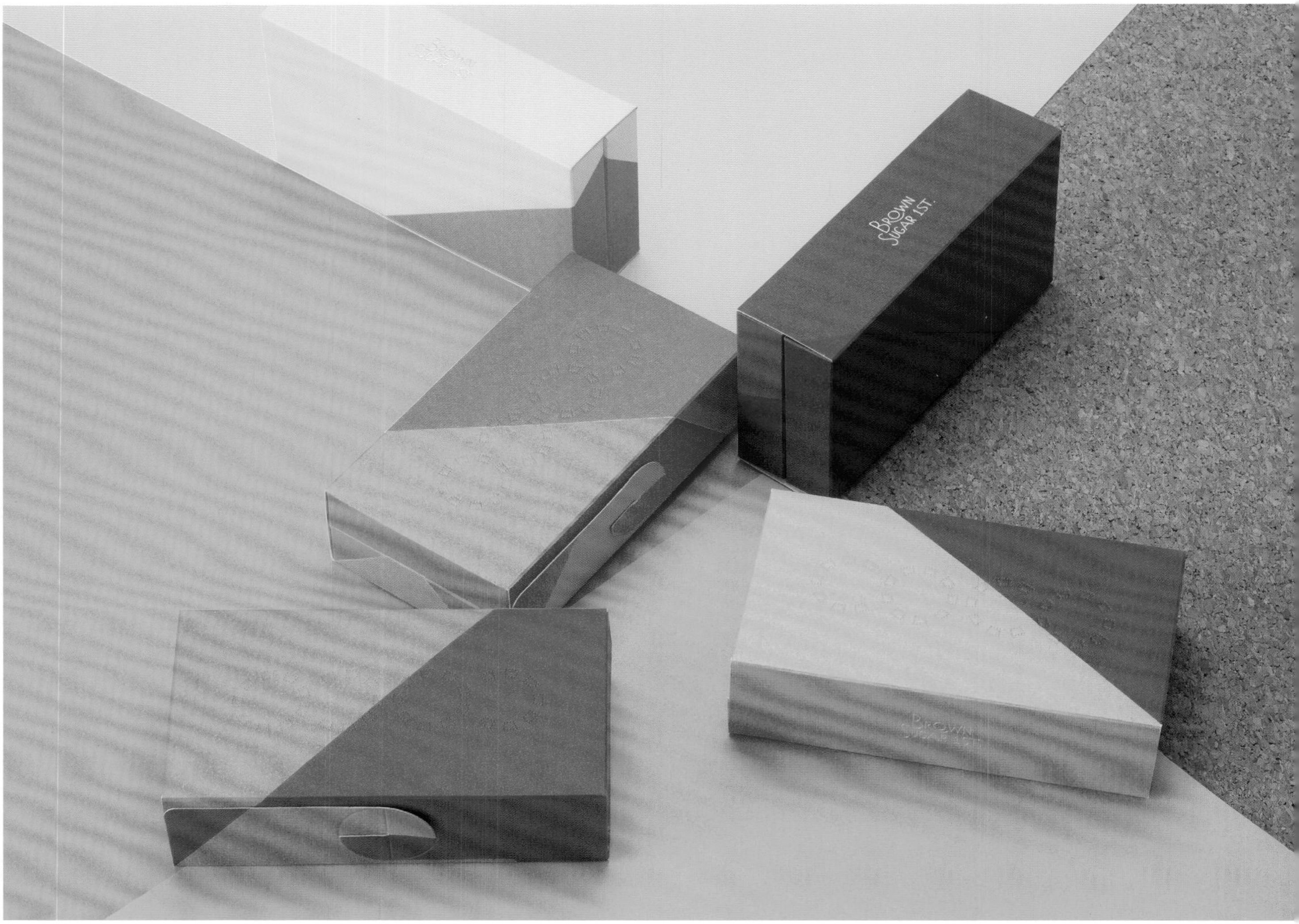

Brown Sugar 1st.'s Coco Cookies

Design: *Keiko Akatsuka*

The coco cookies made by Brown Sugar 1st. are pop and cute tasting like "LOCO" in Hawaii. And these are all organic, so happy sweets! Anyway, good foods should be fashionable and kind for girls with their clutch bag.

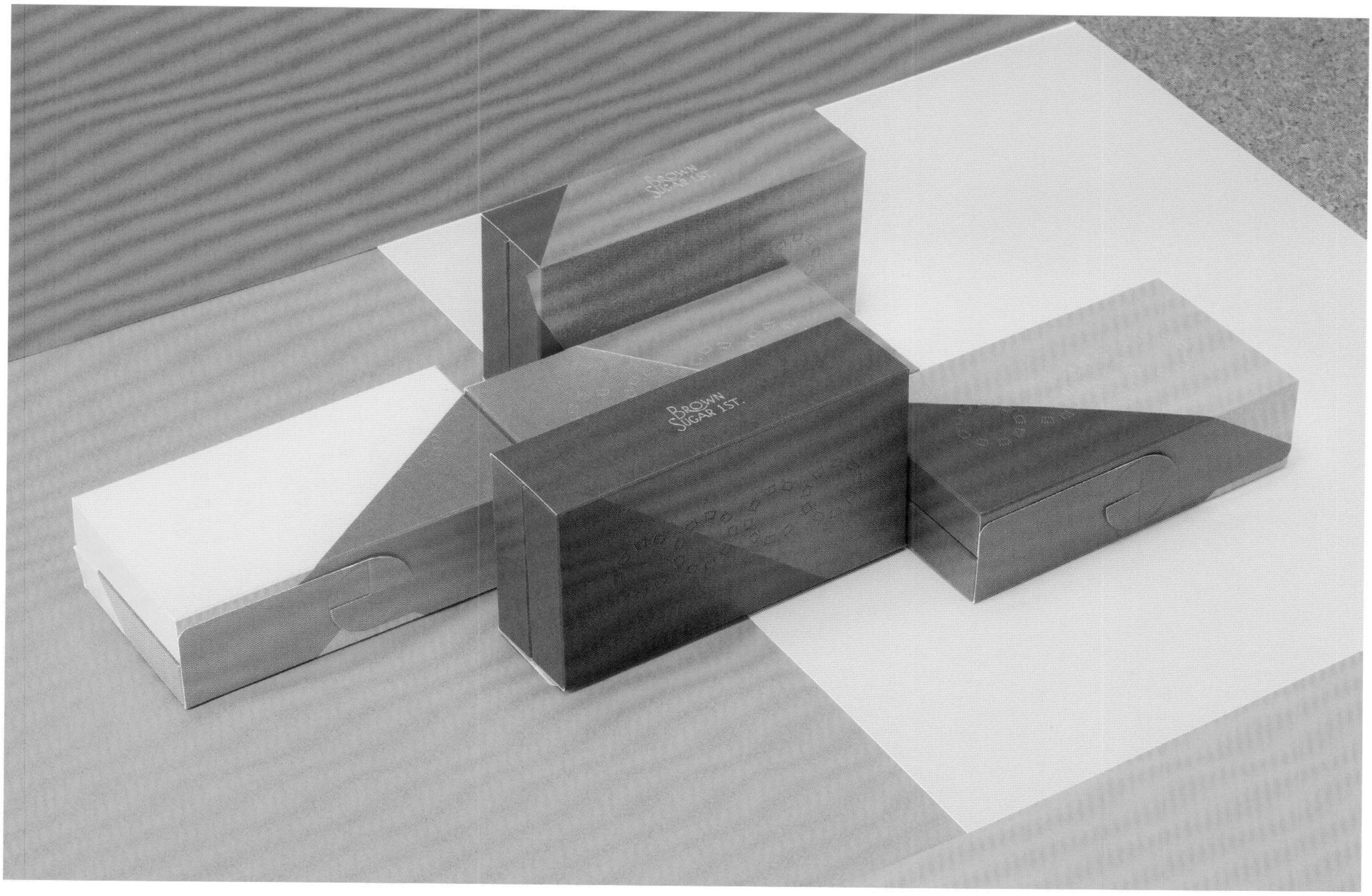
BROWN SUGAR 1ST.

BROWN SUGAR 1ST.
BROWN SUGAR 1ST.
BROWN SUGAR 1ST.
BROWN SUGAR 1ST.

Adobe XD Rebranding

Graphic Design: *You Zhang*
Project Direction: *Shawn Cheris*

Adobe XD is centered on pushing forward new ideas and designs, and the designers strive on keeping experience fresh and exciting. The branding should reflect it. So the designers decided to find a new visual representation that can speak for them.

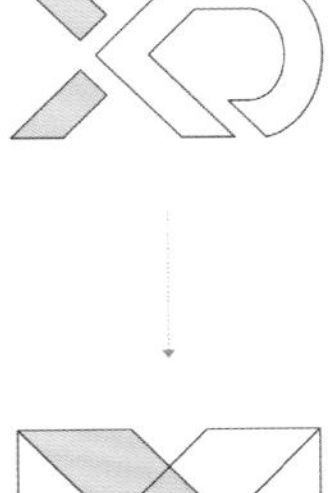

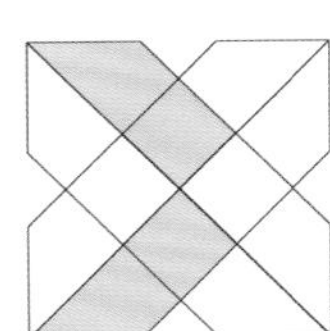

ADOBE
EXPERIENCE
DESIGN

ADOBE
EXPERIENCE
DESIGN

ADOBE
EXPERIENCE
DESIGN

ADOBE
EXPERIENCE
DESIGN

ADOBE
EXPERIENCE
DESIGN

MADRID

PARIS

NEW YORK

LONDON

Choco & Co

Design: *Isabel de Peque*

Packaging, naming, and branding for a chocolate bars collection for a coffee and chocolate company based in Madrid, New York, Paris, and London. Four different kinds of chocolate, one for each city. The packaging colors were chosen according to the style and colors of each city.

Mixed Figures

Olaf Nell

Design: *Dimitris Kostinis*

Olaf Nell is a Swedish architect and designer. He created his company in order to produce distinct and exemplary architecture appropriate to purpose and place. He puts great attention to design at all levels, starting with the smallest detail to the creation of larger space surrounding every one of us and its connection to the environment. His style is bold, modern and influenced by his Swedish roots.

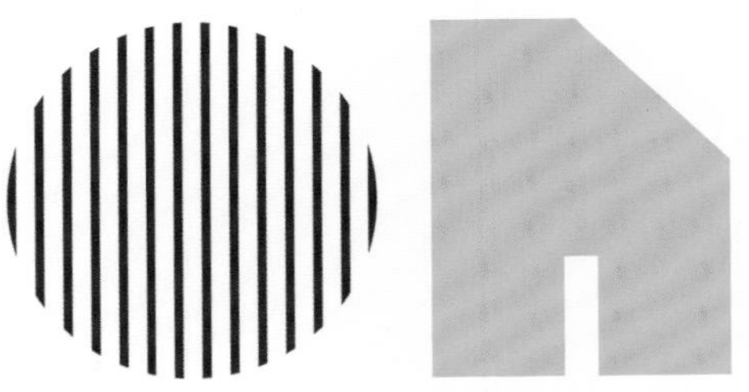

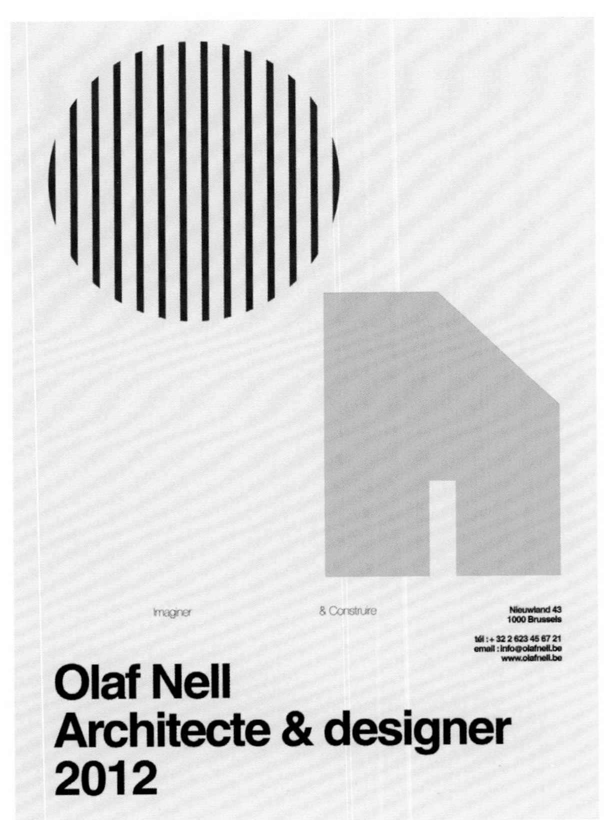

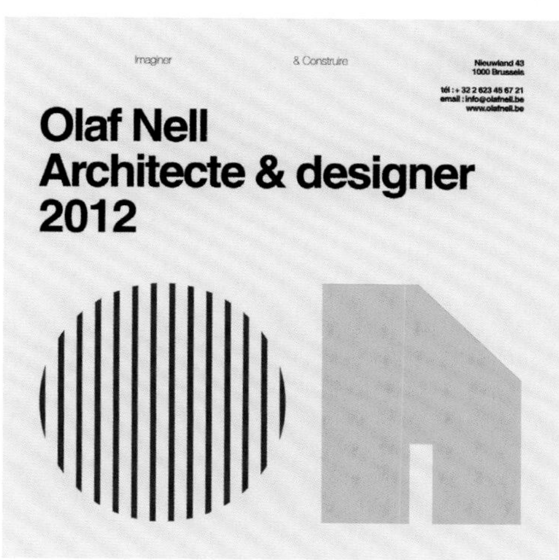
Imaginer
& Construire
Nieuwland 43
1000 Brussels
tél : + 32 2 623 45 67 21
email : info@olafnell.be
www.olafnell.be
Olaf Nell
Architecte & designer
2012

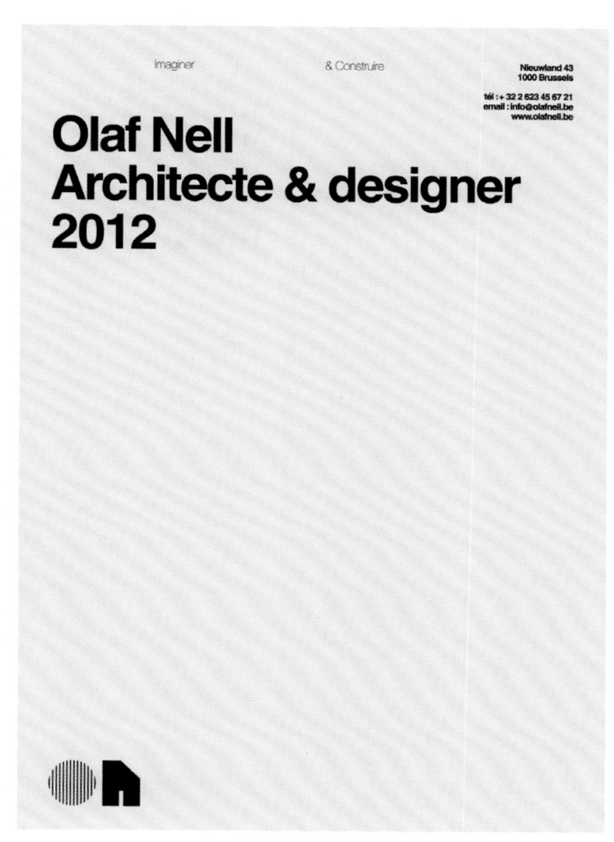
Imaginer
& Construire
Nieuwland 43
1000 Brussels
tél : + 32 2 623 45 67 21
email : info@olafnell.be
www.olafnell.be
Olaf Nell
Architecte & designer
2012

Olaf Nell®

Olaf Nell
Architecte
Imaginer
&
Construire
Nieuwland 43
1000 Brussels
tél : + 32 2 623 45 67 21
email : info@olafnell.be
www.olafnell.be

Olaf Nell
Architecte & designer
2012

RDTEX

Agency: *Ermolaev Bureau*
Creative Direction: *Vlad Ermolaev*
Design: *Vlad Ermolaev, Ekaterina Zolotuhina*

The designers used a new, more understandable and better matching the new strategy abbreviation expansion for RDTEX: "Reasonable Directive Technologies". The new visual style is built on the basis of a unique module grid on which the graphics of three geometrical figures is created and each figure has its own meaning: A circle is a symbol of perfection, irradiation, and mind; A triangle is a symbol of management, action, and work; A square is a symbol of basis, order, and support. Each of these figures corresponds with the company's sub-brand: information systems, management consulting, technological consulting and it is shown in the new company identity: each sub-brand has its own graphics, which is a part of a united visual system in the main master-brand style.

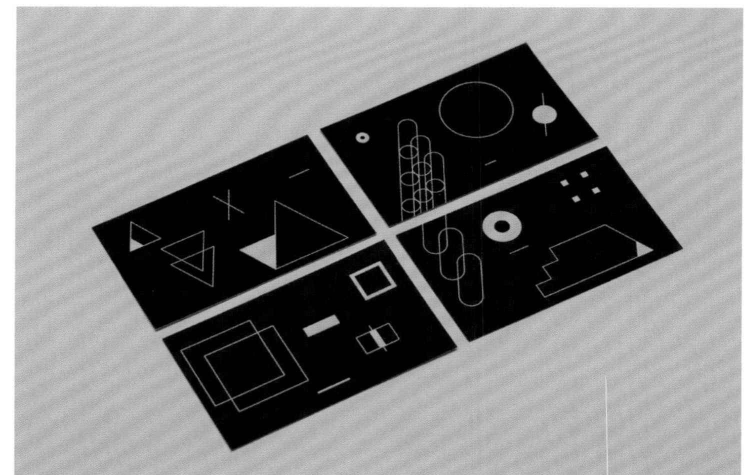

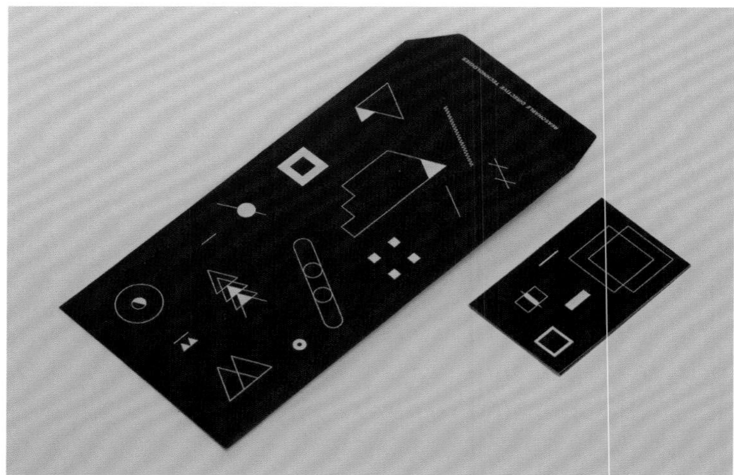

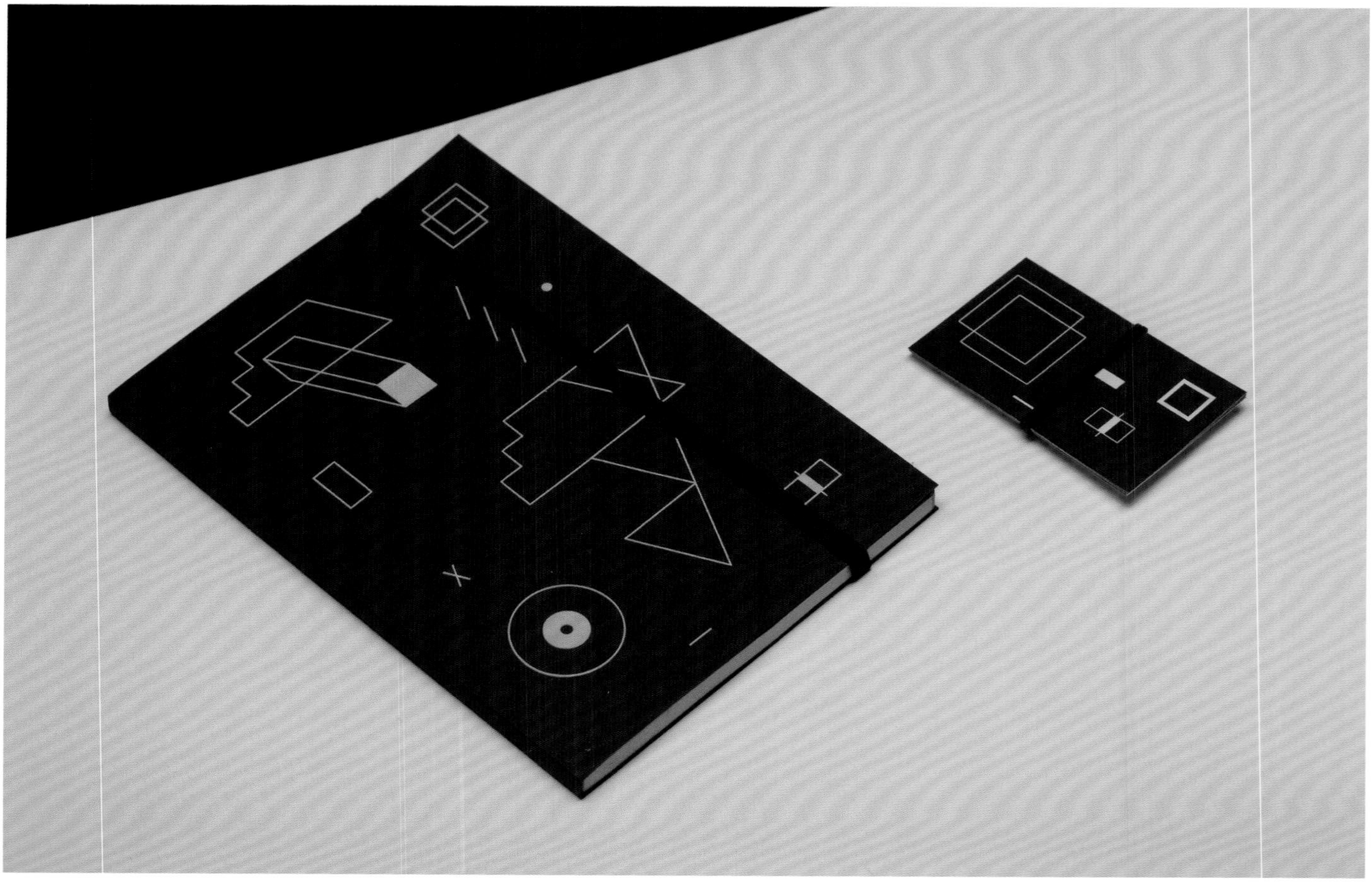

REASONABLE DIRECTIVE TECHNOLOGIES

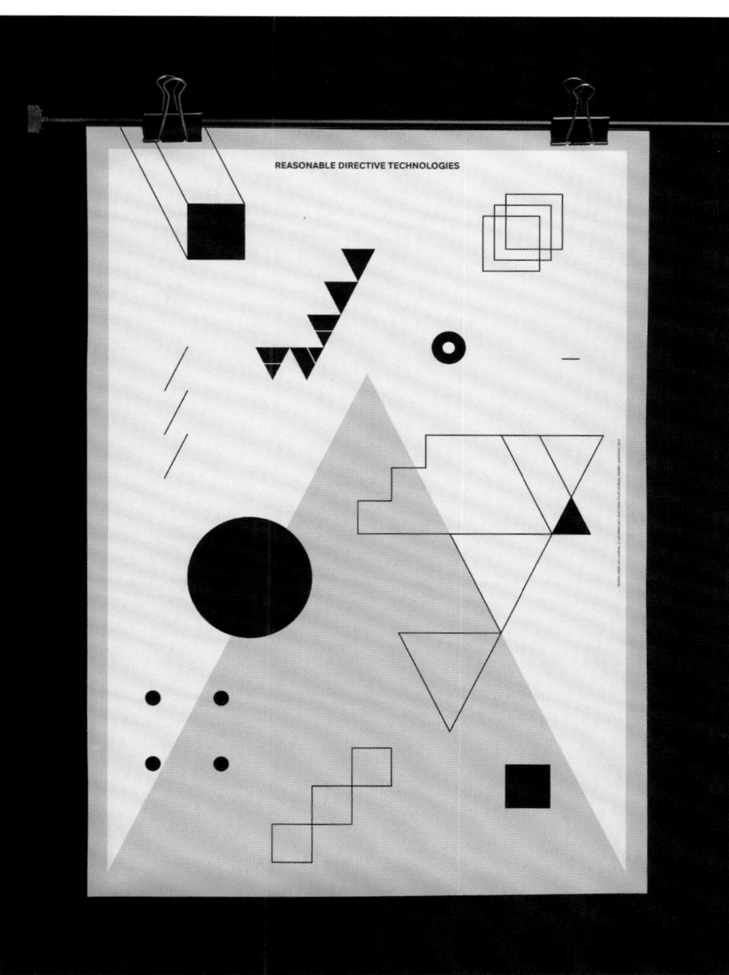
REASONABLE DIRECTIVE TECHNOLOGIES

RDTEX
REASONABLE
DIRECTIVE
TECHNOLOGIES
По вопросам сотрудничества
обращайтесь в РДТЕХ:
Россия, 117105, г. Москва,
ул. Нагатинская, д. 1, стр. 40
тел/факс: 8 (495) 995-09-99
marketing@rdtex.ru
www.rdtex.ru

Logo & Identity of Photographer Ylia Litvishko

Design: *Rina Rusyaeva*

The photograph style of this project is black and white photo, that's why the designer selected this color gamma. The geometry shapes is base in any composition in design and photos, logo constructed on base of simple shapes – circle, triangle, and rectangle.

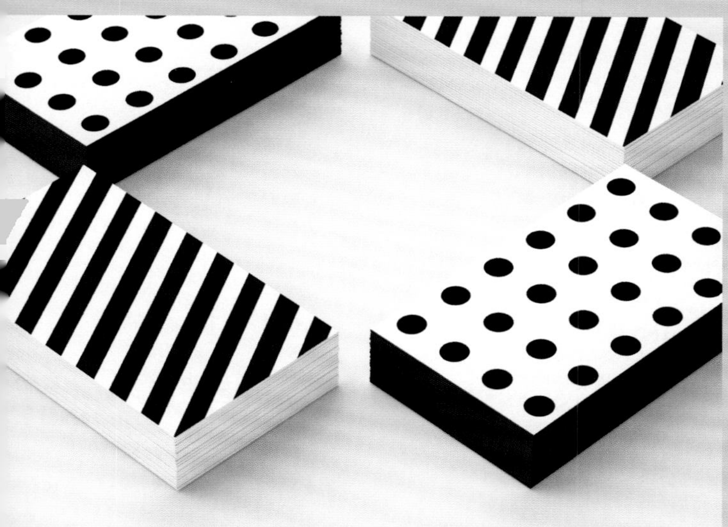

ЮЛ
ЮЛИЯ
ЛИТВИШКО
ФОТОГРАФ

ЮЛИЯ
ЛИТВИШКО
АНДРЕЙ И ОЛЬГА
НАША СВАДЬБА
23.09.2013
ЮЛ

ПОДАРОЧНЫЙ
СЕРТИФИКАТ
НА ПРОВЕДЕНИЕ
ФОТОСЕССИИ
ЮЛ

MTRL Kyoto

Agency: *Enhanced Inc.*
Art Direction: *Hiromi Maeo*
Creative Direction: *Tatsuya Iwasaki*
Photography: *Akira Moriuchi, Mayumi Ishikawa, Tatsuya Iwasaki, Takashi Maki*

MTRL is a new initiative by creative agency Loftwork running Fab Cafe in five countries, a cafe where FAB and creators meet. MTRL regularly provides unique materials and digital FAB equipment such as 3D printers. By renovating a 120 years old building, modern newness is added to MTRL Kyoto also inheriting building's memories. Collecting materials with potential that feeds innovation, MTRL ties materials (i.e. traditional wood, metal, and textile), new technologies (i.e. sensors) and creatives.

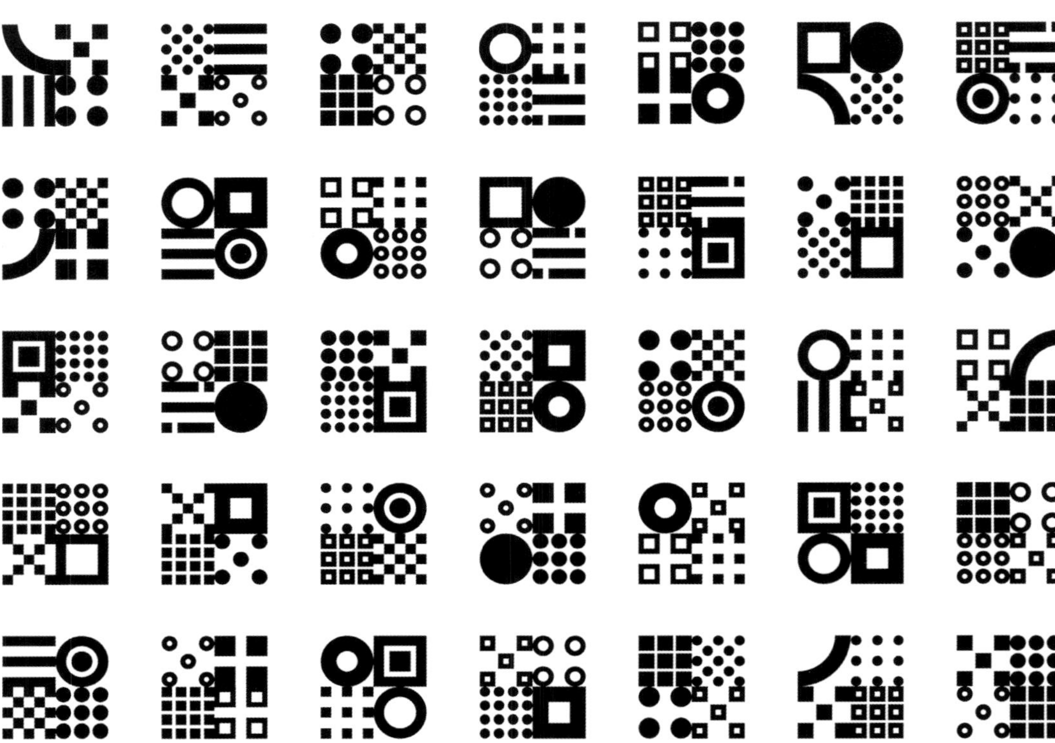

NOV.2015 OPEN
MTRL
DROP IN SPACE
FOR CREATIVE WORKS
KYOTO

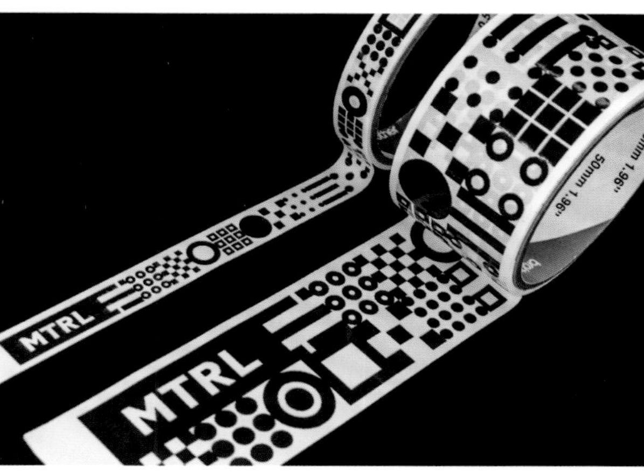
MTRL
MTRL
50mm 1.96"

MTRL
MTRL
DROP IN SPACE
FOR CREATIVE WORKS
TOKYO
KYOTO

Warwick Street Social

Design: *JB Studio*
Photography: *Paul John Bayfield*

Identity designed for the Warwick Street Social (formerly the Mad Moose). An urban meeting place located in the heart of Norwich's Golden Triangle, serving classic dishes with a modern twist. The concept behind the identity draws inspiration from the venues location by incorporating a triangle within the logo mark, which is invariably executed in gold across various applications, including gold foiled stationery, beer labels, exterior signage, and window graphics. The word mark also references the venues location, especially the street on which it can be found.

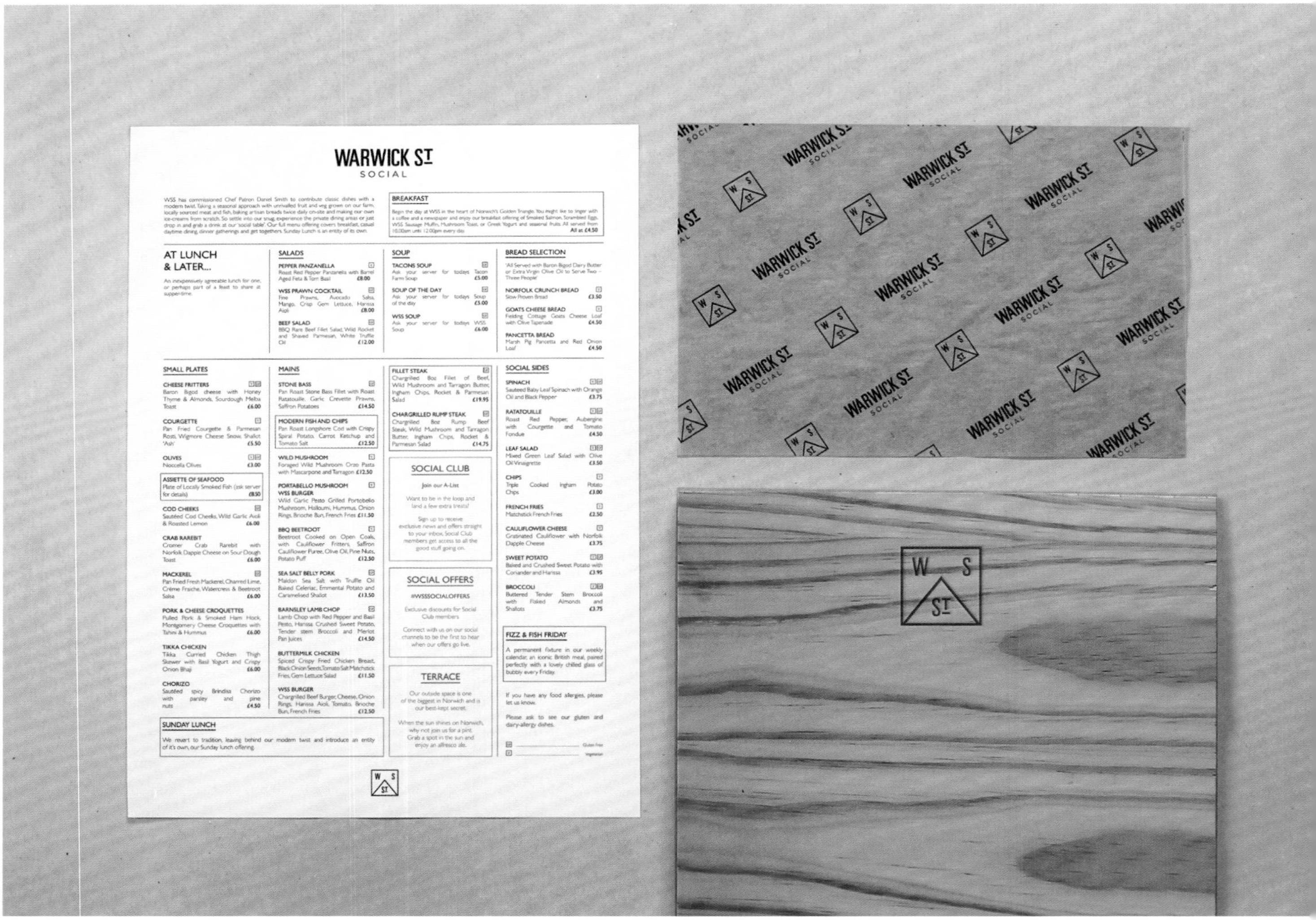

W
S
ST

W
S
ST

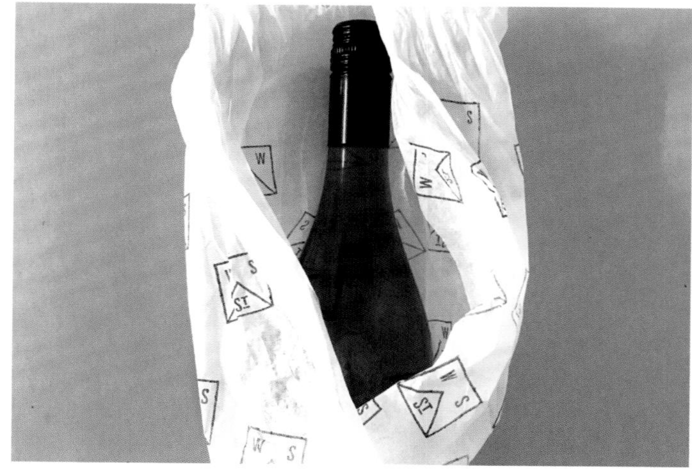

W
S
ST
WARWICK ST
SOCIAL

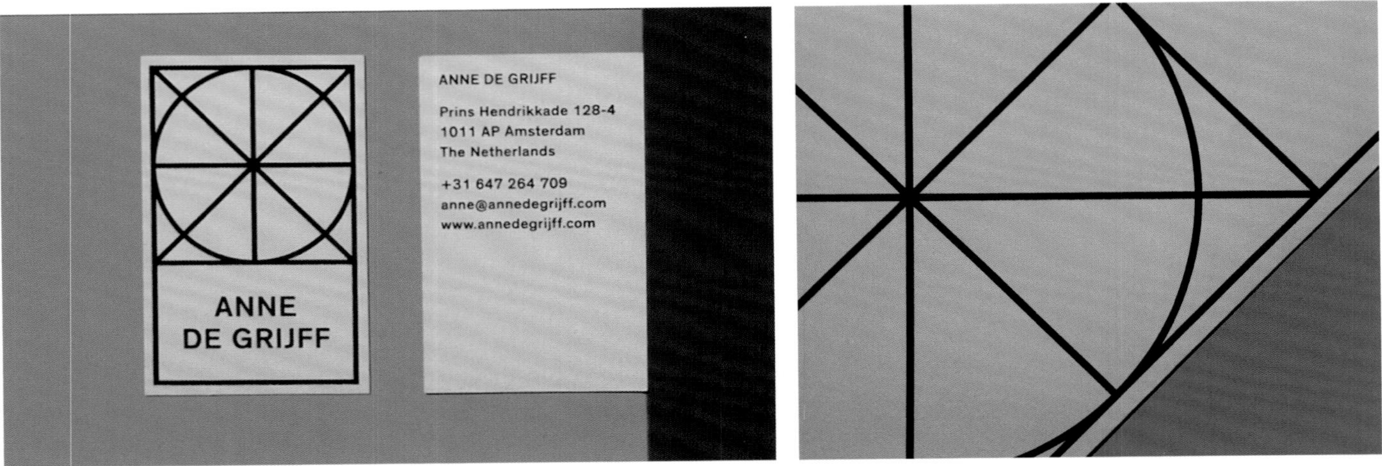

Anne de Grijff

Design: *Mainstudio*
Photography: *Koos van Breukel, Diana Scherer*

Anne de Grijff is a Dutch fashion designer and this identity system was incorporated into her newest collection. She creates capsules for each of what she has termed, "characters". The brand's identity is centered upon the concept of "made-to measure", using "leather and jerseys, pure wool, luxurious synthetics, and fine silks". Reflecting that material palette is a flexible grid incorporating the shapes: a square, circle, cross, and plus sign. The framing bold lines of the identity's graphics can be deconstructed and reconfigured into countless compositions to create an infinite number of such shapes. The identity has functioned as a template for the brand's other designed items, such as hangtags, bags, and stationary. The site's landing page extends vertically in Roman numerals to structure its navigation: characters, wardrobe, salon, curriculum, and contact; while Dutch photographer Koos Breukel captures De Grijff's characters, the core of the brand's digital communication.

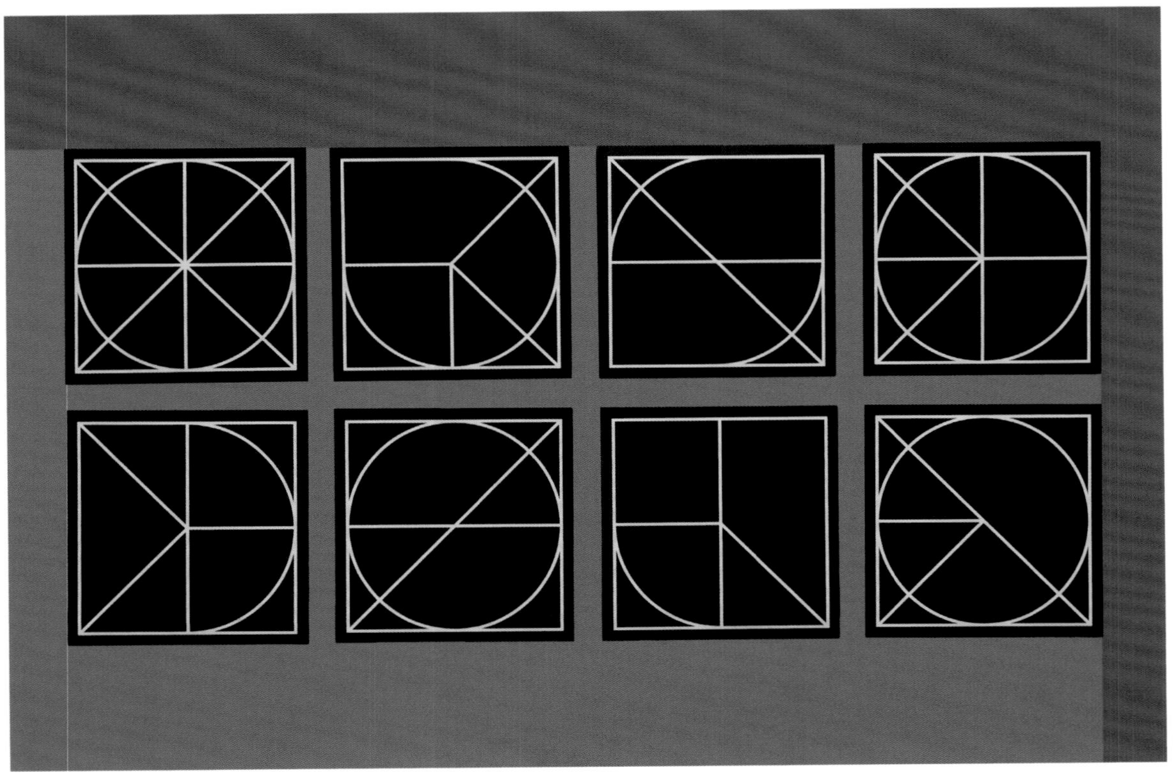

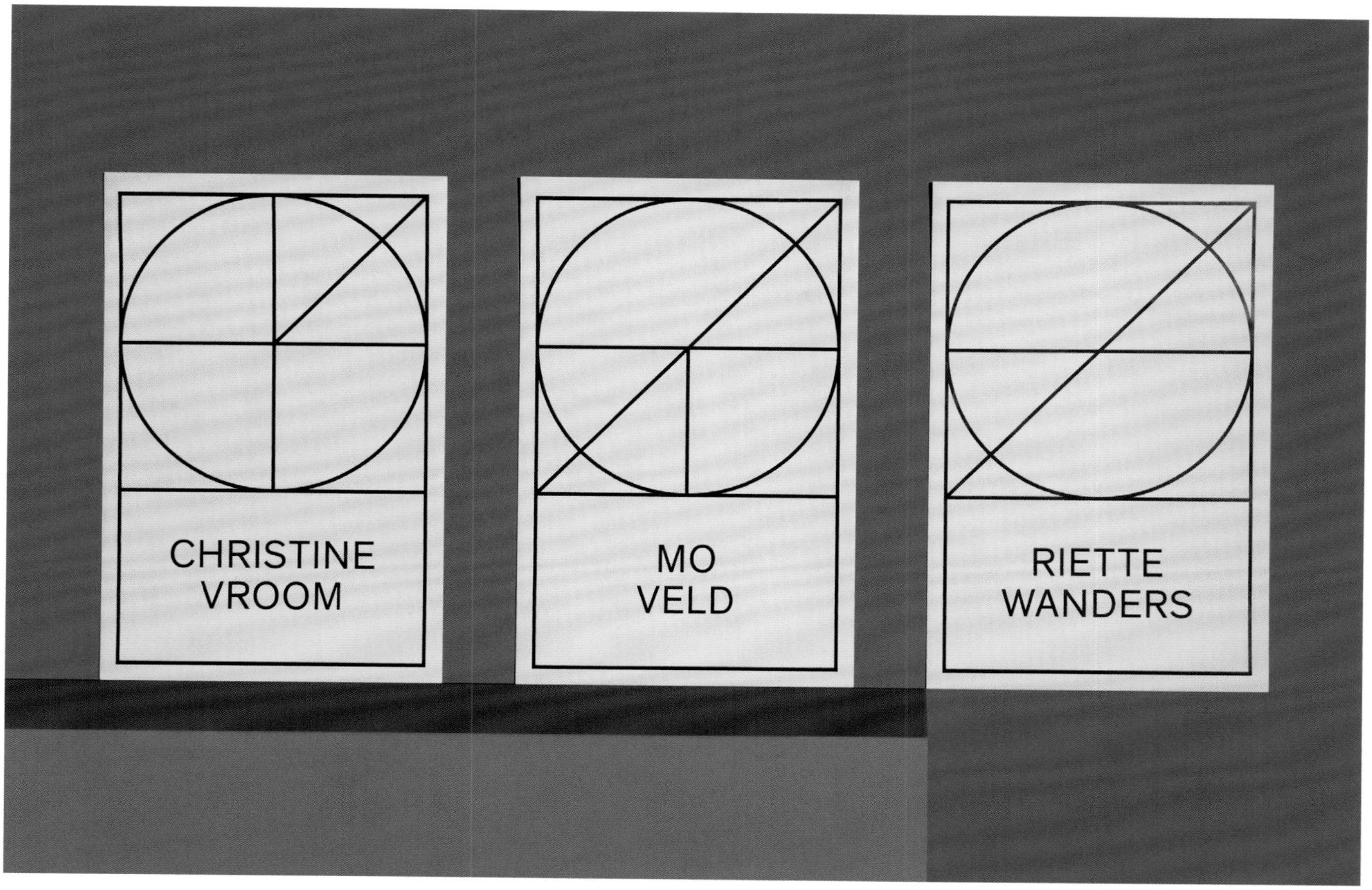

CHRISTINE
VROOM

MO
VELD

RIETTE
WANDERS

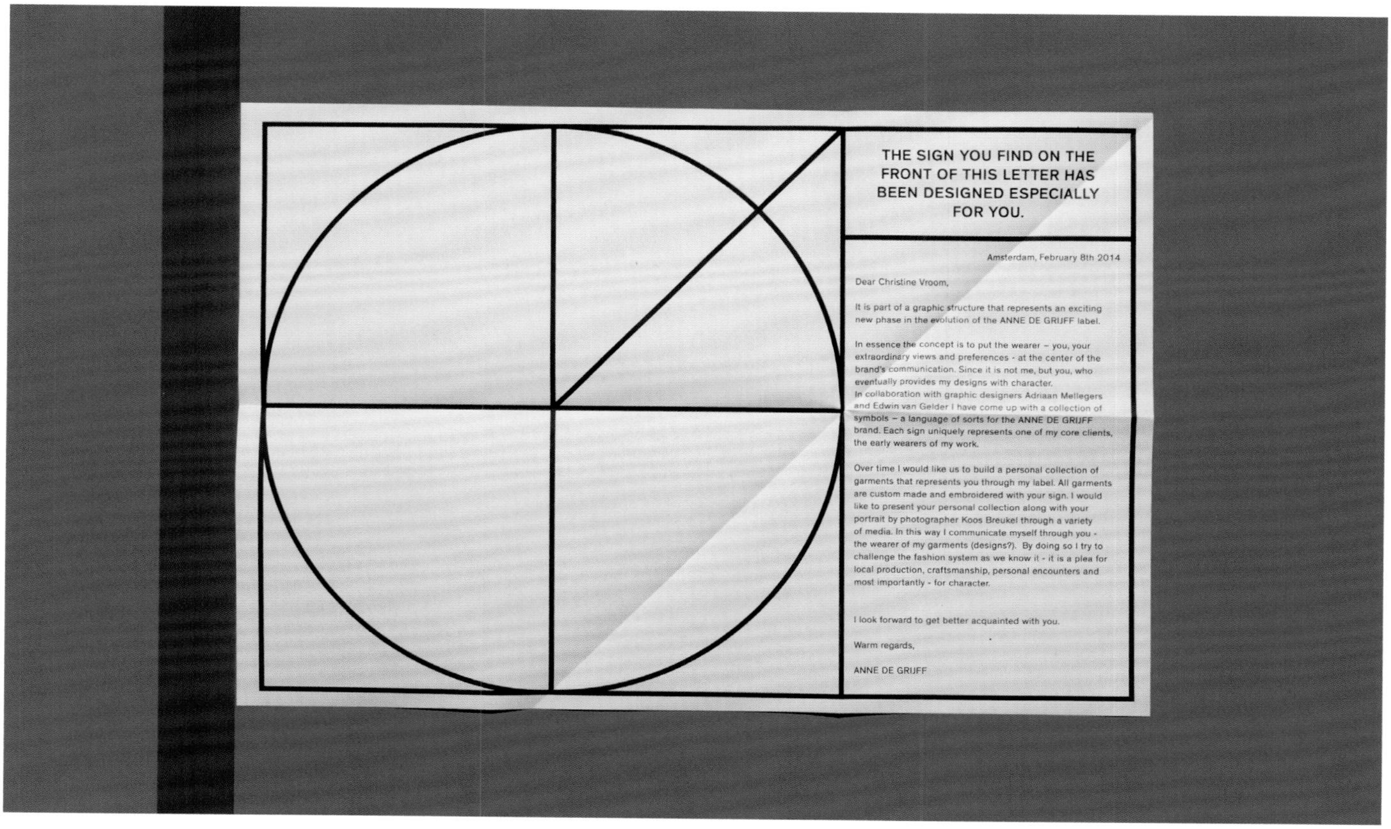

THE SIGN YOU FIND ON THE
FRONT OF THIS LETTER HAS
BEEN DESIGNED ESPECIALLY
FOR YOU.

Amsterdam, February 8th 2014

Dear Christine Vroom,

It is part of a graphic structure that represents an exciting new phase in the evolution of the ANNE DE GRIJFF label.

In essence the concept is to put the wearer – you, your extraordinary views and preferences - at the center of the brand's communication. Since it is not me, but you, who eventually provides my designs with character.
In collaboration with graphic designers Adriaan Mellegers and Edwin van Gelder I have come up with a collection of symbols – a language of sorts for the ANNE DE GRIJFF brand. Each sign uniquely represents one of my core clients, the early wearers of my work.

Over time I would like us to build a personal collection of garments that represents you through my label. All garments are custom made and embroidered with your sign. I would like to present your personal collection along with your portrait by photographer Koos Breukel through a variety of media. In this way I communicate myself through you - the wearer of my garments (designs?). By doing so I try to challenge the fashion system as we know it - it is a plea for local production, craftsmanship, personal encounters and most importantly - for character.

I look forward to get better acquainted with you.

Warm regards,

ANNE DE GRIJFF

BARTENEVA & VEBER

Agency: *Shishki Agency*
Design: *Konstantin Lobanov*

B&V's main competitive advantages are the throughout solutions that they offer as well as an ability to apply new technology when facing architectural and interior design challenges. That is why the designers decided to use sketching images as a metaphor for engineering mentality.

Designers and architects have different outlooks on each project for the reason that tasks are never the same. Thus, the designers offered a dynamic visual identity system. They did not create a single universal logo for the studio, but offered guidelines on how to create it. The designers use the logo as a pattern and fill the blank space with it designing the pattern millimeter by millimeter.

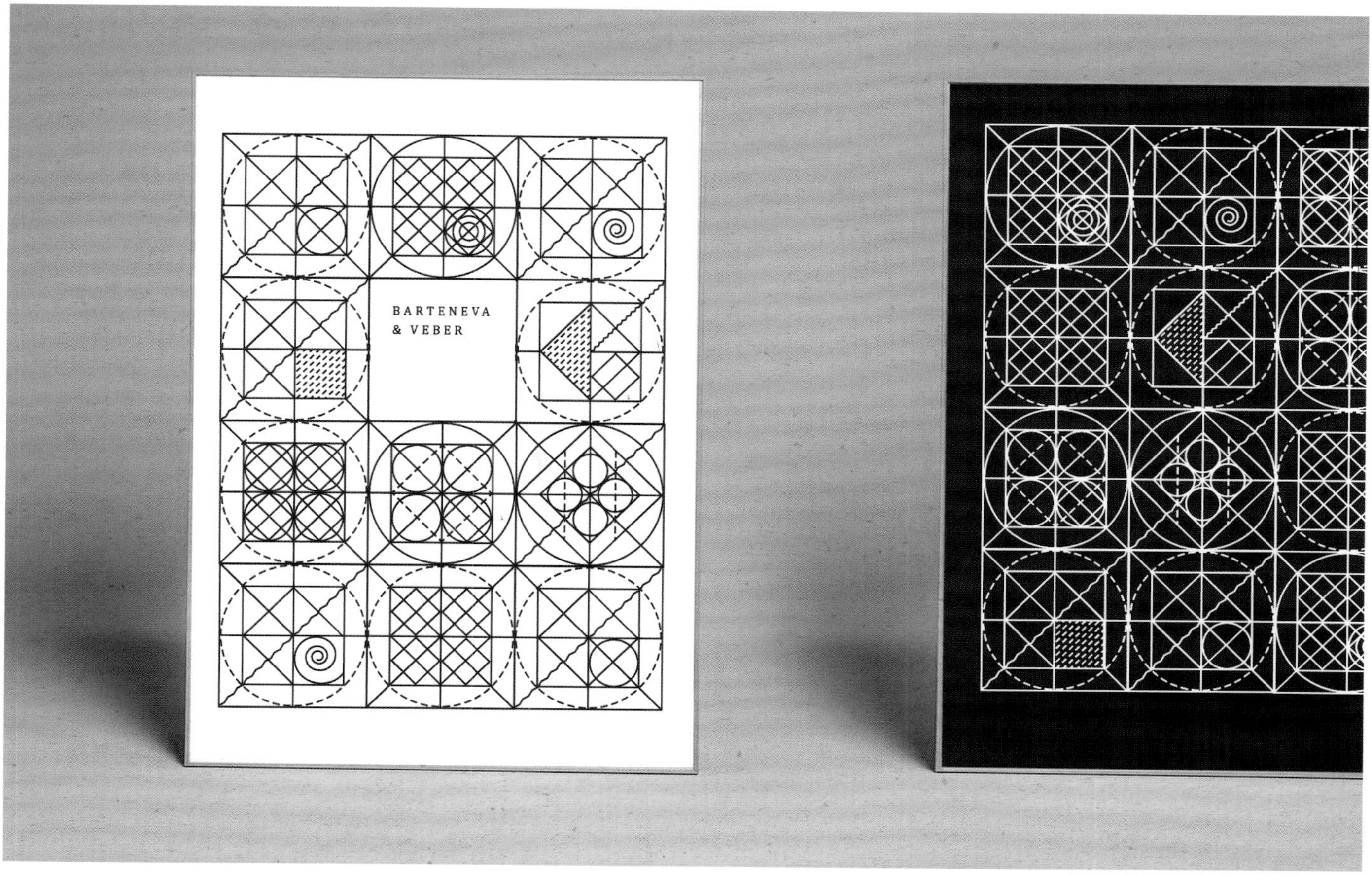

BARTENEVA
& VEBER

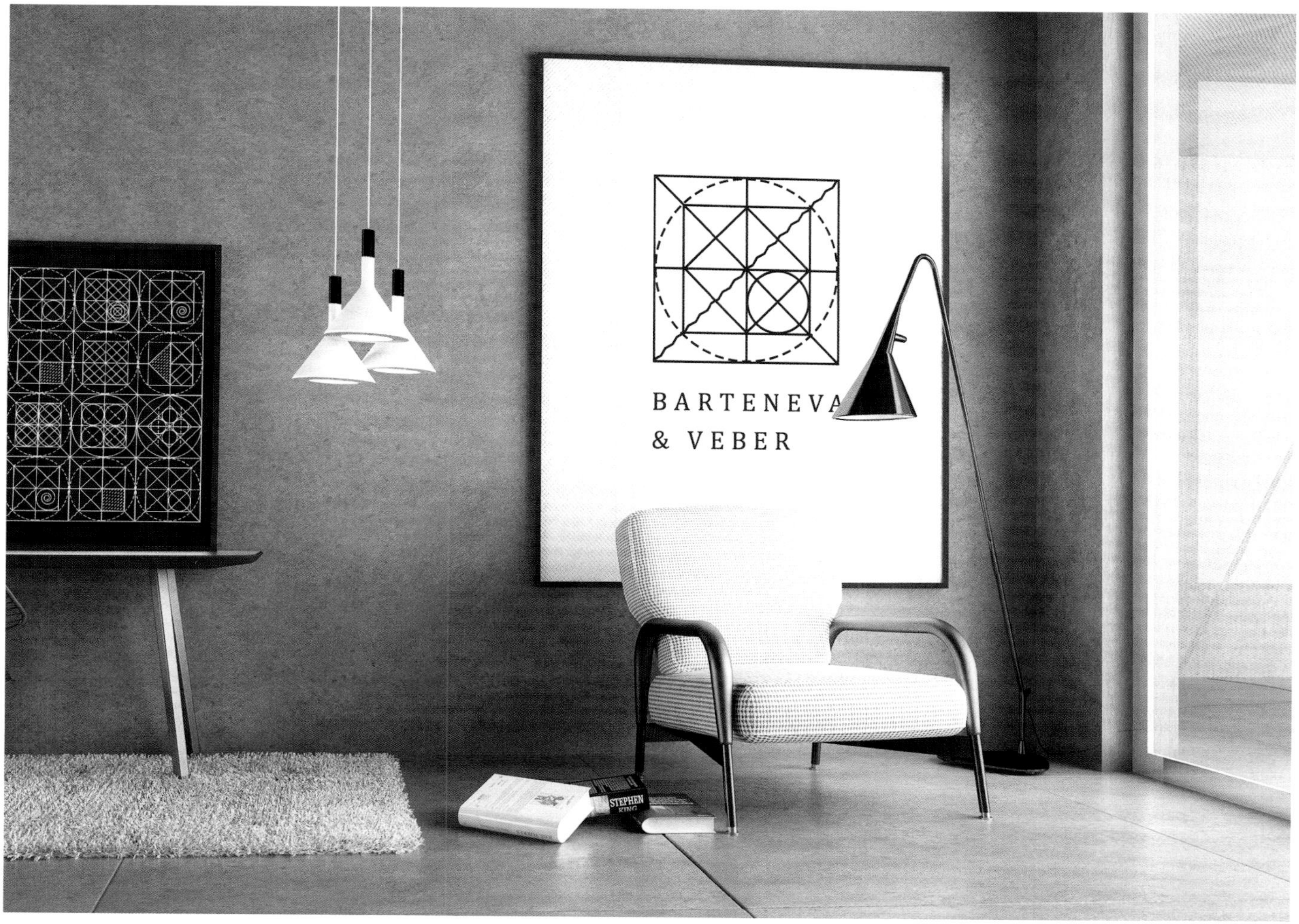

BARTENEVA
& VEBER

Barcelona Pensa

Agency: *Studio Carreras*
Art Direction: *Genis Carreras*

The project consists of a visual system to communicate the different events of the 2nd edition of the philosophy festival Barcelona Pensa. The plurality of symbols created (more than 40) becomes the identity of the festival itself, present across all online and offline applications.

17/11-3/12
Pensar la fi:
Cinema apocalíptic
i filosofia

Barcelona
Pensa

#BCNPensa
www.barcelonapensa.cat

Universitat de Barcelona
Generalitat de Catalunya
Departament de Cultura
FilmoTeca de Catalunya

II Festival de Filosofia
Del 16 al 21 de Novembre de 2015

Barcelona
Pensa

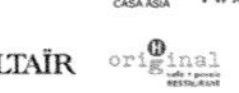

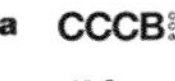

DILLUNS 16/11	
Les revoltes lògiques: 150 anys d'Alicia al país de les meravelles	9-19.30h | Facultat de Filosofia
El filòsof metge i el filòsof artista	18h | Llibreria Calders
El joc com a problema filosòfic	19h | C.C. Golferichs
Cafè filosòfic: "El valor de la veritat"	19.30h | La Central
II Cabaret Filosòfic: "Animalpensando"	20h | L'Horiginal
DIMARTS 17/11	
Animals que pensen: l'origen de la filosofia (visita guiada)	*Diversos horaris* | Museu d'Arqueologia de Catalunya
Pensament xinès	19h | Casa Àsia
La filosofia del quotidià	19h | Llibreria Calders
Pensar la fi: Cinema apocalíptic i Filosofia	19.30h | Filmoteca de Catalunya
Arquitectura en transformació	19.45h | COAC
DIMECRES 18/11	
Viquimarató	10-14h | Facultat de Filosofia
Ètica i neurociència	17h | Hospital Clínic
Fotofilosofia	18h | Facultat de Filosofia
Ments i màquines	18h | Arts Santa Mònica
Ex-posicions: autorepresentacions a l'era Youtube	18.30h | La Virreina Centre de la imatge
"Thinking through Our Ears: Aeshetics and Politics of Listening" amb Peter Szendy	19h | MACBA
Cafè filosòfic: "Estrangeria i hospitalitat: un problema també filosòfic?"	19.30h | Llibreria +Bernat
DIJOUS 19/11	
Pensar la tècnica	9.45-14h | Facultat de Filosofia
Antic règim i revolució a Hegel i Mozart + Concert Mozart	17h i 19.30h | Paranimf de la UB
Pensar en vinyetes	18.30h | Llibreria Gigamesh
Pensar la fi: Cinema apocalíptic i Filosofia	18.30h | Filmoteca de Catalunya
El filòsof davant la física contemporània I	19h | C.C. Golferichs
Amor i Humor	19h | Palau Mola
Cafè filosòfic: "La filosofia, el desig i el paradís"	19.30h | La Central
DIVENDRES 20/11	
Jugar a Pensar. Jornades de Filosofia Lúdica	11-13h | Teatre Plataforma I+D. E. Eòlia
L'eròtica socràtica	18h | C.C. Can Deu
L'ARPV: fotografia, realitat augmentada i espai públic	18.30h | La Virreina Centre de la imatge
Filosofia Japonesa	19h | Casa Àsia
El filòsof davant la física contemporània II	19h | C.C. Golferichs
Conferència de Giacomo Marramao	19h | CCCB
Café filosòfic: "¿Es posible adquirir conocimiento de las ficciones?"	19.30h | Llibreria +Bernat
DISSABTE 21/11	
Taller-debat sobre la discapacitat intel·lectual	10-14h | CCCB
La filosofia també és cosa de nens/es	11.30-13h | CCCB
Taller d'aforismes	11-13h | Biblioteca Vila de Gracia
Futur de coneixement o d'ignorància?	11h | Ateneu Barcelonès
El pensador en moviment	18h | Llibreria Altaïr
Flash Philosophy	19h | La Cervesera Artesana
Pensar la fi: Cinema apocalíptic i Filosofia	19.30h | Filmoteca de Catalunya
Recital indisciplinat	20.30h | Inusual Project

1000 Followers Celebration Poster Series

Agency: *Feten Studio*
Design: *Sara Bautista*
Illustration: *Alex de la Fuente*

Feten studio celebrates 1000 followers in his opening with a poster series based on simple geometric shapes representing "1000" in different ways. A twelve column grid, the corporate color, and minimalism with geometry are the key to this poster series.

www.behance.net/fetenstudio

www.fetenstudio.com

We are over one thousand!

Thank you all for all your love.

www.behance.net/fetenstudio
www.fetenstudio.com
We are over
one thousand!
Thank you all for all your love.

www.behance.net/fetenstudio
www.fetenstudio.com
We are over
one thousand!
Thank you all for all your love.

www.behance.net/fetenstudio
www.fetenstudio.com
We are over
one thousand!
Thank you all for all your love.
10 x
100

www.behance.net/fetenstudio
www.fetenstudio.com
We are over
one thousand!
Thank you all for all your love.

Papa Palheta Brand Experience

Design: *Foreign Policy*

Taking their brand further to provide better user experience even online, the Papa Palheta Experience Kit is designed to reflect their philosophy of having strong coffee roots down to sustainability. With meticulous consideration of the sensory elements within the kit, a card printed on recycled pulp paper made with blended coffee chaff (an underused by product of roasting coffee) prompts the user to repurpose it whether as a bookmark or thank-you card.

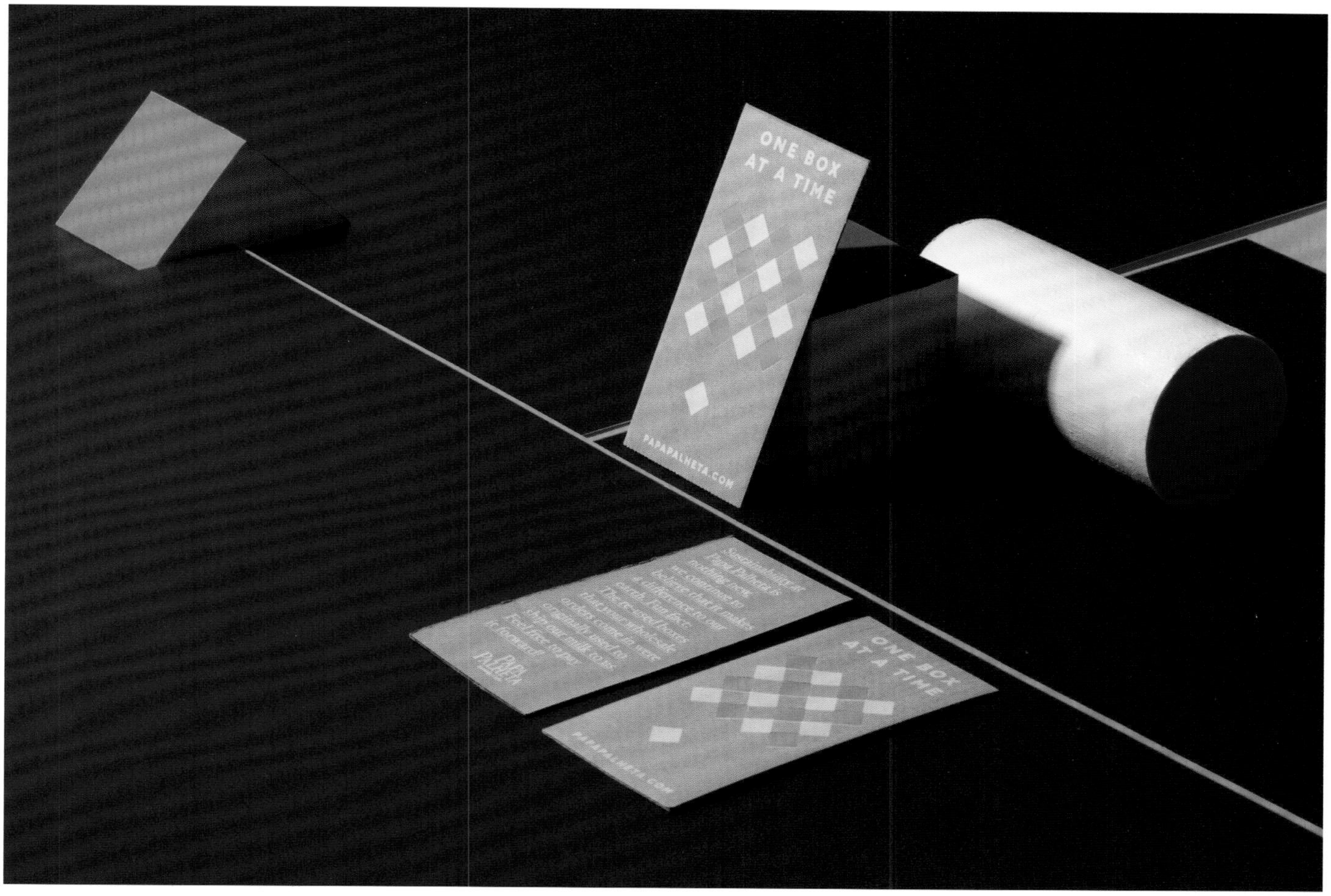
ONE BOX
AT A TIME
PAPAPALHETA.COM
ONE BOX
AT A TIME
PAPAPALHETA.COM

PAPA PALHETA

PRINZIP

Agency: *AM/PM Creative Agency*
Art Direction: *Andrey Trofimenko*
Design: *Andrey Trofimenko, Anna Kostiv, Artem Vlasov*

PRINZIP is one of the biggest real estate companies in Yekaterinburg. The basic geometric figures symbolize the three directions of the company: planning, constructing, and social design. The three of these comprise the whole, and serve as the foundation for the identity system.

The designers have followed the Golden Ratio; It, being the simplest and the purest compositional tool, simplifies the usage of the identity system. It is also easy to adapt the elements of identity for usage in any environment. Pick whichever textures, colors, fabrics, materials, apply it to various scales, and yet the system would still be intact. The identity is applicable in any B2B or B2C communications and serves as an overarching brand for all the projects of PRINZIP.

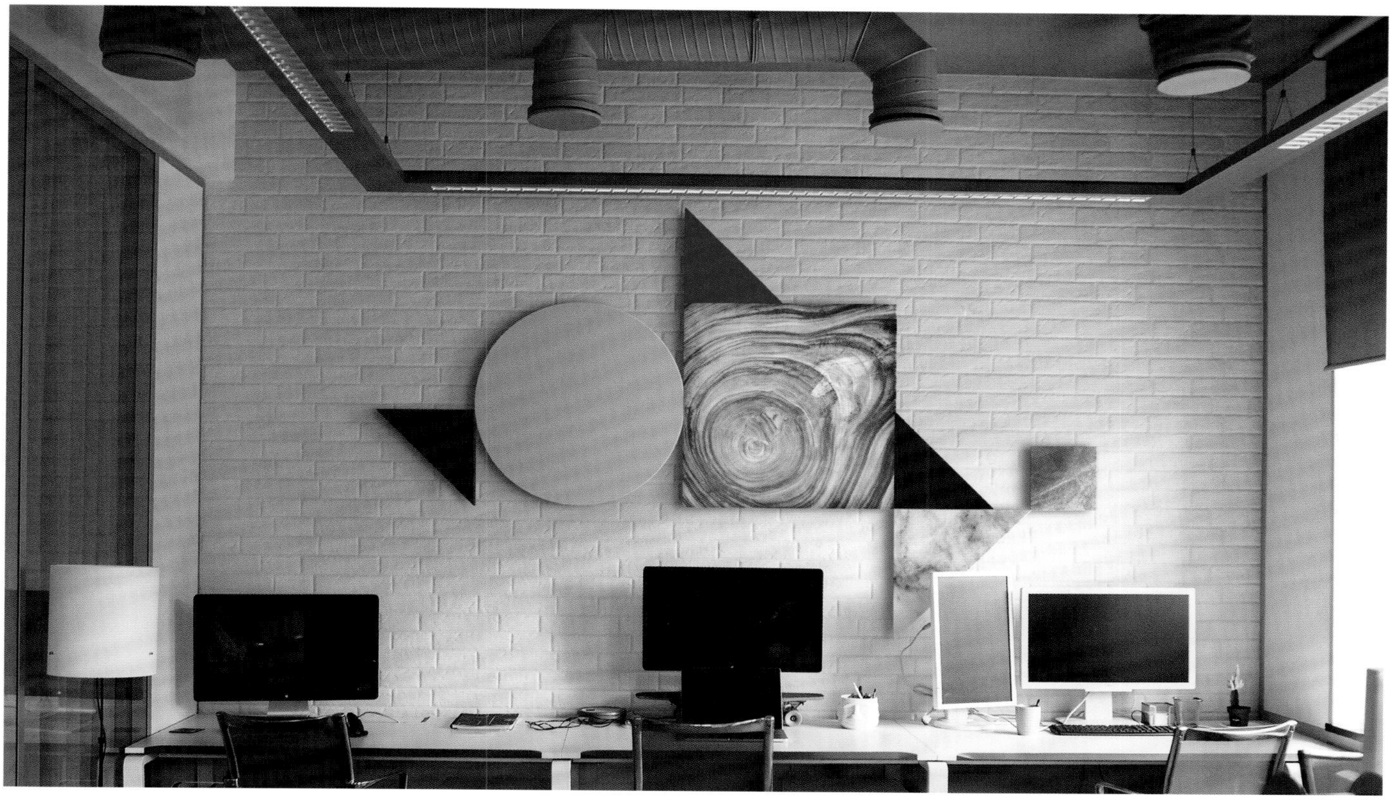

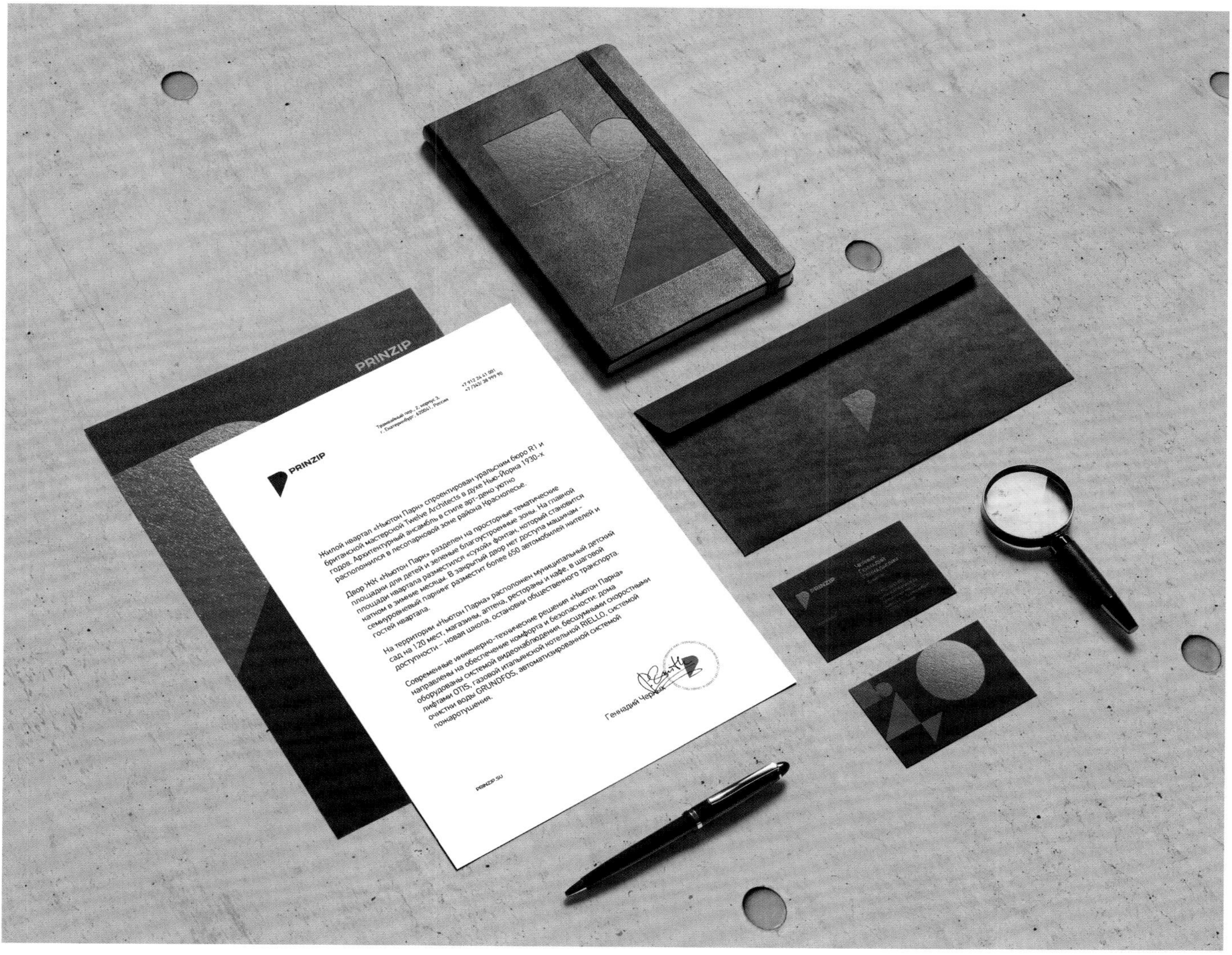

HICKS

***Design:** Design by Face*

Identity system and stationery for a new-generation real estate group in Chihuahua, Mexico. Hicks intents to build a state-of-the-art mixed-use project alongside architect Fernando Romero in Chihuahua, Mexico. The designers developed their new identity system, which was divided into three different companies from the same HICKS group, each of them specialized in a specific complementary area. The designers created a very simple, yet modern visual system where each company is based on a specific set of geometric patterns and classic color palette. A very elegant, timeless identity that reflects the finesse and sharp vision of the brand.

HICKS Solutions
HICKS Capital
HICKS Development
HICKS Solutions

Drama Theater Strela

Design: *Anna Mikhaylova*

Visual identity for Drama Theater Strela. Drama Theater Strela is the only full-fledged theater in the town of Zhukovsky, which is fully updated and therefore requires a new way of having a distinctive voice. The main task is to create the most budget style (as on visual communication will be allocated to the financing of small and possibly non-constant), downtime and understandable to local residents.

Style theater is on the one hand – this is the introduction of a new (that allows the theater to be relevant and meet the capital level). And on the other – it is a historical reference to the avant-garde: a historically significant period in culture. As well as the theater, as your reference point in the cultural life of the city, leads the and committed to a new way. Therefore, based on the logo incorporated the image of the compass.

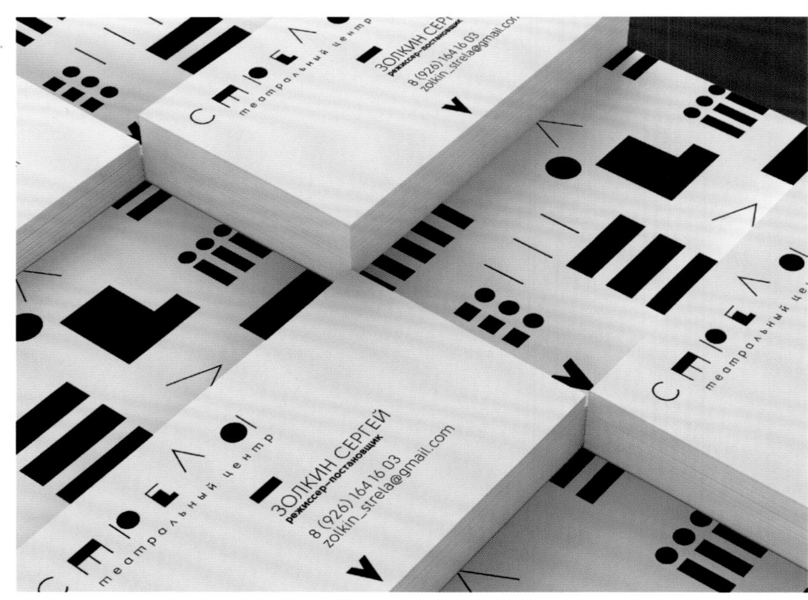

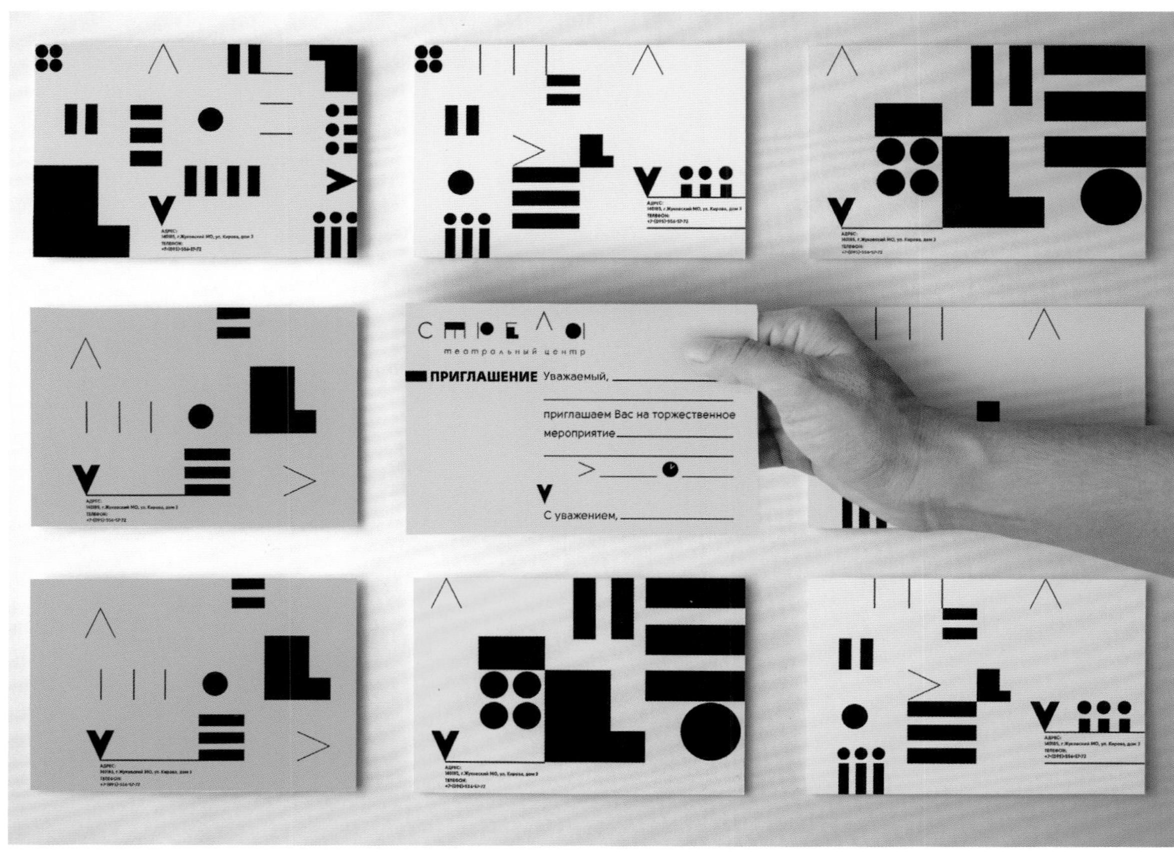

театральный центр
ПРИГЛАШЕНИЕ Уважаемый,
приглашаем Вас на торжественное
мероприятие
С уважением,

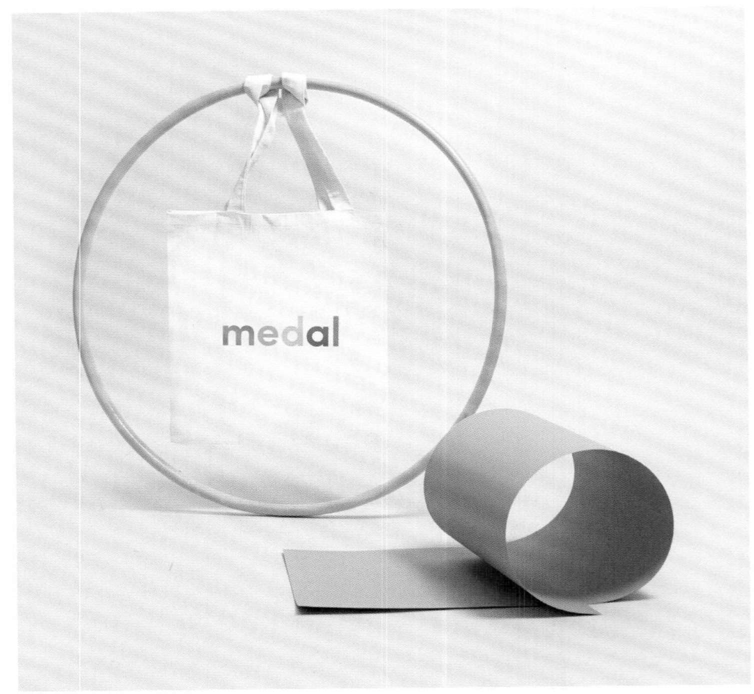

Medal

Design: *Futura*

Medal is a system designed to facilitate the education of slow learning individuals or with a mental disability. The name Medal is an acronym for the complete name in Spanish that means: "Method of Individual Education". The designers proposed this naming once they understood that the system allows each student to advance at his own rhythm, so this is not just about special education but an individual approach.

The branding concept is based on the foundations of Medal: bold and simple stimulation, bright colors and basic geometrical figures. The selection of typography for the wordmark, and the fact that the designers only use lowercase is because that's the way in which Medal teaches how to read and write, leaving capital letters and script typography for a future step.

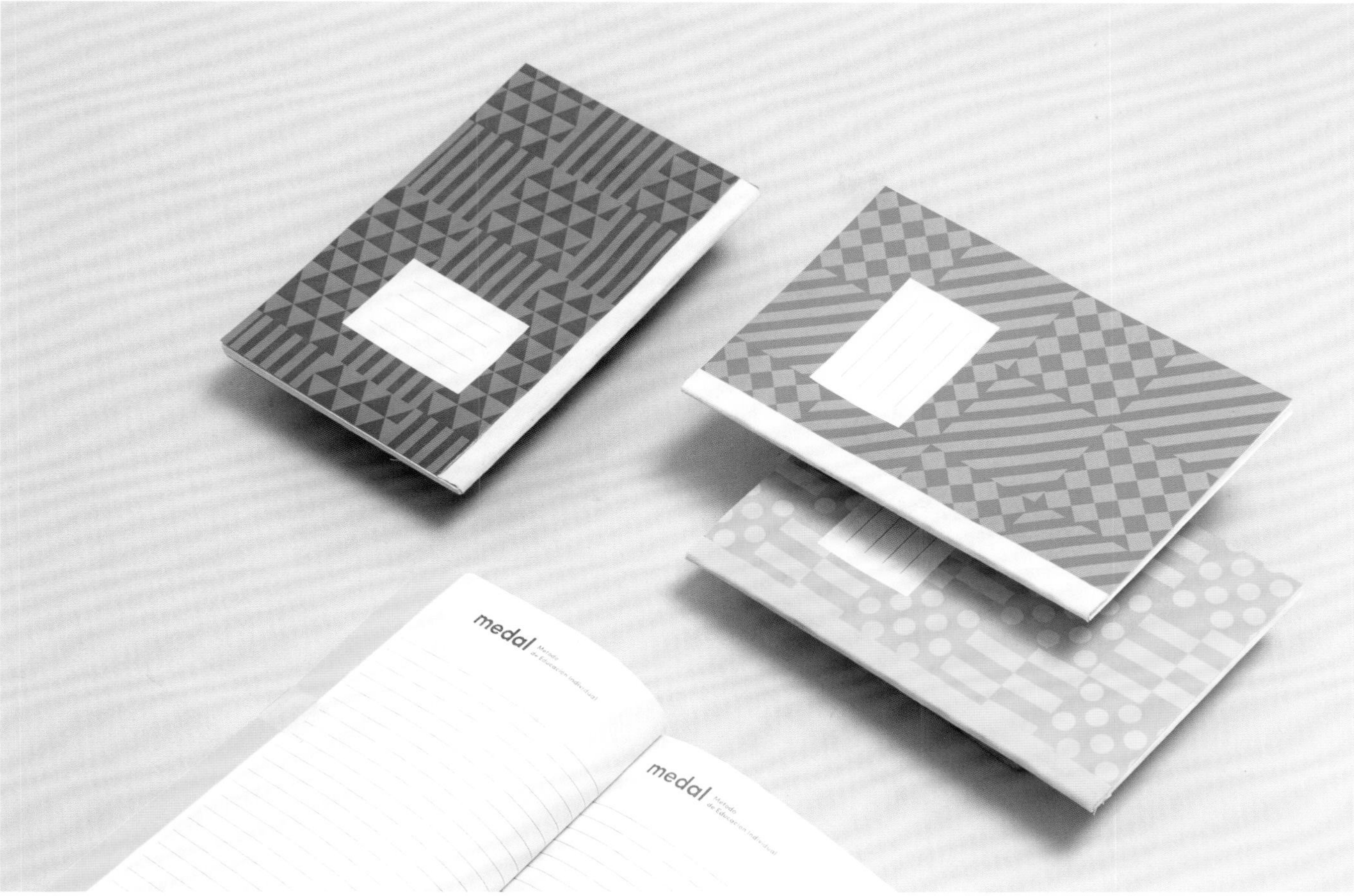

medal

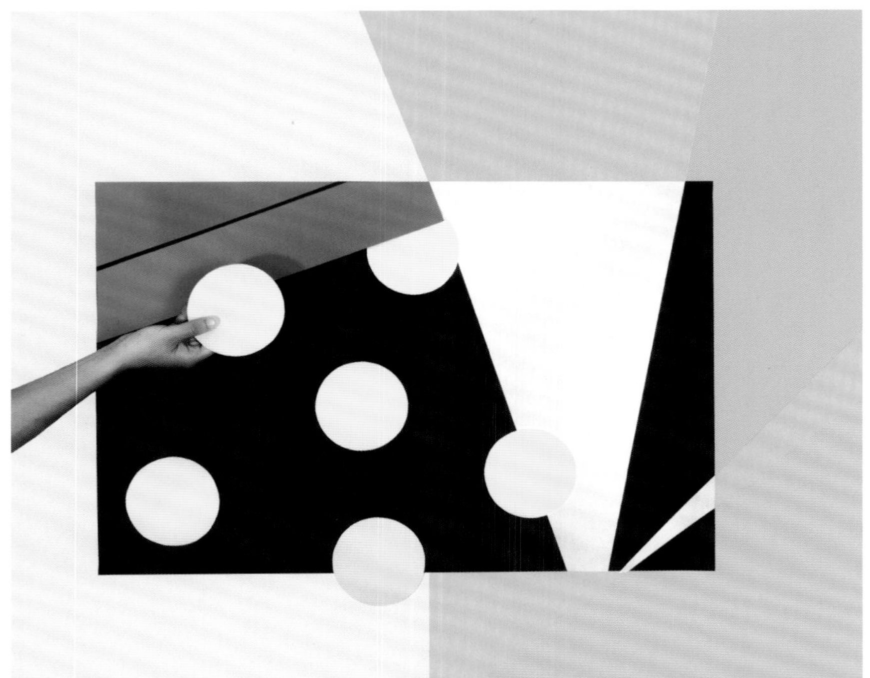

Local Bliss

Design: *Sabbath Visuals*
Photography: *Alain Noguez*

Art direction, branding, and web design for online magazine Local Bliss. It is a new online magazine, dedicated to promote local and international talent from various disciplines, including music, fashion, and design. Local Bliss leads union and communication as mediums for happiness. The brand concept works around cultures diversity, duality of forms and equality of individuals as part of the society. The design solution is presented by a strong and classical wordmark plus a responsive editorial system, based on content hierachy. The brand system has the ability to adapt to different environments in case needed, using patterns, symbols and extended color palettes.

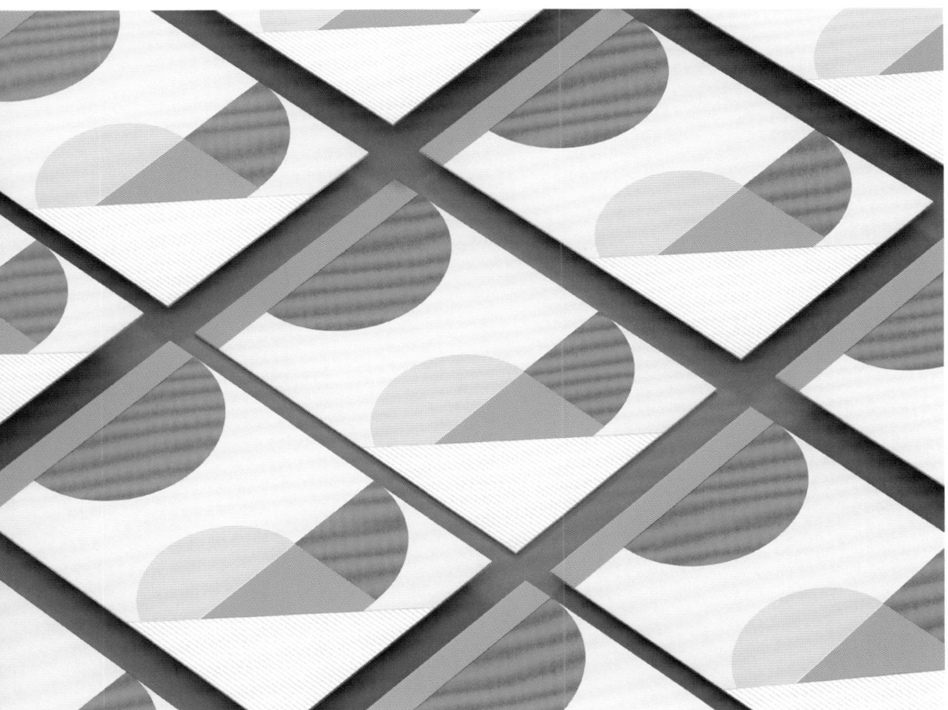

Port – arte

Design: *Sabbath Visuals*
Photography: *Vania Bazúa, Mike Rodríguez, Homero Ruíz*

Port – arte is a soft pop clothing brand based in Monterrey, Mexico. Focus on everyday utopias as emotion and connectivity, to inspire a contemplative plan for enriching life. Port – arte believes the universe is a canvas, where everyone portraits a particular reality. The brand creates his own environment as result of his personality and behavior, with the intention to gather people. The identity is based on variants of CMYK, representing the birth or creation of art and life as a dynamic. The symbol is created by basic forms of geometry to engage, the balance of the color system.

Youtube Insights

Creative Direction: *R/GA Sao Paulo*
Art Direction: *Pedro Veneziano*
Editorial Design: *Pharus Design*

Youtube Brazil made a study based on their most influential users, gathering a bunch of insights so that new brands can learn new ways to reach their users. The task was to come up with a branding solution that embodies this explosion of ideas and the way they are disrupting the market. The design approach was to embody the 3D illustrations into a solid, modular expression that blurs the line between CGI complexity and Graphic Design refinement. The use of symbols with modernist proportions, along with the color pallet, helped segmenting the four groups and open space to various brand expressions.

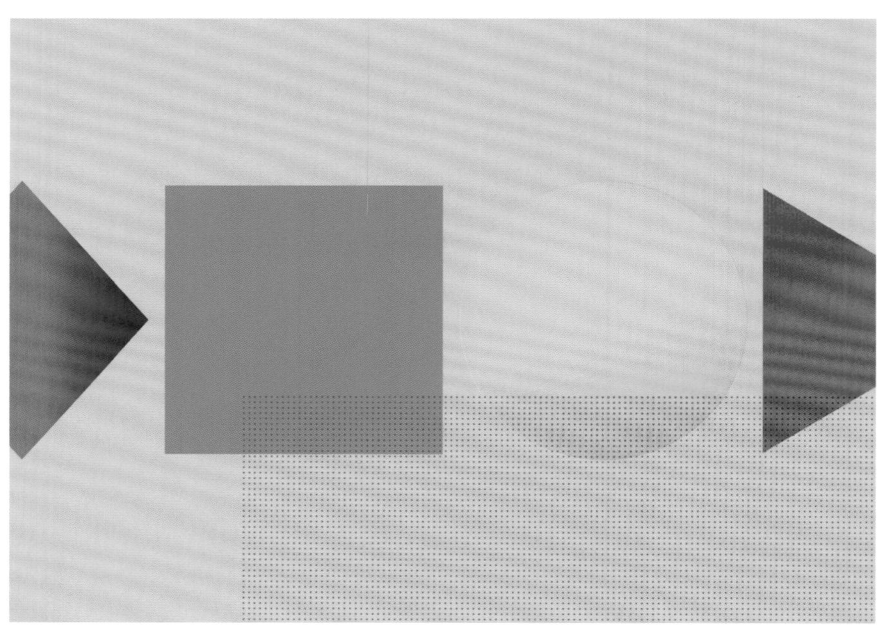

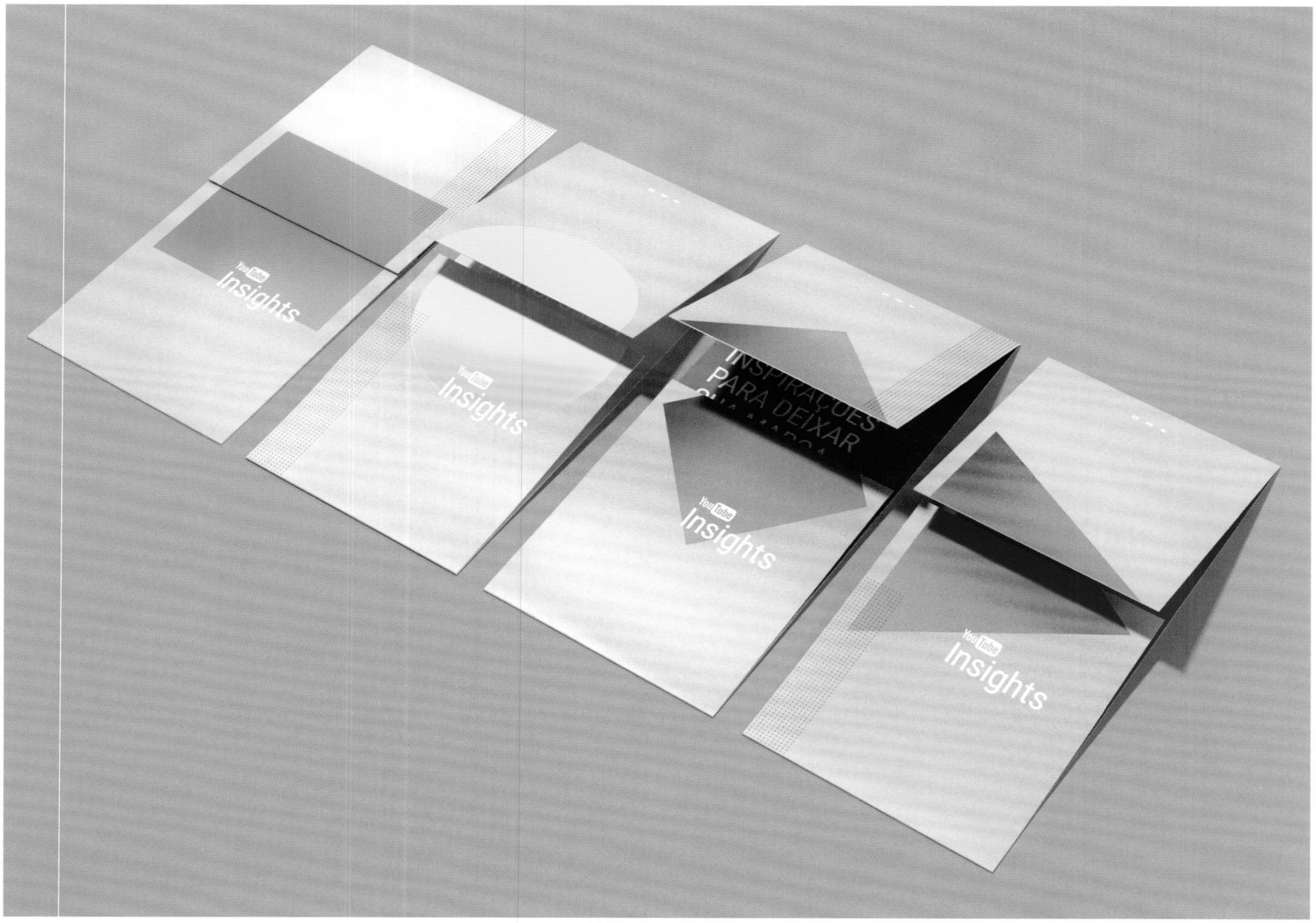

Insights
MUSIC
O PODER
QUE TRANS-
FORMA A
CULTURA

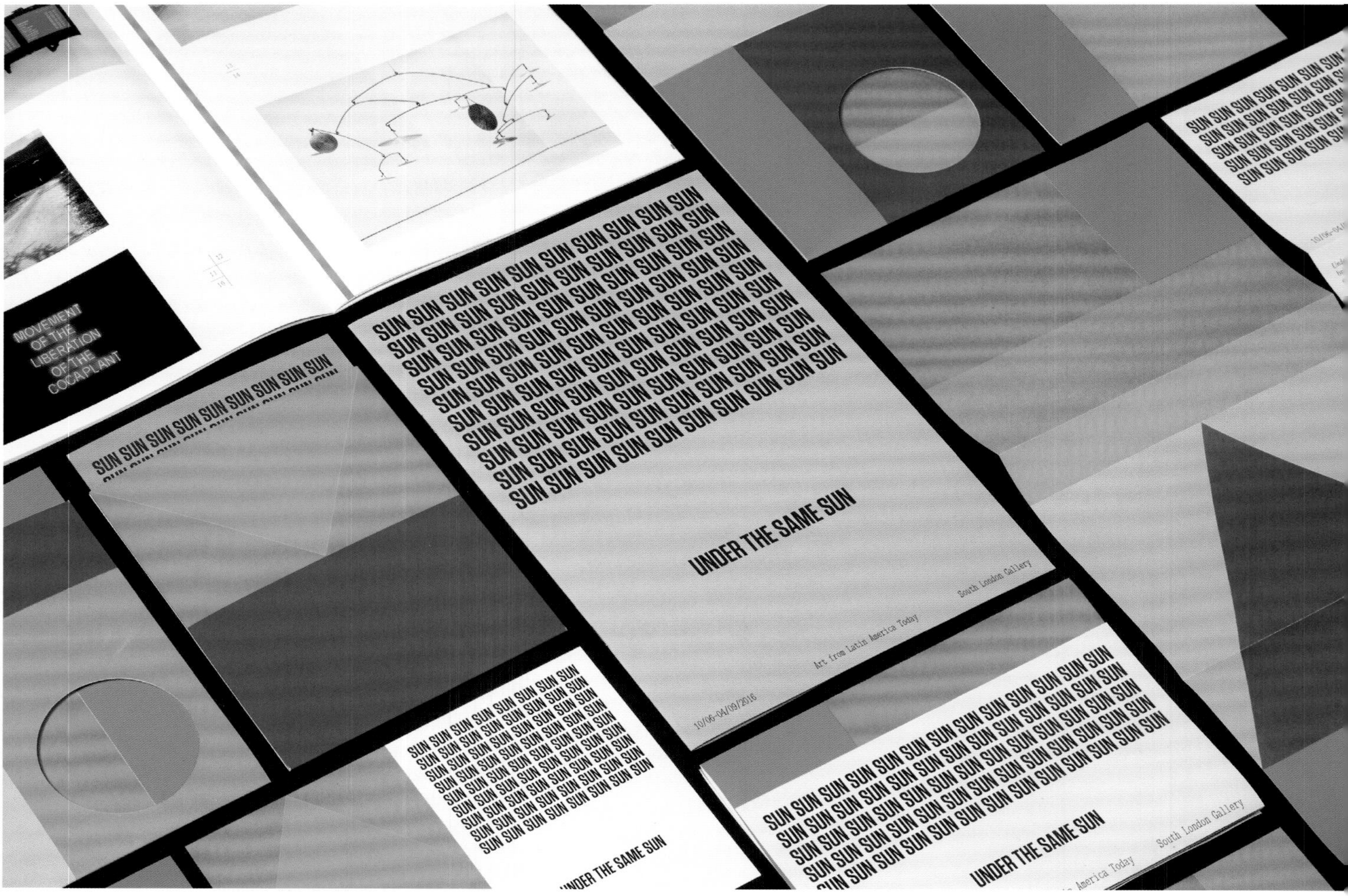

Under the Same Sun

Design: *OK-RM*

Art from Latin America Today, presented by South London Gallery, curated by Pablo León de la Barra for the Guggenheim UBS MAP Global Art Initiative.

SUN SUN SUN SUN SUN SUN SUN
SUN SUN SUN SUN SUN SUN SUN
SUN SUN SUN SUN SUN SUN SUN
SUN SUN SUN SUN SUN SUN SUN
SUN SUN SUN SUN SUN SUN SUN
UNDER THE SAME SUN
Art from
Latin America Today
South London Gallery
10/06-04/09/2016
SLG
VAUXHALL

Kizsports & Gym

***Design:** Loke Kah Wai*

Kizsports & Gym is a child development centered by combining education with fun and fitness. Focus on children play to learn and learn to play in a safe and friendly environment. To emphasize that Kizsports & Gym is a play school that focuses on both physical fitness as well as education to build kids' character and imagination. The keywords are imagination, creative, challenge, discipline, fun, joyful, and idea. Each shape is a block and each block represents a challenge. The shapes forms different objects when it's shifted.

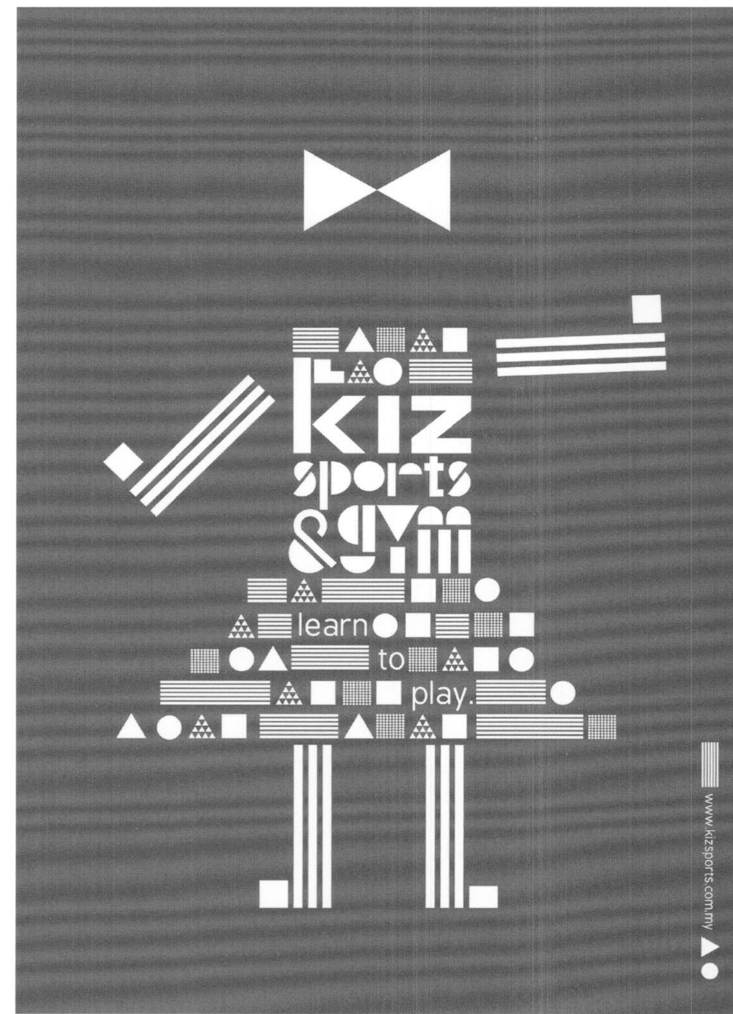

support graphic elements.

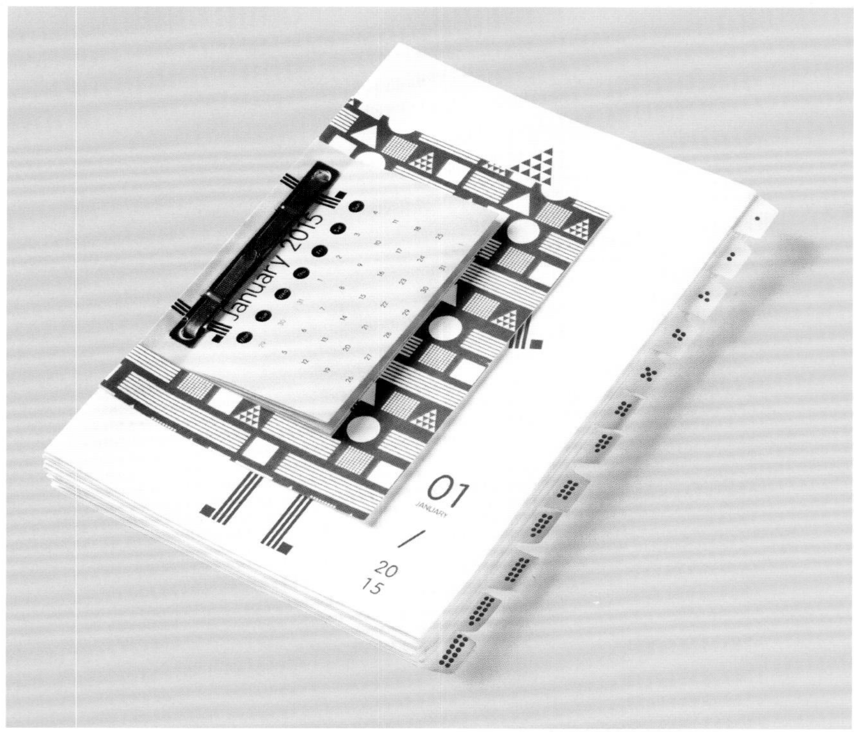

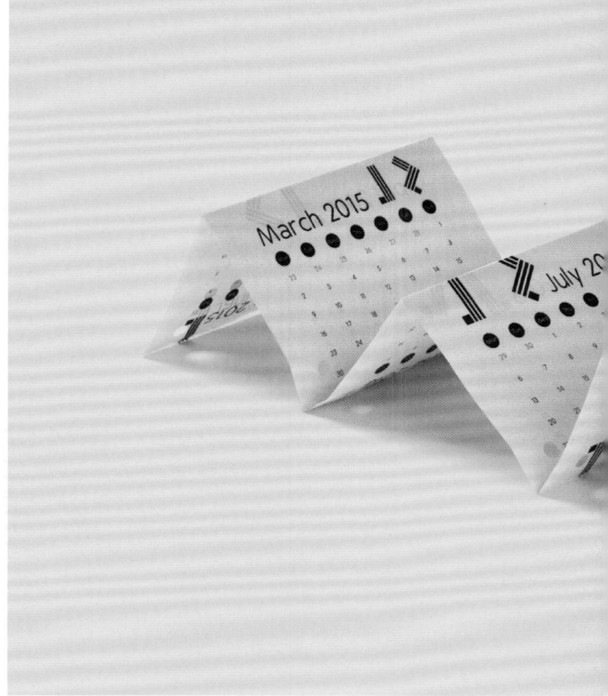

kiz
sports
&gym
Learn
thru
play
www.kizsports.com.my

kiz
sports
&gym
Play
to
learn
www.kizsports.com.my

November 2015

www.kizsports.com.my
Lithin. Administrator
T: 010 8936 212
E: admin@kizsportsgym.com.my
A: No 5, Persiaran Residen, Desa
Parkcity, 52200 Kuala Lumpur
T: 03 6280 8333
F: 03 6280 8222

Latina

Agency: *Brandlab*
Art Direction: *Juan Carlos Yto*
Design: *Romina De'Luise*

Latina is one of the largest media channel with the most audience in Peru. It is also the first channel that gave a special importance to they're brand, breaking with the status they had in their category. A dynamic identity was designed, which varies with the type of content and programs the channel generates. This revalued the brand and its celebrities.

Latina
Latina
(01) 219 1000 Av. San Felipe 968 – Jesús María latina.pe

Latina

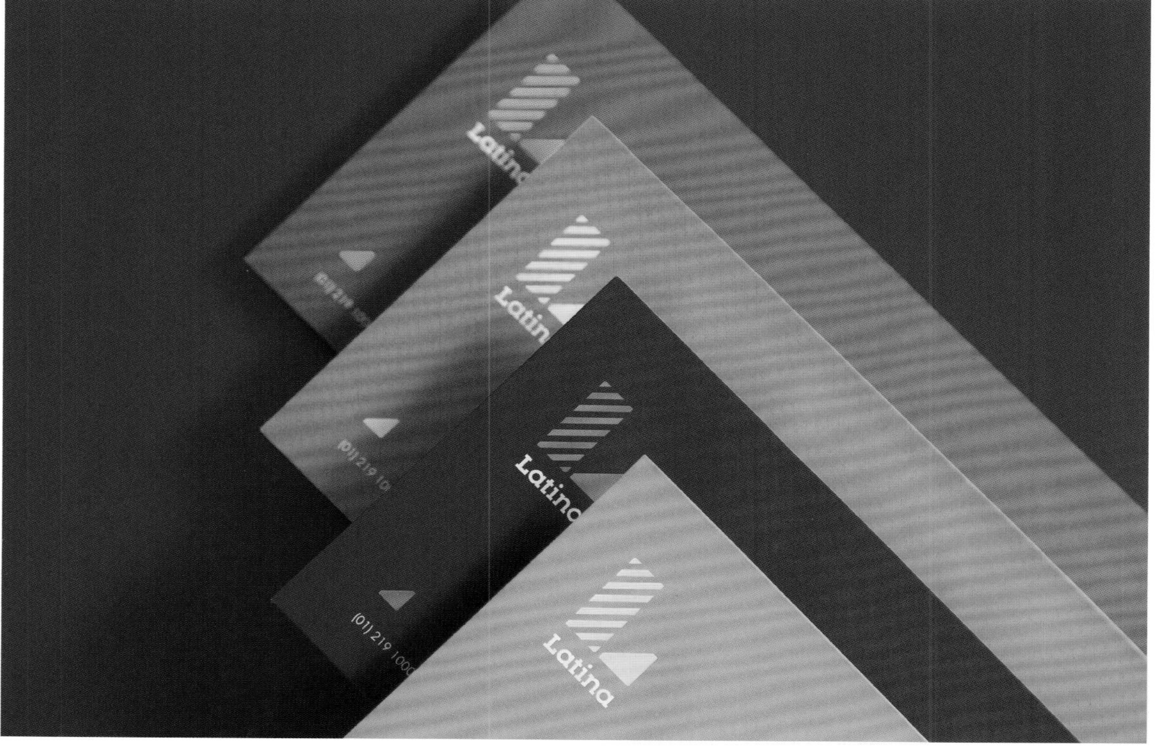
Latina
(01) 219 1000

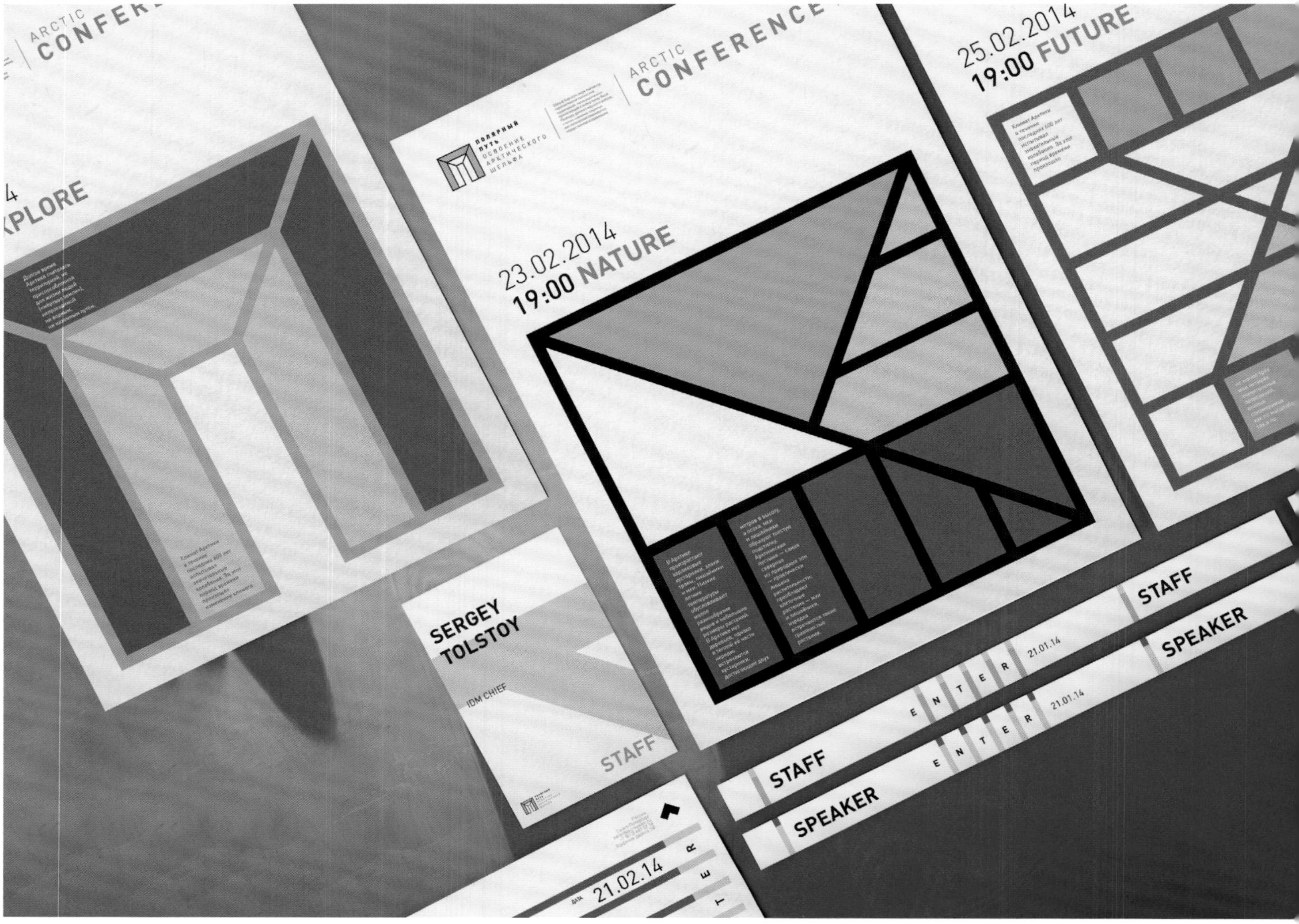

Polar Way

Designer: *Masha Portnova*

Polar Way is a special project with the main purpose of creating conditions in Arctic that will let the local fauna live safely. The logo symbol consists of two letters "П" (first letters of the naming), that forms a special arch, showing the way to the goal achievement. Several icons, based on the logo structure, emphasizes the objects that should be paid the main attention to.

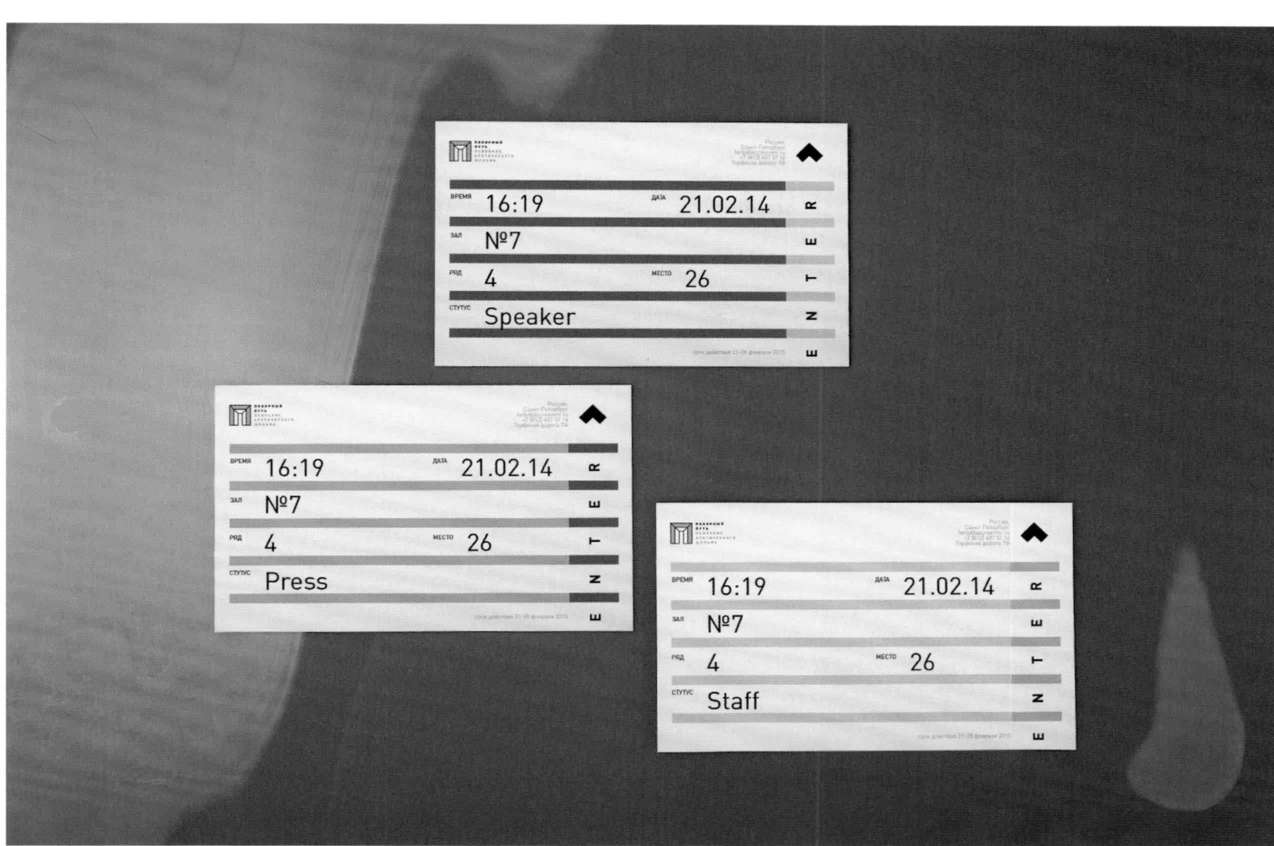

16:19
21.02.14
№7
4
26
Speaker
Press
Staff
ENTER

UPCOMING EVENTS
21.02.2014
19:00 HOME
22.02.2014
19:00 ANIMALS
23.02.2014
19:00 NATURE
24.02.2014
19:00 TECHNOLOGIES
25.02.2014
19:00 FUTURE
26.02.2014
19:00 EXPLORE
'14
ARCTIC
CONFERENCE

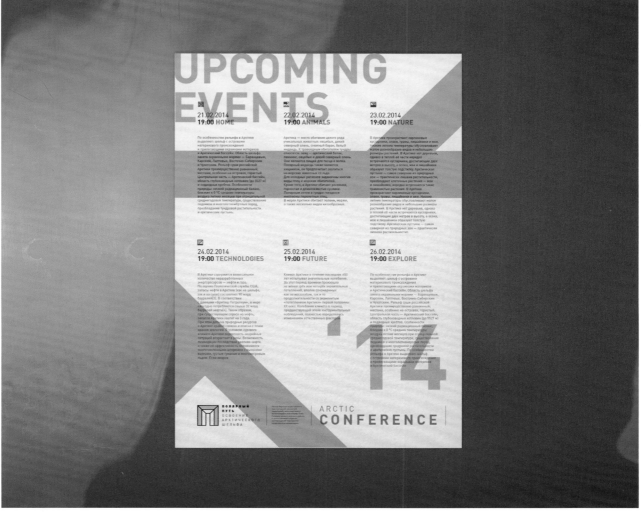

ADI Awards

Design: *TwoPoints.Net*

The ADI and their prestigious Delta Awards were founded in 1960. The first icon was designed by one of the founding members, former president of the ADI, designer of the torch of the 1992 Summer Olympics and winner of the Spanish National Design Prize (1987), Andre Ricard. TwoPoints was commissioned by the former ADI president Viviana Narotzky to create a formally coherent, yet flexible visual identity.

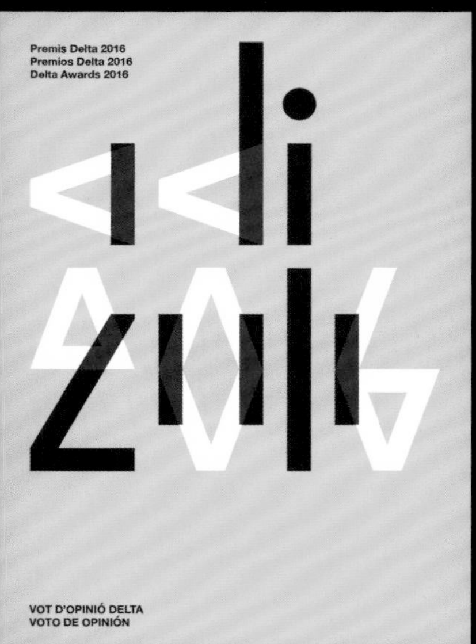

Premis Delta 2016
Premios Delta 2016
Delta Awards 2016
VOT D'OPINIÓ DELTA
VOTO DE OPINIÓN

Medalles ADI 2016
Medallas ADI 2016
ADI Medals 2016
ADI-FAD
Disseny Hub Barcelona
Badajoz, 175-177
08018 Barcelona
premis.adifad.org
Premis als estudiants al millor projecte de disseny industrial
Premio para estudiantes al mejor proyecto de diseño industrial
Període d'inscripció: 02/11/2015 al 11/01/2016
Periodo de inscripción: 02/11/2015 al 11/01/2016
Contacto
T (34) 932 566 770
F (34) 932 566 771
medalla@adifad.org

PREMIS ADI 2016
Δ Premis Delta
O Medalles ADI
O Premi ADI Cultura
Des de l'ADI-FAD us convidem al lliurament dels Premis ADI 2016, on es donaran a conèixer els guanyadors dels Premis Delta, les Medalles ADI i el Premi ADI Cultura, i que tindrà lloc en el marc del FADFest.
Data 9 de juny de 2016
Lloc Sala A. Disseny Hub Barcelona
19:30 Copa i Xurros
20:30 Acte de lliurament dels Premis ADI 2016.
22:30 Festa dels Premis ADI amb l'exposició: 'El Millor Disseny de l'Any'.
L'aforament de l'esdeveniment és limitat. Es prega confirmació al 932 566 770 o a premisadi@adifad.org
Col·laborador Premium
Sabadell Fundació
PREMIOS ADI 2016
Δ Premios Delta
O Medallas ADI
O Premio ADI Cultura
Desde ADI-FAD os invitamos a la entrega de los Premios ADI 2016, dónde se darán a conocer los ganadores de los Premios Delta, las Medallas ADI y el Premio ADI Cultura, y que tendrá lugar en el marco del FADFest.
Fecha 9 de junio de 2016
Lugar Sala A. Disseny Hub Barcelona
19:30 Copa y Churros
20:30 Acto de entrega de los Premios ADI 2016.
22:30 Fiesta de de los Premios ADI con la exposición: 'El Mejor Diseño del Año'.
El aforo del evento es limitado. Se ruega confirmación al 932 566 770 o a premisadi@adifad.org
Colaborador Premium

Premis ADI 2016
Premios ADI 2016
ADI Awards 2016

Premis ADI 2016
Premios ADI 2016
ADI Awards 2016
ADI-FAD
Disseny Hub Barcelona
Badajoz, 175-177
08018 Barcelona
T (34) 932 566 770
F (34) 932 566 771
adi@adifad.org
premis.adifad.org

Delta
38a Convocatòria internacional al millor disseny de producte
38ª Convocatoria internacional al mejor diseño de producto
38th International call to the best product design
Medalla ADI
29a Convocatòria per a estudiants al millor projecte de disseny de producte
29ª Convocatoria para estudiantes al mejor proyecto de diseño de producto
29th Award to best product design project for students
ADI Cultura
1a Convocatòria per a projectes que ajuden al foment i l'actualització social i conceptual del disseny de producte.
1ª Convocatoria para proyectos que ayudan al fomento y a la actualización social y conceptual del diseño de producto.
1st Cultural projects call to the promotion of product design and social and conceptual update for product design
Inscripcions obertes
Inscripciones abiertas
Call for entries
24/11/2015
—11/02/2016
Més informació a
Más información en
More info at
premis.adifad.org

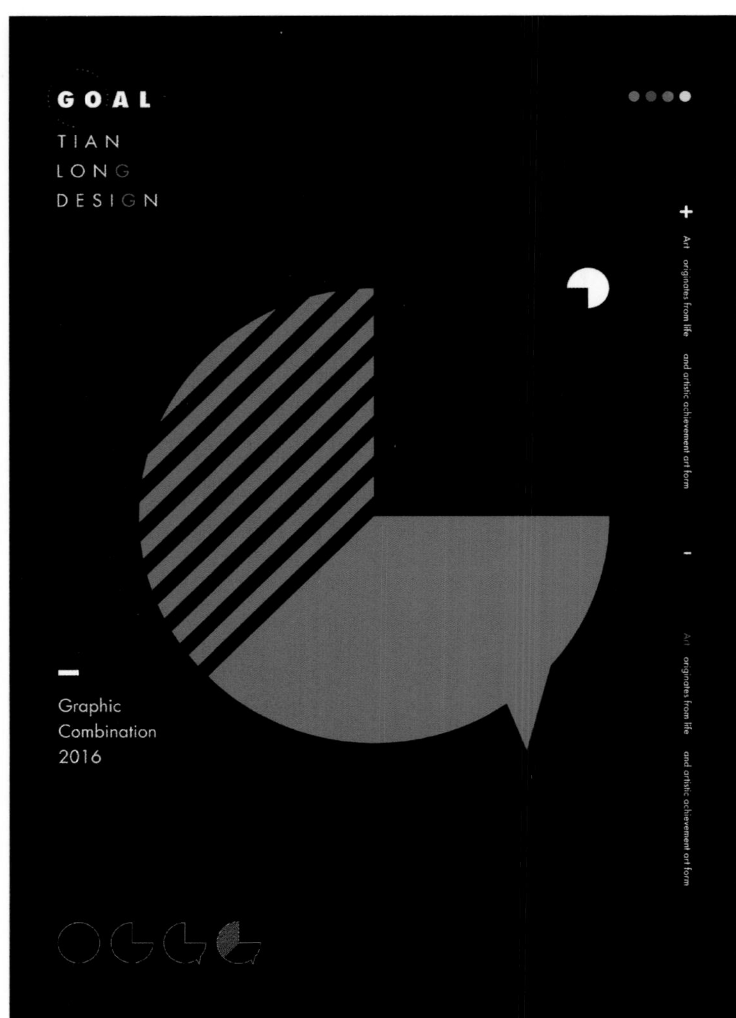

Goal

Design: *Tianlong Design*

A series of creative posters with the theme of goal and dream.

GOAL
TIAN
LONG
DESIGN
Art originates from life and artistic achievement art form
Graphic
Combination
2016

GOAL
TIAN
LONG
DESIGN
Art originates from life and artistic achievement art form
Graphic
Combination
2016

GOAL
TIAN
LONG
DESIGN
Art originates from life
TIANLONG DESIGN
Graphic
Combination
2016

Plus Renewable

Design: *Jan Weidemuller, Guam Lin*
Art Direction : *Brian Dai, Jan Weidemuller*

Plus is a renewable energy company located in Taiwan, China. To reflect the idea of unity in diversity, the designers developed a modular design principle. Based on a single shape, the "+" mark, the designers refined three distinctive elements that create a consistent look while allowing us to express individual personalities. Every shape based on a simple motion of the plus logo. Rotation, multiplication, and addition, which reflecting the dynamics of the solar energy business.

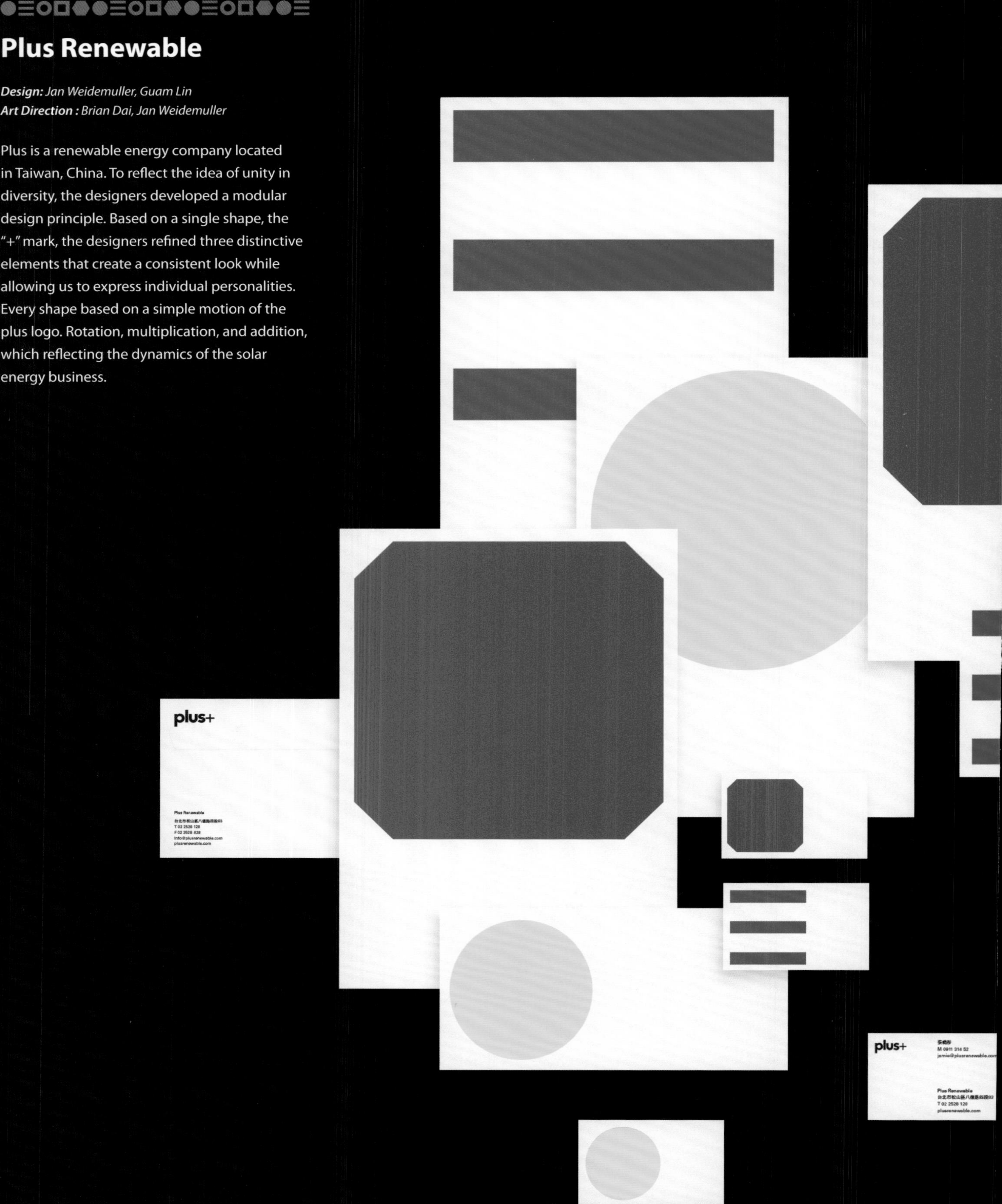

plus+
plus+

Troppo

***Design:** JoJo Dong*

The designer always wanted to explore combination of lines, shapes and colors. Troppo is an architecture company whose design is focusing on energy efficient such as solar/water collection/wind generated power as well as clean elegant lines. The inspiration was from the sun, the water, and the place as the three fundamental elements to work with, the shapes and color are selected in accordance with the idea itself.

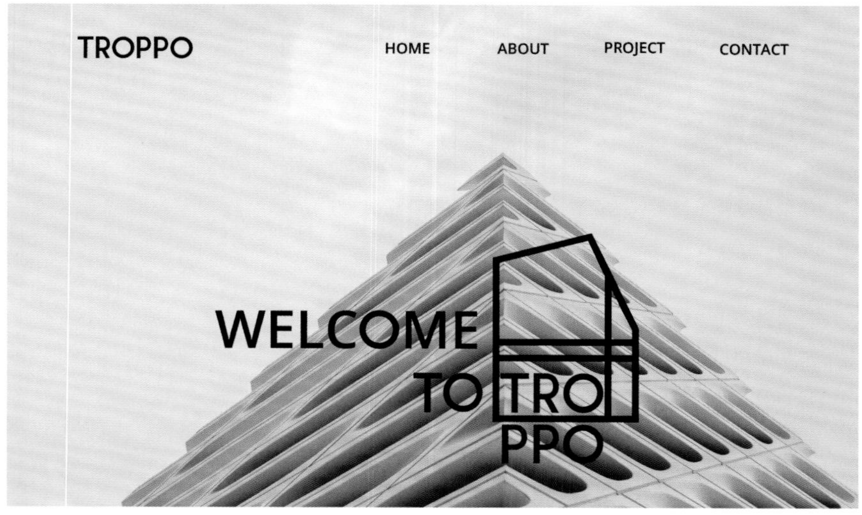

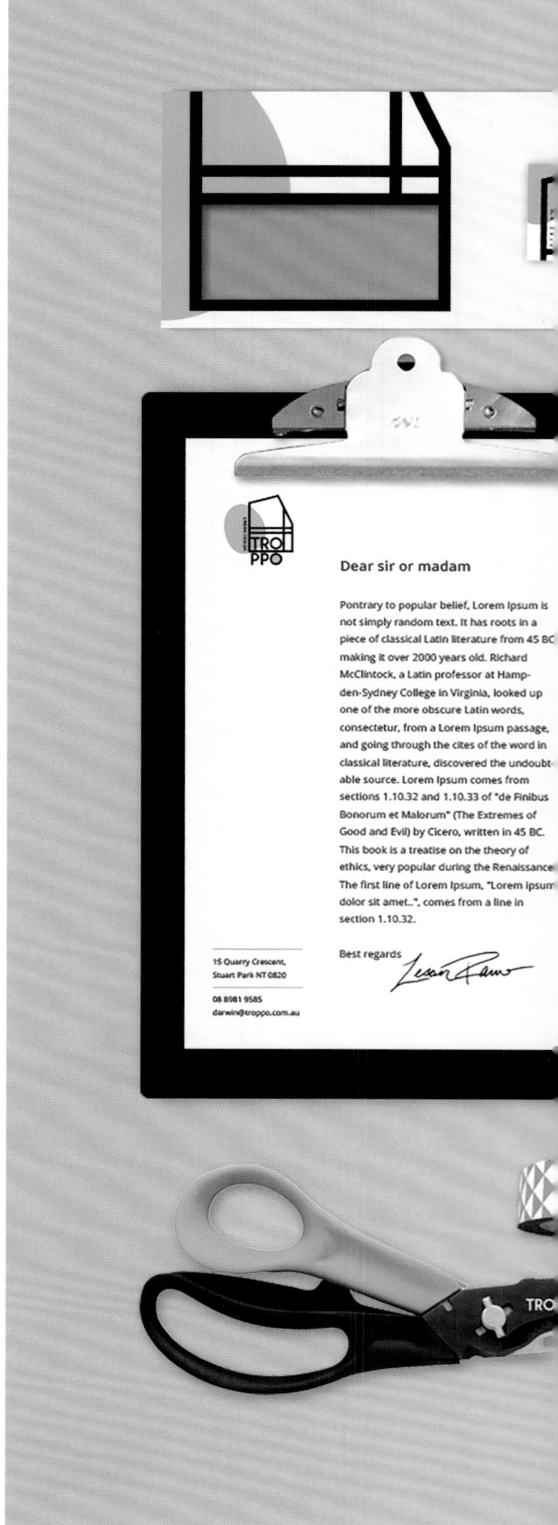

TRO
PPO
INTERIORS
TRO
PPO
TROPPO
TROPPO
TROPPO
TROPPO
TRO
PPO
TROPPO
HOME
ABOUT
PROJECT
CONTACT
WELCOME
TO TRO
PPO
URBAN DESIGN
TRO
PPO
INTERIORS
TRO
PPO

Techwave

Agency: *Enhanced Inc.*
Design: *Hiromi Maeo*

Techwave is a Japanese new website which connects people and the community to an enterprise and works to bring innovation to the consciousness of people and the way of society by managing an event, developing a new business, and focusing on a variety of channels while concentrating on delivering technology related news all over the world. Since the revitalization of the economy in Japan, they perform cooperating with a real capable innovator and aim to be an ultimate owned media which supports them.

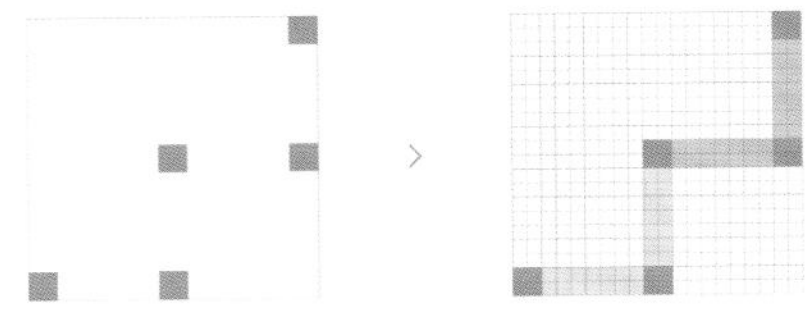

Hidden letter "T"

Technology to support the consciousness innovation of people from an invisible part

Letter "W"

The wave of information that TECHWAVE media handles.

Growth chart

Economic revitalization, Transfer to the new stage

Partnership

People, Community, Enterprise, Writers guild, and Imaginia network

Accumulation

Accumulation of small uniqueness

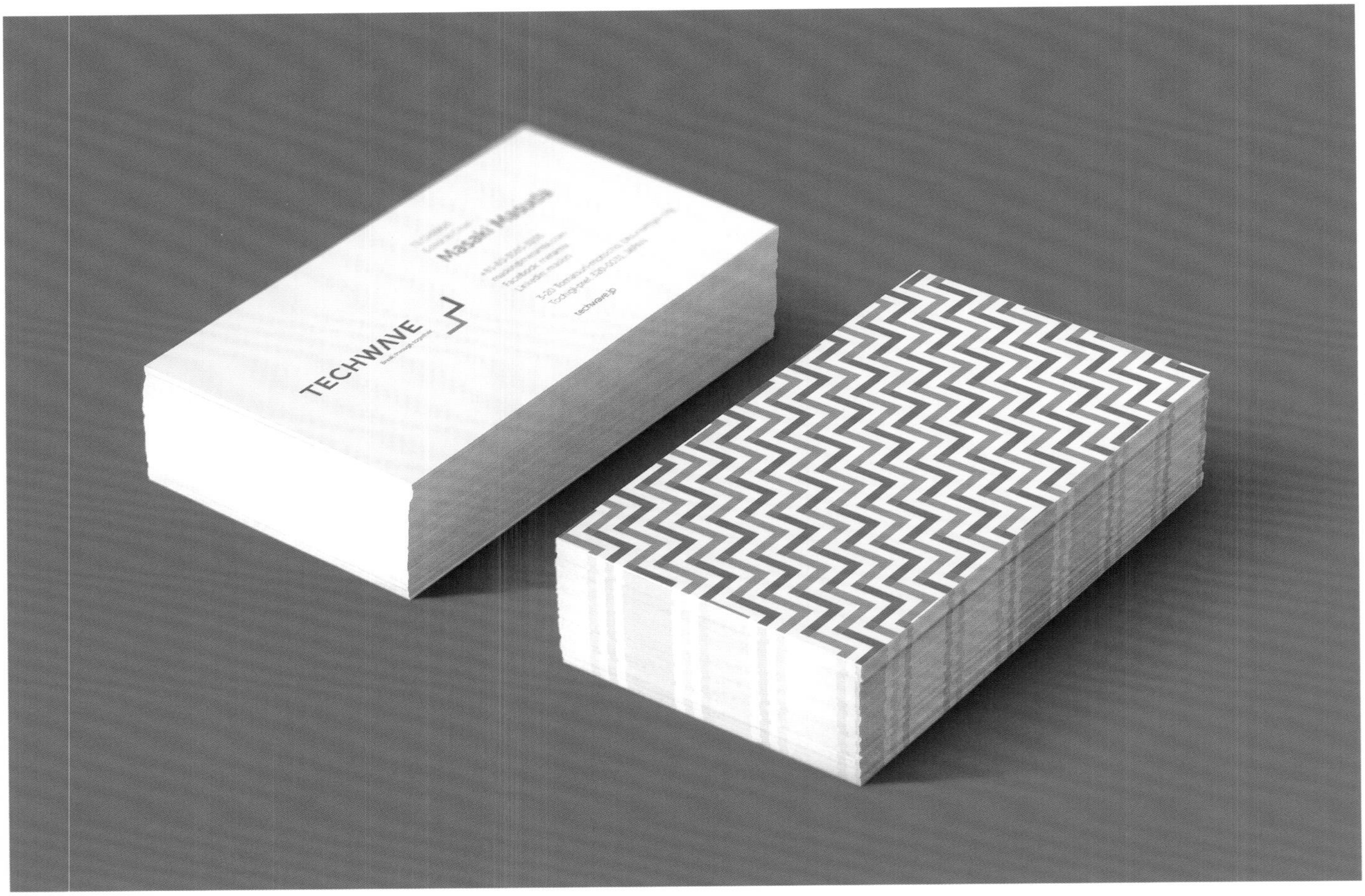

BMA Estates

Design: *JB Studio*

Identity developed for newly formed lettings and estate agents BMA Estates. The logo makes use of a conveniently positioned letter "E", which provides an opportunity to incorporate a simple graphic synonymous with property. The key device can be used in isolation or as part of a word mark and features on all applications, including brochures, stationery, advertising, signage, sale boards, umbrellas, and even the company cars.

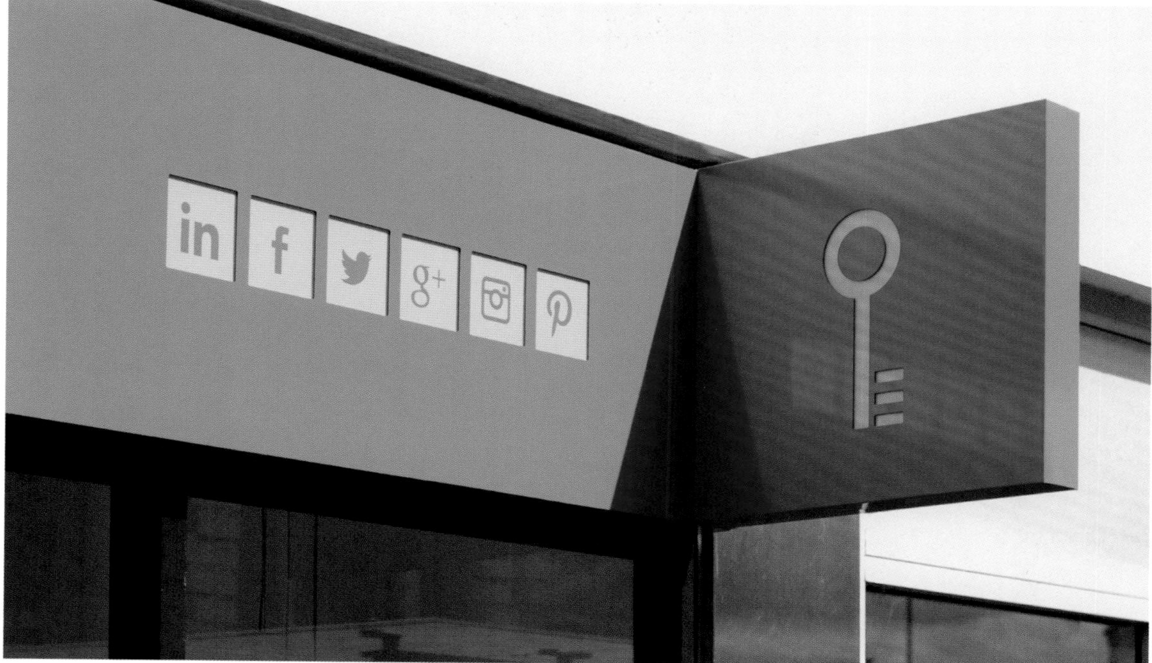

MOK

Design: *Matthias Deckx*
Photography: *Michiel Stegen*

MOK Specialty Coffee Roastery & Bar is a fast growing specialty coffee roastery and is now one of the leading micro roasters in Belgium. Matthias designed a refreshing new look for the brand, from logo and typography to choosing the right materials for the new packaging.

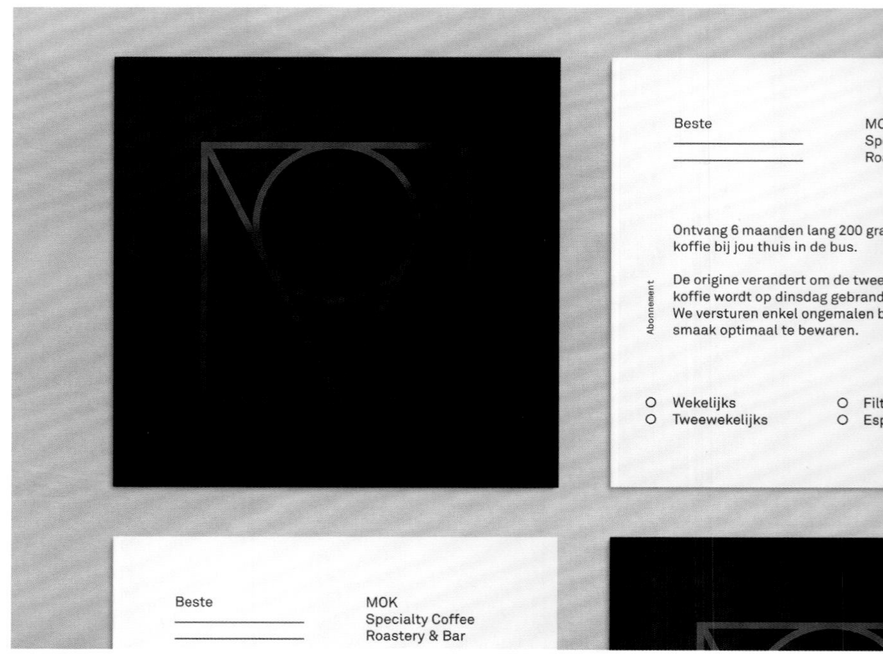

Rich Kid
Blend
Espresso blend
Process: Semi-washed
Variety: Heirloom
Tasting notes: Fruity with slight sugary notes of caramel, dark chocolate and the sweetness of cassis.
Roast date:
MOK
Specialty Coffee
Roastery & Bar
Pour Boy
Blend
Filter blend
Process: Natural & dried
Variety: Mixed heirloom
Tasting notes: Delicate peach tea acidity and slightly fruity with a touch of citrus.
Roast date:
MOK
Specialty Coffee
Roastery & Bar
Deca
Blend
Omni blend
Process: Pulped natural
Variety: Mixed heirloom
Tasting notes: Delicate peach tea acidity and slightly fruity with a touch of citrus.
Roast date:
MOK
Specialty Coffee
Roastery & Bar

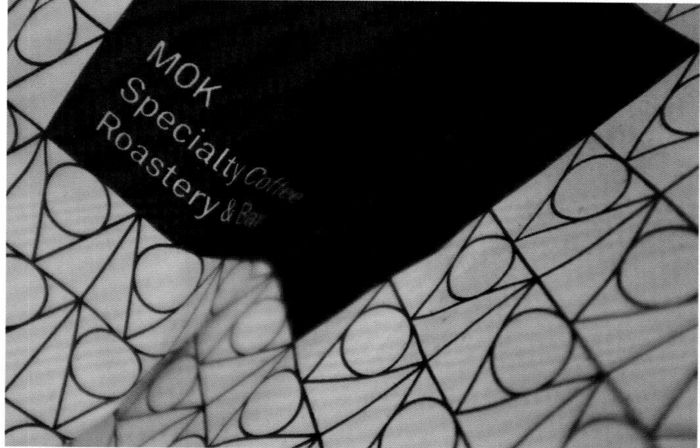
MOK
Specialty Coffee
Roastery & Bar

MOK
Specialty Coffee
Roastery & Bar

Targi Rzeczy Ladnych

Design: *Paprotnik Studio*

Branding for Warsaw design fairs – Pretty Things Fair. The Fairs support young brands by creating a space where designers can exchange ideas and opinions with visitors and buyers. The designers created a coherent system of visual identification, which works on different media and space in a public area. The designers chose simple geometrical shapes to divide different fairs section of sellers and participants.

Trinitat Special Edition

***Design:** Yuta Takahashi*

Yuta Takahashi designed the "Trinitat / Vol.1 and Vol.2 Special Edition" written by Michael Debus. The book design as a whole has an impact that intersects contrast, modern, and minimal impressions.

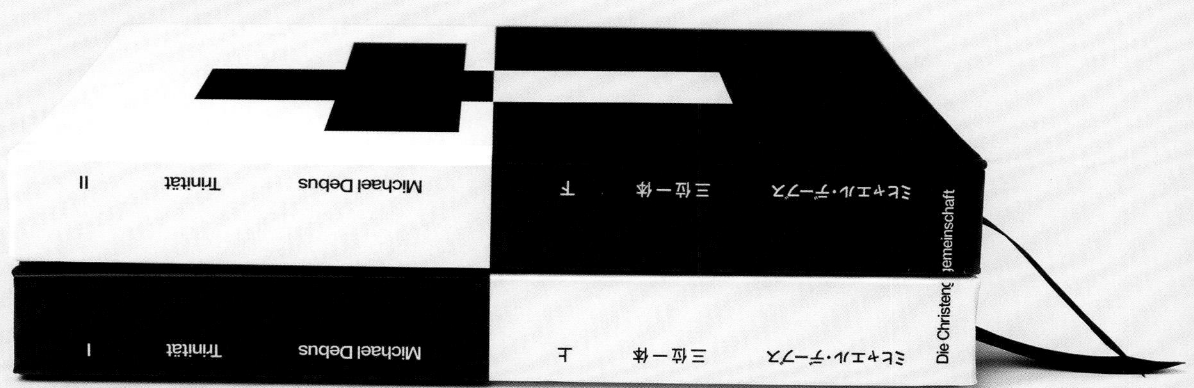

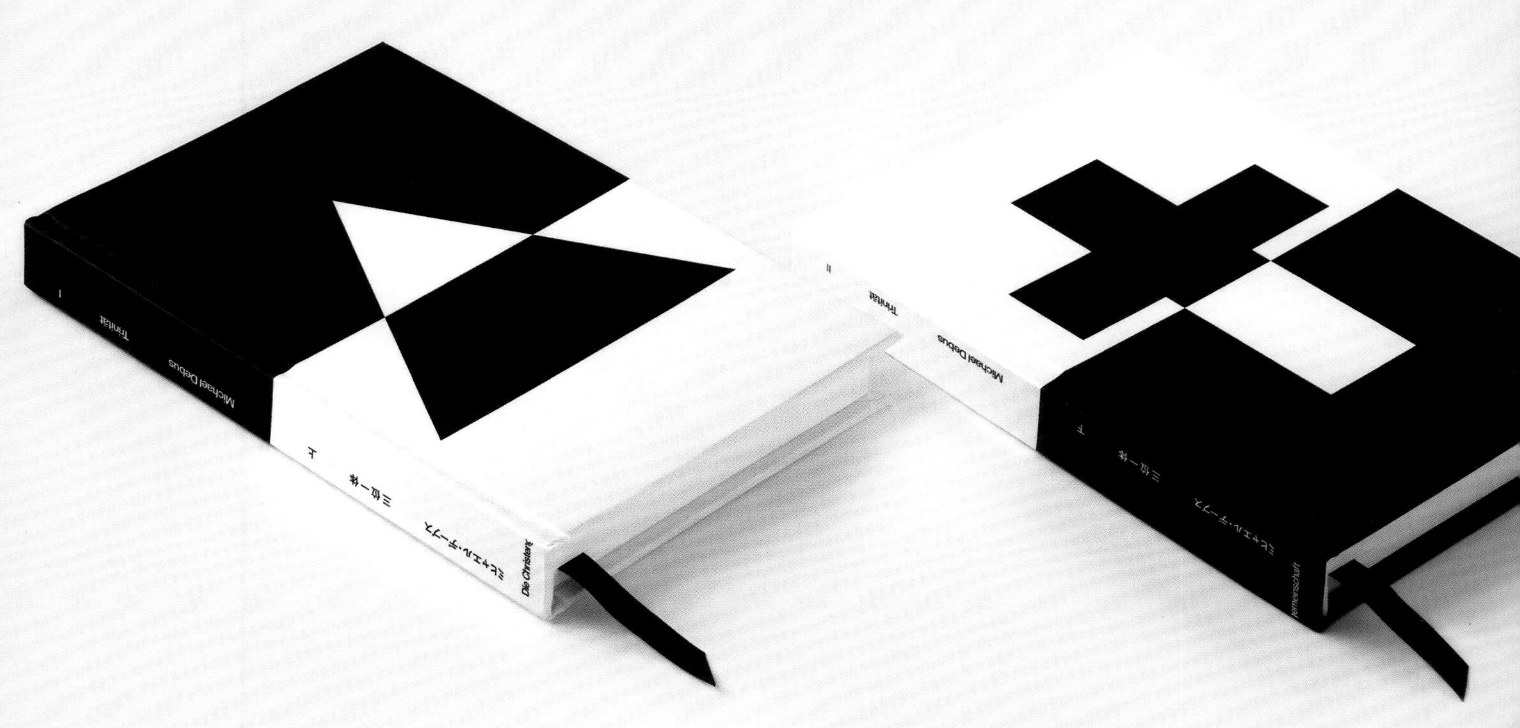

Intelectuall Property Center of Georgia

Agency: *Windfor's Communication*
Design: *Zakharia Mesropov, Ruslan Beridze*

The designers recognized the clear difference between Copyright, Trade Marks, Design, New Breeds, and Geographical Indications – very distinct, but equally valuable units run by IP agency along with Patents. The designers went on to study the daily working process of the agency in 6 units – analyzing what came in and how it got processed. The designers saw IP experts working their magic with sketches, formulas, computer codes, blocks of text, musical notes, etc. The graphic mark is based on the simple forms, which shapes inspiration. The symbol becomes the central element of branding – unifying distinct fields of Intellectual Property.

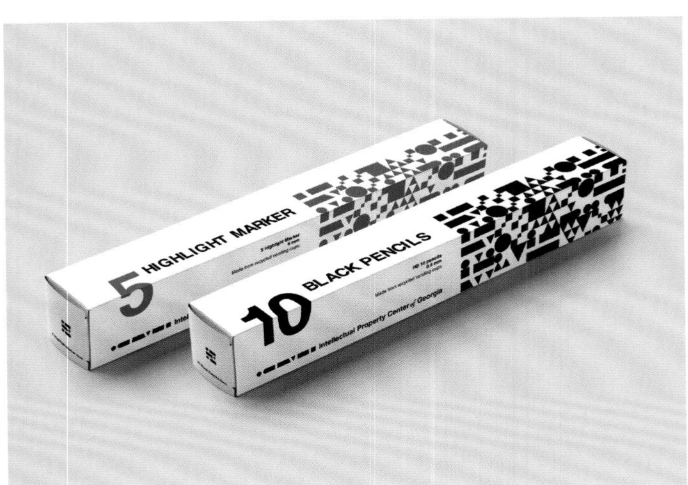

Intellectual Property Center of Georgia
Intellectual
Property
Center of Georgia
Dimitri Vachnadze
Project manager

Trademark Dept.
Intellectual
Property
Center of Georgia
Intellectual
property
center of Georgia.
Intellectual
property
center of Georgia.

National Audiovisual Institute

Agency: *UVMW*
Creative Direction: *Jacek Walesiak, Robert Mendel*
Design: *Jacek Walesiak, Robert Mendel, Darius Chapuis*

After a stage of analyses and consultations with a large group of The National Audiovisual Institute(NInA) managers brought the designers to a conclusion that the NInA sign had to be changed, to keep it working as the overriding logotype of the whole Institute. The designers changed the sign to a circle with an embedded triangle, symbolizing the "play" button and at the same time being a "call to action" assigned not only like a tag to the logotypes of various projects, but also to the whole new identification based on a modular net assuming the use of circles and triangles a building blocks of all possible graphic messages to tell about NInA's activity.

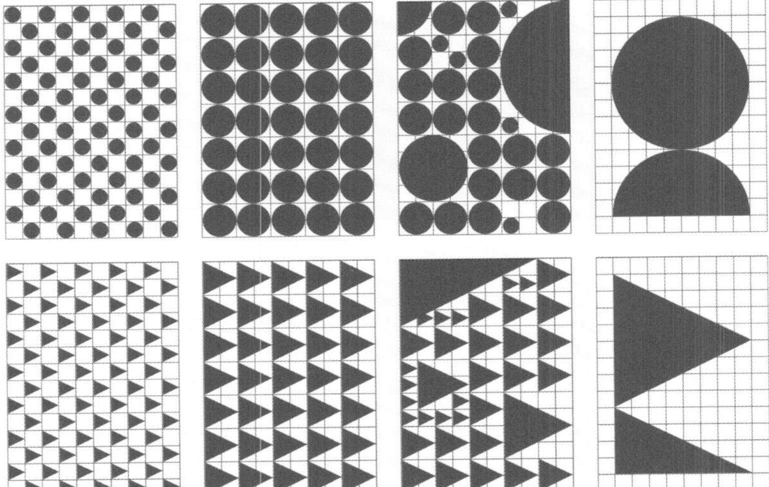

NARODOWY
INSTYTUT
AUDIOWIZUALNY
NInA

L.Dz........... | NInA | 2014

20.11.2014, Warszawa

Pani / Pan
Imię i Nazwisko
Nazwa Stanowiska

Szanowny Panie,

Lorem ipsum dolor sit amet, consectetur adipiscing elit. Aenean euismod elit urna, eu semper neque eleifend vel. Suspendisse sed purus eu mi interdum aliquam. Suspendisse quis nunc accumsan, efficitur eros varius, scelerisque purus. Praesent augue urna, porttitor vehicula lacus quis, blandit sagittis ipsum. Nunc quam massa, viverra nec consectetur non, ultricies nec nibh. Donec tincidunt mauris gravida, elementum turpis luctus, viverra sapien. Duis eget vulputate nibh. Aliquam erat volutpat. Nullam porta sagittis neque auctor egestas. Duis sed egestas turpis. Suspendisse tincidunt consectetur tellus, ultricies semper ipsum posuere ut. Aliquam consequat cursus quam tempus maximus. Fusce mattis consequat finibus.

Aenean ac orci mollis, sagittis elit a, sagittis lorem. Sed nec augue in arcu venenatis tempor nec id felis. Sed efficitur lectus at fermentum tristique. Cras vel nisl sollicitudin, condimentum lectus et, euismod massa. Pellentesque id tortor maximus, auctor nisl nec, porta quam. Quisque sed justo ut lectus finibus luctus. Aenean quis sapien et justo porttitor scelerisque at sit amet nunc.

Mauris vitae dictum lectus. Pellentesque pellentesque elit eu leo ullamcorper cursus. Nullam urna eros, vehicula vel vehicula mattis, ullamcorper ut nunc. Nam bibendum, sapien eget euismod ultrices, sem lacus feugiat tellus, non sollicitudin dui nulla vitae orci. Nam malesuada orci mi, non vehicula magna fringilla nec. Morbi rhoncus volutpat placerat. Praesent vitae lectus ante. Suspendisse vel nisl vehicula, rutrum turpis ac, fringilla mauris. Aenean ac orci mollis, sagittis elit a, sagittis lorem. Nam malesuada orci mi, non vehicula magna fringilla nec. Morbi rhoncus volutpat placerat. Praesent vitae lectus ante. Suspendisse vel nisl vehicula, rutrum turpis ac, fringilla mauris.

Z wyrazami szacunku
Imię i Nazwisko
Nazwa Stanowiska

Narodowy Instytut Audiowizualny
ul. Wałbrzyska 3/5 | 02-739 Warszawa | t: +48 22 380 49 00 | f: +48 22 380 49 01 | sekretariat@nina.gov.pl | NIP 525-234-20-56

Sztuka przynosi nam dowód, że istnieje coś innego niż nicość.
NInA

NARODOWY
INSTYTUT
AUDIOWIZUALNY
NInA

Narodowy Instytut Audiowizualny
National Audiovisual Institute
ul. Wałbrzyska 3/5 | 02-739 Warszawa
t: +48 22 380 49 00 | f: +48 22 380 49 01
NIP 525-234-20-56

Letni cykl
filmowy o sztuce
NInA
Zapraszamy serdecznie!
www.nina.gov.pl
NARODOWY
INSTYTUT
AUDIOWIZUALNY
NInA

NARODOWY
INSTYTUT
AUDIOWIZUALNY
NInA
Filmy drogi

Letni cykl muzyczny:
Nowe brzmienia

Creativita

Design: *Lemongraphic*

Creativita is a design studio based in the Kingdom of Bahrain. This brand identity was created based on the combination of pixels and multiple colors.

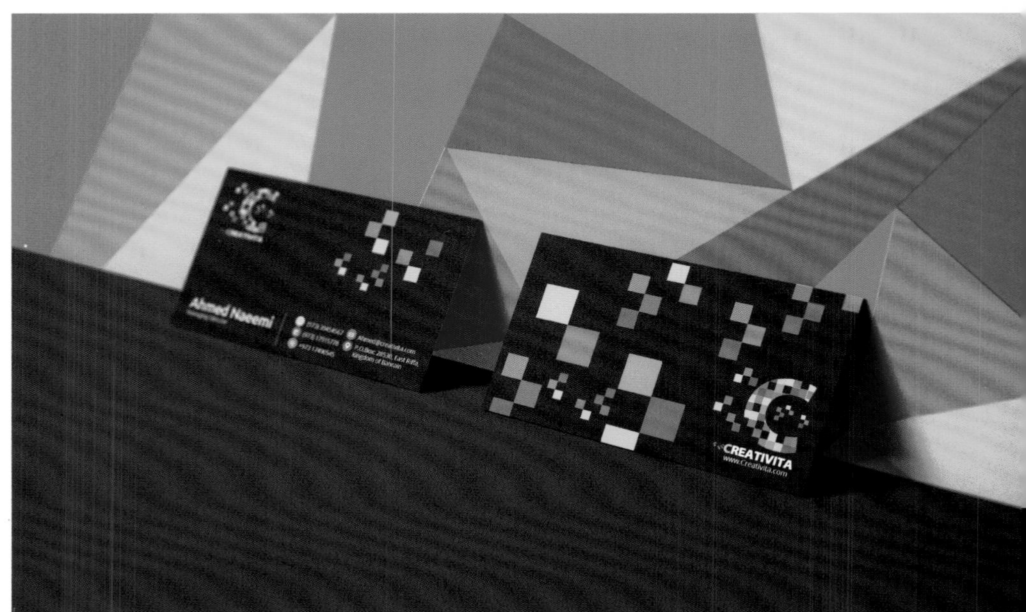

CREATIVITY
IS A DRUG
THAT
DESIGNER
CAN'T
LIVE
WITHOUT

CREATIVITA

Summer Business Cards

Design: *Maxime Archambault*

Summer Business Cards is an exploration into shape and color. It has 24 different backgrounds that can be assembled like a puzzle. The cards are handmade using screen printing and spray cans for the side. Each future client deserves special attention and unique visual solution; this is what this work tries to illustrate.

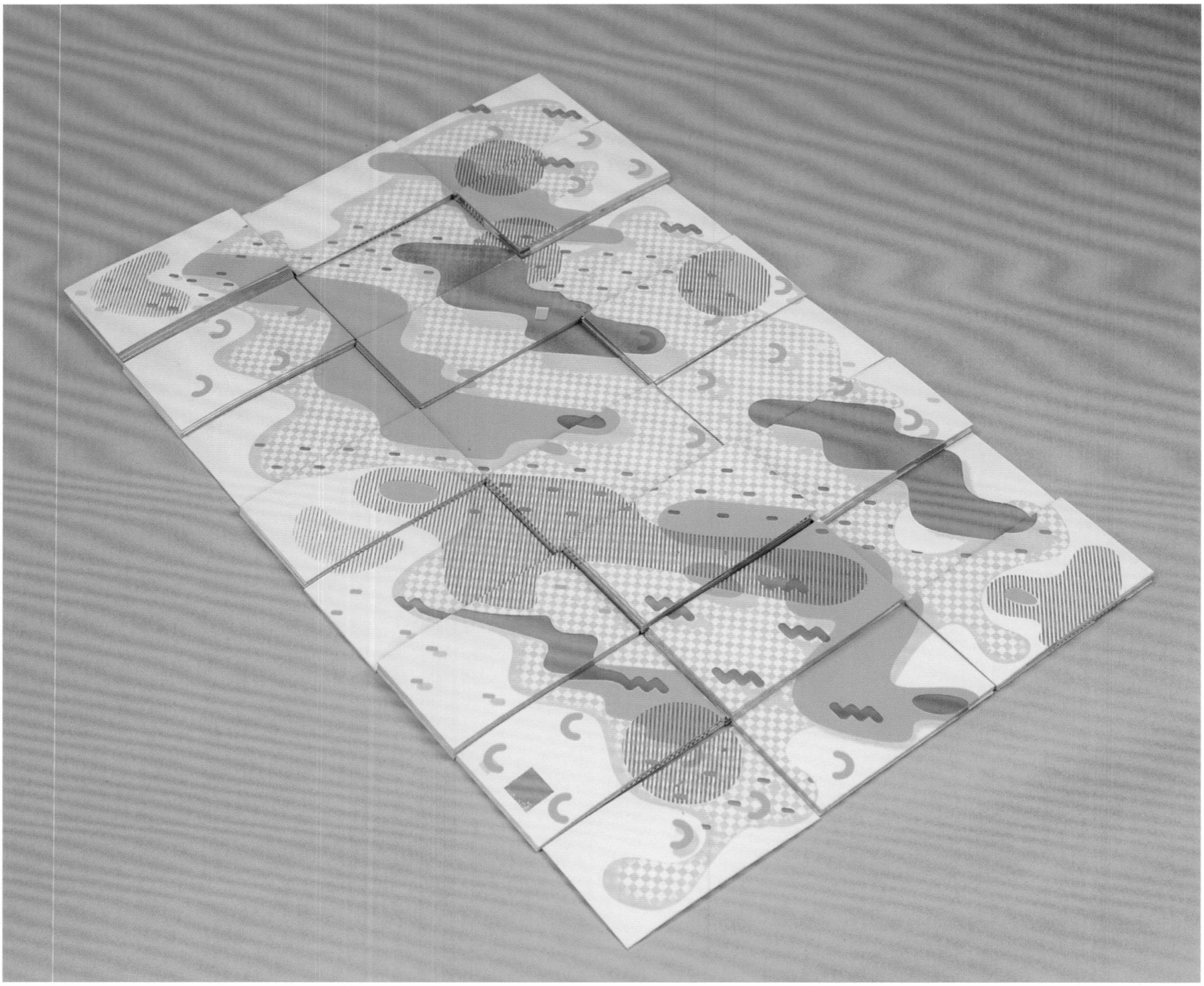

Three Dimensions

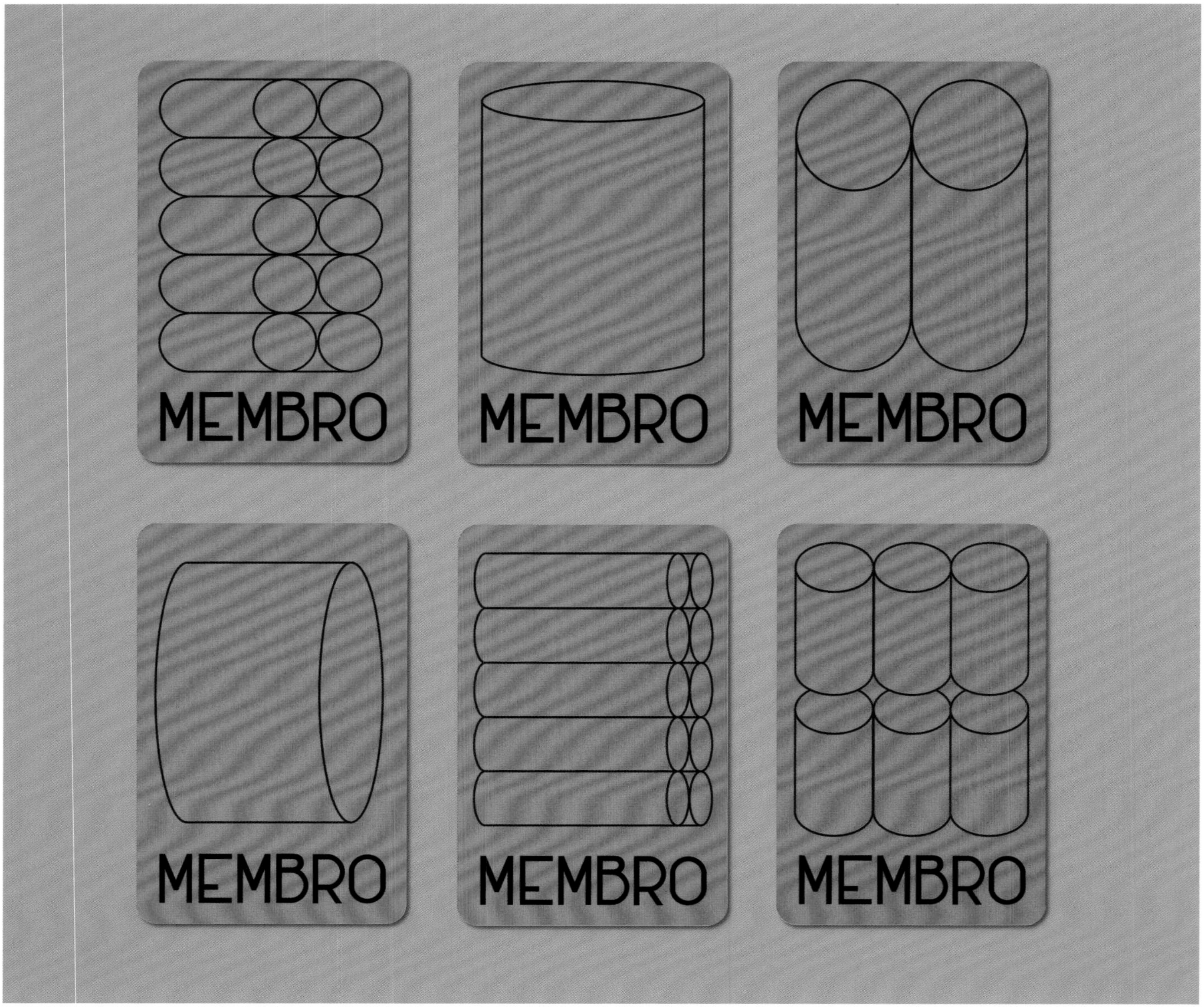

Panificadora

Agency: *Yarza Twins*
Design: *Eva Yarza, Marta Yarza*

Panificadora was meant to be demolished to construct a new neighborhood of luxury flats. Inspired by the rehabilitation of TATE Modern in London and Matadero in Madrid, the designers decided to stop the demolition and to promote the creation of a space for culture and arts in our hometown, Vigo.

Panificadora is an old bread factory based in one of the main streets of Vigo, Spain, despite being in ruins for over 20 years, it is still considered the most important architectural legacy in the city.

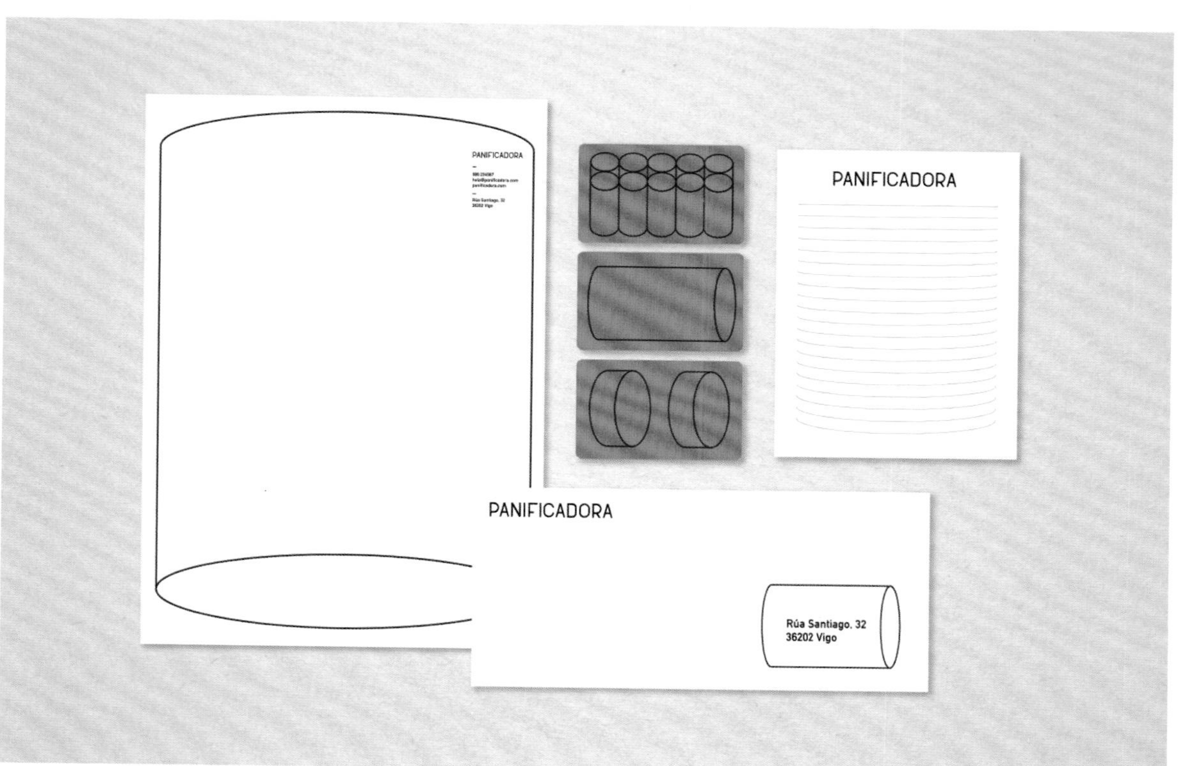
PANIFICADORA
PANIFICADORA
PANIFICADORA
Rúa Santiago, 32
36202 Vigo

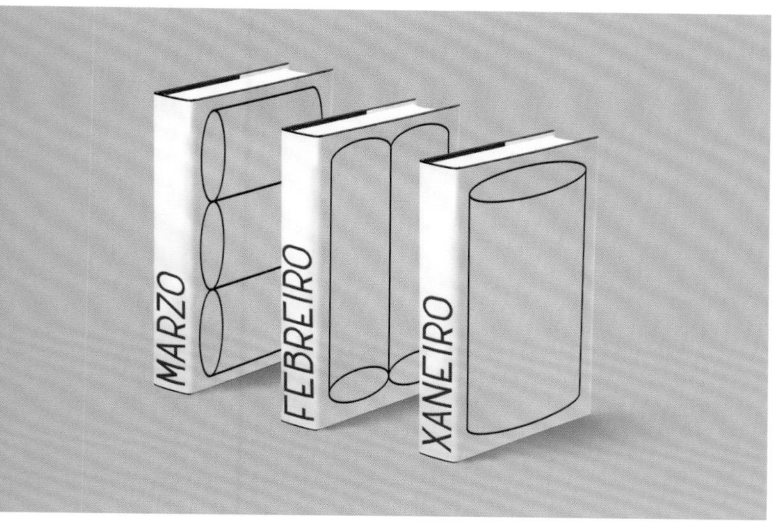
MARZO
FEBREIRO
XANEIRO

CLAUDIA MATE
LUIS SEOANE
30.01.15 – 28.02.15
Acceso pola porta principal
MAURIZIO CATTELAN
30.01.15 – 28.02.15
Acceso pola porta principal
LOLA DUPRE
30.01.15 – 28.02.15
Acceso pola porta principal
IAGO EIROS
30.01.15 – 28.02.15
Acceso pola porta principal
CASTELAO
30.01.15 – 28.02.15
Acceso pola porta principal
ZHANG XIAOGANG
30.01.15 – 28.02.15
Acceso pola porta principal
OLEG DOU
30.01.15 – 28.02.15
Acceso pola porta principal
YARZA TWINS
30.01.15 – 28.02.15
Acceso pola porta principal

O SORRISO ESQUECIDO
PANIFICADORA
OLEG DOU

Architecture Festival

Design: *Apolline Robert, Allen O'toole*

"Architecture Festival" is a festival dedicated exclusively to contemporary architecture of the 2000s. The concept behind the logo was to create a visual object that could be adapted to both printed and digital media. The dotted lines recall the construction lines of an architectural building. The pictogram in the middle represents a 3D volume and embodies the identity of the festival of architecture. The logo frames the visual space of all the proposed formats. May the format be long, high, small or wide, the logo always shows its adaptability.

ar
ch
it
ec
tu
re
fe
st
iv
al.
20
15

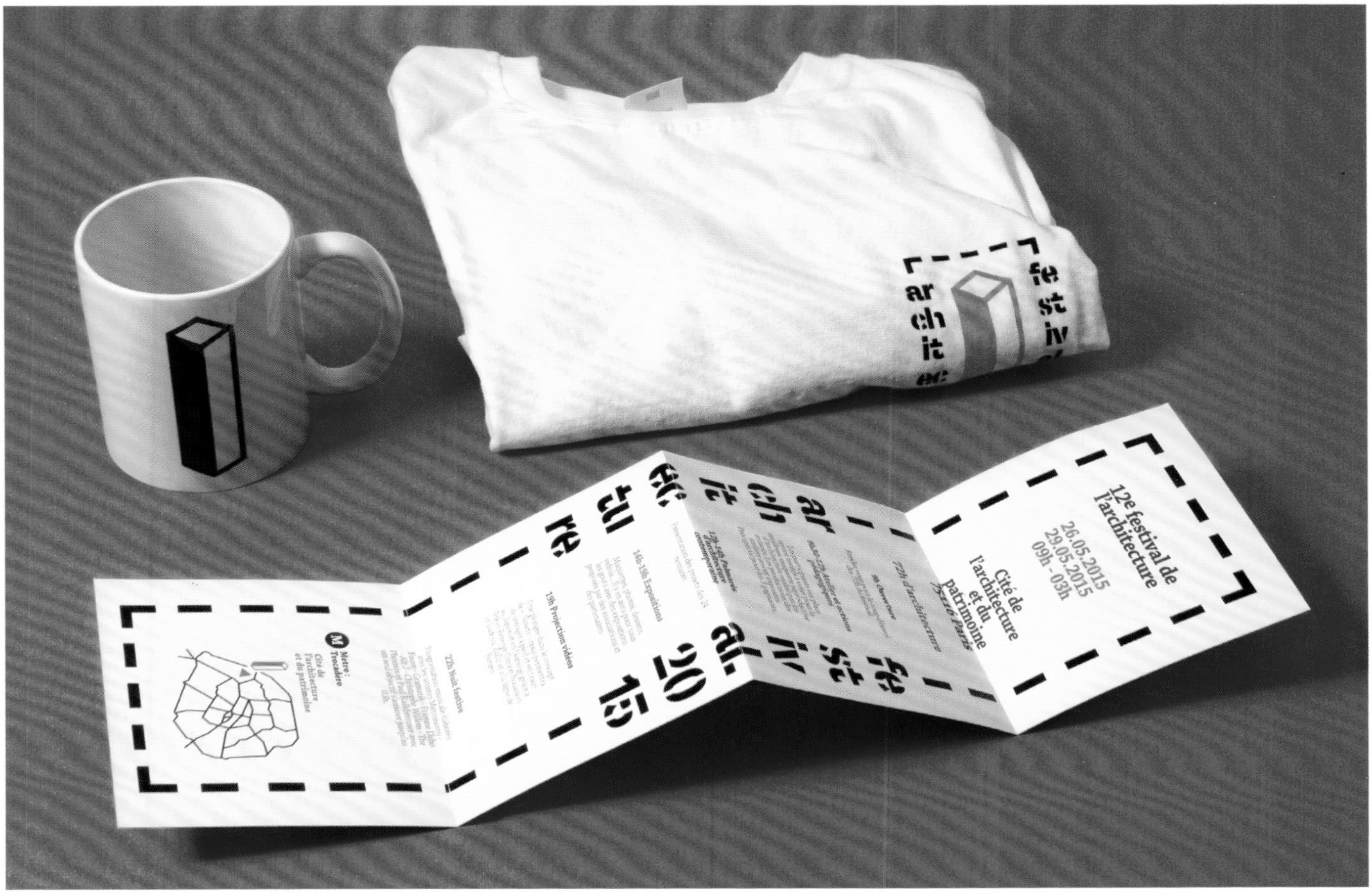
12e festival de
l'architecture
26.05.2015
29.05.2015
09h - 03h
Cité de
l'architecture
et du
patrimoine
ar
ch
it
ec
tu
re
fe
st
iv
al.
20
15

Andrea Sopranzi – Personal Branding

Design: *Andrea Sopranzi*

Geometry, minimalism and elegance. These are the keywords for the designer's personal logo, which combines a geometric construction with an A – for Andrea – written in Apercu Medium. The visual identity is colorful yet sober, clean and pleasing with a fresh and vibrant look, reflecting the designer's graphic works and aesthetic tastes.

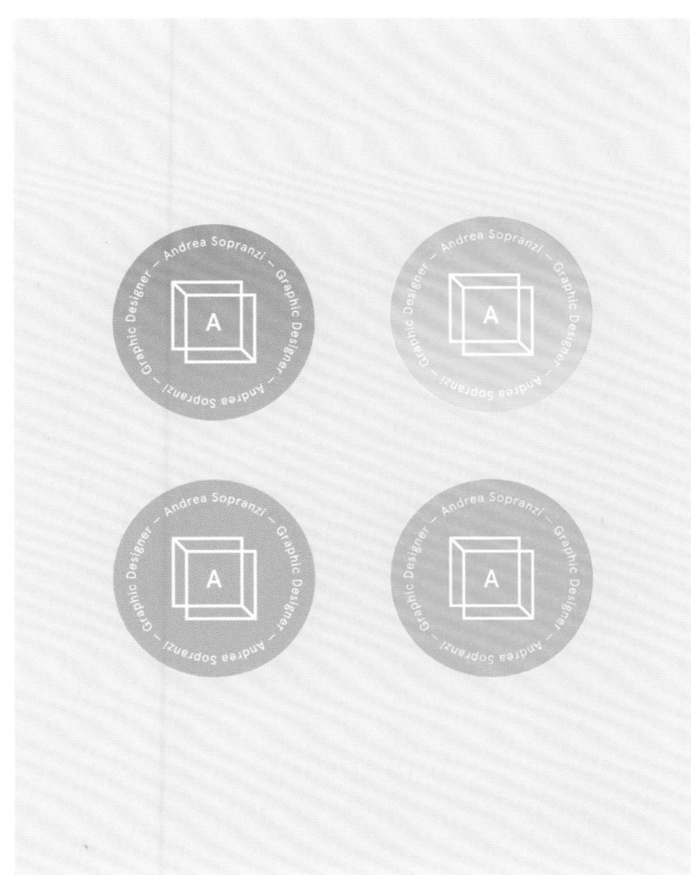
Andrea Sopranzi – Graphic Designer – Andrea Sopranzi – Graphic Designer
A
Andrea Sopranzi – Graphic Designer – Andrea Sopranzi – Graphic Designer
A
Andrea Sopranzi – Graphic Designer – Andrea Sopranzi – Graphic Designer
A
Andrea Sopranzi – Graphic Designer – Andrea Sopranzi – Graphic Designer
A

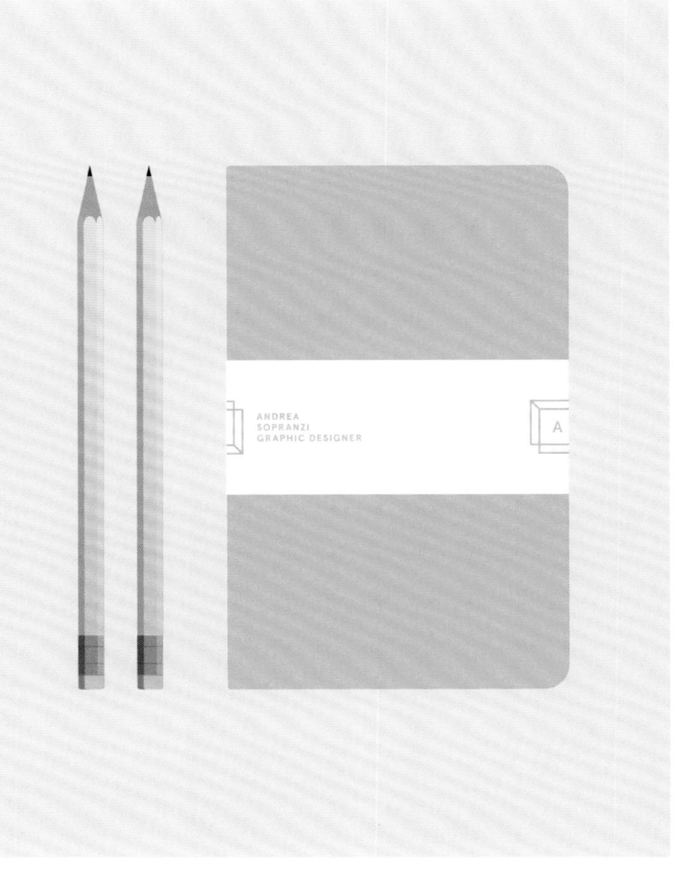
ANDREA
SOPRANZI
GRAPHIC DESIGNER
A

10 Cabinets of Magaziners Exhibition

Design: *Ray Chen*
Illustration: *Rose Lin QR*
Curation: *Rocky Liang*

This is a multi-media exhibition at The MIX-PLACE, featuring ten significant "magaziners". A bunch of talents have inspired the tendency of multi-culture, sparking the new era of creativity of magazines and print media. The design of the exhibition draws inspiration from the word "Magazine" which originates from Arabic word "makhzan", meaning the "drawer of storage". Each magazine is an independent drawer, and the "magaziner" is accordingly the one who fills up the content and pulls up the drawer. Therefore, lines and geometrical shapes were applied to the design to echo the key element of "drawers".

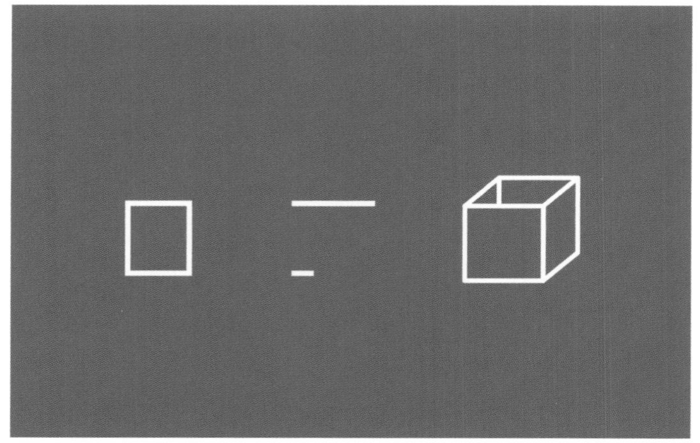

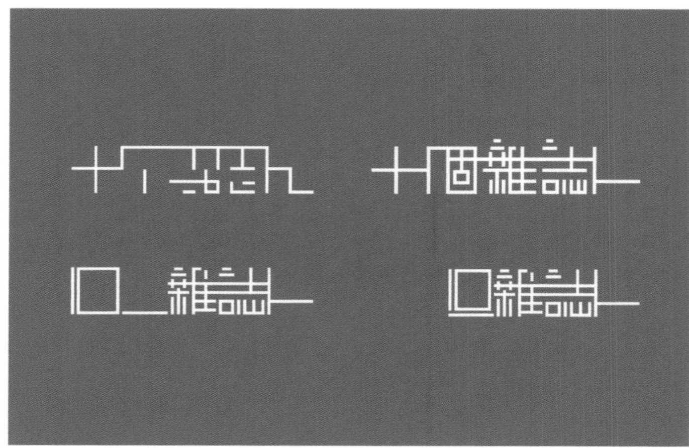

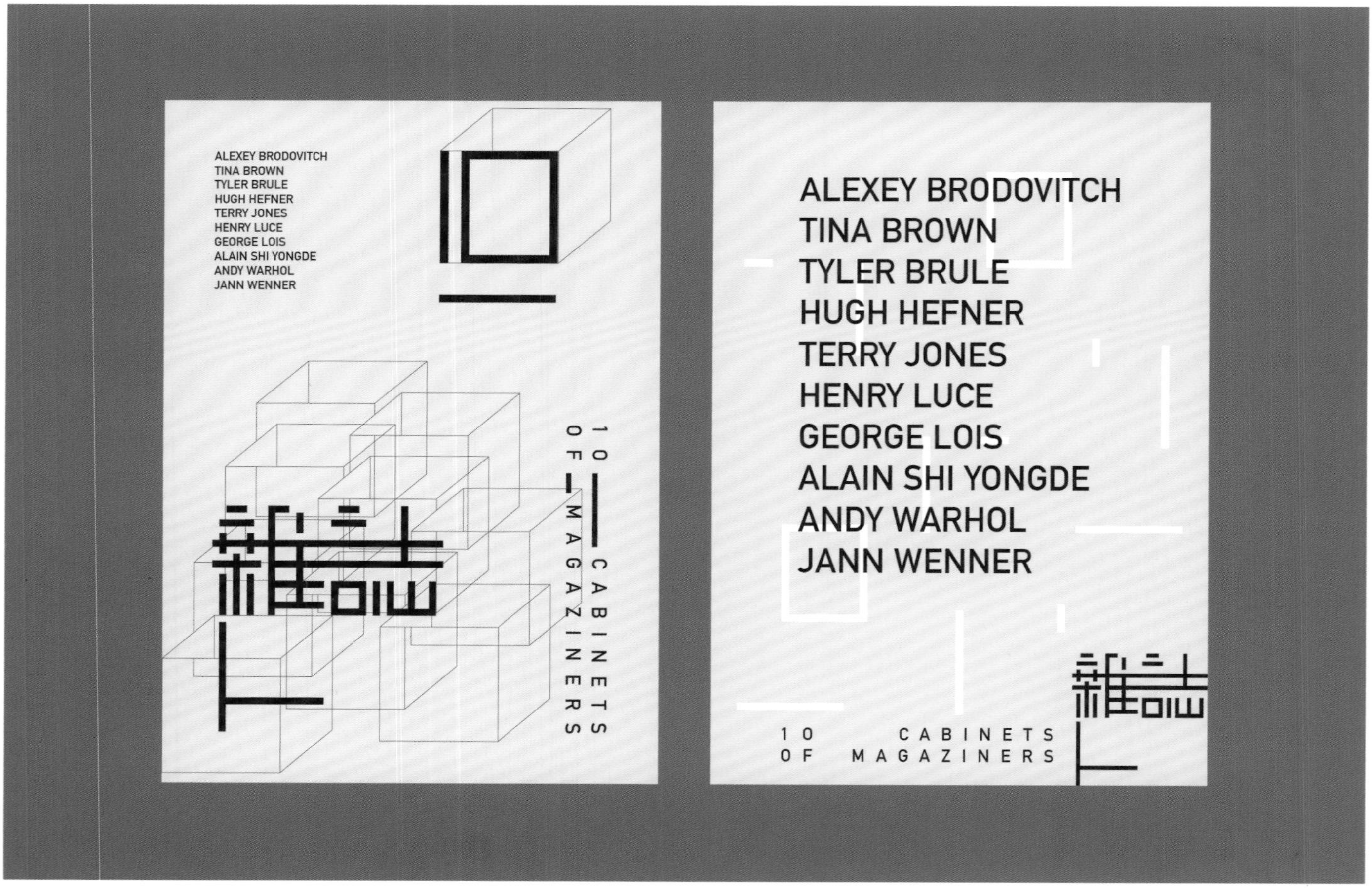

ALEXEY BRODOVITCH
TINA BROWN
TYLER BRULE
HUGH HEFNER
TERRY JONES
HENRY LUCE
GEORGE LOIS
ALAIN SHI YONGDE
ANDY WARHOL
JANN WENNER

10 CABINETS OF MAGAZINERS

ALEXEY BRODOVITCH
TINA BROWN
TYLER BRULE
HUGH HEFNER
TERRY JONES
HENRY LUCE
GEORGE LOIS
ALAIN SHI YONGDE
ANDY WARHOL
JANN WENNER

10 CABINETS OF MAGAZINERS

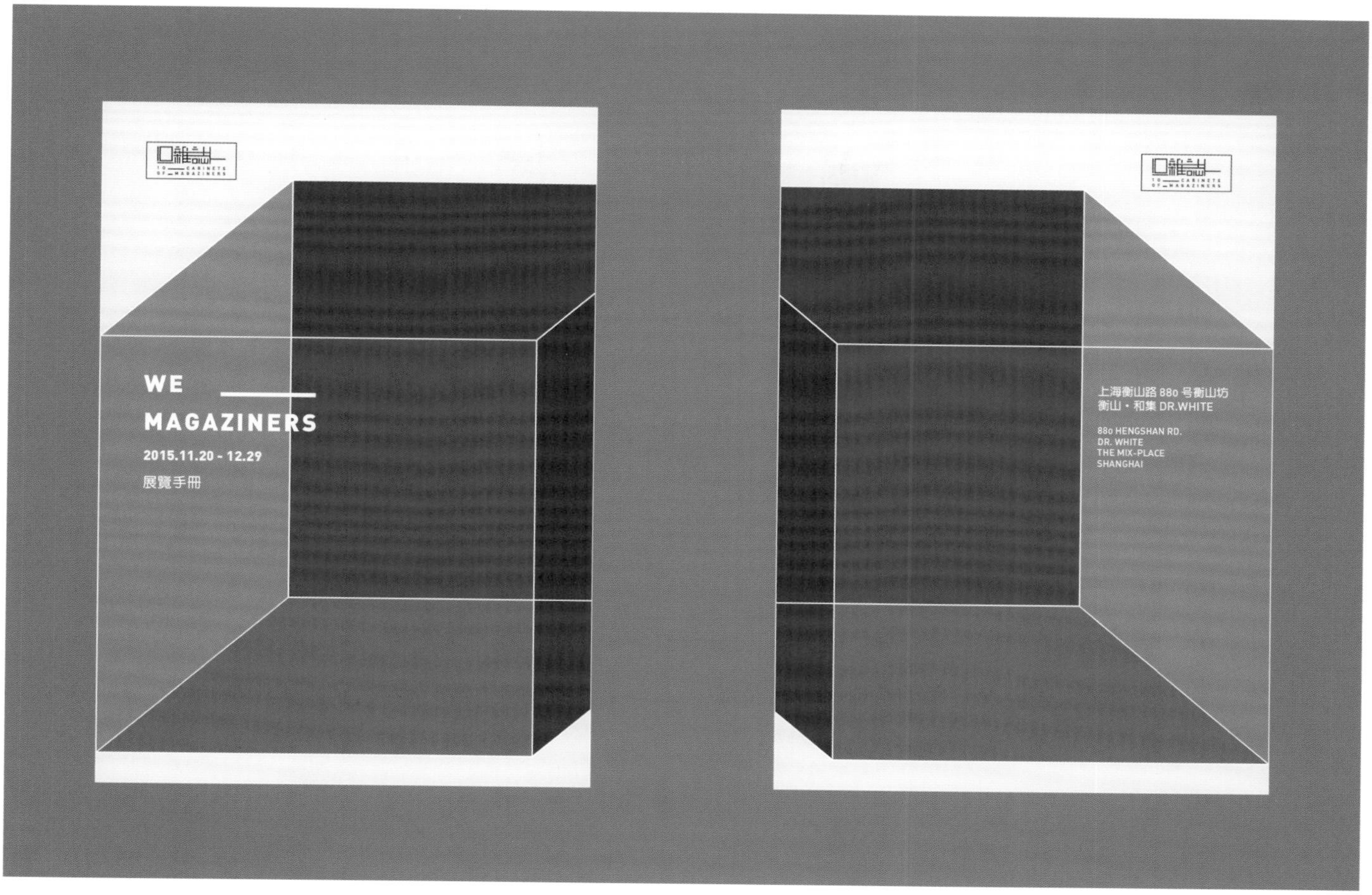

WE
MAGAZINERS
2015.11.20 - 12.29
展覽手冊

上海衡山路 880 号衡山坊
衡山・和集 DR.WHITE
880 HENGSHAN RD.
DR. WHITE
THE MIX-PLACE
SHANGHAI

10 CABINETS OF MAGAZINERS

Punter

Design: *Aleix Font*

Punter is a company that manufactures, design pieces, molds and different precision elements for different sectors of machinery. The idea of the image of the symbol is based on the courtly and intersections that the different elements produce themselves.

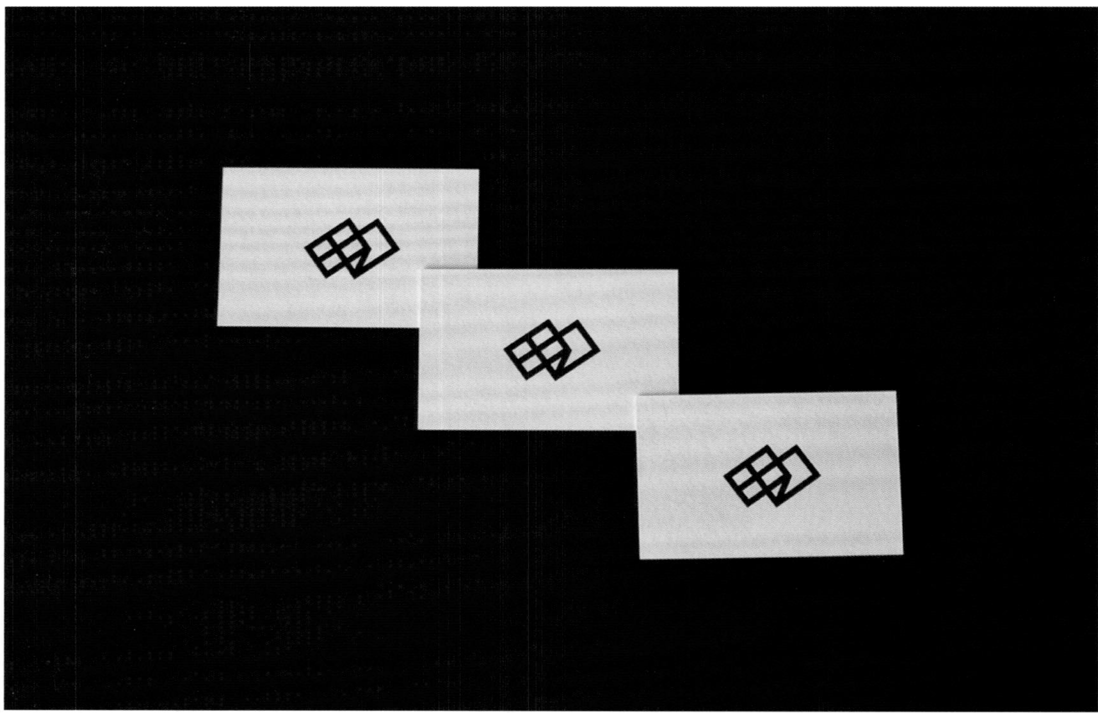

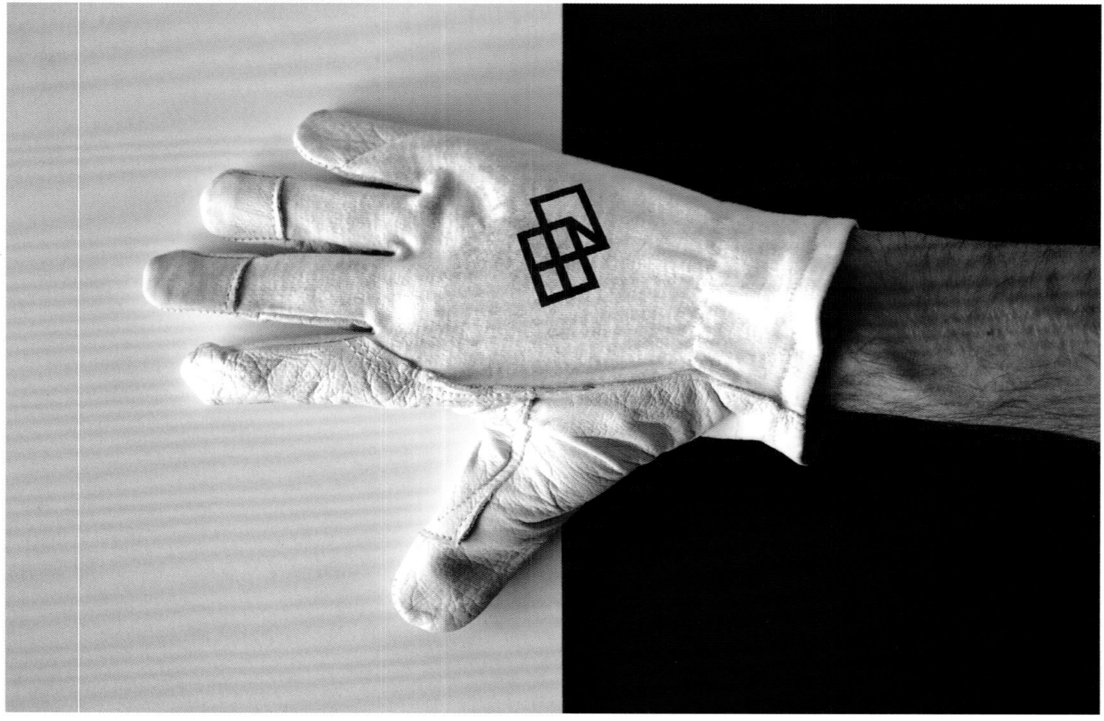

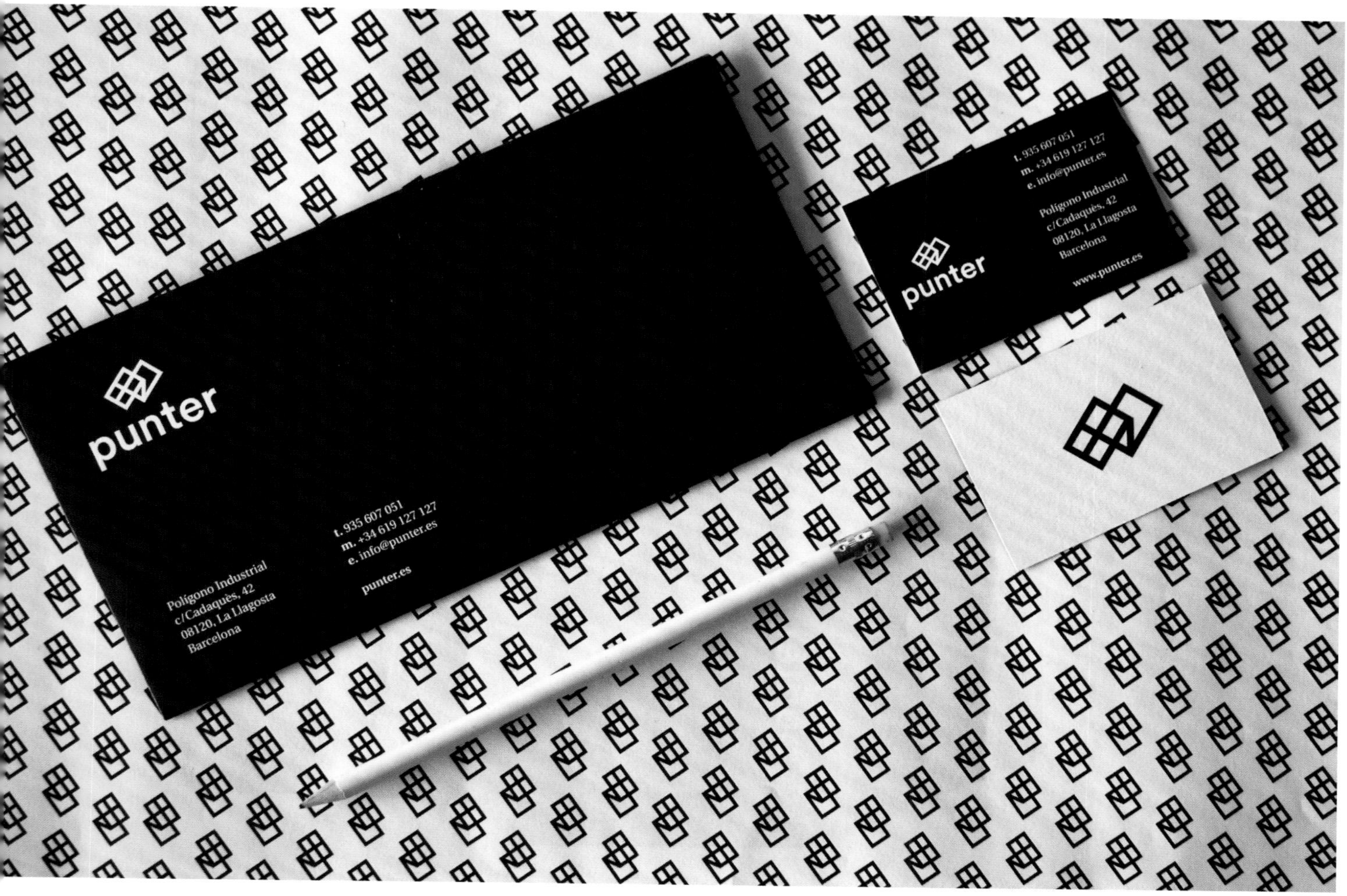

punter

Polígono Industrial
c/Cadaquès, 42
08120, La Llagosta
Barcelona

t. 935 607 051
m. +34 619 127 127
e. info@punter.es

punter.es

t. 935 607 051
m. +34 619 127 127
e. info@punter.es

Polígono Industrial
c/Cadaquès, 42
08120, La Llagosta
Barcelona

www.punter.es

punter

Antonio Rodríguez
c/Corró, 15
Granollers, 08400
Barcelona

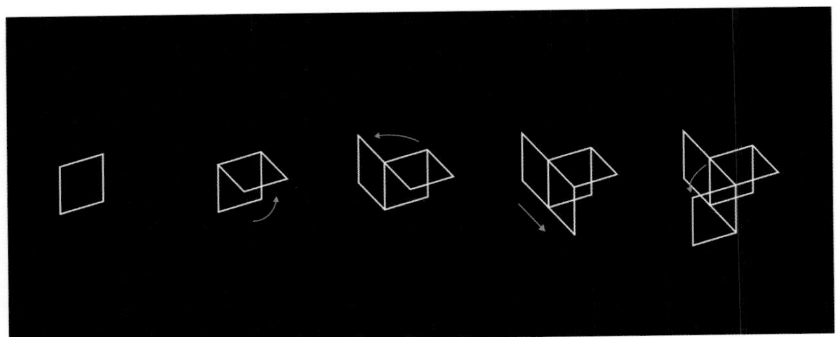

High Performance Doors

Agency: *Me Post Branding*
Design: *Eva Miguel, Mirco Colonna*
Photography: *Michael Cambpell*

Brand identity design work for High Performance Doors. The identity reflects the key principles of the brand: heritage, design, precision, technology, security and trust. The logo is based on the movements of an automatic door opening in three different ways – sliding, swinging and balancing – represented in an axonometric view.

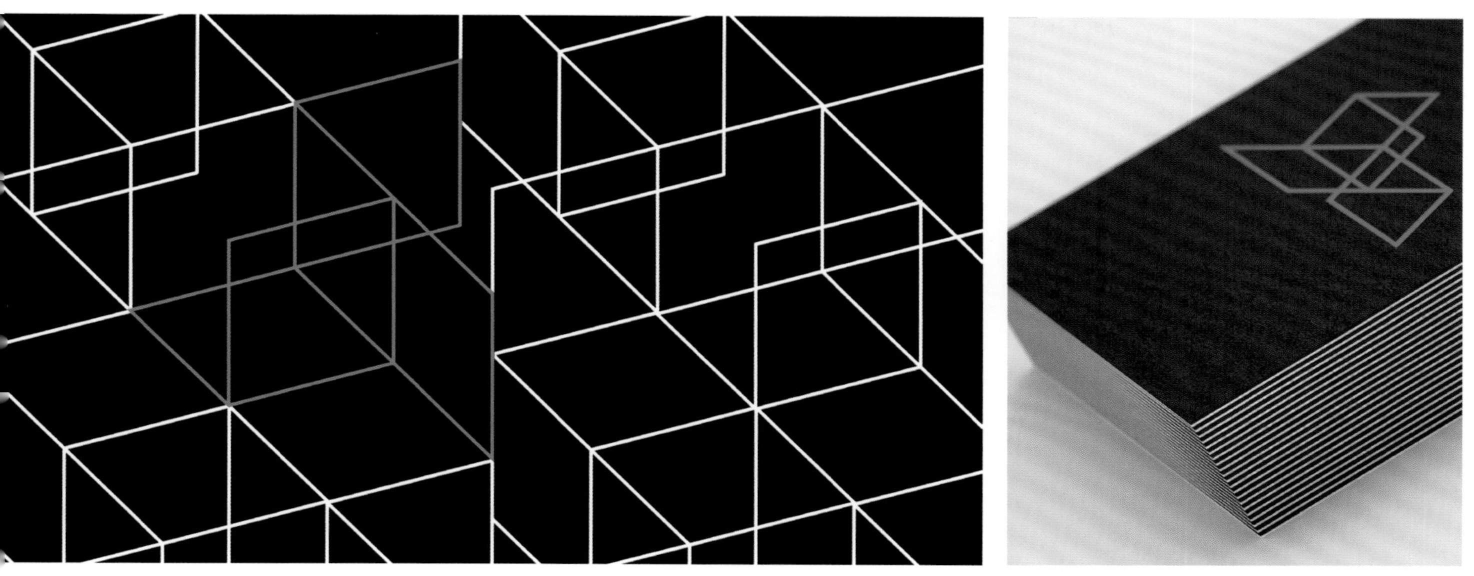

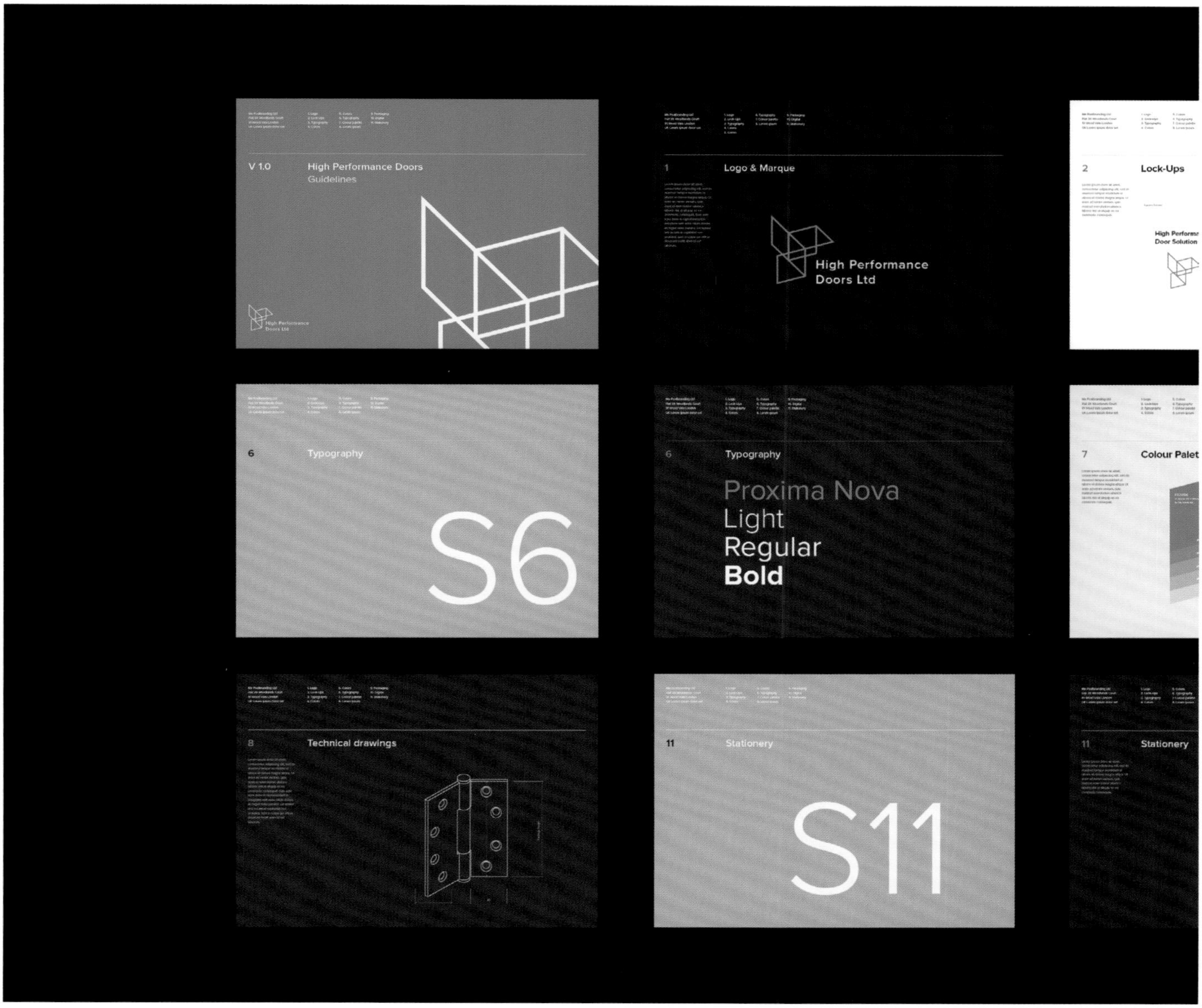

V 1.0

High Performance Doors
Guidelines

High Performance Doors Ltd

1

Logo & Marque

High Performance Doors Ltd

2

Lock-Ups

6

Typography

S6

6

Typography

Proxima Nova
Light
Regular
Bold

7

Colour Palet

8

Technical drawings

11

Stationery

S11

11

Stationery

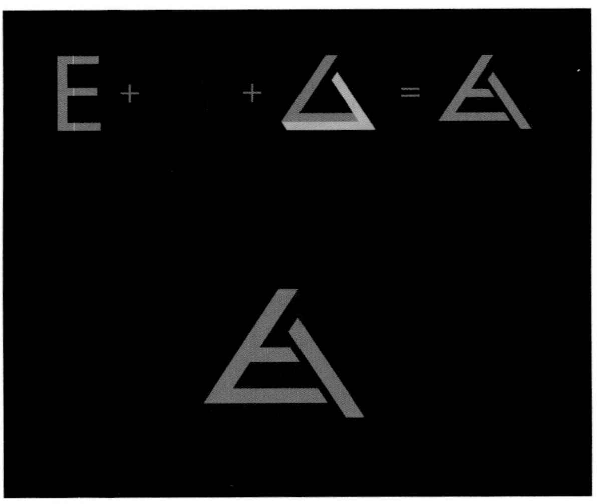

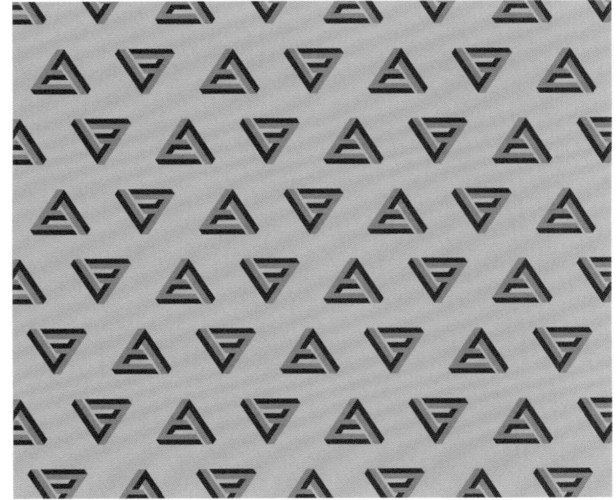

Enrica Acone's Personal Brand

Design: *Enrica Acone*

The Penrose triangle fascinates for its peculiarity of existing as a two-dimensional representation but not as a structure in the space, in spite of the strong sense of three-dimensionality that it communicates. With few changes, Enrica Acone transformed it so that its lines trace the initials of her name and still retain the charming dualistic perception of the Penrose triangle.

ENRICA ACONE

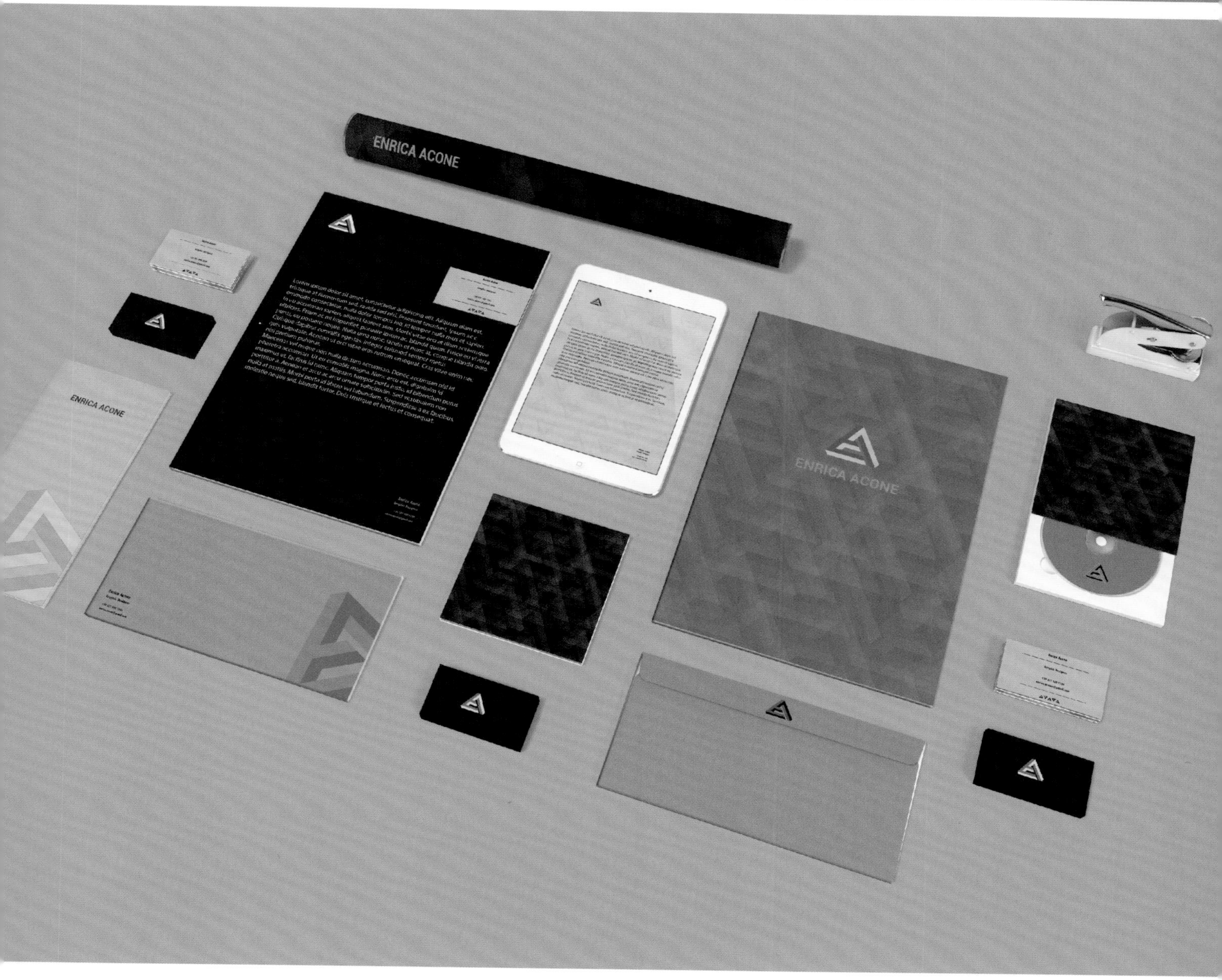

La Fête de la Science

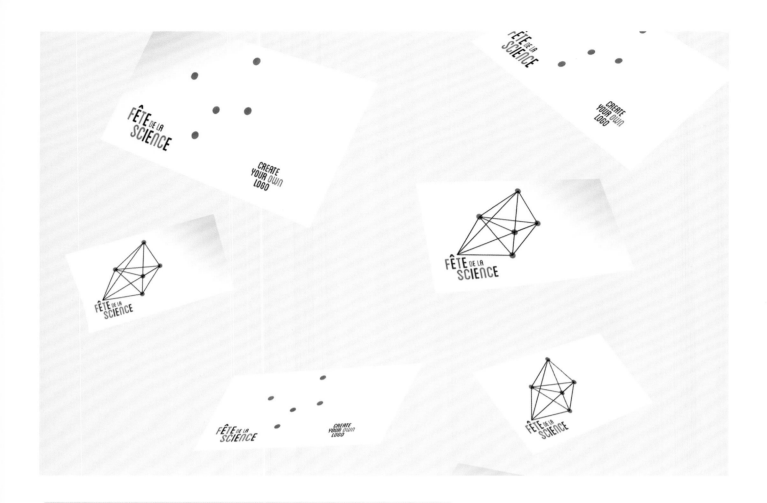

Design: *Quentin Degrange, Antoine Puyfages*
Agency: *Neon Agency*

"La Fête de la Science" is a family event about science all around France. It brings science for everyone through playful animations and stands to learn. This event offers workshop to discover science while having fun.

The theme of this event was the geometry, so the designer created five connected animated dots, which represents a network of the five domains of science: physics, biology, maths, astronomy, research.

DU 26/09
AU 4/10 2014
DE 3 À 99+ ANS,
POUR TOUS
FÊTE DE LA SCIENCE
Partout en
Rhône-Alpes
ATELIERS DE RECHERCHE
APPRENTISSAGE DE LA SCIENCE
POUR TOUT LE MONDE
www.fetedelascience.fr

DU 26/09
AU 4/10 2014
DE 3 À 99+ ANS,
POUR TOUS
FÊTE DE LA SCIENCE
Partout en
Rhône-Alpes
ATELIERS DE RECHERCHE
APPRENTISSAGE DE LA SCIENCE
POUR TOUT LE MONDE
www.fetedelascience.fr

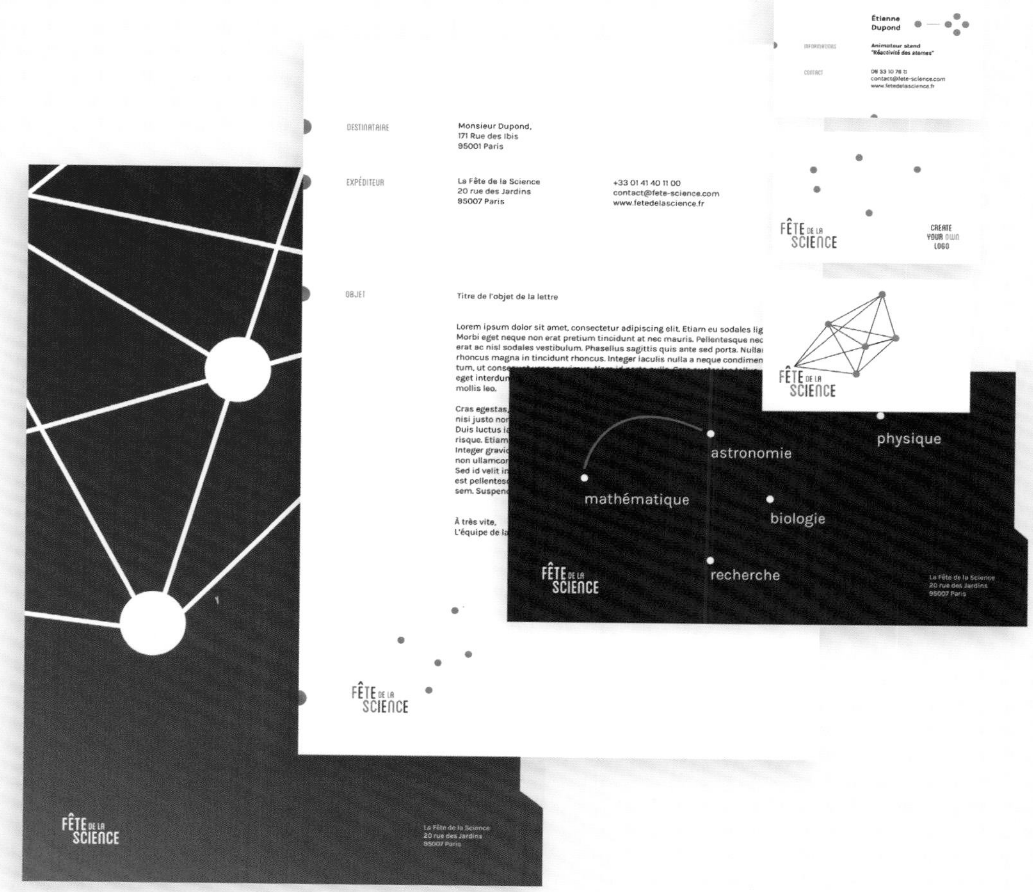
Monsieur Dupond,
171 Rue des Ibis
95001 Paris
La Fête de la Science
20 rue des Jardins
95007 Paris
+33 01 41 40 11 00
contact@fete-science.com
www.fetedelascience.fr
Titre de l'objet de la lettre
astronomie
physique
mathématique
biologie
recherche
FÊTE DE LA SCIENCE
CREATE YOUR OWN LOGO

Quartz Records

Design: *Rada Jeliazkova*

This is the visual identity of a fictional records company called Quartz. The quarts mineral is famous for its diversity in color and shape. The designer tried to express its nature through the design meanwhile combining it with a modern pop look. The designers imagined the company centered around music styles such as indie rock, pop and electronic. With that in mind, a selection of cheerful and uplifting color palette was chosen. The main inspiration for the company's identity and the posters for the opening party was the Memphis design style.

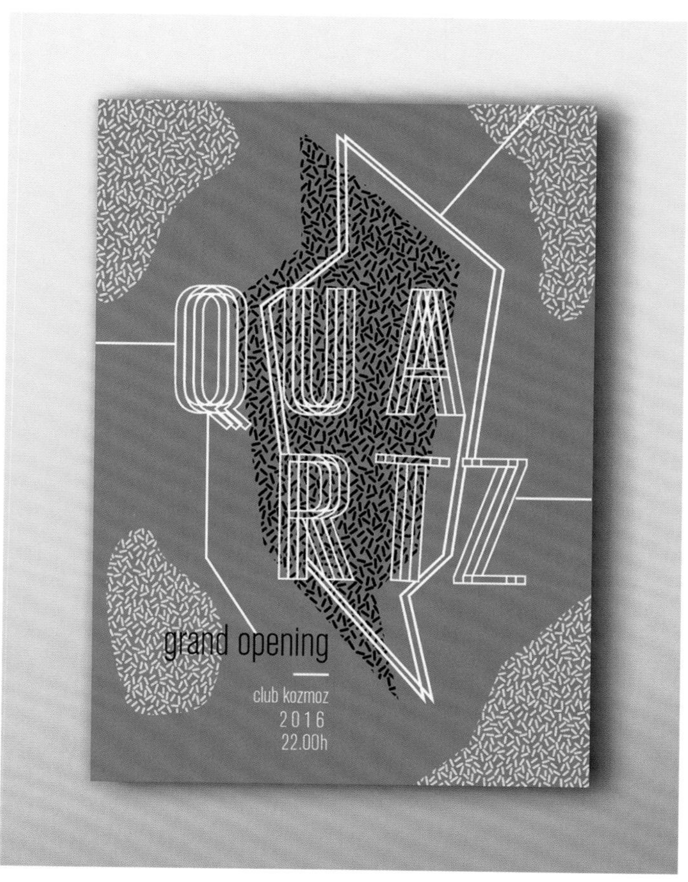
QUARTZ
grand opening
club kozmoz
2016
22.00h

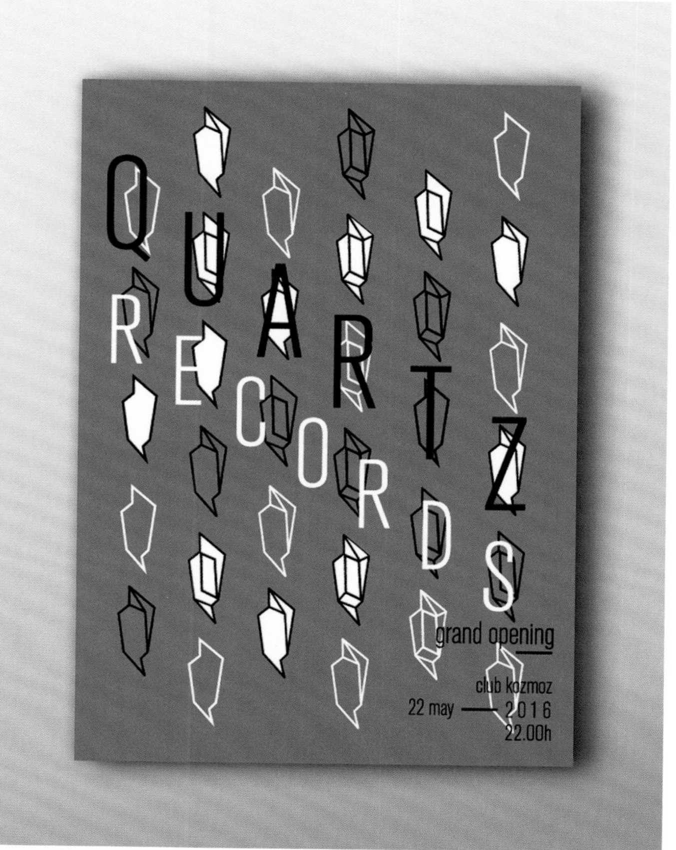
QUARTZ
RECORDS
grand opening
club kozmoz
22 may 2016
22.00h

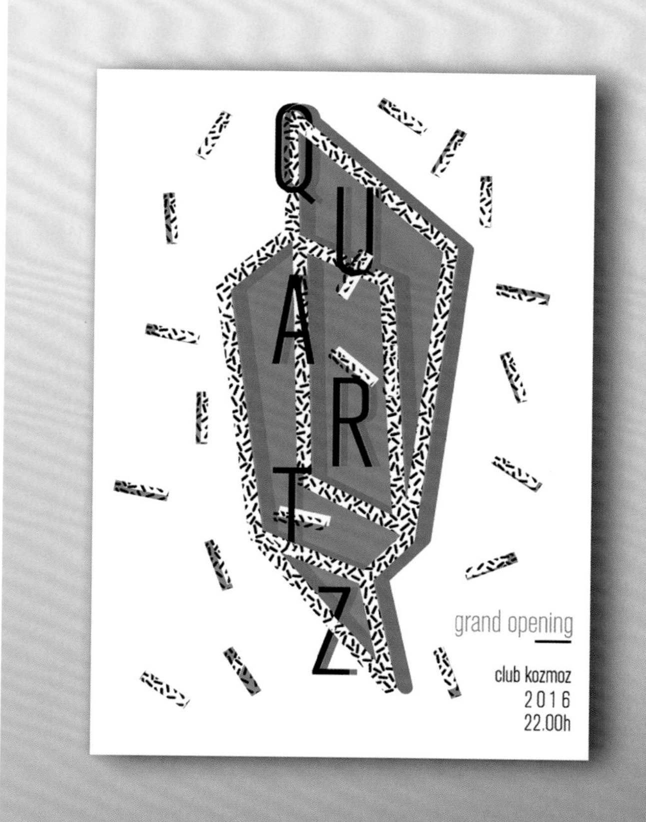
QUARTZ
grand opening
club kozmoz
2016
22.00h

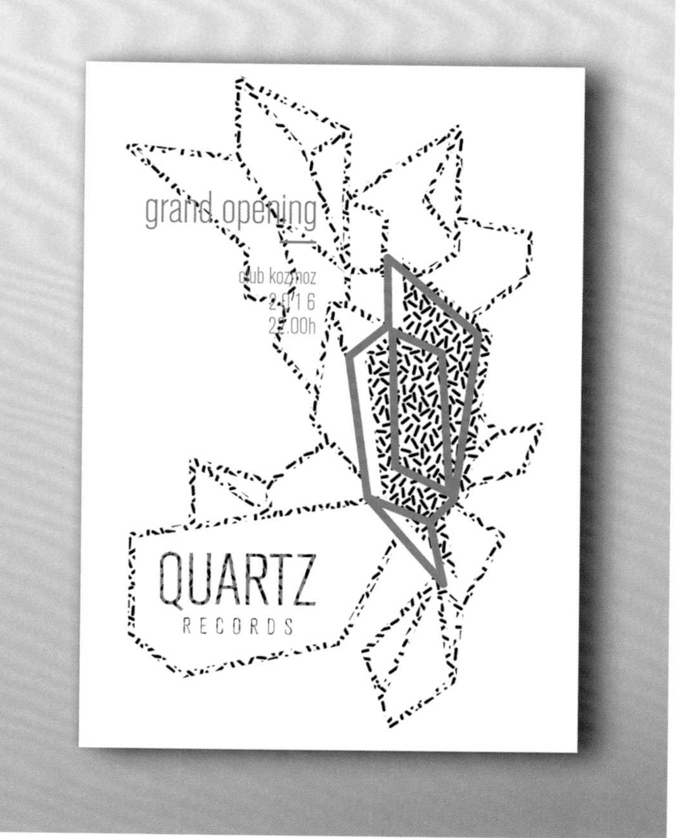
grand opening
club kozmoz
2016
22.00h
QUARTZ
RECORDS

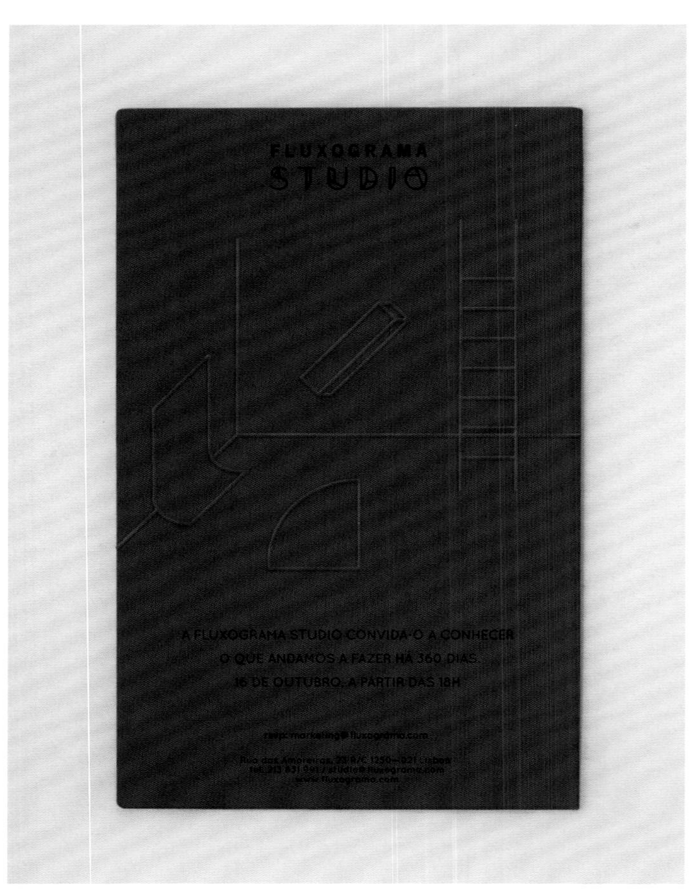

Fluxograma Studio

Agency: *Sam Baron & Co*
Creative Direction: *Sam Baron / Studio AH—HA*
Photography: *Diogo Alves / Studio AH—HA*

Communication project for the new concept store of Fluxograma, a company specialized in office furniture. The branding and display of the shop answered to a constant need of change, using 2D and 3D elements that move, together with the furniture, around the space. The showroom/shop works as a lab of ideas that changes every three months. The goal is to create different moods and environments; showing different approaches to the client for regular offices spaces – such as meeting and waiting rooms, lobbies, libraries, archives, open spaces, etc. The shop is also a printed newsletter where they showcase objects that complement the services that this office brand provides. The newsletter plays with images and lines in the same mood as the display but still in a very experimental way, creating a visual coherence through all materials.

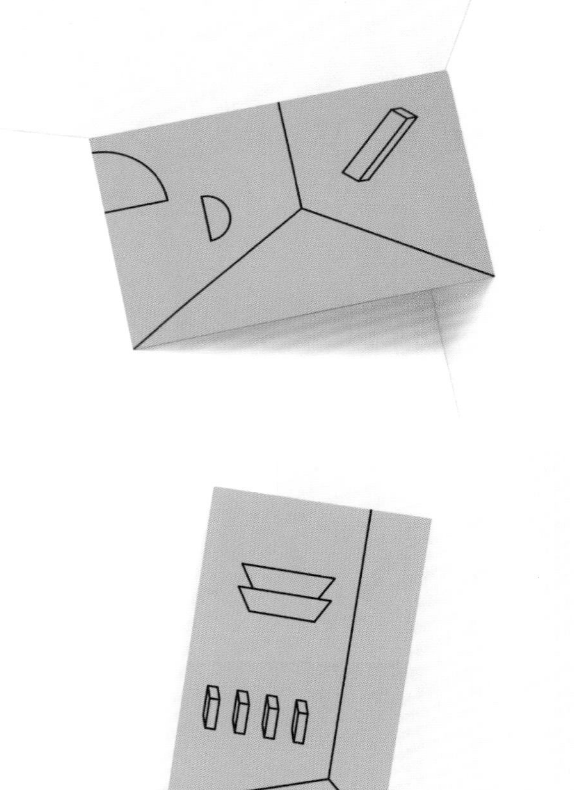

FLUXOGRAMA

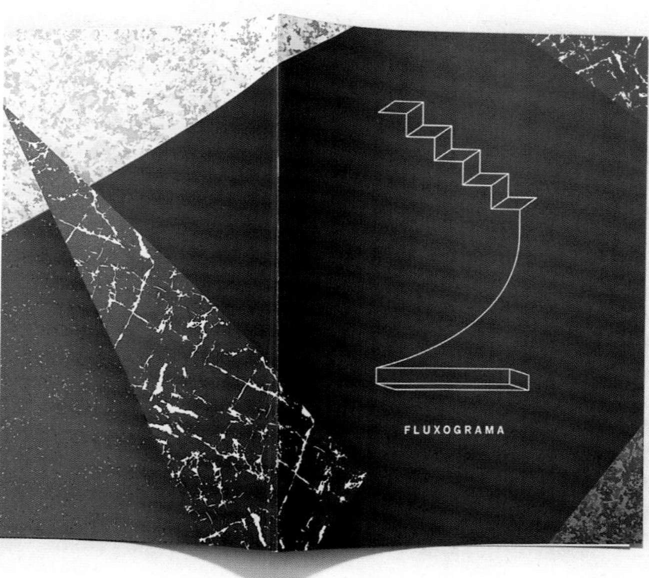
FLUXOGRAMA

FLUXOGRAMA
STUDIO
lounge chair + mesa Betty
by Christoph Lenni
Maxdesign

FLUXOGRAMA
STUDIO

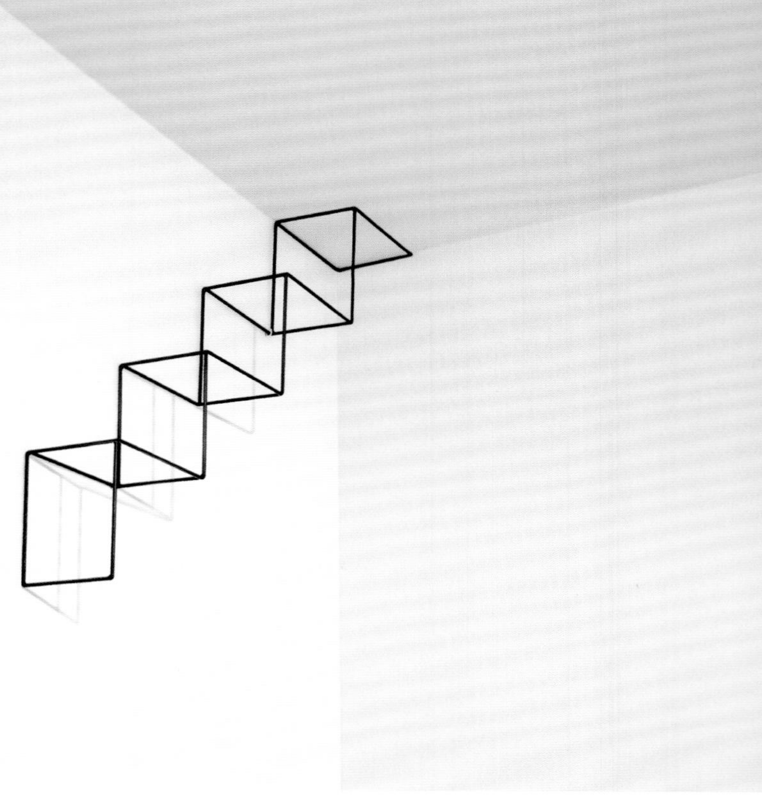

26th Golden Melody Award

Agency: *JL DESIGN*
Creative Direction: *David Tsai*
Lead Design: *Hsiang Ju Hung*
Design & Animation: *Hsijen Liu, Jim Hsu, Julian Chen, Daniel Chang, Jarvis Lim, Orange Chen, Davy Liu*

JL DESIGN is in charge of the visual direction for the Golden Melody Award Ceremony for a second consecutive year. The main visual concept for the 26th Golden Melody Award Ceremony pays tribute to Taiwan, China as the source of inspiration for music. Named "Original Soundtrack of Taiwan", the design takes cue from the sight and sound of Taiwan and invokes a collective memory of the land.

GMA LOGO DESIGN PROCESS

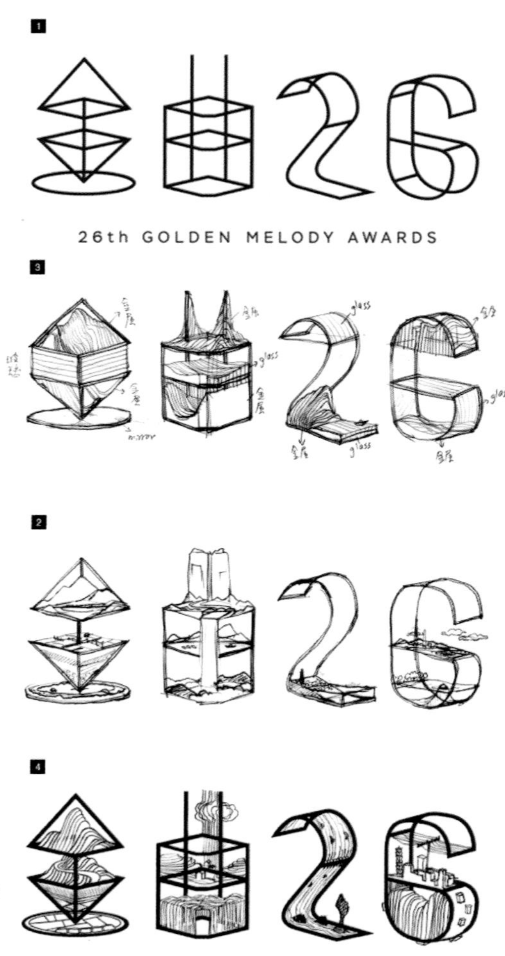

GOLDEN MELODY AWARDS
頒 獎 典 禮

GOLDEN MELODY AWARDS
頒 獎 典 禮

GOLDEN MELODY AWARDS
頒 獎 典 禮
26th GOLDEN MELODY AWARDS

De Cecco Pasta

Design: *Ben Hutchings*

Visual identity and packaging for De Cecco Pasta. The De Cecco company produces hundreds of different types of pasta and pasta-related products, and this concept attempts to categorize this into a minimalistic yet sophisticated brand identity. Each product is easily identifiable and differentiated by its bold titling and numeric typographic system. Completed under the instruction of Louise Fili.

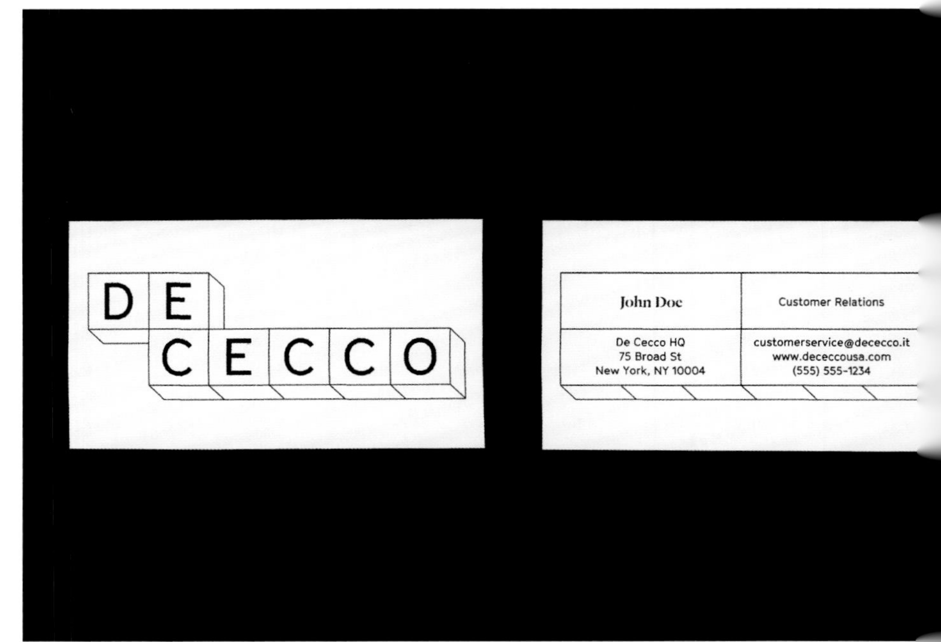

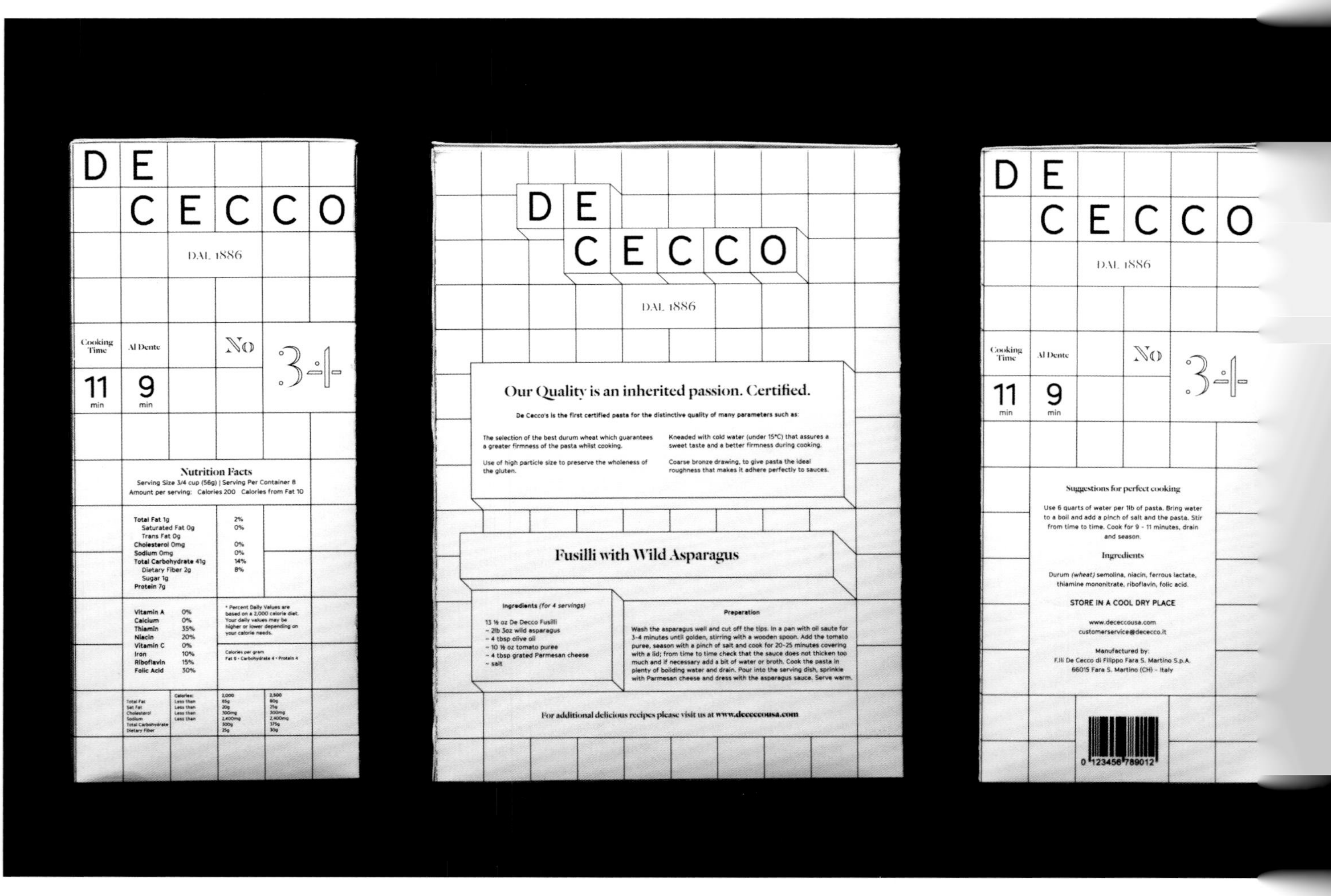

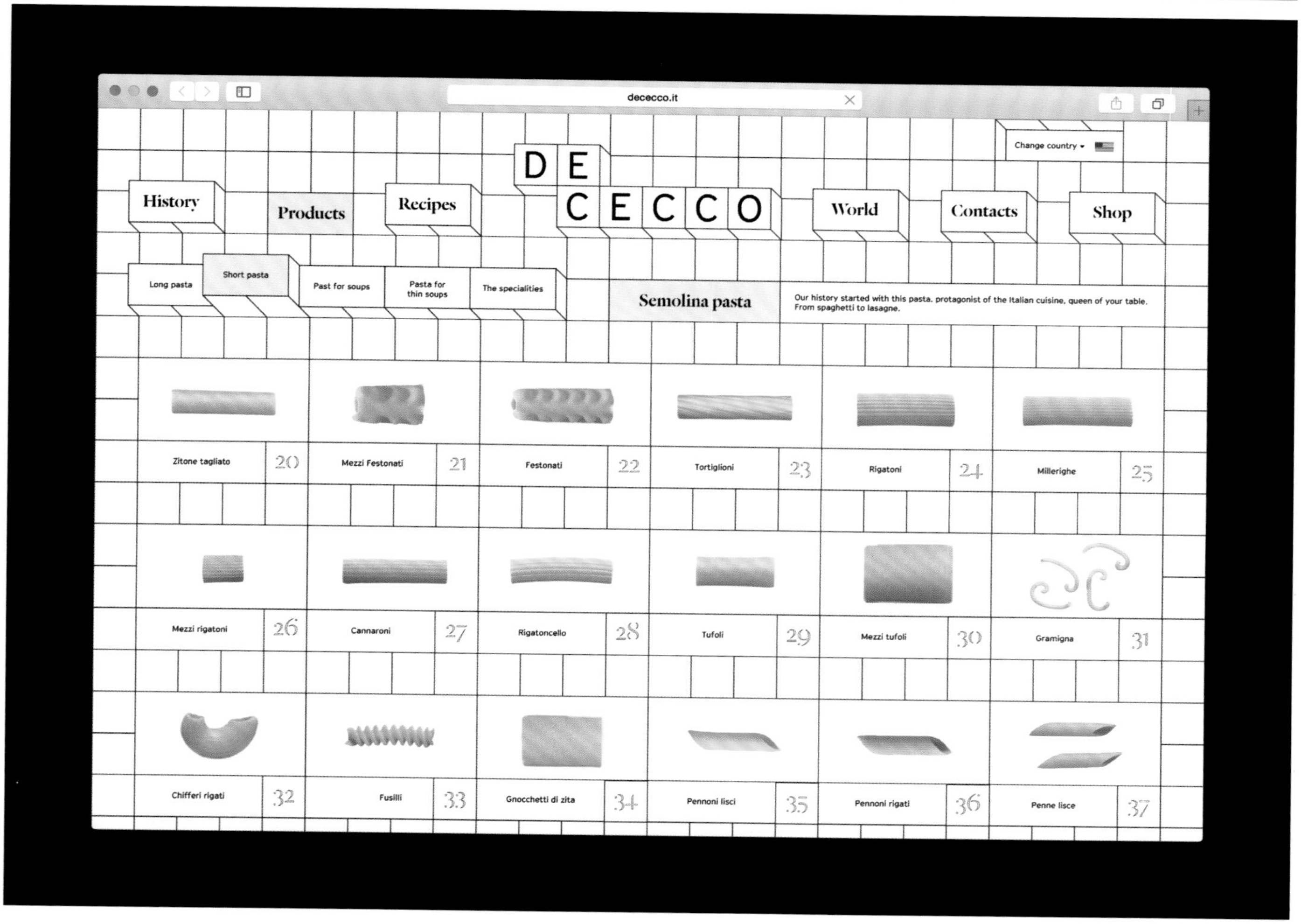

dececco.it
Change country
DE
CECCO
History
Products
Recipes
World
Contacts
Shop
Long pasta
Short pasta
Past for soups
Pasta for thin soups
The specialities
Semolina pasta
Our history started with this pasta, protagonist of the Italian cuisine, queen of your table. From spaghetti to lasagne.
Zitone tagliato 20
Mezzi Festonati 21
Festonati 22
Tortiglioni 23
Rigatoni 24
Millerighe 25
Mezzi rigatoni 26
Cannaroni 27
Rigatoncello 28
Tufoli 29
Mezzi tufoli 30
Gramigna 31
Chifferi rigati 32
Fusilli 33
Gnocchetti di zita 34
Pennoni lisci 35
Pennoni rigati 36
Penne lisce 37

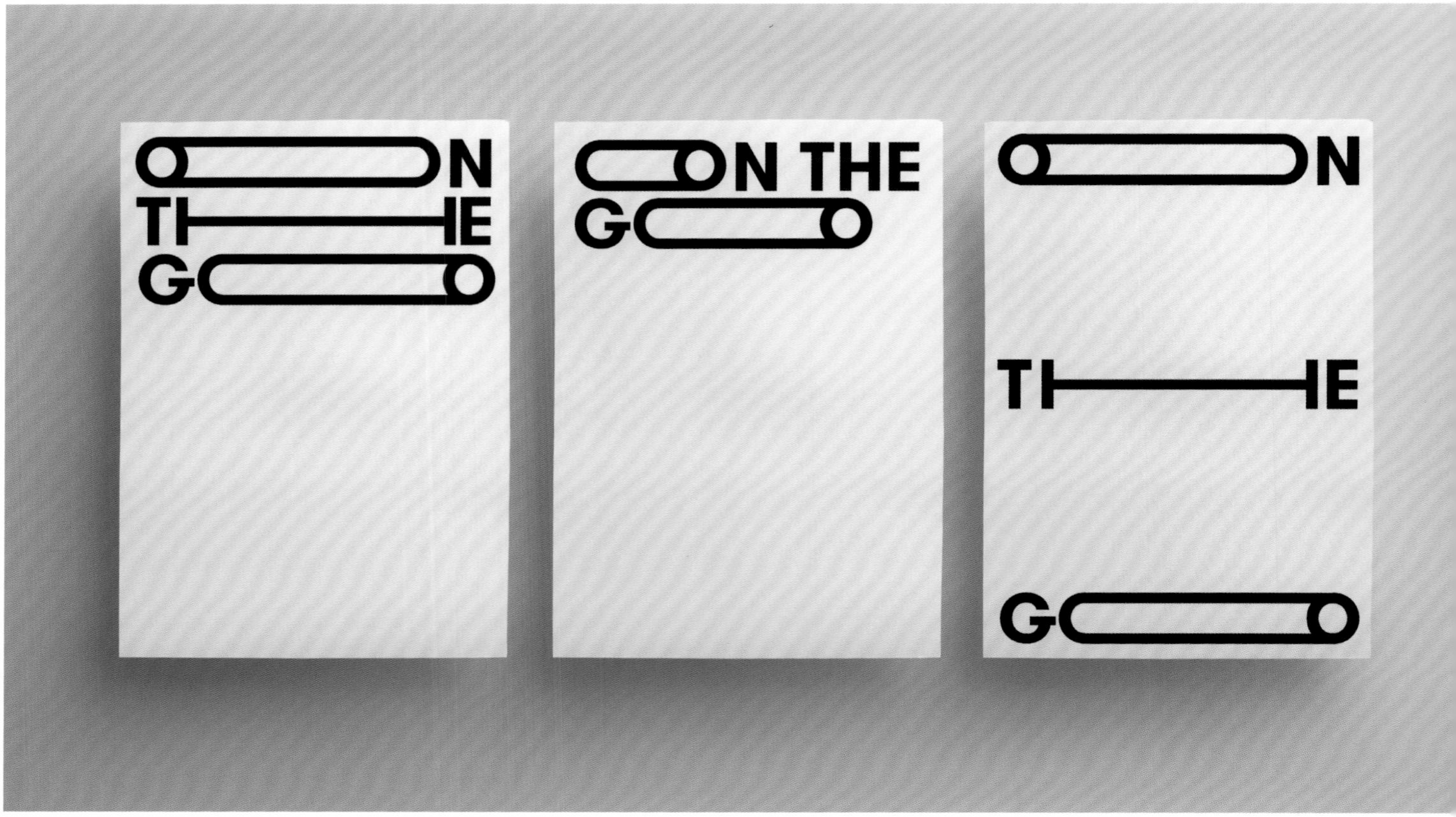

On the Go

Design: *Moby Digg*

The photo exhibition On the Go, which will be presented in 30 countries, explores the cultural differences as well as similarities between Asia and Europe under the guidance of an international jury based in Singapore. The visual identity, Moby Digg has designed, is characterized by the use of the basic colors as well as basic forms and shapes. Those were translated into subtile animations, which enriched the user experience on the exhibition microsite, which has been planned, designed and developed by Moby Digg as well. Next to the microsite's purpose of providing information, it was also the central hub for all participants to upload and share their submissions with followers and friends to collect votes. Next to the implementation of the exhibition concept and its design, Moby Digg produced and published a book, presenting the winning submissions, as well as several collateral communication measures, like posters, postcards and folders.

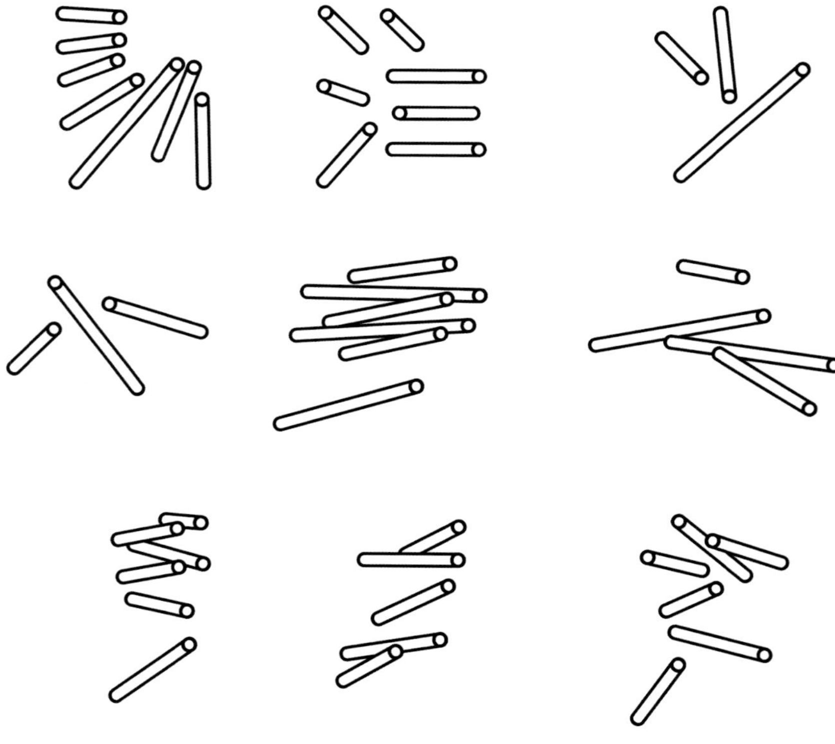

N THE
ASEF P
ASEF

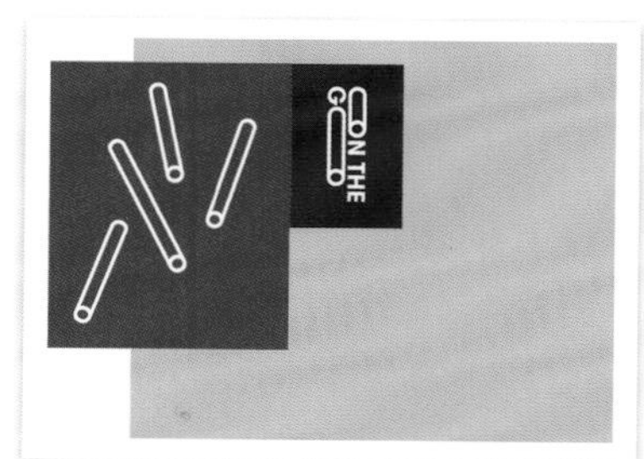

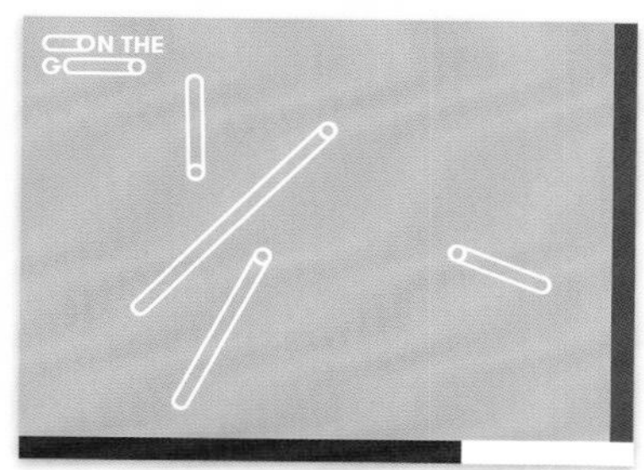

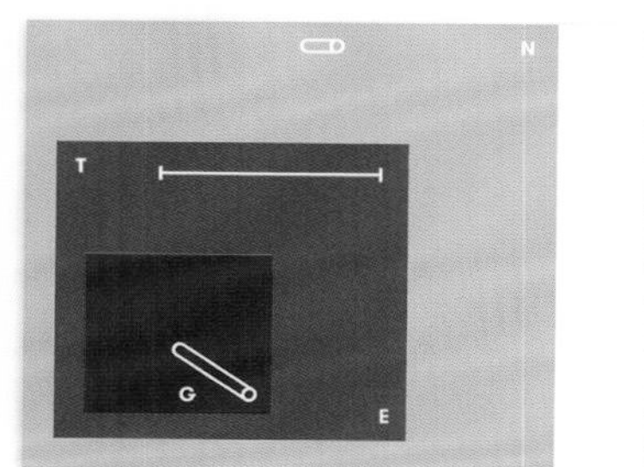

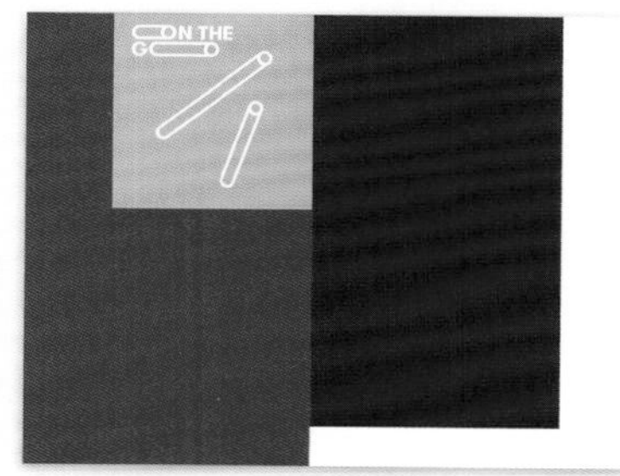

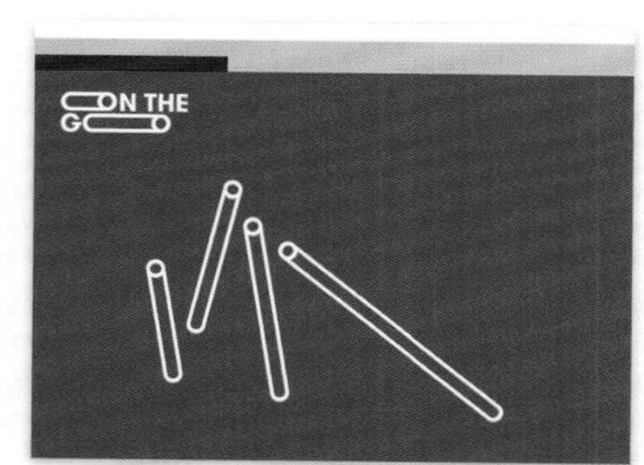

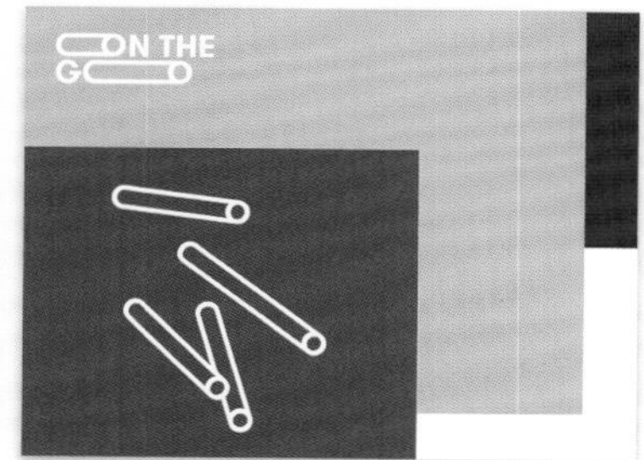

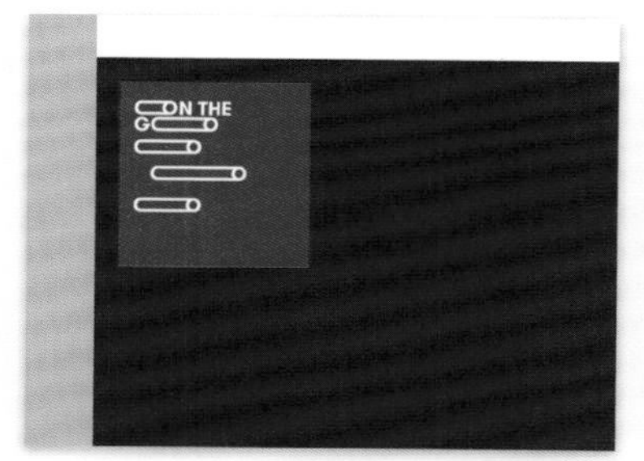

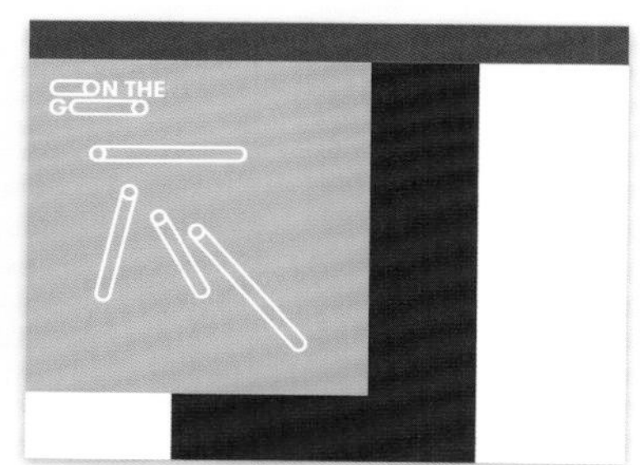

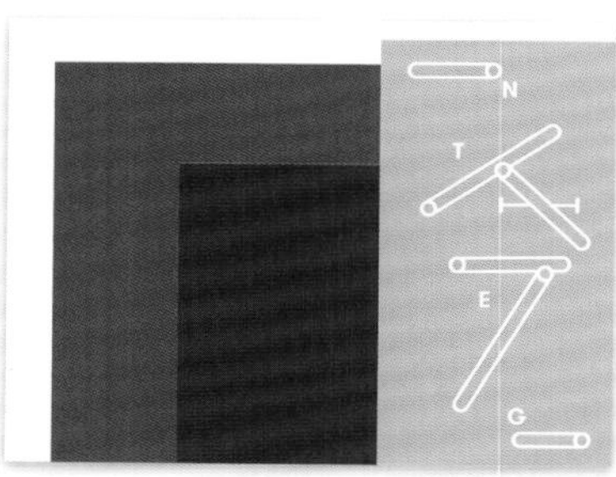

CSG Editorial Design

Design: *Quentin Degrange, Antoine Puyfages*
Agency: *Neon Agency*

Design of the booklet for the "Centre Social et Socioculturel de Gerland (CSG)" from Lyon, France.

The theme of this year was "generator of activities" focused on communities (kids, adults) in constant excitement. The designer used a neon color to catch eyes. Simplicity in the reading, the design aiming to be reassuring and not elitist. Different shapes were also used to create a graphical language.

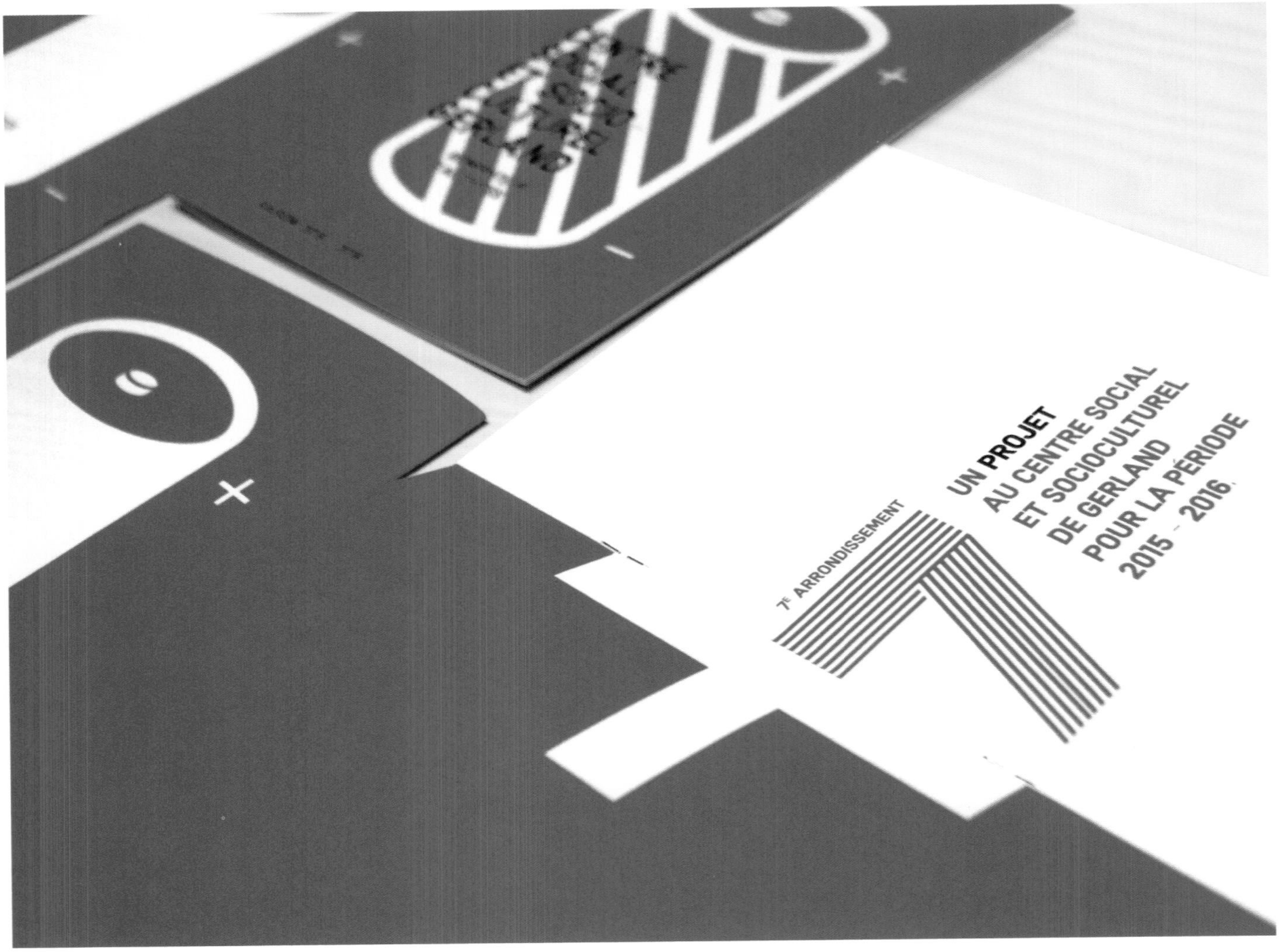

Twig Collaborative

Agency: *Kite Creative*
Creative direction: *Maya Saikali*
Design: *Salma Shamel, Angie Raslan*

Twig is a collaborative creative platform that brings together architects, designers, and artists to bring about distinctive works and experiences. The reference to the Arabic roots and the collaborative practice where the key attributes that inspired the brand creation. The identity explores a ground that combines architectural elements created through the letter T from the Latin and TAA from Arabic. The final emblem is an active form that conveys modularity, merger and simplicity through its diverse usage.

New York Mozart Festival

Design: *Ben Hutchings*

Identity for a fictional festival based in the Culture Shed in midtown Manhattan celebrating the life and work of Wolfgang Amadeus Mozart through classic recitals and modern adaptations. The identity works around the animated "M" which serves as the logo and also a frame for imagery, which can be blown up for use on a poster or used on smaller collateral such as tickets. The visual language presents itself as being daring and immediate through the striking limited color palette, which intends to attract the interest of younger audiences perhaps unfamiliar with the work of the composer.

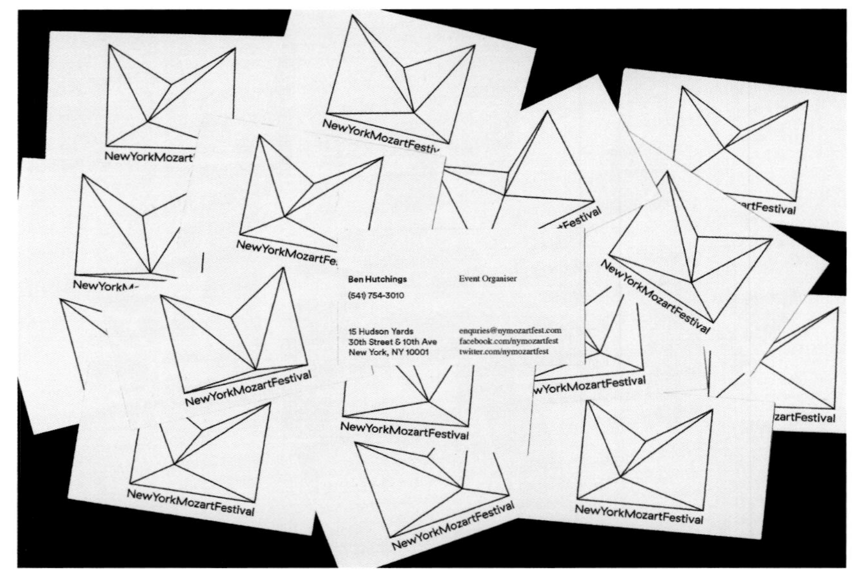

The New York Mozart Festival is being held between Friday 12th - Sunday 21st August 2016.

The Culture Shed is located on 30th Street between 10th & 11th Ave. Nearest subway station is 34th St Hudson Yards.

To purchase tickets, make reservations and general inquiries go to *nymozartfest.com* or call *(541) 754-3010* weekdays 9am-6pm.

Interested in participating in the New York Mozart Festival 2016? For more information and applications go to nymozartfest.com/takepart

NO.8 IN C MAJOR, K.246 AT THE CULTURE SHED

Mozart Concerto Series
Friday August 19th, 8-11pm
at the Culture Shed

15 Hudson Yards
30th Street & 10th Ave
New York, NY 10001

Join the New York Philharmonic Orchestra for an evening of the much celebrated musical journey that is Mozart's Piano Concerto No. 8.

For the full series of events and to book tickets go to: *nymozartfest.com*

NewYorkMozartFestival

NewYorkMozartFestival

ABOUT THE FESTIVAL

The New York Mozart Festival is an annual film and music festival that showcases the music of Wolfgang Amadeus Mozart through classic recitals and modern adaptations.

Over the course of the 10 day festival, the provocative work of Mozart will be celebrated through a range of films, live music, talks and more.

The festival is based in the Culture Shed, an innovative, accessible home for the creative industries in the Hudson Yards district.

WHAT'S ON

Through the course of the festival many different events will celebrate the incredible work of Mozart - highlights including:

AMADEUS DISCUSSION & PANEL
Saturday August 13th – 8.00pm, Culture Shed 4th Floor

THE GENIUS OF MOZART
Friday August 17th – 2.00pm, Culture Shed 2nd Floor

NO.8 IN C MAJOR, K.246
Friday August 19th – 8.00pm, Culture Shed 4th Floor

15 Hudson Yards
30th Street & 10th Ave
New York, NY 10001

The Culture Shed is located on 30th Street between 10th & 11th Ave. Nearest subway station is 34th St Hudson Yards.

2016 EVENT SCHEDULE

FRIDAY 12TH

3.00pm	No.8 in C Major, K.246 Culture Shed, Auditorium | 3hrs (approx)
5.00pm	Film Music Gala Culture Shed, Floor 3| 3hrs (approx)
8.30pm	Explosions in the Sky Culture Shed, Main Courtyard | 3hrs (approx)
10.00pm	Free live music at the Culture Shed Culture Shed, Rooftop| 3hrs (approx)

SATURDAY 13TH

1.00pm	Amadeus Live Culture Shed, Auditorium | 3hrs (approx)
6.00pm	Violin Sonata No. 12 in G Culture Shed, Exhibition Hall A | 3hrs (approx)
9.00pm	Piano Concerto No. 1 in F major, K. 37 Culture Shed, Auditorium | 3hrs (approx)
10.30pm	Mozart in the Jungle Culture Shed, Floor 2| 3hrs (approx)
10.30pm	Late Night Jazz Culture Shed, Floor 3| 3hrs (approx)

SUNDAY 14TH

11.00am	Serenade No. 7 in D major Culture Shed, Exhibition Hall B | 3hrs (approx)
3.00pm	Free Sunday Music - John Crawford Culture Shed, Exhibition Hall A | 3hrs (approx)
8.00pm	The New York Philharmonic Orchestra Culture Shed, Auditorium | 3hrs (approx)
9.00pm	Mozart in the Jungle Culture Shed, Floor 2 | 3hrs (approx)
10.30pm	Late Night Jazz Culture Shed, Floor 3| 3hrs (approx)

MONDAY 15TH

2.00pm	Film Music Gala Culture Shed, Floor 3| 3hrs (approx)
5.00pm	Symphonic Mozart Culture Shed, Main Courtyard | 3hrs (approx)
8.00pm	No.8 in C Major, K.246 Culture Shed, Auditorium | 3hrs (approx)
9.00pm	Violin Sonata No. 12 in G Culture Shed, Exhibition Hall A | 3hrs (approx)
11.00pm	Late Night Jazz Culture Shed, Floor 3 | 3hrs (approx)

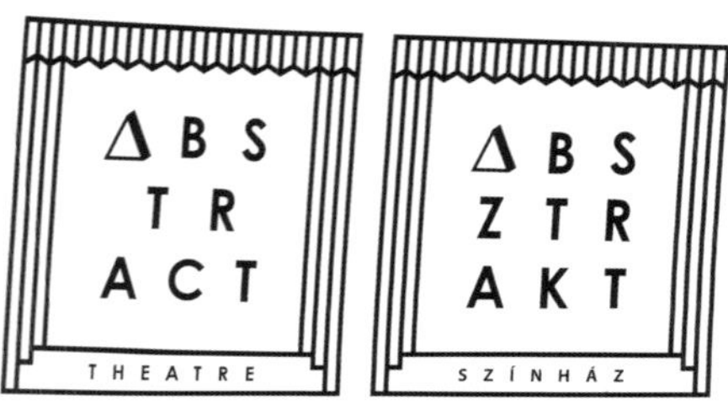

Abstract Theatre

Design: *Sarolta Agnes Erdelyiis*
Photography: *Kelemen Richard*

This project is a "cultural mission" of a performance which evokes that playful and experimental scenic style which was created in the school of Bauhaus in the 1920's. Moving paintings, vibrant compositions, and mechanical ballet were made and finally completed with the stylized moves of the dancers. Typography appeared as an important compositional element of the performance which was based on the synthesis of light, shapes, moves and sounds. The designer created the logo, posters, ticket, web page, brochure, and a souvenir for this performance.

Jegyek az ismert jegypénztáraknál,
vagy rendelje meg online!
www.abstract_theatre.com
ABSTRACT THEATRE

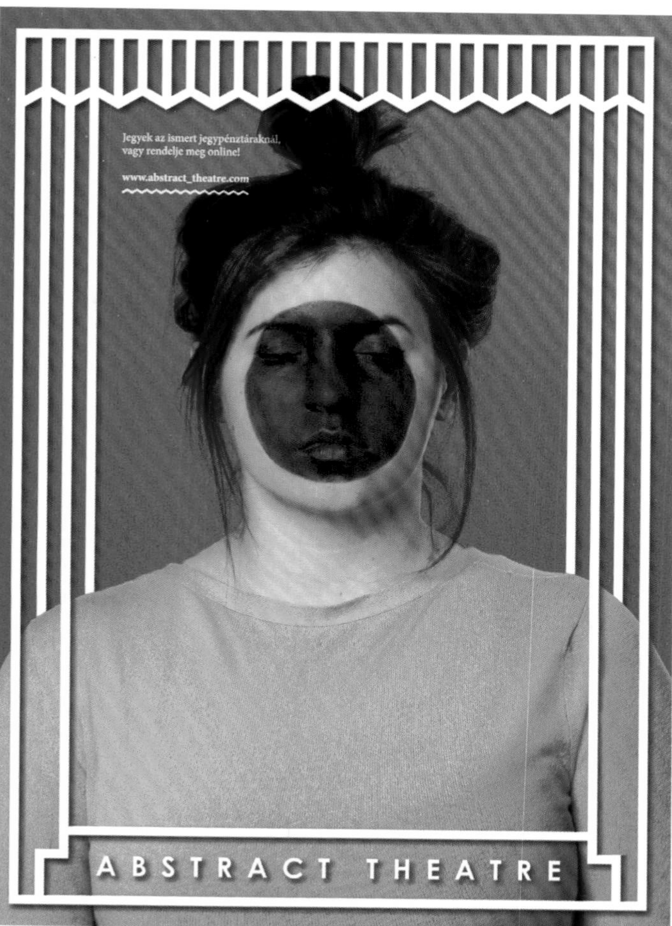
Jegyek az ismert jegypénztáraknál,
vagy rendelje meg online!
www.abstract_theatre.com
ABSTRACT THEATRE

ABS
ZTR
AKT
ABS
TR
ACT
THEATRE

Autistic Art

Agency: *Y&R Budapest*
Art Direction: *Laszlo Polgar*

Autistic Art is a Hungarian design brand of Autistic Art Foundation that supports autistic people by organizing regular drawing activities for them. Then they put this artwork onto design products that get a unique artisan look.

The identity was based on a symbol: a window. A window, which is a bridge between their unique inner world and the outside society. The logo is dynamic because it can feature an infinite number of artworks – embodying the diversity of the disorder spectrum called autism. The light streaming through the window shows a pattern made by an autistic artist – a different one on every product.

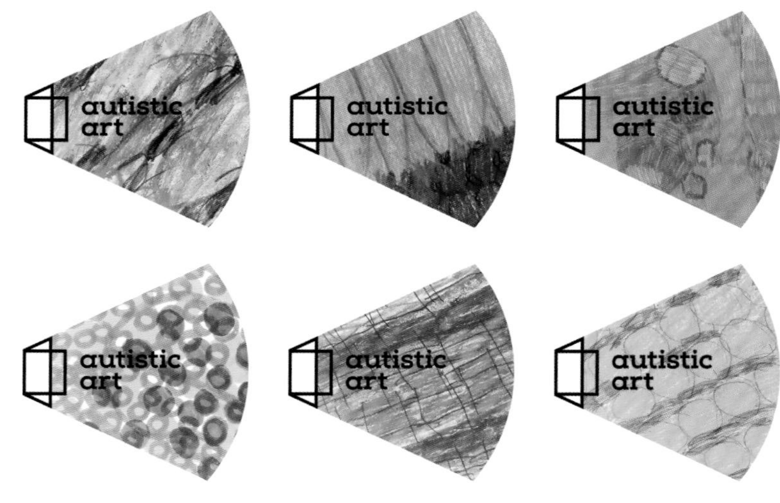

autistic
art

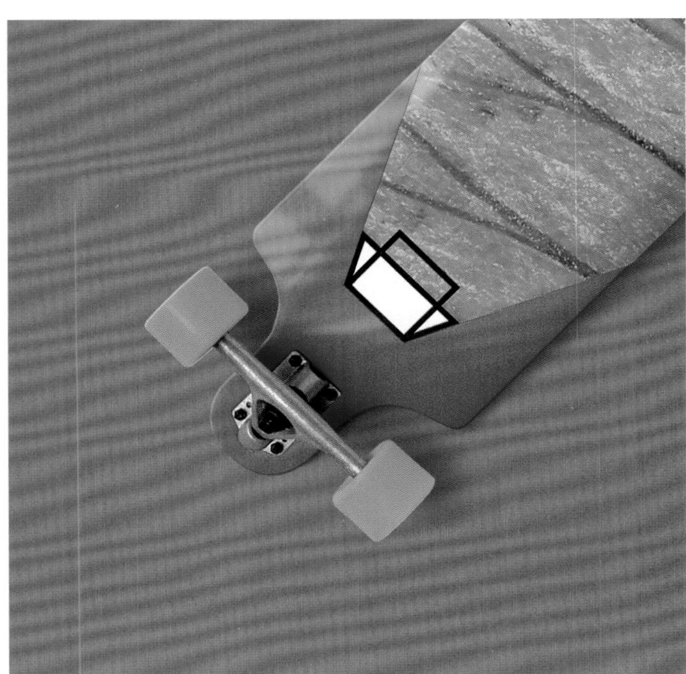

kézműves csokoládé
válogatás
autistic
art

Pixelated Realities

Design: *Veronika Wonder*

Identity design for community organization Pixelated Realities. Pixilated Realities create a platform that connects the community of enthusiasts to 3D scan real world and VRlise the reality into Metaverse, and promote the movement for preservation of important architectural monuments and buildings of Ukraine.

The conception of the project is the elements for the designer's dynamic identity. This identity contains objects that reminds beam of laser in various form, also calibrating setups points for 3D laser and stereometry figures that reminds people about process of creating architecture buildings. You can use this objects in different order and make from them a logo, as well as using the objects as a pattern or just like single object in some print or souvenir goods.

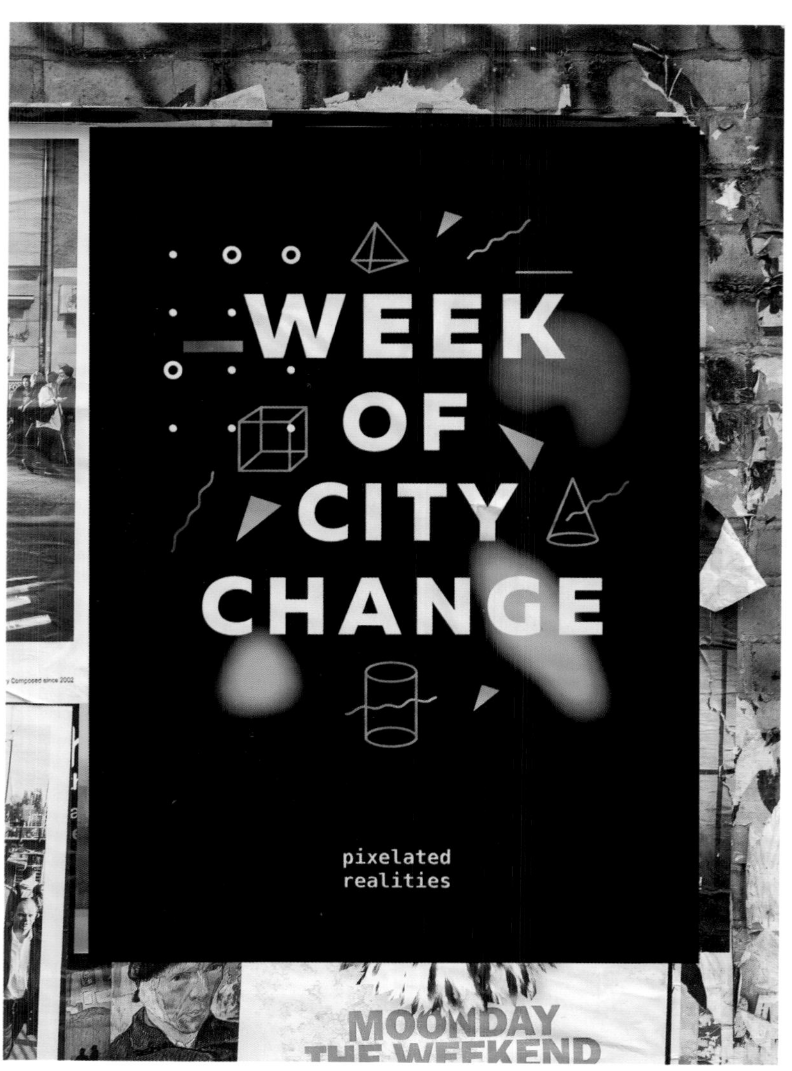

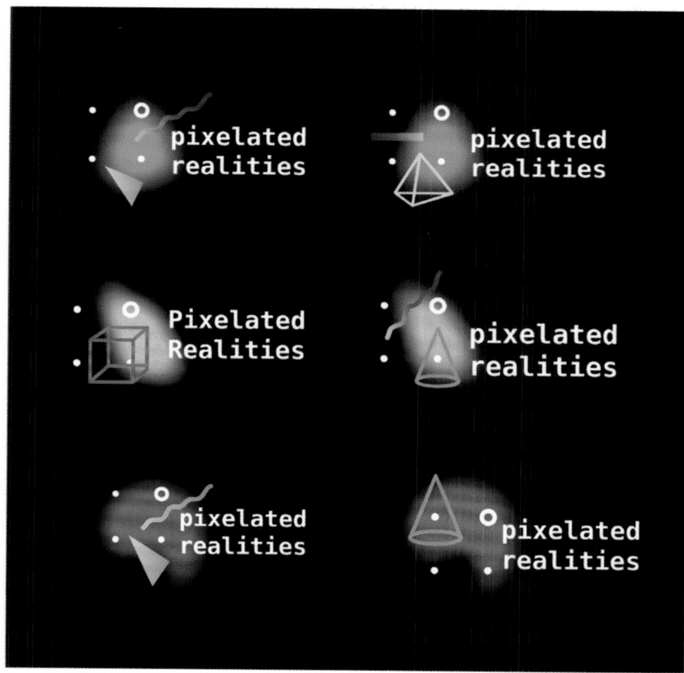

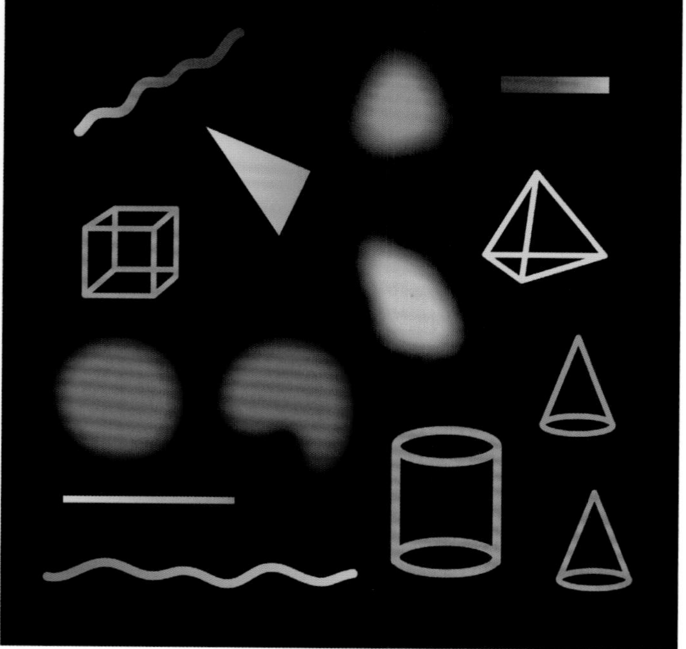

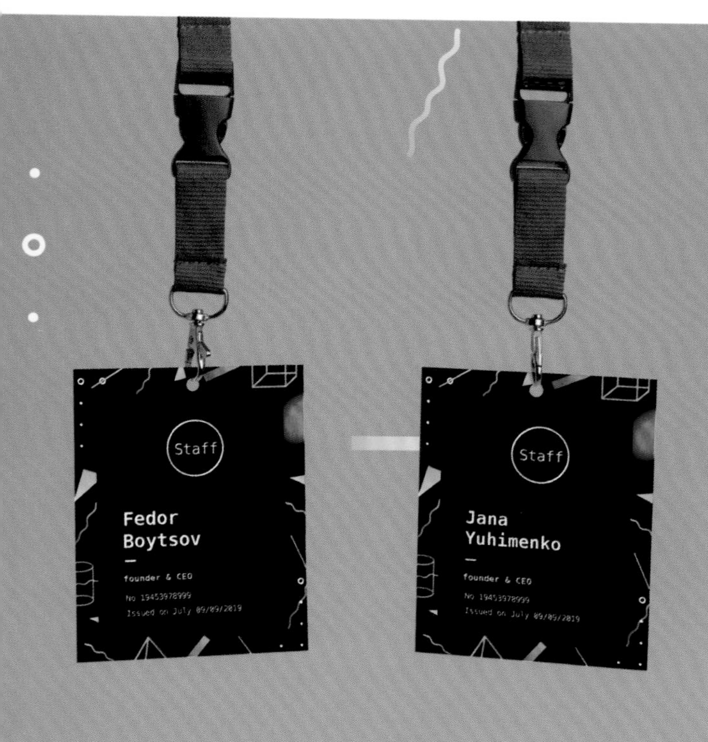
Staff
Fedor
Boytsov
founder & CEO
Staff
Jana
Yuhimenko
founder & CEO

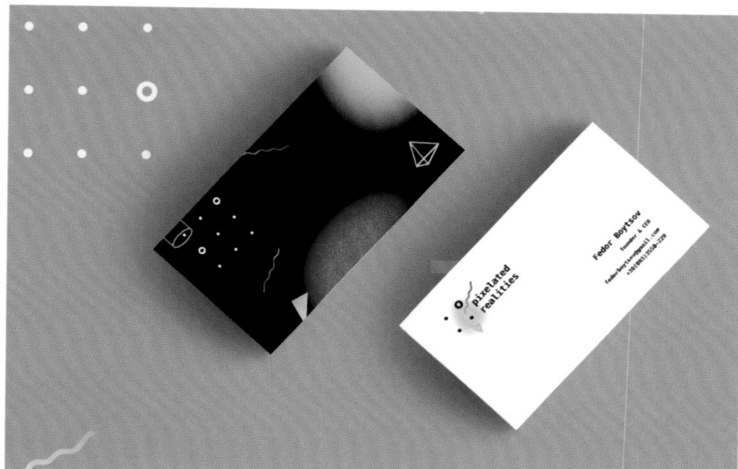
pixelated
realities
Fedor Boytsov

pixelated
realities
pixelated
realities

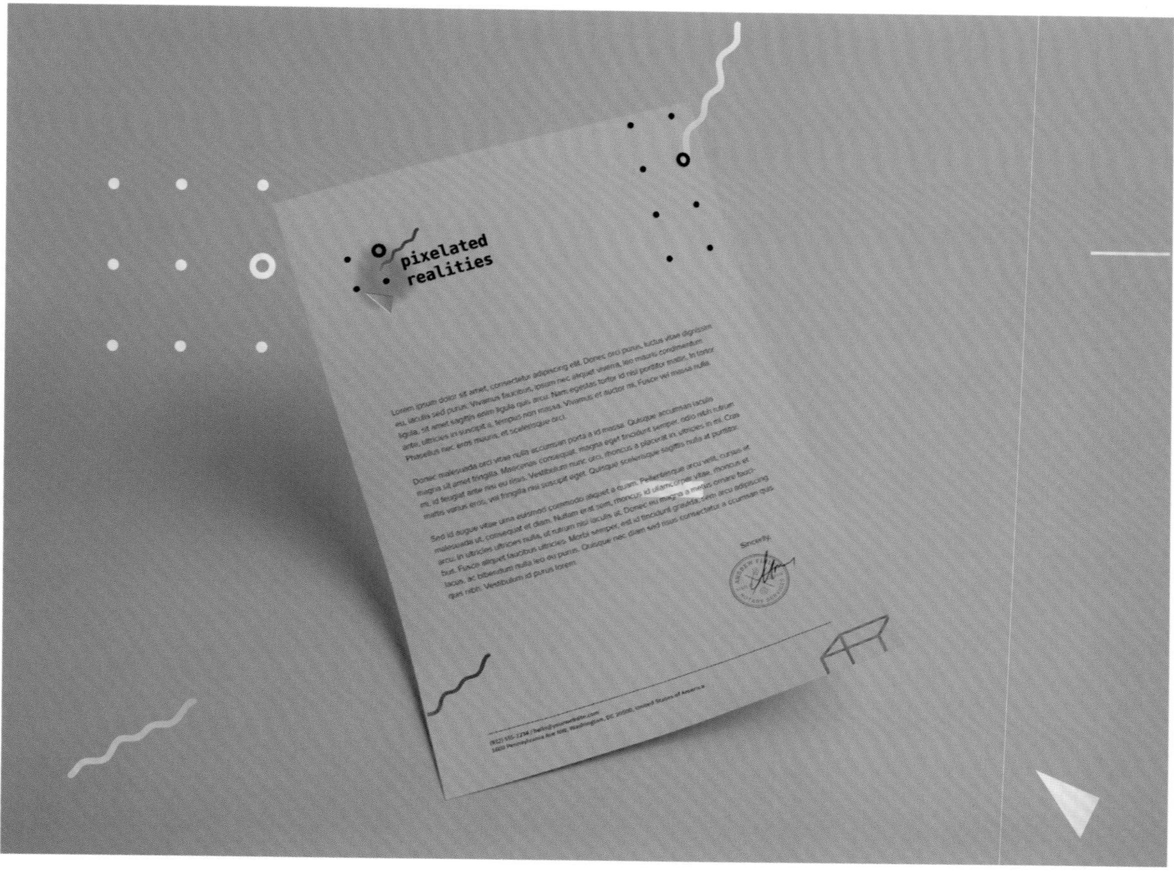
pixelated
realities

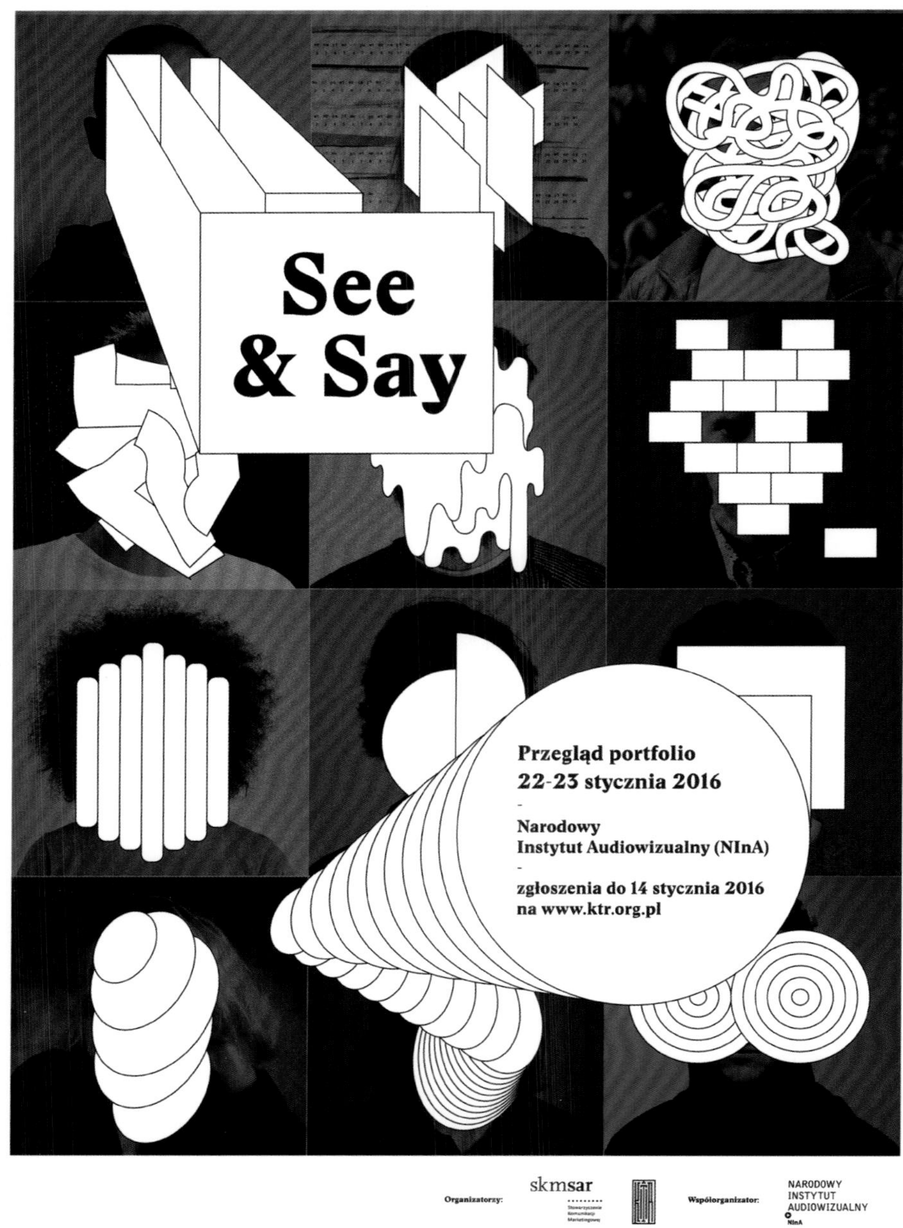

See & Say

Agency: *UVMW*
Creative Direction: *Robert Mendel, Jacek Walesiak, Piotr Matejkowski*
Design: *Jacek Walesiak, Robert Mendel, Michał Małolepszy, Sławek Czajkowski*

See & Say is a free portfolio consultation event organized by Marketing Communication Association SKM SAR. The idea was to communicate the event while using the potential of the specialists' image. They are the ones that guarantee providing reliable knowledge for the participants.

The designers based the communication on animated GIF files, posted on Facebook as the deadline approached. A graphic mask was designed for each of the specialists. After it dissolved one saw information about the competition along with the name of the juror. After the introduction of our campaign the number of applicants rose by 100% in relation to the previous year's event.

Se
& S
-
Gry
Kreatywność w technologii
Ilustracja
Animacja/Video
Reklama
Muzyka/Sound design
Fotografia
Design/Projektowanie
Moda
Creative Writing
Instalacje/Wideoinstalacje
-
Zgłoszenia do
14 stycznia
skmsar
NARODOWY
INSTYTUT
AUDIOWIZUALNY

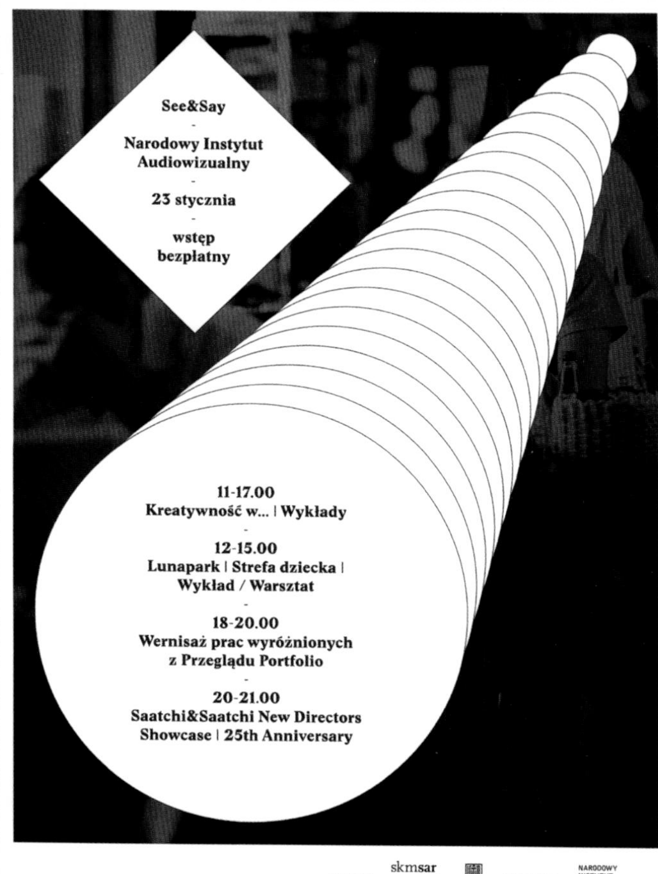
See&Say
-
Narodowy Instytut
Audiowizualny
-
23 stycznia
-
wstęp
bezpłatny
11-17.00
Kreatywność w... | Wykłady
-
12-15.00
Lunapark | Strefa dziecka |
Wykład / Warsztat
-
18-20.00
Wernisaż prac wyróżnionych
z Przeglądu Portfolio
-
20-21.00
Saatchi&Saatchi New Directors
Showcase | 25th Anniversary
skmsar
NARODOWY
INSTYTUT
AUDIOWIZUALNY

See
& Say
Przegląd Portfolio
-
Wyróżnienia 2016
skmsar
NARODOWY
INSTYTUT
AUDIOWIZUALNY

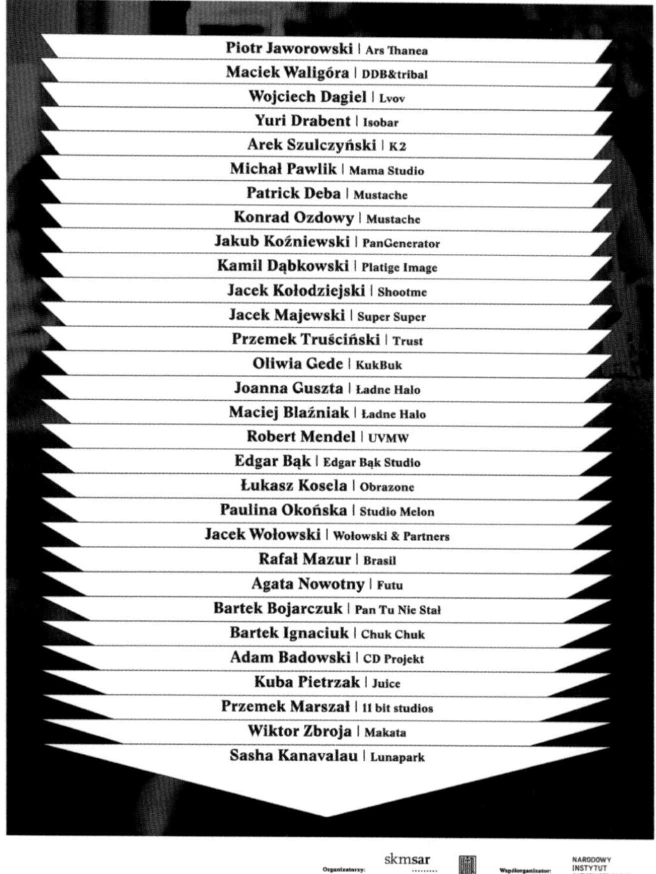
Piotr Jaworowski | Ars Thanea
Maciek Waligóra | DDB&tribal
Wojciech Dagiel | Lvov
Yuri Drabent | Isobar
Arek Szulczyński | K2
Michał Pawlik | Mama Studio
Patrick Deba | Mustache
Konrad Ozdowy | Mustache
Jakub Koźniewski | PanGenerator
Kamil Dąbkowski | Platige Image
Jacek Kołodziejski | Shootme
Jacek Majewski | Super Super
Przemek Truściński | Trust
Oliwia Gede | KukBuk
Joanna Guszta | Ładne Halo
Maciej Blaźniak | Ładne Halo
Robert Mendel | UVMW
Edgar Bąk | Edgar Bąk Studio
Łukasz Kosela | Obrazone
Paulina Okońska | Studio Melon
Jacek Wołowski | Wołowski & Partners
Rafał Mazur | Brasil
Agata Nowotny | Futu
Bartek Bojarczuk | Pan Tu Nie Stał
Bartek Ignaciuk | Chuk Chuk
Adam Badowski | CD Projekt
Kuba Pietrzak | Juice
Przemek Marszał | 11 bit studios
Wiktor Zbroja | Makata
Sasha Kanavalau | Lunapark
skmsar
NARODOWY
INSTYTUT
AUDIOWIZUALNY

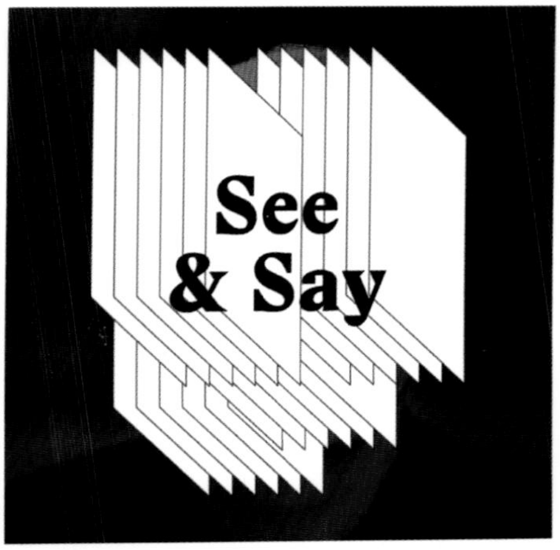
See
& Say
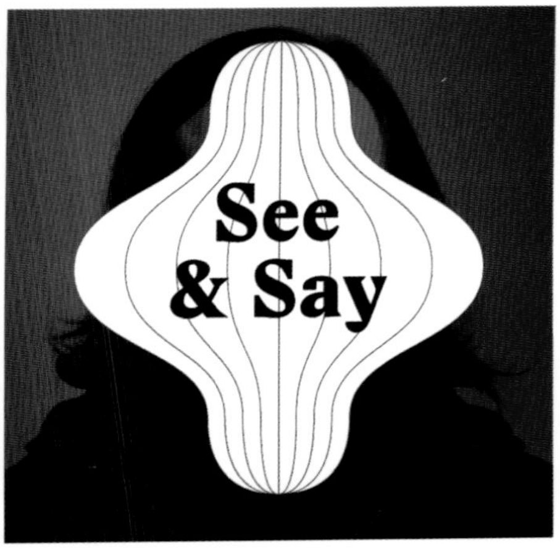
See
& Say
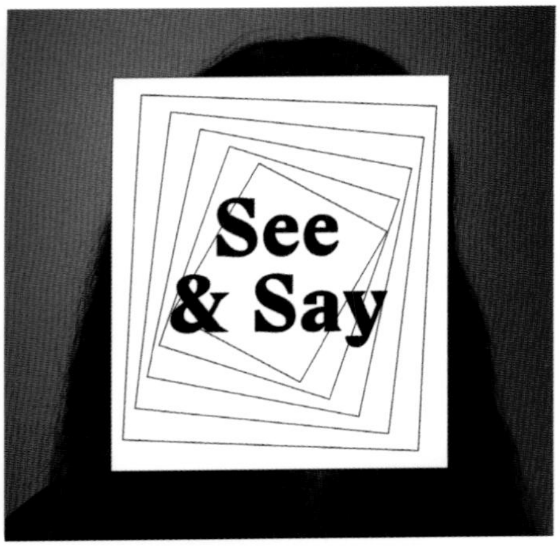
See
& Say
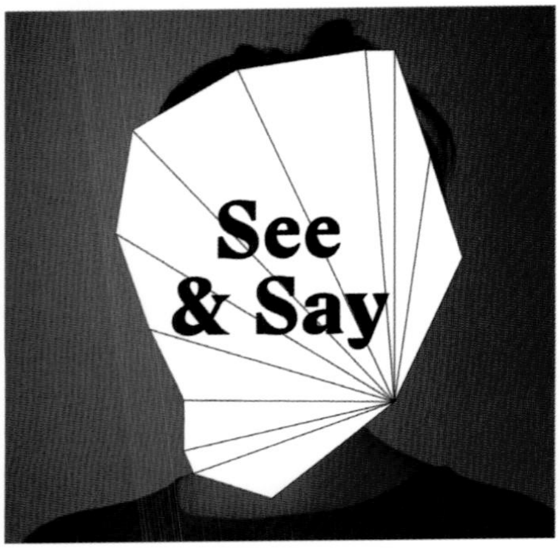
See
& Say
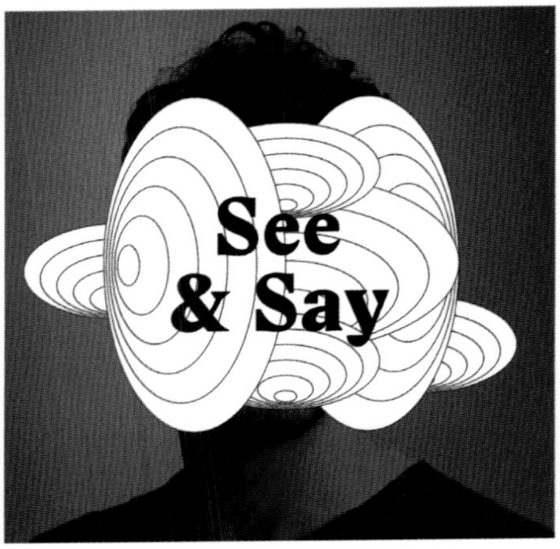
See
& Say
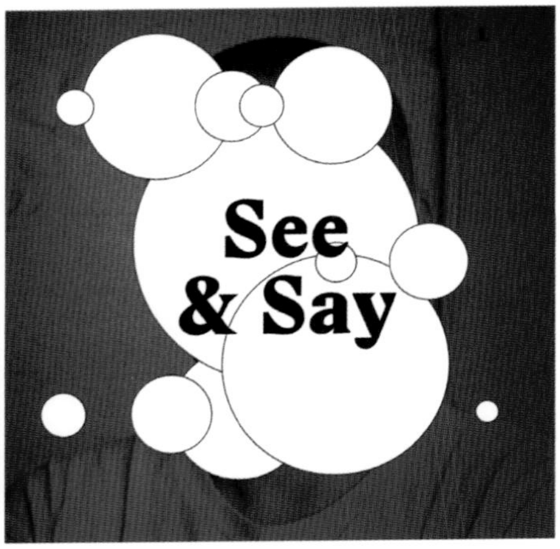
See
& Say
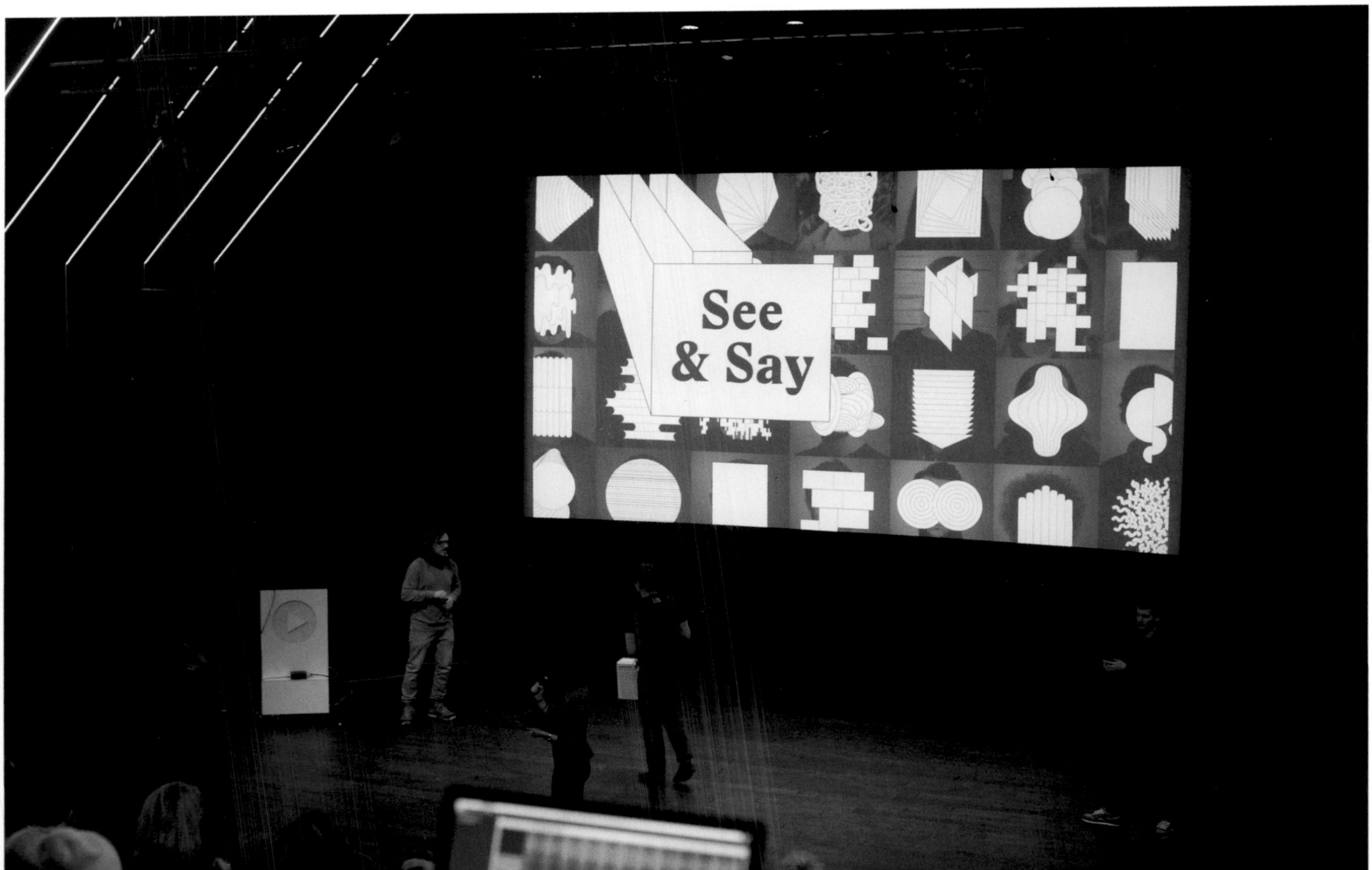
See
& Say

Index

13&5

www.dreizehnundfuenf.de

13&5 is a young graphic design studio specializes in conception and branding. The studio's focus areas are corporate design, web design, editorial design, illustration, hand lettering, and photography.

P.062-063

1983ASIA

www.1983asia.com

1983ASIA is co-founded by Su Su (Tianjin, China) and YAO (Malaysia) in Shenzhen China. As two of the 100 top-most Chinese designers in the world, they are also active participators in International cultural and design exchanges.

P.068-069

ADDA Studio

adda-studio.de

ADDA Studio is a Stuttgart-based design agency, specialized in conceptual design, creation and communication. Since 2009, Christian Vögtlin represents it with his holistic principle of creation, centering the customers' wishes, ideas and views.

P.018-019

Aleix Font

www.aleixfont.com

Aleix Font is a graphic designer based in Barcelona, Spain, focusing on graphic design, art direction, and editorial design.

P.200-201

Allen O'toole

www.allenotoole.fr

Allen O'toole is a design student in third year at the ESAG Penninghen in Paris, France.

P.194-195

AM/PM Creative Agency

ampm-creative.com

AM/PM Creative Agency is based in Yekaterinburg, Russia. AM/PM invents brands, draws corporate identity, and finds advertising solutions and shoots video, or more simply, builds communication between the company and its customers through the auditory-visual impact.

P.150-151

Andrea Sopranzi

www.andreasopranzi.com

Andrea Sopranzi is a graphic and web designer who plan every aspect of visual communication, from corporate design, to graphic art, and advertising.

P.196-197

Andrii Kurylo

behance.net/kurylo

Andrii Kurylo is a Ukraine designer living and working in Kyiv. Andrii loves graphic design and handcraft.

P.072-073

Anna Mikhaylova

behance.net/anneta_mi

Anna Mikhaylova is a designer based in Moscow, Russia, focusing in graphic design, branding, and art direction.

P.154-155

Base Design

basedesign.com

Base Design is a leading international branding firm specializing in brand strategy and identity. Base was founded in Brussels, Belgium in 1993 by Thierry Brunfaut and Dimitri Jeurissen and maintains studios in New York, Brussels, and Geneva.

P.040-041

Ben Hutchings

www.benhutchings.co.uk

Ben Hutchings is an English graphic designer and student currently in his 3rd year at Central Saint Martins in London studying Graphic Design BA (Hons). He is currently based in London, UK.

P.216-217, 222-223

Brandlab

brandlab.pe

Brandlab is specialized consultants in generating and revitalizing brands, using strategy as their main tool. Brandlab covers several design areas: naming, identity, editorial, packaging, environment, and signposting.

P.022-023, 098-099, 166-167

Caio Mattoso

work.cr

Caio Mattoso and Rodrigo Mendes are currently working at Wieden + Kennedy São Paulo as creative directors. They've been working in the advertising industry for the past fifteen years – nine of them, as a creative duo. In parallel to the agency, they opened their own creative lab: a place where they could experiment things independently.

P.112-113

Casey Martin

www.caseymart.in

Casey Martin is a New Jersey-born, Chicago-trained designer and art director who now lives and works in San Francisco, California. Now, he runs his own branding and design studio in SF's Dogpatch district and collaborates with all sorts of clients.

P.116-117

Hanna Sköld

behance.net/hanna_skold
behance.net/saraknipstrom

Hanna Sköld and Sara Knipström are a design duo that met in college where they studied packaging design. Now they are at the beginning of their career and with a passion for creative things they want to develop as designers and make a difference in the design industry.

P.070-071

Hiromi Maeo

behance.net/enhanced_hiromimaeo

Hiromi Maeo is a Japanese designer with over 20 years' experience. He founded Enhanced Inc., and since then Hiromi's main focus has been on corporate branding. His design expertise covers wide ranges of visual representation for brands, including CI/VI development, art direction, etc.

P.016-017, 136-137, 178

Isabel de Peque

www.isabeldepeque.com

Isabel de Peque is an art director and independent designer, specialized in packaging design and branding development. Isabel has a broad experience in cosmetics and perfumery; and currently immersed in gourmet sector.

P.128

Jack Morgan

jackmorgan.com

Jack Morgan is a self-taught brand identity designer and marketer, specializing in the conception, design and launch of disruptive new brands, alongside guerilla marketing campaigns for existing household names like Google, Duolingo, PayPal, Hyundai, BBC, Hugo Boss and more.

P.094

Jan Weidemuller

weidemuller.com

Jan Weidemuller is a graphic designer and art director based in Berlin, Germany. Jan's expertise ranges from identity, digital, and typography design.

P.174-175

JB Studio

www.jordanblyth.com

Founded by Jordan Blyth, JB Studio is a small (in numbers, big on ideas) creative design studio, specializing in identity design and brand development.

P.092-093, 138-139, 179

JL DESIGN

jl.design

JL DESIGN is the first motion graphic design studio in Taiwan, China to specialize in channel branding. JL DESIGN's works has not only gained recognition abroad but garnered numerous international awards.

P.054-055, 214-215

JoJo Dong

behance.net/dongboshu0689

JoJo is a graphic designer who's based in Brisbane, Australia. She is passionate about design, enjoys watching an idea grow from sketch to a creative solution. JoJo's technical knowledge of graphic and motion design, combined with her innate creative abilities, results in an effortless and outstanding creative work.

P.176-177

Kati Forner

katiforner.com

Kati is a Los Angeles based designer with over 10 years of experience in print, digital, and production.

P.038-039

Keiko Akatsuka

www.keikored.tv

Keiko Akatsuka is a freelance designer based in Japan, and flexible also to oversea.

P.124-125

Kite Creative

www.kitecreative.com

Kite is a Beirut based creative agency specialized in branding. Based on a methodological process, Kite develops comprehensive identity systems and their derivatives: publications, exhibitions, posters, signage, and packaging.

P.221

Konstantin Lobanov

behance.net/otokoe

Konstantin Lobanov is an independent graphic designer based in Saint-Petersburg, Russia with experience in branding, visual identity, and illustration.

P.142-143

Laszlo Polgar

behance.net/polgarlaszlo

Laszlo Polgar is an art director and graphic designer based in Budapest, Hungary, focusing on advertising, web design, and sculpting.

P.226-227

Lemongraphic

www.lemongraphic.sg

Lemongraphic is a multimedia design house established in 2007 by Rayz Ong. Rayz Ong is a Singaporean art director who specializes in vector illustration, interactive, and information design. Character design is his true love.

P.188-189

Leo Porto

behance.net/leoporto

Leo Porto is a designer from Brazil, currently based in New York and working at Collins.

P.100-101

Lid&Wiken

www.lidwiken.no

Lid&Wiken is a multidisciplinary design and storytelling studio based in Norway. Lid&Wiken deliver solutions for graphic design and advertising, digitally or printed.

P.036-037, 048-049

Loke Kah Wai

behance.net/francesloke

Loke Kah Wai is a graphic designer based in Kuala Lumpur, Malaysia, focusing on graphic design, typography, and illustration.

P.164-165

Mainstudio

www.mainstudio.com

Mainstudio is an Amsterdam based graphic design studio, founded by Edwin van Gelder in 2005. The studio creates projects deriving from the intersection of art, architecture and fashion, including publications, digital media, and visual identities.

P.026-029, 140-141

Marco Vincit

beer.marcovincit.com

Marco Vincit is a multidisciplinary designer and front-end developer living in Brazil. Despite a degree in Graphic Design, Marco's greatest passion is the digital design.

P.046

Masha Portnova

mashaportnova.com

Masha Portnova is a young designer living between Saint-Petersburg and New York. Web and graphic design are the main spheres of interest. Lines, angles, open colors, clear message and simplicity are the main inspiration tools that she creates her works with.

P.168-169

Matthias Deckx

matthiasdeckx.be

Matthias Deckx is a designer working in the fields of art, culture and commerce. He specializes in a wide range of disciplines including identity design, digital design, and web development.

P.180-181

Maurizio Pagnozzi

www.mauriziopagnozzi.com

Maurizio Pagnozzi is an Italian designer based in London, specializing in branding, corporate identity and packaging.

P.090-091

Maxime Archambault

maximearchambault.com

Maxime Archambault is a multidisciplinary designer that thing that visual solution need to be well design and fun.

P.190

Me Post Branding

mepostbranding.com

Me Post Branding (aka Me,) is a London based design and brand consultancy that creates strong visual concepts to inspire people and activate brands. Founded in 2013 by Mirco Colonna and Eva Miguel, the studio has conceived produces and publishes commercial and cultural projects for national and international clients across different industries.

P.202-203

mischen

www.mischen-berlin.de

Mischen is a Berlin-based design studio founded in 2005. It is specialized in designing books, corporate designs and packagings. mischen's work has received a number of awards, among others the German Design Award, TDC New York, TDC Tokyo, 100 Best Posters, and Laus.

P.047

Moby Digg

www.mobydigg.de

Moby Digg is a Munich based digital design studio, working in the fields of branding, identity and coding. Moby Digg strongly focuses on the creation of simple but decisive identities and disruptive cultural projects. As part of a collaborative practice, Korbinian Lenzer and Maximilian Heitsch founded Moby Digg originally in Buenos Aires.

P.024-025, 104-105, 218-219

Moving Studio

www.movingstudio.co.uk

Moving Studio is an independent design studio based in Leicester, UK, focusing on projects that combine print design, branding, 3D design and motion graphics. The agency works with high profile clients and small independent businesses alike, focusing on producing work with high visual impact.

P.020-021

MTN Company

www.mtncompany.it

MTN Company is a creative communication agency, created in Cava de' Tirreni, Salerno, Italy in 2001. MTN is a team of expert professionals, trained in various disciplines, including corporate identity, art direction, packaging design, exhibit and display designs, posters, leaflets catalogue and web services.

P.064-065

Natalia Zerko

behance.net/nataliazerko

Natalia Zerko is a graphic designer and illustrator based in Poznan, Poland. Aside from branding project for various clients, Natalia's an art director and illustrator. Her work can be seen showcased on multiple design-related websites.

P.030-031

Noeeko

www.noeeko.com

Noeeko is a small design studio based in Warsaw, Poland. Their aim is to create a coherent, original and effective design solution that communicates clients' key messages. They work with large corporate brands and public organizations as well as small businesses, lifestyle brands, restaurants, and artists.

P.108-109

OK-RM

www.ok-rm.co.uk

Founded in 2008 by Oliver Knight and Rory McGrath, OK-RM is a collaborative practice engaged in ongoing partnerships with artists, curators, editors, architects, designers and institutions.

P.162-163

Paperlux

www.paperlux.com

The full circle of natural creativity is completed when the intuitive minds of the 11 pioneering spirits from Hamburg's Schanzenviertel district perform their craft. Here is where inspiration, abstraction, passion, palpability and aesthetics are transformed into concept, branding, corporate and editorial design, event communication, typography, illustration, and art.

P.110-111

Paprotnik Studio

behance.net/paprotnik

Paprotnik Studio is a creative studio based in Warsaw. The studio mainly focuses on branding, creating visual identification, illustration, animation, and web design.

P.182

Pedro Gonzalez

behance.net/pedrogonzalez

Pedro Gonzalez is a graphic designer based in Curitiba, Brazil. The focus of Pedro's work is developing visual identities, branding solutions and other associated material for small and big clients.

P.084-085

Pedro Veneziano

pedroveneziano.com

Pedro Veneziano is a 23-year-old Brazilian graphic artist living in São Paulo. Already worked with studios like Sagmeister&Walsh and Vault49, and clients such as Youtube and Spotify.

P.160-161

Pocket Oslo

www.pocketoslo.com

Pocket is an independent brand consultancy founded back in 2009. The world has changed a lot since then, so has Pocket. Today, the mindset of the consumers, the market and the technology are in constant change, and it needs to reflect the way Pocket collaborates with its clients.

P.042-043

Puntuale

www.silviavirgillo.it

Founded by Silvia Virgillo, Puntuale is a graphic design studio based in Torino, Italy.

P.056-057

Quentin Degrange

www.degrangequentin.com

Quentin Degrange is a French freelance graphic designer, art director and UI designer. He has been collaborating with many institutions which wish to improve credibility and visibility through a real graphical singularity.

P.206-207, 220

Rada Jeliazkova

www.cargocollective.com/radada

Rada Jeliazkova is a graphic designer based in Sofia, Bulgaria, focusing on branding, packaging, and editorial design.

P.208-209

Ray Chen

behance.net/weavepopweave

Graduating from London College of Communication, Ray Chen worked as a senior designer at The MIX-PLACE, Shanghai. He is now based in Xiamen and Taiwan, China with Rose Lin QR, forming "shame:onyou", a multi-disciplinary graphic branding studio who wishes to bring wit and courage to graphic and product design.

P.198-199

Riccardo Vicentelli

www.riccardovicentelli.com

Riccardo Vicentelli is an Italian designer, fan of innovations, inventions, communication, and technology. Riccardo focuses on branding (logo design and visual identity), graphic design (print design and digital design), packaging (label design), and web design (website and UI design).

P.078-079

Rina Rusyaeva

behance.net/rina-rusyaeva

Rina Rusyaeva is a designer and illustrator based in Krasnodar, Russia.

P.134-135

Rocket & Wink

rocketandwink.com

Rocket & Wink. Since May 2011, Rocket Man and Nature Boy are a team. And they see themselves as more than just condiment waiters at an empty breakfast buffet. They dish up in all categories – design, illustration, literature, product development, and conception. And always at full throttle.

P.086-087

Sabbath Visuals

www.sabbathvisuals.com

Sabbath is a multidisciplinary creative consultancy based in Monterrey, Mexico. Formed by passionate individuals dedicated to set higher standards and evolve to create new visuals and methods of thinking.

P.158-159

Sarolta Agnes Erdelyiis

cargocollective.com/saroltamagnes

Sarolta Agnes Erdelyiis a Hungarian graphic designer based in Budapest. She is interested in the theoretical part of visual representation, visual education and visual perception. Her works have been exhibited at various venues both in Hungary and abroad.

P.224-225

Savvy Studio

savvy-studio.net

Savvy Studio is a branding and architecture design practice based in New York, Mexico City and Monterrey. Savvy's expertise involves working around the globe on different ventures including boutique hotels, restaurants, retail spaces, art galleries and museums.

P.050-051

Studio AH—HA

www.studioahha.com

Carolina and Catarina started Studio AH—HA to pursue varied creative interests across a variety of mediums: from brand strategy to interior design, naming and identity work, advertising, new media, traditional and fine print, retail and product design, photography and illustration.

P.010-011, 060-061, 210-213

Studio Carreras

www.studiocarreras.com

Studio Carreras is the graphic design and illustration studio of Genis Carreras, specialized in branding, print, editorial, and digital projects. After working 9 years in different branding and design agencies from London, Carreras decides to start his own studio that focuses on color and simple shapes to create bold and timeless pieces of visual communication.

P.144-145

Studio Flag

designbyflag.com

Studio Flag is an art directors group for all creative fields. The studio focuses on brand identity, print design, package, web, GUI, and digital media design.

P.044-045

Studio Hands

www.studiohands.nl

Studio Hands is a design agency based in Arnhem, the Netherlands. For all kinds of ambitious clients from all over the world, the team designs visual identities, campaigns, and publications.

P.082-083

Studio Iknoki

www.iknoki.com

Studio Iknoki is a graphic design and art direction studio working within different fields of visual communication. The studio designs visual identity systems, visual strategies and tools for agencies, institutions, and brands.

P.106-107

Tadas Bujanauska

tadasbujanauskas.com

Graduated from Towson University, Maryland, USA, Tadas Bujanauskas is a multidisciplinary designer who creates visual identities and works in the fields of illustration, print design, and art direction. He aims to deliver aesthetically pleasing design with a strong sense of minimalism and cleanness.

P.058-059

The Bakery Design Studio

www.madebythebakery.com

The Bakery Design Studio works in different media with clients worldwide. The team is young, but experienced. The disciplines it works in include identity, custom typography, packaging, art direction, and almost anything else one could think of.

P.034

Thomas Wightman

www.thomaswightman.co.uk

Thomas Wightman is a graphic designer currently working in London, UK. His work includes print design, typography, branding, sculpture, paper craft, and motion graphics. He always enjoy challenging himself when answering a brief, exploring the best solution whatever the media.

P.114-115

Tianlong Design

behance.net/tianlong_design

Born in 1988, Zhang Tianlong is a senior graphic designer and art director.

P.172-173

Toby Ng

www.toby-ng.com

Toby Ng graduated in Central St. Martins, London in Graphic Design. Specializing in graphic design and brand identity, Ng rigorously tackles design challenges with wit and aesthetically meaningful communications.

P.080-081

Toormix

www.toormix.com

Toormix is a design studio based in Barcelona working to help clients boost their business through design. Founded in 2000 by Oriol Armengou and Ferran Mitjans, Toormix is an experienced team that works in close collaboration with local and international clients with a clear focus on innovation and brand development.

P.120-121

TwoPoints.Net

www.twopoints.net

The design studio TwoPoints.Net was founded in 2007 with the aim to do exceptional design work. Work that is tailored to the client's needs, work that excites the client's customers, work that hasn't been done before, work that does more than work.

P.170-171

Typical Organization

www.typical-organization.com

Founded in 2013 by Kostas Vlachakis and Joshua Olsthoorn, Typical organization is an Athens, Greece based design studio working internationally on Typical matters. Shaping the mostly undefined "Type" behind the already existing matter. Typical organization is advocated not to add new surfaces to the existing but instead aspiring to discover the "typical" structure of any relevant subject.

P.035

UVMW

uv-warsaw.com

UVMW design studio was founded by Robert Mendel and Jacek Walesiak. UVMW gives long-term support in marketing for companies and organizations, caring for the quality and compatibility of the message with the brand's identity.

P.052-053, 186-187, 230-232

Vasilis Pallas

www.vasilispallas.com

Vasilis is a young graphic and web designer from Athens, Greece. He studied Graphic and Web Design at AKTO College of Art and Design from where he graduated with honors in 2013.

P.088-089

Veronika Wonder

behance.net/veronika_wonder

Veronika Wonder is a Ukrainian graphic designer currently working in Berlin, Germany.

P.228-229

VOLTA Brand Shaping Studio

www.volta.pt

VOLTA is a branding, design and digital dedicated Studio, with offices in Porto and Lisbon. VOLTA is part of WYgroup, the biggest group of creative companies in Portugal.

P.118-119

Windfor's Communication

www.windfors.ge

Founded in 2004, Windfor's Communication is one of the leaders in the Georgian advertising market. It is a full-service creative agency. Exclusively in the country, it represents a greater holding of different advertising service companies, offering the widest range and the highest quality of services.

P.184-185

Yarza Twins

www.yarzatwins.com

Yarza Twins is an international multi-tasking studio based in London that creates the awesomeness in each of their projects, being branding, moving image, illustration, typography and set design.

P.192-193

You Zhang

behance.net/youzhang

You(Emma) Zhang is an experience designer and graphic designer based in San Francisco, USA, currently working in Adobe System Inc.

P.126-127

Yuta Takahashi

www.yutatakahashi.jp

Yuta is an art director and designer based in Japan. Yuta's design studio is simple and minimal, with clean and modern design as its forte. It offers a wide variety of solutions in branding, graphic design, packaging design, editorial design, logo design, illustration, web design, UI & UX design, and others.

P.012-013, 014-015, 183

Acknowledgements

We would like to thank all of the designers involved for granting us permission to publish their works, as well as all of the photographers who have generously allowed us to use their images. We are also very grateful to many other people whose names do not appear in the credits but who made specific contributions and provided support. Without these people, we would not have been able to share these beautiful works with readers around the world. Our editorial team includes editor Annie Lai and book designer Wu Yanting, to whom we are truly grateful.